"David is a national treasure. His first book was great. This book . . . is even better. A must read for citizens everywhere asking the hard questions about 911."

— Meria Heller, *producer/host of* The Meria Heller Show

"It is rather obvious that the 9/11 commission aimed more to bring closure than to investigate the anomalies surrounding the event. For the dominant media in the U.S. they have largely succeeded. All the more reason why it is important that its failure even to mention these anomalies not go unnoticed. For those who still seek the truth and hope for a serious investigation of the facts, Griffin's careful analysis of the report is essential reading."

— John B. Cobb, Jr., Professor of Theology, Emeritus, Claremont School of Theology

"This is a painstaking and devastating demolition of the lies transmitted by *The 9/11 Commission Report,* and also the new lies invented by it in an effort to reconcile the government's impossible chronologies. Time after time, David Ray Griffin uses credible eyewitness accounts to refute the Report's methods and allegations, particularly with respect to the stand-down and shoot-down orders issued on that infamous September 11 and the attack on the Pentagon. Those concerned with preserving our Republic in these troubled times should pay particular attention to his focus on the disturbing behavior of the core group who appear on that day to have misdirected the defenses of our country. In the coming national debate over 9/11, Griffin's book will strengthen the cause of those who believe that the best defense for democracy is not blind fealty to leaders, but the truth."

— Peter Dale Scott, author of *Drugs, Oil, and War*

Praise for David Ray Griffin's
The New Pearl Harbor: Disturbing Questions about the Bush Administration and 9/11

"This is an important, extraordinarily well-reasoned and provocative book that should be widely read. Griffin raises disturbing questions that deserve thoughtful and truthful answers from our government."

— *Marcus Raskin, co-founder of the Institute for Policy Studies*

"David Ray Griffin has done admirable and painstaking research in reviewing the mysteries surrounding the 9-11 attacks. It is the most persuasive argument I have seen for further investigation of the Bush administration's relationship to that historic and troubling event."
—*Howard Zinn, author of* A People's History of the United States

"David Ray Griffin has written what America may most of all need—a dispassionate, balanced, and exhaustively researched and documented account of the implausible gaps and misrepresentations of the Bush administration's official story of 9/11. Sensitive to the 'conspiracy theory' mind-stop that has disconnected his fellow Americans from the facts of this history-steering event, Griffin painstakingly marshals the evidence pro and con, and follows it where it leads. A courageously impeccable work."
— *John McMurtry, author of* Value Wars: The Global Market versus the Life Economy, *Fellow of the Royal Society of Canada and Professor of Philosophy, University of Guelph*

"It will be painful, and disturbing, to turn the pages of this thoughtful and meticulously researched book. But turn we must. For we owe the truth to those who died, and nothing less."
—*Colleen Kelly, sister of Bill Kelly, Jr., who was killed in the North Tower of the World Trade Center on 9/11, and co-founder of September 11th Families for Peaceful Tomorrows*

"This is a very important book. David Ray Griffin's carefully researched and documented study demonstrates a high level of probability that the Bush administration was complicit in allowing 9/11 to happen in order to further war plans that had already been made. A must-read for anyone concerned about American foreign policy under the present administration."
—*Rosemary Radford Ruether, Carpenter Professor of Feminist Theology, Graduate Theological Union, Berkeley, California*

"David Griffin's book is an excellent exposé of so many of the deeply troubling questions that must still be answered fully and transparently if democratic control over political and military leaders is to mean anything at all."
—*Michael Meacher, British member of Parliament, and former Minister of the Environment*

THE
9/11
COMMISSION REPORT

Omissions and Distortions

by DAVID RAY GRIFFIN

OLIVE
BRANCH
PRESS

An imprint of Interlink Publishing Group, Inc.
Northampton, Massachusetts

First published in 2005 by

OLIVE BRANCH PRESS
An imprint of Interlink Publishing Group, Inc.
46 Crosby Street, Northampton, Massachusetts 01060
www.interlinkbooks.com

Library of Congress Cataloging-in-Publication Data
Griffin, David Ray, 1939–
The 9/11 Commission report : omissions and distortions / by David Ray Griffin.
p. cm.
Includes bibliographical references and index.
ISBN 1-56656-584-7 (pbk.)
1. National Commission on Terrorist Attacks upon the United States. 9/11
Commission report. 2. September 11 Terrorist Attacks, 2001.
3. Terrorism—Government policy—United States. 4. Terrorism—United
States—Prevention. 5. War on Terrorism, 2001– 6. Intelligence
service—United States—Evaluation. I. Title.
HV6432.7.G745 2004
973.931—dc22

2004023282

Cover image © AP Wide World Photos
Book design by Juliana Spear

Printed and bound in Canada by Webcom

CONTENTS

ACKNOWLEDGMENTS

In *The New Pearl Harbor*, I made clear in the endnotes that I was heavily dependent on 9/11 books by Michel Chossudovsky, Thierry Meyssan, Nafeez Ahmed, Eric Hufschmid, and the 9/11 timeline created by Paul Thompson. Because I have not done this in the present book, I wish to emphasize my continuing dependence on their work and that of the many researchers upon whom they drew.

Because my greatest dependence was on Paul Thompson's timeline, which was available only on the Internet—originally at the Center for Cooperative Research—I am pleased that Paul and the Center have now published *The Terror Timeline: Year by Year, Day by Day, Minute by Minute*, which appeared just in time for me to employ it a few places.

I am also grateful for various kinds of help from many other people, especially Daniel Athearn, Tal Avitzur, Fred Burks, Elias Davidsson, Tod Fletcher, Nico Haupt, Kyle Hence, Jim Hoffman, Eric Hufschmid, Allison Jaqua, Peter and Trudy Johnson-Lenz, Michael Kane, David Kubiak, Peter Lance, Nicholas Levis, Derek Mitchell (at the Center for Cooperative Research), Pat Patterson, Allen Poteschman, Morgan Reynolds, Peter Dale Scott, Paul Thompson, Craig Unger, and Barrie Zwicker. I thank them all for taking time from the own work to help with my effort. My greatest ongoing indebtedness is to my wife, Ann Jaqua.

This book had its origin in a lecture I gave in Eugene, Oregon, six days after the appearance of *The 9/11 Commission Report*, at the invitation of a group headed by Mary Addams and Mark Rabinowitz. I thank them for the stimulation provided by their timely invitation.

I wish, finally, to thank the hundreds of people who have written to express their appreciation for *The New Pearl Harbor* and to report on their efforts to publicize its existence—with some of them saying that they had bought a dozen, or 50, or even 100 copies to give away. The extraordinary response to that book, which revealed that it met a deeply felt need, was surely instrumental in getting me—shortly after completing the Afterword for its second edition—to sit back down at the computer to write the present book. I hope it will help bring the many problems in the official story—and now in the authorized defense of the official story—into the open.

INTRODUCTION

In the third week of July of 2004—almost three years after the 9/11 attacks—the long-awaited report of the 9/11 Commission[1] was finally published. It quickly became widely accepted as the definitive account of 9/11. It was thus treated, for example, on a National Public Radio program about the 9/11 hearings that I heard September 7, 2004. Describing *The 9/11 Commission Report* as the most complete record of the events surrounding 9/11, this NPR program assumed that the Commission's report could be used as an unquestionable source of information. Mentioning several points in the report that contradicted previously held beliefs, the narrator said before each point: "We now know." She said, for example, that we now know that Vice President Cheney's authorization for the US military to shoot down hijacked airliners came too late to bring down any of the airliners. In the present book, I question whether this report really deserves to be treated as the definitive account of 9/11.

Such an examination is surely in order because, regardless of one's opinion about its historical accuracy, *The 9/11 Commission Report* is one of the most important documents ever produced in the United States.

WHY *THE 9/11 COMMISSION REPORT* IS IMPORTANT

The 9/11 Commission Report is important, first, simply because 9/11 itself was one of the most important events of modern history. It has occasioned, among other things, a "war on terror" that has had significant consequences in many parts of the world, especially Afghanistan and Iraq.

This report is important, second, because the 9/11 Commission was mandated to provide the definitive account of "facts and circumstances relating to the terrorist attacks of September 11, 2001" (xv).[2] The Commission sought, we are told in the Preface by Chairman Thomas Kean and Vice Chairman Lee Hamilton, "to provide the fullest possible account of the events surrounding 9/11" (xvi).

A third reason why this report is important is that the 9/11 Commission, having reached its conclusions as to why the attacks of 9/11 were able to succeed, has used these conclusions to suggest structural changes, the most important of which would be the creation of a National Intelligence Director (411–15). This proposal is based on the conclusion that the attacks of 9/11 were able to succeed because of "deep institutional failings" (265), especially the fact that "no one was firmly in charge" (400).

THREE OBVIOUS REASONS FOR EXAMINING THE REPORT

We thereby have three obvious reasons for examining the report carefully to see whether its conclusions are justified by the available evidence. We want to know, first, whether the Bush administration's "war on terror" was an appropriate response to 9/11; second, whether the report of the 9/11 Commission should be accepted as the definitive account; and, third, whether the success of the attacks would have been less likely if the recommended structural changes had already been in place.

There has been some discussion of the first question, especially whether the war on Iraq was an appropriate response. But there has been little if any public discussion of the second question. Rather, the Commission's report has for the most part simply been accepted as the definitive account of 9/11. Nevertheless, the third question has already been given a positive answer, with leaders of both parties rushing to endorse the recommendations of the Commission—in spite of the fact that these recommendations presuppose a positive answer to the second question, which has not been discussed. Surely before we endorse a proposal based on the Commission's analysis of why the attacks were able to succeed, we need to discuss whether this analysis is convincing.

A FOURTH REASON: THE POSSIBILITY OF A COVER-UP

This issue brings us to yet another reason why a careful scrutiny of *The 9/11 Commission Report* is of great importance. Most Americans evidently believe that the Bush administration had more information about the impending attacks than it has admitted. In 2002, the Atlanta Journal-Constitution conducted a poll on this question, asking its readers if they were "satisfied the Bush administration had no advance warning of the September 11 attacks." Only 52 percent of the respondents said they were. A surprising 46 percent said "No, I think officials knew it was coming," while 2 percent said "I'm not sure. Congress should investigate."[3] This means that almost 50 percent of the 23,000 people who responded—before the poll was suddenly withdrawn from the paper's website—suspected that the Bush administration was covering up advance warnings it had received.

More recently, a CBS/ *New York Times* poll taken April 23–27, 2004, found that 56 percent of the American public believed that the Bush administration was "mostly telling the truth but hiding something" about what it knew prior to September 11, while 16 percent believed that it was "mostly lying."[4] This means that by that date an astonishing 72 percent of the American people believed the Bush administration to be guilty of a cover-up, at least to some degree, of relevant information it had prior to the attacks of 9/11.

More recently yet, a poll taken by Zogby International in August 2004 asked residents of New York if they agreed with the view that "some leaders in the US government knew in advance that attacks were planned on or around September 11, 2001, and . . . consciously failed to act." The poll found that 41 percent of the residents of the state of New York agreed (while 11 percent made no statement, leaving only 48 percent who disagreed). That view was even endorsed by nearly 30 percent of the registered Republicans and over 38 percent of the people in the state describing themselves as "very conservative." The results were even more astonishing in New York City, where 49 percent of the residents agreed with the stated view. This latter figure was the basis for the story's headline: "Half of New Yorkers Believe US Leaders Had Foreknowledge of Impending 9–11 Attacks and 'Consciously Failed' to Act." Still more people—56 percent of the state's residents and 66 percent of the city's— called for an investigation by the US Congress or New York Attorney General Elliot Spitzer to deal with "still unanswered questions."[5]

In Canada, where there has been more public discussion of the problems in the official account, the number of people who suspect a cover-up of advance knowledge is evidently even greater. A national poll released May 20, 2004 asked people if they agreed with this statement: "Individuals within the US Government including the White House had prior knowledge of the plans for the events of September 11th, and failed to take appropriate action to stop them." A surprising 63 percent said that they agreed.[6]

At this writing (September 2004), I know of no poll in the United States asking about complicity in the stronger sense, according to which the Bush administration would have been involved in the planning and execution of the attacks. This question has been asked, however, in Canada and some European countries. In the Canadian poll, mentioned above, 16 percent of the respondents said they believed that individuals within the US government were involved in the planning and execution. In Germany—as a front-page story in the *Wall Street Journal* pointed out—a poll in July 2003 revealed that 20 percent of the population said that "the US government ordered the attacks itself." This story mentioned that books arguing this case have been very popular in France and Italy as well as Germany.[7]

As these polls show, many people, far from thinking with the 9/11 Commission that the problem was that "no one was firmly in charge," believe instead that the attacks were able to succeed only because someone *was* in charge, giving "stand-down" orders that removed various institutional safeguards through which any planned attacks of this nature would have normally been thwarted. In my previous book on the subject, *The New Pearl Harbor*,[8] I summarized much of the evidence that has been gathered to support this view.

A fourth reason to scrutinize the 9/11 Commission's final report, therefore, is to see whether it puts these suspicions to rest—the suspicion that the Bush administration planned the 9/11 attacks as well as the more widespread suspicion that the Bush administration was at least complicit in the sense of deliberately not preventing them. In this critique, I will primarily address this fourth question (the answer to which will also suggest answers to the first three questions).

PERSPECTIVE AND SELECTION

The chairman and the vice chairman of the 9/11 Commission said, as we saw, that their aim was "to provide the fullest possible account of the events surrounding 9/11." Of course, they could not have meant that statement literally, because there were trillions of "events surrounding 9/11." What they meant was that they tried to give the fullest account of those events surrounding 9/11 that are relevant to understanding why the attacks of 9/11 occurred.

This point raises the question of how they would have determined, out of all the events "surrounding" 9/11, which ones were relevant to understanding it. What was the Commission's principle of selection by which it determined which events surrounding the 9/11 attacks—events occurring before 9/11, after 9/11, and on 9/11 itself—were to be included in its report?

Every principle of selection presupposes a perspective, a basic way of seeing things, which determines what is considered relevant. For example, if the question is why Bill Jones is not feeling well, believers in Christian Science and believers in modern western medicine will consider quite different factors relevant to answering this question, and believers in traditional Chinese medicine will focus on still other factors. In some cases, these diverse perspectives are complementary, with each having an element of truth. In some cases, one perspective is right and the others wrong. In still other cases, all the extant perspectives are largely wrong. The point at hand, however, is simply that what we consider relevant for understanding some event or condition will largely depend on our overall perspective about it.

Applied to 9/11, this point means that our view of the relevant events surrounding the 9/11 attacks will be largely shaped by our perspective on this event—our basic theory about what happened on 9/11 and why.

TWO BASIC THEORIES ABOUT 9/11

As the preceding discussion has indicated, there are two basic theories about 9/11. Each of these theories is a "conspiracy theory."

One of these is the official conspiracy theory, according to which the attacks of 9/11 were planned and executed solely by al-Qaeda terrorists under the guidance of Osama bin Laden. This theory, according to which 9/11 resulted from a conspiracy among Arab Muslims, is, of course, the conspiracy theory that has been promulgated by the Bush administration and its various agencies, including the Pentagon.

Opposing this official theory is the alternative conspiracy theory, which holds that the attacks of 9/11 were able to succeed only because they were facilitated by the Bush administration and its agencies. "Facilitated" is a deliberately vague word, which allows this theory to have a weak and a strong version. According to the weak version, the Bush administration facilitated the success of the attacks merely in the sense of deliberately failing to prevent them. According to the strong version, the Bush administration was actively involved in the planning and execution of the attacks.[9] For now, however, we can ignore the distinction between these versions, focusing our attention entirely on the crucial contrast— that between the official theory and the alternative theory.

The question of just which "events surrounding 9/11" are deemed relevant for understanding what happened that day will hinge largely on whether this question is approached from the perspective of the official theory or from the perspective of the alternative theory. People who accept the official conspiracy theory will assume that the most important background information involves the history of Osama bin Laden and al-Qaeda. Also important, to be sure, will be events within the US government, especially its intelligence agencies, with the question being why these agencies were not able to uncover the plot in time to prevent the attacks. But all these events within the US government will be studied as examples of various kinds of misunderstanding, confusion, and failure to communicate.

People who accept the alternative conspiracy theory will, by contrast, focus on events suggesting that the attacks were facilitated by agencies and individuals within the US government, whether by obstructing investigations, issuing "stand-down" orders to suspend standard operating procedures, or covering up signs of the government's involvement. These people may or may not find the history of Osama bin Laden particularly relevant. But they will, in any case, be most focused on events suggestive of complicity within the Bush administration itself.

WAS THE 9/11 COMMISSION "NONPARTISAN"?

Chairman Kean and Vice Chairman Hamilton tell us that their Commission "sought to be independent, impartial, thorough, and nonpartisan" (xv). In this book, I will be asking whether these virtues are in fact embodied in *The 9/11 Commission Report*. Let us begin with the question of whether the Commission was "nonpartisan."

With this term, Kean and Hamilton allude to the fact that the Commission was composed of both Democrats and Republicans. This allusion suggests that the Commission would have succeeded in being nonpartisan if the Republicans did not blame everything on the Clinton administration, while being excessively defensive about the Bush administration, and the Democrats did not behave in the opposite way. Those who watched the hearings on television know that there was considerable partisanship during the proceedings. In the end, however, the Commission came together sufficiently to produce a final report endorsed unanimously by all the Democrats and all the Republicans. Kean and Hamilton are obviously proud that the Commission did end up being nonpartisan in this sense, producing the report, as they say, "without dissent" (xv).

The Commission was also said to be nonpartisan in a purely factual sense, namely, that the Commission was comprised of an equal number of members from both parties—five Democrats and five Republicans.

One of the major problems with the Commission, however, was that it was not truly nonpartisan in a factual sense. There are two reasons why it was not. The first is that the chairman was a Republican. The vice chairman was, to be sure, a Democrat, but he was merely the vice chairman, not the co-chairman.

Even more important is the second reason why the Commission was not nonpartisan in a factual sense. The person who served as the Commission's executive director, Philip D. Zelikow, is a Republican. This is important because as executive director, Zelikow was in charge of the Commission's staff, and it was these staff members—not the Commissioners we saw on television—who did most of the actual work of the Commission. The Commissioners would have carried out their own distinctive work—their discussions and interviews—on the basis of the material provided by the staff. Kean and Hamilton refer to this fact in their statement that the "professional staff, headed by Philip Zelikow, . . . conducted the exacting investigative work upon which the Commission has built" (xvi–xvii).

The extent of Zelikow's influence on the Commission's processes has been commented on by Paul Sperry, who wrote, while the Commission was still working, that Zelikow

> arguably has more sway than any member, including the chairman. Zelikow picks the areas of investigation, the briefing materials, the topics for hearings, the witnesses, and the lines of questioning for witnesses. In effect, he sets the agenda and runs the investigation.[10]

This overwhelmingly important fact has been little commented on by the press. Kean and Hamilton have been the public face of the Commission. But the Commission's investigation was essentially run by Zelikow.

Later, Zelikow was in charge of overseeing the writing of the staff reports, many of which went virtually unchanged into the final report. And he was then in charge of editing the final report itself. Kean and Hamilton refer to this fact in their statement that the "professional staff, headed by Philip Zelikow, has contributed innumerable hours to the completion of this report" (xvi). A Republican, therefore, oversaw both the investigative work and the writing of the final report.

WAS THE 9/11 COMMISSION "INDEPENDENT"?

The 9/11 Commission's executive director was not, furthermore, simply any Republican. Philip Zelikow had been very closely associated with the Bush White House. He was on the National Security Council in the Bush I administration, where both he and Condoleezza Rice served as aides to National Security Advisor Brent Scowcroft. During the Clinton years, while the Republicans were out of office, he and Rice co-authored a book.[11] Zelikow also directed the Aspen Strategy Group, which involved Rice and Scowcroft as well as, among others, Dick Cheney and Paul Wolfowitz. Then, he served on the National Security Council's team for the transition between the Clinton and Bush II administrations. In this role, he provided recommendations for Rice, who was becoming the National Security Advisor to the president. Shortly after 9/11, Zelikow was appointed to the President's Foreign Intelligence Advisory Board, on which he served until becoming executive director of the 9/11 Commission in 2003.[12]

Because of his close ties to the Bush White House, Zelikow's appointment was controversial from the outset. The Family Steering Committee for the 9/11 Commission, in fact, repeatedly called for Zelikow's removal.[13] The families were saying, in effect, that Zelikow's appointment made a mockery of the idea that the Commission was "independent."

This allegation was not unreasonable. The 9/11 attacks occurred after the Bush administration had been in office for about seven months. Any thorough investigation would have needed to ask about complicity or at least negligence on the part of this administration. A central part of the Commission's task should have been the investigation of these questions. The Commission needed, therefore, to be completely independent of the White House. And yet the Commission's investigation was to be carried out by a man who was essentially part of the Bush administration. The conflict of interest could not have been clearer. The judicial system would never let a judge preside in a case involving persons who were close friends, colleagues, and former employers of the judge. But Zelikow remained the executive director of the 9/11 Commission. The Commission was not, therefore, "independent."

The Commission made a nod in the direction of acknowledging this problem, but only a nod. The Commission's report says that in preparation for the transition from the National Security Council of the Clinton administration to that of the Bush administration, "Rice had asked University of Virginia history professor Philip Zelikow to advise her on the transition" (199). In the accompanying note, we find this amazing statement: "Rice and Zelikow had been colleagues on the NSC staff during the first Bush administration and were coauthors of a book concerning German unification. . . . As the Executive Director of the Commission, Zelikow has recused himself from our work on the Clinton–Bush transition at the National Security Council" (509n165). The first part of this statement acknowledges the problem. Then the second part suggests that it was solved merely by having Zelikow recuse himself from discussions involving the brief period during which he helped with the transition.

The assumption implicit in this "solution" is that Zelikow's association with Rice and the Bush administration more generally would have been a problem only with regard to discussions in which he was directly involved—"as if," in Paul Sperry's words, "any potential conflicts he might have would end there."[14] But that is a wholly untenable assumption—as we would, again, immediately recognize in an analogous judicial case. If a case involving a close friend or business associate of Sandra Day O'Connor came before the US Supreme Court, we would not expect her to recuse herself only with regard to some decision in which she had personally been involved. We would recognize that it would be unrealistic to expect her to be objective and impartial in the case as a whole.

As executive director of the 9/11 Commission, Zelikow was in charge of an investigation that would accuse or absolve people with whom he was politically, personally, and ideologically intertwined. The problem of bias could by no means be limited to events occurring during the brief period during which he participated in the transition process. The fact that the Commission could pretend otherwise is a major mark against its honesty.

WAS THE 9/11 COMMISSION "IMPARTIAL"?

After seeing how the 9/11 Commissioners met their stated aims to be independent and nonpartisan, let us ask now how they fared in their quest for impartiality.

An impartial investigation into the "facts and circumstances relating to the terrorist attacks of September 11" would have begun its work like any good crime investigation, collecting evidence and testimonies under oath from all those who might have something to contribute. It would have tried to investigate equally the two basic theories about the attacks: that the attacks were planned and carried out solely by followers of Osama bin Laden, and that the attacks were able to succeed only because of the complicity of the Bush administration itself.

Different crime cases, of course, require different approaches. In some murder cases, for example, there is no suspect. In such cases, the investigators must simply begin their work without any theory as to the guilty party. It is only through this theory-neutral investigation that a theory as to the guilty party may emerge. In other cases, there may be two prime suspects from the outset. In these cases, it is most important that the investigation not focus on only one of them. The violation of this rule is, in fact, one of the most common sources of false convictions. Even if the investigators are strongly convinced that Suspect A is guilty, they must look with equal rigor at evidence that might point to the guilt of Suspect B (while also remaining alert to any possible evidence suggesting that someone other than either of these initial suspects might actually be the guilty party).

The case of 9/11 was analogous to this second kind of murder case, in which there were two likely suspects. There was considerable evidence pointing to the guilt of al-Qaeda operatives, with much of this evidence coming from sources within the US government. There was a good prima facie case for this theory. But there were many things that reasonably led many observers to suspect that the US government itself was behind, or at least complicit in, the attacks. It is surely understandable that there was a strong predisposition on the part of the Commission towards the first of these theories. But as in any crime investigation, the Commission should have looked equally at evidence supportive of the alternative theory—with one piece of this evidence being the very fact that the White House tried to prevent any serious investigation of the matter.[15]

The importance of taking this approach was, in fact, acknowledged by Chairman Kean, who said:

There are a lot of theories about 9/11, and as long as there is any
document out there that bears on any of those theories, we're
going to leave questions unanswered. And we cannot leave
questions unanswered.[16]

In speaking of "theories" here, Kean was, to be sure, probably referring
to particular sub-theories within the overall official theory. But the
validity of his point applies as well to the distinction between the
official theory as such and the alternative theory. Before the
Commission began zeroing in on various sub-theories within the
official theory, accordingly, it should have asked if that official theory as
such is supported by more evidence than is the alternative theory. (The
Commission should have also, of course, remained open to evidence for
yet other theories, but for simplicity's sake we can limit the present
discussion to the need to deal evenhandedly with the two most
prevalent theories.) Such an investigation would have been an
"impartial" one, at least if the evidence for the competing theories was
treated in an evenhanded way.

The Commission's report, however, reveals no sign that the
Commission was ever impartial in this sense. Indeed, the Commission
seems simply to have presupposed the truth of the official conspiracy
theory from the outset. Far from examining the evidence for the two
theories in an evenhanded way, the Commission's report for the most
part—as the ensuing chapters will show—simply ignores all the "events
surrounding 9/11" that have been cited as evidence for the alternative
conspiracy theory.

The partiality of the 9/11 Commission's report is so extreme, in
fact, that it even fails to acknowledges the existence of the alternative
theory. The Commission was surely aware of this theory. Those who
know the types of evidence on which it rests can see places, here and
there in the report, in which the Commission appears implicitly to be
trying to refute some piece of this evidence. But this alternative theory
was evidently regarded by the Commission as the theory—to adopt a
phrase used by Zelikow himself in another connection—"that dare not
speak its name."[17]

We should, of course, be disappointed by the fact that the 9/11
Commission was so partial. Given the Commission's lack of independence
from the White House, however, we should not be surprised. As executive

director, Zelikow was in position to determine which of the "events surrounding 9/11" would be investigated and which not. He was, therefore, in position to have the research staff's "exacting investigative work" directed entirely to matters that were consistent with the theory about 9/11 promulgated by the White House. Events supportive of the alternative theory, even if they had been reported in mainstream publications, could for the most part be ignored.

The Commission's lack of impartiality—which is evident throughout the report, as the remainder of this critique will show—can thereby be explained, at least in large part, by the Commission's lack of independence from the White House. Just as we would not have expected an investigation carried out by George Bush, Dick Cheney, or Condoleezza Rice to be impartial, neither should we expect an investigation directed by their man inside the 9/11 Commission, Philip Zelikow, to be impartial. Zelikow, in fact, publicly likened discussing alternative theories about 9/11 to "whacking moles."[18]

Special commissions often come to be named after the individuals who shared them. The 9/11 Commission has, accordingly, sometimes been called the "Kean Commission." But both the work and the final report of the 9/11 Commission were probably shaped even more by Philip Zelikow. We should, therefore, speak of the "Kean–Zelikow Commission" and the "Kean–Zelikow Report."

WAS THE 9/11 COMMISSION "THOROUGH"?

Besides seeking to be nonpartisan, independent, and impartial, the Commission, said Kean and Hamilton, sought to be thorough. For the Commission's report to have embodied this virtue, it would have needed to do precisely what Kean suggested in the indented quotation above—track down every bit of evidence with bearing on any of the theories about 9/11. I have already indicated that the Commission's report did not achieve thoroughness in this sense. The report's lack of thoroughness is, in fact, one of its outstanding characteristics, signaled by the word "omissions" in the subtitle of the present critique.

The fact that the Commission's final report is characterized by significant omissions was the central point of an open letter to the US Congress, signed by 25 individuals "who have worked within various government agencies (FBI, CIA, FAA, DIA, Customs) responsible for national security and public safety." In this letter, sent September 13, 2004, they say:

> Omission is one of the major flaws in the Commission's report. We are aware of significant issues and cases that were duly reported to the Commission by those of us with direct knowledge, but somehow escaped attention. Serious problems and shortcomings within government agencies likewise were reported to the Commission but were not included in the report. The report simply does not get at key problems within the intelligence, aviation security, and law enforcement communities. The omission of such serious and applicable issues and information by itself renders the report flawed, and casts doubt on the validity of many of its recommendations.[19]

This letter offers no theory as to why the "significant issues and cases that were duly reported to the Commission" were omitted from its final report, saying simply that they "somehow escaped attention." In the present critique, I will suggest that these omissions are by no means random, but reveal a pattern.

This pattern is part and parcel of the fact that the Commission did seek thoroughness in some respects. It is, for one thing, quite thorough with regard to its recital of events surrounding 9/11 that are consistent with the official conspiracy theory promulgated by the Bush administration. The Commission, for example, goes into great detail about Osama bin Laden, the rise of al-Qaeda, and the lives of the (alleged) hijackers. The Commission also evidently sought, implicitly, to give a thorough defense of the White House, the Justice Department, the FBI, and the CIA by thoroughly omitting, or explaining away, any reports that could be used to suggest complicity on their parts. The Commission also clearly sought to provide a thorough defense of the US military against any suggestion that it was responsible for the success of the attacks of 9/11, whether through complicity or incompetence. In many respects, therefore, the Kean–Zelikow Report embodies the virtue of thoroughness.

With regard to thoroughness in what should have been the most important sense, however, the Commission failed disgracefully. The Commission's mandate, as Kean and Hamilton pointed out, was to investigate "facts and circumstances relating to the terrorist attacks of

September 11" and then to provide "the fullest possible account" of those facts and circumstances. What the Commission actually did, however, was only to provide a fairly full account of those facts and circumstances that are consistent with the official conspiracy theory about 9/11. Every fact inconsistent with this theory is either distorted or entirely omitted.

I have suggested that if the Commission's final product should in reality be called the Kean–Zelikow Report, we should not be surprised by these omissions and distortions. I suspect, nevertheless, that many readers will be shocked, as I was, by the sheer number of the omissions and the audacity of the distortions.

THE NATURE AND STRUCTURE OF THIS CRITIQUE

Critiques of *The 9/11 Commission Report* can legitimately take many possible approaches. The present critique, I have indicated, evaluates this report from the standpoint of the main alternative to the official theory about 9/11. It asks how evidence supportive of this alternative theory—much of which was summarized in my previous book about 9/11, *The New Pearl Harbor*—is treated in the Commission's report. This evidence, by suggesting that the official account is false, thereby suggests that those who provided this account probably conspired to allow or perhaps even arrange the attacks. One central purpose of the Kean–Zelikow Report, although it remains merely implicit, is to defend the truth of the official account against arguments based on such evidence. The present critique evaluates the success of this attempt.

My examination of this attempt consists of two parts. In the first part, I point out evidence against the official account that is either distorted or simply ignored by the report. In the second part, I look at the report's treatment of the charge that the 9/11 Commission has tried most strongly to refute—the charge that on 9/11 itself the US military, if it had followed its own standard procedures, would have been able to prevent the attacks.

This critique's subtitle—Omissions and Distortions—refers most obviously to the material in Part I. It may at first glance seem less appropriate for Part II, which focuses on the Commission's new version of the official explanation as to why the US military failed to prevent the attacks of 9/11. But this subtitle is also appropriate for this part, because the Commission is able to construct this new explanation in a way that appears plausible, at least to readers without prior knowledge of the relevant facts, only by omitting or distorting many of those facts.

This book does not necessarily presuppose that readers have read *The New Pearl Harbor*. But having a copy handy—preferably the second, updated edition—will certainly be helpful.

PART ONE

The Commission's Omissions and Distortions

CHAPTER ONE

The Alleged Hijackers

As I explained in the Introduction, the 9/11 Commission for the most part simply omits evidence that would cast doubt on the official account of 9/11. When it does refer to evidence of this type, it typically mentions only part of it accurately, omitting or distorting the remainder. The present chapter illustrates this criticism in relation to the Commission's response to problems that have emerged with respect to the alleged hijackers.

SIX ALLEGED HIJACKERS STILL ALIVE

One problem is that at least six of the nineteen men officially identified as the suicide hijackers reportedly showed up alive after 9/11. For example, Waleed al-Shehri—said to have been on American Airlines Flight 11, which hit the North Tower of the World Trade Center—was interviewed after 9/11 by a London-based newspaper.[1] He also, the Associated Press reported, spoke on September 22 to the US embassy in Morocco, explaining that he lives in Casablanca, working as a pilot for Royal Air Maroc.[2]

Likewise, Ahmed al-Nami and Saeed al-Ghamdi—both said to have been on United Airlines Flight 93, which crashed in Pennsylvania—were shocked, they told *Telegraph* reporter David Harrison, to hear that they had died in this crash. Al-Nami, who was working as an administrative supervisor with Saudi Arabian Airlines at the time, added: "I had never even heard of Pennsylvania." Al-Ghamdi said he had been in Tunis the previous ten months learning to fly an Airbus.[3] According to the BBC, *Asharq Al Awsat*, a London-based Arabic newspaper, also reported having interviewed al-Ghamdi.[4]

The Saudi embassy in Washington reported that three other alleged hijackers—Mohand al-Shehri, Salem al-Hazmi, and Abdulaziz al-Omari—were all alive and living in Saudi Arabia.[5] Salem al-Hazmi, who was accused of hijacking Flight 77, "had just returned to work at a petrochemical complex in the industrial eastern city of Yanbou after a holiday in Saudi Arabia when the hijackers struck," David Harrison reported.[6] Al-Omari, supposedly the pilot of Flight 11 but in reality working as a pilot for Saudi Airlines, "visited the US consulate in Jeddah to demand an explanation" for the US claim that he was a hijacker, and a dead one at that.[7]

In spite of these revelations by mainstream news sources, however, *The 9/11 Commission Report* simply repeats, in the first few pages (1–5), the FBI's original list of nineteen names, then later gives their photographs (238–39). The Commission's report fails to mention the fact that at least six of the identifications have been shown to be incorrect. The report goes into considerable detail about these six men (231–42, 524–525nn91,98,105,106), even speculating that Waleed al-Shehri was probably responsible for stabbing one of the flight attendants on AA Flight 11 (5). How can we believe that the Commission's report was based on "exacting investigative work," as we were told by Kean and Hamilton in the Preface, if the staff did not even learn, from sources such as the Associated Press, the *Telegraph*, and the BBC, that six of the men originally identified as the hijackers were still alive? Of course, it is possible that the Commission did know this but simply failed to tell us. But would that not be worse yet?

OMISSIONS ABOUT MOHAMED ATTA

The results of the research with regard to Mohamed Atta, said to be the ringleader of the hijackers, are also inadequate. As I pointed out in *The New Pearl Harbor*, stories in the mainstream press, including *Newsweek* and the *San Francisco Chronicle*, had reported that Atta had engaged in behavior—such as gambling, drinking alcohol, and having lap dances performed for him—that seemed to undermine the portrayal of him as a devout Muslim, ready to meet his Maker.[8] In the meantime, investigative reporter Daniel Hopsicker has reported that while Atta was in Florida, he lived with a prostitute, drank heavily, used cocaine, and ate pork chops.[9]

The 9/11 Commission Report, however, fails to mention any of these reports. It instead portrays Atta as not only religious but as having become "fanatically so" (161). Although the Commission mentions that Atta met other operatives in Las Vegas shortly before 9/11, it says that it saw "no credible evidence explaining why, on this occasion and others, the operatives flew to or met in Las Vegas" (248). However, according to a *Wall Street Journal* editorial:

In Florida, several of the hijackers—including reputed ringleader Mohamed Atta—spent $200 to $300 each on lap dances in the Pink Pony strip club. . . . [I]n Las Vegas, at least six of the hijackers spent time living it up on the Strip on various occasions between May and August.[10]

Are we to conclude that the 9/11 Commissioners knew of this report but did not mention it simply because they did not consider it "credible"? Or did the staff, in spite of its reputed extensive research, not learn of this and the similar reports in *Newsweek* and the *San Francisco Chronicle*? Or did the Commissioners deliberately fail to mention reports that would cast doubt on the official portrayal of Atta and the other alleged hijackers as devout Muslims?

The official story about Atta is thrown even further into question by indications that materials pointing to his role in the hijacking were intended to be found. Two of Atta's bags, which failed to get loaded onto Flight 11, contained flight simulation manuals for Boeing airplanes, a copy of the Koran, a religious cassette tape, a note to other hijackers about mental preparation, and Atta's will, passport, and international driver's license.[11] But why would Atta have intended to take such things on a plane he expected to be totally destroyed? Seymour Hersh later wrote in the *New Yorker* that

many of the investigators believe that some of the initial clues that were uncovered about the terrorists' identities and preparations, such as flight manuals, were meant to be found. A former high-level intelligence official told me, "Whatever trail was left was left deliberately—for the FBI to chase."[12]

The 9/11 Commissioners, however, do not even mention the strangeness of all this. Did they simply assume that it would not have occurred to Atta that a plane headed for self-destruction in a fiery inferno would be the worst possible place for his will?

HANI HANJOUR: THE BEST PILOT OR THE WORST?

Also problematic is the Commission's discussion of Hani Hanjour, supposedly the pilot of AA Flight 77, which is said to have crashed into the Pentagon. As I reported in *The New Pearl Harbor*, people at flight schools attended by Hanjour had described him as a horrible pilot, and yet the aircraft that crashed into the Pentagon's west wing was shown by radar to have been able to hit this part of the Pentagon only by executing a very difficult maneuver. As the Commission itself points out, when the aircraft was 5 miles from the Pentagon, it "began a 330-degree turn. At the end of the turn, it was descending through 2,200 feet" (9). The report does underplay the difficulty of the maneuver somewhat by saying that the pilot "then advanced the throttles to maximum power and dove towards the Pentagon" (9) In reality, the aircraft, rather than hitting the Pentagon from above, as it would had it "dove," came in almost horizontally, having approached the west wing from tree-top level. For a plane to do this while going at full throttle would take a very highly skilled pilot. Even simply executing the downward spiral, which the Commission does describe, would have been difficult enough. As a story in the *Washington Post* said, the pilot "executed a pivot so tight that it reminded observers of a fighter jet maneuver.... Aviation sources said the plane was flown with extraordinary skill, making it highly likely that a trained pilot was at the helm."[13]

The Kean–Zelikow Commission deals with this problem by saying contradictory things. On the one hand, it reports that Hanjour's application to become a pilot was repeatedly rejected, that he was considered a "terrible pilot," and that as late as July 2001 he still had such poor piloting skills that an instructor refused to go up with him a second time (225–26, 520n56, 242). But then the report tells us—in explaining why Hanjour was reportedly chosen to pilot the airplane assigned to hit the Pentagon—that he was "the operation's most experienced pilot" (530n147). Whereas the Commission in most cases simply omits problematic evidence, it in this case did acknowledge, at least implicitly, the existence of a problem. But it then dealt with this problem by ignoring its implications, failing to ask how such a terrible pilot could have executed such a difficult maneuver. Having ignored this question, the Commission could then report, without evident embarrassment, that "[a]s a former pilot, the President was struck by the apparent sophistication of the operation and some of the piloting, especially Hanjour's high-speed dive into the Pentagon" (334).

EVIDENCE FOR ANY OF THE ALLEGED HIJACKERS?

As we have seen, serious questions have been raised about at least eight of the alleged hijackers. But there is an even more radical question: Do we have any publicly available proof that any of the 19 men named by the FBI and the 9/11 Commission were on any of the four planes that day? The shocking answer is: No. We have been told that their names were on the flight manifests. But the flight manifests that have been released have no Arab names on them.[14] Students of this subject who have tried to get final flight manifests from the airlines have been refused.[15] Presumably the 9/11 Commission, with its subpoena power, could have obtained copies of the actual passenger manifests from United and American Airlines and cleared up the question of whether the names of the alleged hijackers were on them. But the Commission's report, besides not containing copies of these manifests, reveals no sign that this issue was even discussed. The Commission evidently simply repeated the official story about 19 Arab hijackers with no investigation into serious questions that have been raised about it.

The Commission's treatment of the alleged hijackers—a central feature of the official conspiracy theory presupposed by the Commission—does not bode well for the rest of the report. One might suppose, of course, that the Commission's treatment of the alleged hijackers was an aberration— one due, perhaps, to the fact that this topic was assigned to one of the poorer researchers. We will see, however, that the low quality of this part of the Kean–Zelikow Report is no exception.

CHAPTER TWO

The Collapse of the World Trade Center Buildings

As I pointed out in my previous book, there are severe problems with the official account of the collapses of the Twin Towers and Building 7 of the World Trade Center (WTC), according to which they were caused by fire. One way to test *The 9/11 Commission Report* is to examine how it treats these problems. I will begin this discussion by mentioning six of them.

SIX PROBLEMS IN THE OFFICIAL ACCOUNT

One problem is that fire had never before caused steel-frame high-rise buildings to collapse, even when the fire was a very energetic, all-consuming one, such as the 1991 fire at One Meridian Plaza in Philadelphia.[1] Indeed, tests had even been performed to see if very hot fires could cause steel-frame buildings to collapse, as the report on Building 7 of the WTC by FEMA (the Federal Emergency Management Agency) pointed out.[2] The Commission says that to its knowledge, "none of the [fire] chiefs present believed that a total collapse of either tower was possible" (302).[3] This might be regarded as an implicit acknowledgment on the Commission's part that no such collapse had ever occurred before. But if so, it remains implicit.

A second problem is that the fires, especially in the South Tower and WTC-7, were quite small. We have all seen the pictures of the giant fireball immediately after the South Tower was hit. This fireball did not signal a raging fire inside, however, but the opposite. There was such a big fireball outside because the building was struck near a corner, so that much of the jet fuel burned up outside. There was, accordingly, not much fuel to feed the fire inside. Photographs show, in fact, that not a single floor beyond the fire's starting location was hot enough to ignite paper or plastic or to break windows. How could anyone suppose that such a fire could weaken steel sufficiently to induce a collapse?[4] With regard to WTC-7, which was not even struck by an airplane, photographs show that there were fires only on the seventh and twelfth floors of this 47-story building. And yet it collapsed, while Buildings 5 and 6, which had raging fires, did not.[5]

A third problem is that if the Twin Towers had been brought down by the heat of their fires (perhaps combined with the impact of the airplanes), the North Tower should have collapsed first. It was struck seventeen minutes before the South Tower. It also had larger and hotter fires. The difference was suggested by a *New York Times* report that although "probably well over 50" people jumped or fell from the North Tower, no one fell or jumped from the South Tower.[6] However, the South Tower collapsed first, 29 minutes before the North Tower did, as the Commission itself acknowledges (285). In other words, although the South Tower had smaller fires, it collapsed in 56 minutes, whereas the North Tower, with bigger fires, collapsed only after an hour and 42 minutes.[7] As one critic put it, "The Wrong Tower Fell First,"[8] suggesting that something other than fire brought the buildings down.

A fourth problem is that, even had the fires been raging throughout the Twin Towers and Building 7, they would not have been nearly hot enough to melt steel, because ordinary hydrocarbon fires—such as fires based on jet fuel (kerosene)—can at most rise to 1700° Fahrenheit, whereas steel begins to melt only at about 2770° F.[9]

A fifth problem is that the collapse of Building 7 was recognized as being especially difficult to explain. FEMA, which was given the task, admitted that the best possible explanation it could come up with had "only a low probability of occurrence."[10]

A sixth problem is that the collapses of the Twin Towers and WTC-7 had ten characteristics that are standard features of "controlled demolition" collapses, which are produced by explosives placed throughout a building and set to go off in a particular order. Namely:

1. Each collapse occurred at virtually free-fall speed.
2. Each building collapsed straight down, for the most part into its own footprint.[11]
3. Virtually all the concrete was turned into very fine dust.
4. In the case of the Twin Towers, the dust was blown out horizontally for 200 feet or more.[12]
5. The collapses were total, leaving no steel columns sticking up hundreds of feet into the air.
6. Videos of the collapses reveal "demolition waves," meaning "confluent rows of small explosions."[13]

7. Most of the steel beams and columns came down in sections that were no more than 30 feet long.[14]

8. According to many witnesses, explosions occurred within the buildings.[15]

9. Each collapse was associated with detectable seismic vibrations (suggestive of underground explosions).

10. Each collapse produced molten steel (which would be produced by explosives), resulting in "hot spots" that remained for months.[16]

Although authors of *The 9/11 Commission Report* reportedly aspired to make it "the fullest possible account of the events surrounding 9/11," it does not explicitly acknowledge, let alone solve, any of these problems.

THE TWIN TOWERS: OMITTING THE CORE COLUMNS

The report does implicitly acknowledge that the North Tower collapsed straight down, primarily into its own footprint, by speaking of its "pancake" collapse (308). But it offers no reflections on how a fire could have produced such a collapse.[17] The report also mentions that the "South Tower collapsed in 10 seconds" (305), which would be at virtually free-fall speed. But the report gives no indication that any of the Commission's members expressed curiosity as to how fire could cause a 110-floor steel-frame building to collapse so rapidly.

With regard to the more basic question—Why did the Twin Towers collapse at all?—the Commission implies an answer by saying that

> the outside of each tower was covered by a frame of 14-inch-wide steel columns. . . . These exterior walls bore most of the weight of the building. The interior core of the buildings was a hollow steel shaft, in which elevators and stairwells were grouped. (541n1)

This implicit explanation, however, involves a complete falsification, because the core of each tower was composed not of "a hollow steel shaft" but of 47 massive steel columns, in between which were the elevators and stairwells. At its base, each column was 14 by 36 inches, with 4-inch-thick walls. It then tapered up to 1/4-inch walls in the upper floors, which had far less weight to support.[18] It was these massive steel columns that "bore most of the weight of the buildings." One of the major problems with the official account is why, even if the fire could have somehow caused the floors of the building to "pancake" (as the generally accepted explanation has it), the resulting pile of rubble was only a few stories high.

Why were these massive steel columns not still sticking up hundreds of feet into the air?[19] The Commission avoids this embarrassing problem by simply denying the existence of these massive steel columns—thereby either demonstrating enormous ignorance or telling an enormous lie.

THE COLLAPSE OF WTC-7 AND SILVERSTEIN'S STATEMENT

The Commission avoids another embarrassing problem—explaining how WTC-7 could have collapsed, also at virtually free-fall speed—by simply not mentioning the collapse of this building. Building 7 of the WTC was 47 stories high, so it would have been considered a giant skyscraper if it had been anywhere other than next to the 110-story Twin Towers. But the collapse of such a huge building was not even considered worthy of comment by the Commission. Did the Commission not know about this collapse? Or did the Commission simply not mention it because the Commission—unlike FEMA—considered this building's collapse unproblematic? Or did the Commission not mention this collapse because it knew that there was no explanation that met the two necessary criteria: being plausible while being consistent with the official account of 9/11?

A particularly glaring omission in relation to this collapse is the Commission's failure to discuss a provocative statement made by Larry Silverstein, who—as the Commission's only mention of him points out[20]—had taken out a long lease on the World Trade Center only six weeks before 9/11 (281). In a PBS documentary entitled "America Rebuilds," originally aired in September of 2002, Silverstein made the following statement about Building 7:

> I remember getting a call from the, er, fire department commander, telling me that they were not sure they were gonna be able to contain the fire, and I said, "We've had such terrible loss of life, maybe the smartest thing to do is to pull it." And they made that decision to pull and we watched the building collapse.[21]

Because "pulling" a building is slang for having it demolished by explosives, this statement seems to say that Silverstein and the fire department decided to have the building deliberately destroyed. And if the building was in fact "pulled," this would explain the fact that the collapse of the building looked just like a collapse produced by explosives. As CBS anchorman Dan Rather noted on the evening of 9/11, the collapse of Building 7 was "reminiscent of those pictures we've all seen too much on television before when a building was deliberately destroyed by well-placed dynamite to knock it down."[22]

If Silverstein really did admit that Building 7 was deliberately destroyed, many questions would need to be raised. One would be why Silverstein and others who knew how this building collapsed did not inform FEMA. Silverstein could have saved FEMA the embarrassment of publishing, four months before his statement, a report with a scenario about how this building might have collapsed that FEMA itself called quite improbable.

An even more serious question would be why Silverstein and the New York Fire Department would have decided that Building 7 could not be saved. After all, as we saw above, fire was not raging through this 47-floor building. There were fires only on the seventh and twelfth floors—fires that the building's sprinkling system should have extinguished.[23] As the Alex Jones show asked: "Why would they even be considering pulling the building when it only had two small pockets of fire visible?"[24] The Commission relieved itself of answering this question, however, by not mentioning Silverstein's statement or even the mysterious fact that WTC-7 collapsed.

It might be argued, to be sure, that Silverstein's statement is susceptible of a different interpretation. But the 9/11 Commission, given the task of investigating "facts and circumstances relating to the terrorist attacks of September 11," should have interviewed Silverstein, asking him what he meant. The results of this interview and a related investigation should have been included in the report to the American people.

SIMILARITIES BETWEEN THE TWIN TOWERS AND WTC-7

If the Commission had concluded that the collapse of WTC-7 was in fact an example of controlled demolition, it would then logically have needed to ask if the same was true of the Twin Towers—at least if their collapses were similar to the collapse of Building 7. And indeed they were. They were not, to be sure, identical in all respects. The collapse of each tower began in the upper floors, near the point of the airplane's impact, whereas the collapse of WTC-7 followed the pattern of a typical demolition, in which the collapse begins at the bottom. Otherwise, however, the collapses of all three buildings shared the standard features of controlled demolitions mentioned earlier. The Commission does not mention any of these similarities, of course, since it does not even mention that Building 7 collapsed.

There was also an important similarity in the way the steel from all three buildings was treated after 9/11. Virtually all of it was quickly removed from the scene, before any forensic examination could be carried out,[25] then sold to scrap dealers and exported to other countries, such as China and Korea. This fact is possibly significant because, if explosives had been used to break the steel columns, these columns would have had tell-tale signs of the impact of these explosives. Generally, removing any evidence from the scene of a crime is a federal offense. But in this case, the FBI allowed this removal to go forward. The *New York Times* complained, saying: "The decision to rapidly recycle the steel columns, beams and trusses from the WTC in the days immediately after 9/11 means definitive answers may never be known." The next week, an essay in *Fire Engineering* said: "The destruction and removal of evidence must stop immediately."[26] But it went ahead at full speed.

The excuse given by authorities was that victims of the collapses might still be alive in the rubble, so that it was necessary to remove the steel quickly so that rescuers could get to them. This excuse, however, brings up another reason why focusing on the collapse of Building 7 is especially important: Everyone had been evacuated from the building many hours before it collapsed at about 5:30 PM, so there would have been no victims hidden in the rubble. And yet the steel from Building 7 was removed just as quickly. One will, however, look in vain in *The 9/11 Commission Report* for any mention of these matters.

THE OMISSION OF GIULIANI'S STATEMENT

The statement by Larry Silverstein is not the only provocative statement that should have been investigated. Rudolph Giuliani, who was then the mayor of New York City, said while talking to Peter Jennings on *ABC News*:

> We were operating out of there [the Emergency Command Center on the 23rd floor of WTC-7] when we were told that the World Trade Center was gonna collapse, and it did collapse before we could get out of the building.[27]

This is a remarkable statement. There was no publicly available reason to believe that the Twin Towers were going to collapse. After all, steel-frame high-rise buildings had never before collapsed because of fire, and the fires in the Twin Towers were not even raging, all-consuming fires. This is especially true of the South Tower, which collapsed first. The firemen going up the stairs in the South Tower certainly did not think it was about to collapse. And yet Giuliani's statement suggests that he somehow knew—he says he was told by someone—that the towers were going to collapse. Should the Commission not have asked Giuliani some questions about this statement, such as: Who told him the towers were about to collapse? How could anyone have known this in advance? But the Commission's report makes no mention of Giuliani's statement.

THE OMISSION OF PRESIDENT BUSH'S RELATIVES

Of course, if the Twin Towers as well as WTC-7 had been fitted with explosives so that they could be "pulled" at the appropriate time, we would have an explanation as to how some people could have known in advance that the buildings were going to collapse. Relevant to this possibility might be the fact that President Bush's brother, Marvin Bush, and his cousin, Wirt Walker III, were principals in the company that was in charge of security for the World Trade Center, with Walker being the CEO from 1999 until January 2002.[28]

The Kean–Zelikow Commission, if it did not already know about Marvin Bush's connection to this company, could have learned it from Craig Unger's well-known book, *House of Bush, House of Saud,* which included this statement:

> One of many of the ironies of the attack was that Marvin Bush, the president's brother, owned stock in and had served as a director of a company, Stratesec, that handled security for three clients that figured prominently in the attack—United Airlines; Dulles Airport, from which American Airlines Flight 77 was hijacked; and the World Trade Center itself.[29]

Unger also adds the following information:

> [O]ne of Marvin Bush's coinvestors was Mishal al-Sabah, a member of the Kuwaiti royal family, which was rescued and restored to power by Marvin's father during the Gulf War of 1991. The al-Sabah family is the same ruling Kuwaiti family that helped the elder George Bush make his fortune through Zapata Off-Shore forty years earlier. And, of course, it is the family of Nayirah, the fifteen-year-old girl whose false congressional testimony [about Iraqi

soldiers ripping Kuwaiti babies out of incubators] helped launch the Gulf War.[30]

Given all this information available to its research staff, readers should have been able to assume that the Commission would have at least interviewed Marvin Bush and Wirt Walker. But a search of *The 9/11 Commission Report* reveals no mention of either man's name, also no mention of Stratesec or its prior name, Securacom.[31]

To summarize: Many features of the Kean-Zelikow Commission's treatment of the collapses of the World Trade Center buildings—its failure to discuss the fact that fire has never before brought down steel-frame high-rise buildings, its distortion of the truth about the core of the Twin Towers, its failure even to mention the collapse of Building 7, its failure to discuss the similarities of these collapses with those caused by controlled demolition, its failure to deal with the provocative statements by Silverstein and Giuliani, and its failure to mention the positions of the president's brother and cousin—give the impression of an intent to cover up facts that do not fit the Commission's assumption that the attacks of 9/11 were planned and executed solely by members of al-Qaeda.

CHAPTER THREE

The Strike on the Pentagon

T he Commission's report, as we have seen, omits many facts about the alleged hijackers and about the collapses of three buildings of the World Trade Center—facts that would have been included if this report were truly giving us "the fullest possible account of the events surrounding 9/11." This report also fails to discuss many questions that have been raised about the official account of the damage to the Pentagon, according to which it was caused by American Airlines Flight 77 under the control of hijackers. We have already discussed one of these questions—how Hani Hanjour, being a very poor pilot, could have performed the very difficult downward spiral that was necessary for the aircraft to hit the Pentagon's west wing, especially in a giant, cumbersome airliner. But there are many more questions.

WHY THE WEST WING?

A second question involves the very fact that it was the west wing that was struck. A terrorist pilot would surely have wanted to cause as much death and destruction as possible. And yet the west wing was being renovated. Instead of the several thousand people who would normally have been working in the area that was struck, there were only about 800.[1] As a result, whereas a strike on a different part of the Pentagon would have probably killed thousands, the strike on the west wing killed only 125 people employed at the Pentagon—many of whom were civilians working on the renovation (the Commission itself points out that the victims included more civilians than military personnel [314]).[2]

A terrorist using a hijacked airplane to strike the Pentagon would also presumably want to target its top officials. But they were located elsewhere. The strike on the west wing, in fact, reportedly killed none of the top Pentagon officials and only one general.[3] Surely any al-Qaeda terrorists brilliant enough to mastermind a successful attack on the Pentagon would have known that the west wing provided the worst, rather then the best, target. The Kean–Zelikow Commission, however, reveals no curiosity about this anomaly.

THE UNCOLLAPSED FACADE AND ITS SMALL ENTRANCE HOLE

The Commission also fails to mention a photograph that creates a most awkward problem for the official account. This photograph, credited to Corporal Jason Ingersoll of the US Marine Corps (and reprinted in Thierry Meyssan's *Pentagate* and on various websites),[4] shows the west wing shortly after the fire trucks had arrived but before the facade had collapsed. One embarrassing thing about the photograph is simply that it shows this fact—that the facade had not yet collapsed. The fact that this collapse did not occur until 10:15, about a half hour after the strike, was reported the day after 9/11.[5] But it was seldom reported thereafter.[6] Corporal Ingersoll's photograph has, however, remained as a testament to this fact. But the 9/11 Commission's report mentions neither the news stories nor the photograph. It fails, accordingly, to ask a most obvious question: How could a facade, even one that had been recently reinforced, have remained standing for 30 minutes after being hit by a giant airliner weighing over 60 tons and going several hundred miles an hour?

A second embarrassing fact shown by this photograph is that the hole created in this facade was not very big, perhaps no more than 18 feet in diameter. A Boeing 757 has a wingspan of almost 125 feet and a tail that gives it a height of almost 40 feet. How could such a big airplane have created such a small hole? A story in the *Washington Post* the next day reported that the hole was "five stories high and 200 feet wide."[7] Even if the hole had been this big after the facade collapsed (which it was not), but the crucial issue is the size of the hole that was immediately caused by the aircraft that struck the Pentagon.

WHERE'S THE BOEING?

That hole was big enough for part of a Boeing 757 to have entered—its nose. But this fact creates another embarrassing problem. If the nose of a Boeing 757 had gone inside, the rest of the airplane—its wings, engines, fuselage, and tail—would have remained outside. But no Boeing is visible in photographs taken immediately after the strike, either the photograph credited to Corporal Jason Ingersoll, already mentioned, or one taken even earlier—just after the firetrucks arrived—by Tom Horan of the Associated Press (which is reprinted on the cover of Thierry Meyssan's *9/11: The Big Lie* and is also available on Meyssan's website called "Hunt the Boeing"[8]). From reading only the Kean–Zelikow Report, however, one would have no idea that these problems exist. All these inconvenient facts are simply omitted.

One can fully understand why the Commission, if it was intent on defending the official account of the Pentagon strike, would not have wanted to discuss these embarrassing facts. But if the Commission's task was to give "the fullest possible account" of the "facts and circumstances" relating to 9/11 in an "independent, impartial" way, the Commission had a duty to mention these facts, however embarrassing they might be to those who have promulgated the official account.

How might the Kean–Zelikow Commission have defended the official theory while mentioning the fact that the photographs show no airliner? One possibility would have been to endorse what has passed for the official explanation, according to which the entire plane went inside the Pentagon. This is perhaps the theory that the Commission implicitly endorses. But this theory faces difficulties. One is the fact that it must simply ignore Corporal Ingersoll's photograph, which shows that the hole was far too small for a Boeing 757 to have gone inside. Another difficulty involves the testimony of Ed Plaugher, the county fire chief who was in charge of putting out the Pentagon fire. At a press conference the next day, he was asked whether anything was left of the airplane. He replied that there were "some small pieces . . . but not large sections . . . . [T]here's no fuselage sections and that sort of thing."[9] Similar reports were given three days later by Lee Evey, the head of the renovation project, and Terry Mitchell, both of whom said no big pieces from an airplane were visible.[10] These embarrassing facts are also omitted in the report of the 9/11 Commission. Plaugher's testimony from 2001 is not cited, and the names of Evey and Mitchell are not even mentioned.[11]

Had the Commission reported this eyewitness testimony, it might have still defended the official account by endorsing an explanation that has been offered as to why no remains of a Boeing 757 were visible inside the Pentagon. According to this explanation, the fire created within the Pentagon was so hot that it not only melted the airplane, including the tempered steel engines, but even vaporized it.[12] This explanation, however, would bring us back to the problem of the type of fire that would be needed to produce such effects. A fire fed by jet fuel could at most rise to 1,700 degrees Fahrenheit, we recall, but to melt steel a fire would have to be 2,770 degrees. A fire that could completely vaporize steel would have to be still hotter. Furthermore, the claim that the fire was so hot as to melt or even vaporize the steel would not fit well with another part of the official story—the claim that the bodies of the passengers on Flight 77 were identified by their fingerprints.[13] How could a commission whose task was to try to explain what really happened on 9/11 have failed to investigate any of these contradictions?

WHAT ABOUT THE PENTAGON'S ANTI-MISSILE SYSTEM?

One more problem is how a commercial airliner, even if it had gotten to the nation's capital undetected by the FAA and military radar systems, could have actually hit the Pentagon. Is it not true, as has been reported, that the Pentagon is protected by five very sophisticated anti-missile batteries? Is it not true that they are set to fire automatically if the Pentagon is approached by any aircraft not sending out a "friendly" signal from its transponder—meaning any aircraft other than one belonging to the US military? When Thierry Meyssan wrote, "A missile should normally be unable to pass. As for a big Boeing 757-200, it would have strictly no chance," was he not correct? But the 9/11 Commission did not ask these questions.

The Commission did, interestingly, raise this issue in relation to another possible target. One criticism of the official account has been that if the attacks on the WTC had been the work of terrorists wanting to inflict severe damage on the United States, we must wonder why they did not strike the nuclear plant they passed on their way to New York City. An attack on a nuclear plant might have killed tens of thousands of Americans immediately, poisoned many more, and made a large area of the northeastern United States uninhabitable far into the future. Compared with this prospect, the death, destruction, and economic slowdown caused by the attacks on the World Trade Center were quite minimal.

The Commission implicitly provides an answer to this criticism by saying that the terrorists did indeed consider this possibility but rejected it for various reasons. One reason was that the terrorists "thought a nuclear target would be difficult because the airspace around it was restricted, making reconnaissance flights impossible and increasing the likelihood that any plane would be shot down before impact" (245). We can surely hope that US nuclear facilities are well protected. But are we supposed to believe that the Pentagon is less protected? Are we supposed to believe that the terrorists would have assumed that, whereas their hijacked airliner might be shot down if they tried to attack a nuclear power plant, no such danger existed in relation to the Pentagon?

Of all of the problems in the 9/11 Kean–Zelikow Report that appear to reflect deliberate dishonesty in the name of defending the official account, this is surely one of the most extreme. By using the possibility of a shoot-down in the one case while ignoring it in the other, the Kean–Zelikow Commission gives the appearance of having deliberately omitted mention of a very problematic dimension of the official account.

WHERE ARE THE VIDEOS?

Still another problem in the official account is that although we have all seen videos of the airplanes hitting the North and South Towers of the World Trade Center, we have not been exposed to any videos showing that the Pentagon was hit by a Boeing 757. One of the main things that the Pentagon could do to support its claim is to release videos showing an American Airlines Boeing 757 approaching and then striking the Pentagon. But it has not done this.

It is true, to be sure, that on March 7, 2002, after the publication of Thierry Meyssan's claim that the aircraft that hit the Pentagon could not have been a Boeing 757, the Pentagon released a few frames from one its security cameras. These frames were meant to support the official claim.[14] These frames are at best, however, too unclear to support the Pentagon's claim. At worst, say some critics, the frames, insofar as they show anything, show that the aircraft was not a Boeing 757.[15] Besides the ambiguity of these frames, furthermore, their release raises other questions. Why were only five frames released? Was this security camera the only one to catch the aircraft approaching the Pentagon?

The 9/11 Commission could have played an important role in answering such questions and clearing up this controversy. It could have subpoenaed all the videos taken by the Pentagon's outdoor security cameras during the relevant time period. It could have also subpoenaed videos from the nearby Sheraton Hotel and Virginia's Department of Transportation. The Commission could also have looked into a story that the FBI confiscated a video from a nearby gas station immediately after the strike on the Pentagon. According to this story, published in the *Richmond Times* ten days later, an employee at a gas station across the street from the Pentagon that services only military personnel says the gas station's security cameras should have recorded the moment of impact. However, he says, "I've never seen what the pictures looked like. The FBI was here within minutes and took the film."[16]

The 9/11 Commission should have interviewed the gas station attendant, José Velasquez, and the reporter who filed the story, Bill McKelway. But their names are not to be found in *The 9/11 Commission Report*. The Commission should also have subpoenaed the FBI for the confiscated video. And it should have interviewed the FBI agents, finding out when and from whom they received the order to confiscate the video. There is no sign, however, that the Kean–Zelikow Commission did any of these things.

In an interview in which Philip Zelikow said that it is "indisputable" that American 77 hit the Pentagon, he was asked if there were unreleased photographs of the attack that would convince the doubters. He replied "No."[17] This is probably one of the few points on which Zelikow and these doubters would agree.

AN ALTERNATIVE HYPOTHESIS

The problems for the official account that have been mentioned here— the choice of the west wing, the uncollapsed facade, the small entrance hole, the missing Boeing 757, the failure of the anti-missile batteries to protect the Pentagon, the failure of the Pentagon to produce video evidence—have led Meyssan and others to propose that what really hit the Pentagon was a small military airplane or winged missile. This alternative hypothesis fits the physical evidence much better. Indeed, the main support for the hypothesis that Flight 77 hit the Pentagon is the fact that this is what the Pentagon has told us.[18] There were, to be sure, eyewitnesses who reported seeing an American Airliner hit, or at least fly towards, the Pentagon. But eyewitness testimony cannot trump physical evidence, especially if—as in this case—this testimony turns out upon examination to be less clear than it initially seemed and to be balanced by contrary eyewitness testimony (witnesses who reported seeing what seemed to be a winged missile or small military airplane).[19]

Was it not incumbent upon the 9/11 Commission to discuss this alternative hypothesis? If they believed it to be baseless, did they not have the responsibility of telling us why? Also, Secretary of Defense Donald Rumsfeld seemed in one statement to have inadvertently endorsed the missile hypothesis, referring in an interview to "the missile [used] to damage this building."[20] Should the Commission not have asked Rumsfeld on our behalf why he said this? One might suppose, of course, that the Commissioners did not discuss Meyssan's hypothesis (and hence Rumsfeld's apparent confirmation of it) simply because they did not know about it. But Meyssan's suggestion was denounced in official pronouncements by both the FBI and the Pentagon,[21] so those agencies certainly knew about it. If the Kean–Zelikow Commissioners remained ignorant of this hypothesis, therefore, their ignorance would have been inexcusable. But equally inexcusable would be the other possibility—that they knew about it and covered it up.

CHAPTER FOUR

The Behavior of Bush and His Secret Service

One question that has been widely asked, especially since the appearance of Michael Moore's movie *Fahrenheit 9/11*, is why President Bush lingered so long in the classroom in Sarasota, Florida, after being notified about the second strike on the World Trade Center. One would assume that the Commission would have been especially anxious to give a satisfactory answer to this widely asked question. This chapter asks whether it provided such an answer.

THE DAWDLER IN CHIEF

The president had reportedly, after being told about the first crash, referred to it as a "horrible accident." Given that interpretation, it was not terribly strange that he went ahead with the planned "photo opportunity," in which he would be photographed and videotaped with second graders to publicize his educational policy. But after word came that a second plane had crashed into the WTC, it was clear that the nation was suffering an unprecedented terrorist attack. And yet, after getting this report at about 9:05, the president lingered so long in the classroom that even one of his admirers referred to him as "the dawdler in chief."[1] As that description illustrates, many critics of the president's behavior focus on the point that, as commander in chief of America's armed forces, he should have immediately moved into that role, making calls to find out more about what was happening and making sure that the nation's military was springing into action to prevent any more attacks.

WHY WAS THE PRESIDENT NOT WHISKED AWAY?

Other critics, however, have raised an even more serious problem: If the attacks on the World Trade Center were what they were purported to be—a completely surprise attack—the president and the head of his Secret Service detail would have had to assume that Bush himself might have been one of the intended targets. Indeed, one Secret Service agent, having seen the second attack on TV, reportedly said: "We're out of here."[2]

But if he did, he was obviously overruled. At the same time, Vice President Cheney was reportedly being rushed to the shelter under the White House.[3] And yet, commented *The Globe and Mail*, "For some reason, Secret Service agents [do] not hustle [Bush] away." Their failure to do so is astounding, given the fact that, in the words of two critics, "Hijackers could have crashed a plane into Bush's publicized location and his security would have been completely helpless to stop it."[4]

As that statement indicates, Bush's location that day had been well publicized, so any terrorists worth their salt would have known where he was. As far as the Secret Service would have known (given the correctness of the official story), a hijacked airliner might have been racing towards them at that very moment, preparing to crash into the school. The Secret Service agents should have immediately whisked Bush away to some unknown location. And yet this was not done. As the Commission's report points out, the presidential party remained at the school until 9:35, at which time the motorcade departed for the airport (39).

The Commission says that, having asked the president about remaining in the classroom, it received an answer:

> The President told us his instinct was to project calm, not to have the country see an excited reaction at a moment of crisis. The press was standing behind the children; he saw their phones and pagers start to ring. The President felt he should project strength and calm until he could better understand what was happening. (38)

The Commission does not tell us if they found this to be a satisfactory answer. It also does not tell us whether anyone asked the president whether it occurred to him that by staying at the school, he was making all the students and teachers potential targets of a terrorist attack. It does not tell us if anyone suggested to the president that, under the circumstances, a little lack of calm might have been appropriate.

In any case, as the Commission surely knew, it is the Secret Service that makes the decisions in situations like this. In his interview on *Meet the Press*, Vice President Cheney said that "under [such] circumstances, [Secret Service agents] just move. They don't say 'sir' or ask politely. They [simply say] 'we have to leave immediately,' and [grab you]."[5] The Secret Service agents grabbed Cheney, he said, and hustled him to safety. But the Secret Service agents with President Bush simply left him where he was, in a completely exposed position, for half an hour.

The 9/11 Commission should have had some pointed questions for the president's Secret Service detail, to which they should have demanded satisfactory answers. But here is the Commission's entire statement about why the Secret Service did not whisk President Bush to safety once it was clear the country was undergoing an attack by terrorists using hijacked airplanes:

> The Secret Service told us they were anxious to move the President to a safer location, but did not think it imperative for him to run out the door. (39)

It evidently did not occur to any of the Commissioners to point out that there would have been an option somewhere between "run[ning] out the door" and remaining at the school for another half hour. The agents could, for example, have simply walked out the door with the president, gotten into one of the cars, and driven to an undisclosed location. But the Commissioners appear to have accepted the Secret Service's totally unsatisfactory explanation.

To accept that explanation would require us to believe that these highly trained Secret Service agents were, like the president, more concerned about appearances than about the possibility that a hijacked airliner might crash into the school, killing the president and everyone else, including themselves. As far as we can tell, no one on the Commission found this sense of priorities strange. The Kean–Zelikow Commission's evident lack of curiosity is suggested by the fact that its "exacting investigative research" on this matter was evidently limited to an interview with one member of the Secret Service (463n204).

The fact that the president should have been regarded as in real danger is suggested in the account provided of that morning by Richard Clarke, who was the National Coordinator for Security and Counterterrorism. In his 2004 book, *Against All Enemies*, Clarke says that shortly after the onset of the teleconference he was running from the Situation Room in the White House, he and the others paused to listen to the president's speech from the Sarasota school. During this pause, says Clarke, Brian Stafford, the Director of the Secret Service, pulled him aside and said: "We gotta get him out of there to someplace safe. . . and secret," after which Clarke told his assistant to work with Stafford to "[f]igure out where to move the President."[6]

Although this account suggests some later sensitivity to criticism, it does nothing to alleviate the problem. Why did Stafford, whose main job is to protect the president, think of this only after Bush had already been at this publicly announced place for 30 minutes since the time that it was clear that terrorists were using hijacked airplanes to strike valuable targets? Assuming that Stafford did not know who was orchestrating the attacks, he would have had no idea how many more planes had been hijacked. Indeed, about 10 minutes earlier, according to Clarke's narrative, Stafford would have heard Jane Garvey, the head of the FAA, report that as many as 11 planes may have been hijacked.[7] That certainly should have gotten his attention. But he obviously did not call the lead Secret Service agent in Sarasota and order him to move the president immediately. Did he think it was more important to let the president give his televised speech than it was to make sure the president, his traveling party, and everyone else at the school were not killed by another hijacked airliner?

We might think that the 9/11 Commission, which was surely familiar with Clarke's book, would have queried Stafford about Clarke's report about this matter. But there is no sign that it did.

WHY WAS AIR COVER NOT ORDERED?

The Commission also apparently found no reason to press the Secret Service with regard to another decision that—unless it was based on foreknowledge that the president would not be a target of a hijacked airplane—involved gross incompetence. This is the fact that neither during the remaining time at the school, nor during the 10-minute motorcade to the airport, did the Secret Service agents call for fighter jets to protect the motorcade and then Air Force One. When the president's plane took off at about 9:54, therefore, it did so without any air cover.[8] A hijacked airplane under the control of terrorists could have simply rammed into the president's plane as it was taking off.

The Commissioners were, in fact, aware that there should have been fear that Air Force One would be attacked. They reveal this awareness in their statement that "Air Force One departed at about 9:54 without any fixed destination. The objective was to get up in the air—as fast and as high as possible—and then decide where to go" (39). But the Commissioners, as far as we can tell, did not ask the Secret Service why they did not call for air cover, rather than simply having the pilot try to outrun any potential terrorists.

The Secret Service, incidentally, could not have claimed that there were no air force bases in the area with fighters on alert. Even though the US military has been claiming since 9/11 that there were only seven bases in the entire country with fighters on full-time alert (a claim to be discussed in Chapter 12), two of those seven bases are in Florida: Homestead Air Station and Tyndall Air Station, which are, respectively, 185 and 235 miles from Sarasota.[9] Fighter jets to provide air cover for the presidential party could, therefore, have been provided within a matter of minutes. And yet the Secret Service agents, who are trained to do everything possible to protect the president, evidently thought that having air cover for Air Force One was not necessary.

The foolhardiness of this failure to provide air cover was demonstrated by the fact that at about 10:55, the pilot of Air Force One, receiving a report that there was an unidentified aircraft coming towards him, took evasive action, rising to an elevation high above normal air traffic.[10]

The fact that air cover should have been ordered is also shown by the fact that it belatedly was. Just before 10:00, the 9/11 Commission itself reports, "The White House requested . . . fighter escorts for Air Force One" (38). According to Richard Clarke, this request was made after Secret Service Director Brian Stafford, in the same conversation mentioned above, asked Clarke: "When Air Force One takes off, can it have fighter escorts?"[11]

It is doubly difficult to believe that this report reflects historical reality. In the first place, the Director of Secret Service surely did not need to make this request to Richard Clarke. The head of the Secret Service, having the primary responsibility to protect the president, can surely order fighter cover for Air Force One directly. (Indeed, the Commission reports that the Secret Service ordered planes scrambled from Andrews later that morning [44].) The second problem with this report is that Stafford does not get around to making this "request" until after 9:30, although the president's plane was scheduled to lift off about 20 minutes later. So, although Clarke says that he was amazed at how quickly the permission was given after he relayed it to Vice President Cheney, it was not until Air Force One was about to take off that Clarke was reportedly able to relay the request to the Pentagon.[12] It is not clear, furthermore, that the request was actually made at that time, because Cheney later reported that the fighter escort did not arrive until after 11:10[13]—

testimony that fits with the fact that as late as 10:55, the pilot of Air Force One had felt the need to take defensive action.

However, even if things did not actually develop in the way Clarke said, the very fact that he put in this conversation shows that there was sensitivity on someone's part to the fact that air cover should have been provided. The fact that Clarke drew attention to this problem makes the failure of the Kean–Zelikow Commission to press the point all the more significant.

IGNORING THE MORE SERIOUS CHARGE

The Commission's treatment of this issue—of why there was evidently no concern by anyone in the president's party that he would be a target of a terrorist attack—is completely unsatisfactory. It certainly should have been a burning question in the minds of the Commissioners. If the terrorist attacks were a complete surprise, as their report presupposes, then no one at the school that day would have known how many airplanes had been hijacked. "No one in the traveling party," we are told, "had any information during this time that other aircraft were hijacked or missing" (39). Assuming the truth of that statement, it would have been equally true that no one in this traveling party had information that other aircraft had *not* been hijacked, and the Secret Service is surely trained to act in terms of the worst-case scenario.

If a terrorist attack on the nation was underway, the president and his Secret Service agents would have had to suppose that he might have been one of the prime targets. The Kean–Zelikow Report tells us that we were attacked by an enemy that hates America (xvi). What greater success could America-hating terrorists have than to kill the American president? And yet for almost an hour there was no sign that those in charge were worried about this possibility. This fact has been used by some critics to suggest that they were not worried because they knew the targets and knew that the presidential party was not among them. The Commission responded to this charge in its usual way—by simply ignoring it.

The Commission did, by contrast, seek to answer the most publicized charge against the president's behavior that day—the charge that he stayed away from Washington for so long because he was afraid. The Commission repeatedly lets us know that this charge was unfair.

"The only decision made [by the presidential party] during [the period between 9:15 and 9:30]," we are told, "was to return to Washington" (39). But during the motorcade to the airport, the presidential party learned about the attack on the Pentagon, and this led the decision to be reversed, in spite of the president's wishes to the contrary:

> The [lead] Secret Service agent felt strongly that the situation in Washington was too unstable for the President to return there, and [Andrew] Card agreed. The President strongly wanted to return to Washington and only grudgingly agreed to go elsewhere. The issue was still undecided when the President conferred with the Vice President at about the time Air Force One was taking off. The Vice President recalled urging the President not to return to Washington. (39)

The note to this discussion, furthermore, provides "additional sources on the President's desire to return" (463n207). The Kean–Zelikow Commission, accordingly, certainly did not consider it beyond its assigned task to defend the president against the charge that he stayed away from Washington most of the day because he feared for his own safety.

This defense, however, makes it even more puzzling that the Commission did not discuss the much more serious charge—that the real problem was not that he appeared to be afraid later that day, but that neither he nor anyone else in his traveling party seemed to have any fear earlier, when they should have been *very* afraid.

THE DENIAL OF PRESIDENTIAL PARTY KNOWLEDGE

The reason the apparent absence of fear is important is, of course, that it suggests that at least some members of the presidential party, especially the lead Secret Service agent, knew that they were in no danger. That would in turn suggest that they knew what was going on. The 9/11 Commission obviously claims that no one in the traveling party had advance knowledge of the attacks. As we just saw, however, the Commission makes an even stronger denial of presidential party knowledge, saying: "No one in the traveling party had any information during this time that other aircraft were hijacked or missing" (39). This claim is essential. Without it, the decision by the president to continue with the reading lesson and the decision of the Secret Service to remain at the school could not have been rationalized.

Two very good sources, however, have made statements suggesting that the claim is false. One of those sources is Vice President Cheney. Five days after 9/11, Cheney said during an interview, "The Secret Service has an arrangement with the FAA. They had open lines after the World Trade Center was . . . ."[14] Although Cheney stopped himself before finishing the sentence, he was apparently going to say that the Secret Service was in constant communication with the FAA since the first strike on the World Trade Center.

The other source is Richard Clarke. He has reported that during his teleconference, Secret Service director Stafford slipped him a note saying: "Radar shows aircraft headed this way." Clarke then wrote, by way of explanation: "Secret Service had a system that allowed them to see what FAA's radar was seeing."[15] This acknowledgment means that if the FAA knew before 9:00 AM that Flight 77 had been hijacked—which, as we will see in Part II, it did—then the Secret Service also knew this. It also means that the Secret Service would have known, even before Stafford heard Jane Garvey announce it, that the FAA thought that as many as 11 planes may have been hijacked. This would surely mean that the lead Secret Service agent in the presidential party also knew all this. The fact that members of the presidential party were informed about what was going on is further reinforced by Clarke's statement that he had an open line with Captain Deborah Lower, the director of the White House Situation Room, who was traveling with the president.[16]

The Commission's claim that the presidential party had no knowledge about other hijackings is, therefore, almost certainly false. And this conclusion means that there is no publicly acceptable justification for the Commission's apparent acceptance of the Secret Service's explanation for not rushing the president to safety. If the Secret Service knew that Flight 77 and ten other planes were thought by the FAA to be hijacked, its only possible justification for not rushing the president to safety would have been: "We knew that the president was not in danger." But that, of course, could not be said. The failure of the Kean-Zelikow Commission to point out this dilemma provides one of many clues that it was dedicated to something other than revealing the truth about 9/11.

CHAPTER FIVE

Advance Information about the Attacks

The 9/11 Commission's treatment of the question of advance information about the attacks is mixed. On the one hand, the Commission reports some facts that cast doubt on the Bush administration's claim that the 9/11 attacks were a complete surprise. The Commission uses a statement from CIA Director George Tenet, "the system was blinking red" (259), as the title for the chapter. It reports that the CIA had intercepted al-Qaeda messages predicting a "spectacular" attack in the near future. The Commission also printed—supposedly in its entirety—the famous Presidential Daily Brief of August 6, 2001, which contained a memo from the CIA entitled "Bin Ladin Determined to Strike in US"[1]—which, as everyone who was paying attention knows, the administration released only after pressure was exerted by the Commission. This memo, we can see, spoke of activity "consistent with preparations for hijackings or other types of attacks" and of a report that "a group of Bin Ladin supporters was in the US planning attacks with explosives" (262). By printing this memo, the Commission, without directly criticizing the president, showed the falsity of his assertion that the briefing he received on August 6 was purely "historical in nature" (260). On the other hand, the Commission generally accepted the official explanation as to why the plot for the attacks was not uncovered in advance.

THE "LOOKING OVERSEAS" DEFENSE

The Commission by and large accepted the word of intelligence officials that they were primarily expecting attacks "overseas" (263). To explain why no one was apparently expecting the kind of attack that occurred, furthermore, the Commission developed a very fine distinction:

> The September 11 attacks fell into the void between the foreign and domestic threats. The foreign intelligence agencies were watching overseas, alert to foreign threats to US interests there. The domestic

agencies were waiting for evidence of a domestic threat from sleeper cells within the United States. No one was looking for a foreign threat to domestic targets. The threat that was coming was not from sleeper cells. It was foreign—but from foreigners who had infiltrated into the United States. (263)

The Commission does not explain, however, the distinction between foreigners who are members of sleeper cells and foreigners who have infiltrated into the United States. And it certainly does not explain what difference this distinction might have made. Are we supposed to believe that an FBI agent, for example, would say, "I'm not going to investigate the suspicious activities of these foreigners who have infiltrated into the United States, because my task is limited to investigating sleeper cells"?

In any case, the most serious issue is how the Kean–Zelikow Commission could, in spite of the August 6 memo and other information pointing to the likelihood of al-Qaeda attacks in the United States involving hijackings and explosives, claim to believe that US intelligence agencies were expecting attacks only overseas. They could do this only by ignoring, or dismissing, some other advance warnings of the attacks of 9/11, some of which were quite specific.

THE WARNING TO ATTORNEY GENERAL ASHCROFT

Attorney General John Ashcroft, on the basis of a threat assessment he had received from the FBI, reportedly decided some time before 9/11 to quit flying commercial airplanes. This story received considerable attention. "The FBI obviously knew something was in the wind," complained the *San Francisco Chronicle*. "The FBI did advise Ashcroft to stay off commercial aircraft. The rest of us just had to take our chances." CBS's Dan Rather asked, "Why wasn't [this warning] shared with the public at large?"[2] This is surely a question that many Americans wanted answered. A reporter for the Associated Press, however, said that when Ashcroft was asked about this, he walked out of his office rather than answer.[3]

But finally, with the report of the 9/11 Commission, we would surely find out what Ashcroft had to say about this, because the Commission, having subpoena power, could force him to submit to its questions. The issue was clearly of great importance because media reports suggested, as the *Chronicle* pointed out, that the FBI evidently had more specific information about upcoming attacks in the United States, involving commercial airliners, than it had let on. Yet if readers look up all 26 references to Ashcroft in the Commission report,[4] they will find nothing about this matter.[5]

ASHCROFT AND DAVID SCHIPPERS

This is, moreover, not the only omission about reports suggesting that the FBI had rather specific advance information about the attacks. Two days after 9/11, Attorney David Schippers publicly declared that over six weeks prior to 9/11, FBI agents had given him information about attacks planned for "lower Manhattan." This information, Schippers claimed, was highly specific, including the dates, the targets, and the funding sources of the terrorists. Schippers said further that the FBI field agents told him that their investigations had been curtailed by FBI headquarters, which threatened the agents with prosecution if they went public with their information. Finally—to get to the part of Schippers' claim that is most relevant to our present concern—he reported that six weeks prior to 9/11, he tried to warn Attorney General Ashcroft about the attacks, but that Ashcroft would not return his calls.[6]

One might suspect, of course, that the Attorney General's office was receiving all sorts of crank calls and that people in the office ignored the calls from Schippers because they assumed that it was one more of these. David Schippers, however, had been the Chief Investigative Counsel for the US House of Representatives' Judiciary Committee in 1998 and its chief prosecutor for the impeachment of President Clinton in 1999. He should have, accordingly, been both well known and well respected in Republican circles.

We would assume, then, that the Commission would have asked Ashcroft about the claims publicly made by Schippers. Did Ashcroft know about his calls? If so, why did he not return them? But we find no sign in the Commission's report that these questions were asked.

We would also assume that the Commission would have interviewed Schippers, to get the story directly from him. The Commission surely would have been interested to get Schippers' testimony under oath about the apparently highly specific advance knowledge FBI agents had reportedly given him. When one does a search for the name of David Schippers in *The 9/11 Commission Report*, however, one finds not a single reference.

THE FBI FIELD AGENTS

We would also assume that the Commission would have been most anxious to identify and interview under oath, perhaps with lie detectors, the FBI agents who, according to Schippers, had contacted him. This should have been even more the case because Schippers' claims were confirmed by a story in a conservative magazine, *The New American.* According to this story, three FBI agents, interviewed by the author, said "that the information provided to Schippers was widely known within the Bureau before September 11th." One of them reportedly said that some of the FBI field agents—who were some of the "most experienced guys"—"predicted, almost precisely, what happened on September 11th." This agent also reportedly said that it was widely known "all over the Bureau, how these [warnings] were ignored by Washington."[7]

"Washington," of course, meant FBI headquarters, where Thomas Pickard was the Acting Director and Dale Watson the head of counterterrorism. Watson told the Commission that "he felt deeply that something was going to happen" but that "the threat information was 'nebulous'" (265). Wouldn't the Commission have wanted to confront Pickard and Watson with the far-from-nebulous claims of these FBI field agents? When we check all the places in the Commission's report in which Pickard and Watson are mentioned, however, we find no indication that they were asked about these reports. We also find no discussion of any interviews with these FBI field agents.

The Kean–Zelikow Commission concludes that the terrorists succeeded by "exploit[ing] deep institutional failings within our government" (265). This conclusion points ahead to the Commission's recommendations, in which they propose some sweeping institutional changes. But the evidence ignored here by the Commission is evidence of failures due not to structural flaws but to the actions—and nonactions—of particular individuals: John Ashcroft, Thomas Pickard, and Dale Watson.

PUTTING DOWN THE PUT OPTIONS

Although the Commission in general simply ignored all reports suggesting that quite specific advance information about the attacks was available, there is one important exception. The Commission does mention that shortly before 9/11, the option market witnessed some highly suspicious purchases of "put options," which are bets that the price of the stock in question is going to plummet. An extremely high volume of these put options was purchased for the stock of Morgan Stanley Dean Witter, which occupied 22 floors of the World Trade Center, and for the two airlines—United and American—that were used in the attacks. Estimates of the profits after 9/11 have ranged from 10 million to 15 *billion* dollars.[8] This volume of purchases "raises suspicions that the investors," said the *San Francisco Chronicle*, "had advance knowledge of the strikes."[9]

The basis for this suspicion has in the meantime been studied by Allen Poteshman, a professor of finance at the University of Illinois, in an article entitled "Unusual Option Market Activity and the Terrorist Attacks of September 11, 2001." Starting from the fact that it has been widely said that the activity was such as to indicate foreknowledge of the attacks, Poteshman points out that an informed judgment about this matter cannot be made "in the absence of systematic information about the characteristics of option market activity." One needs, in other words, benchmark information in terms of which to evaluate the seemingly unusual purchases of put options in the days before 9/11. Poteshman first provides this benchmark information, then examines the activity related to American and United Airlines in the period between the 5th and 10th of September, 2001. Using an analysis based on "abnormal long put volume," which would reflect "the most straightforward way for terrorists or their associates to have profited from foreknowledge of the attacks," he says that this analysis "does provide evidence that is consistent with the terrorists or their associates having traded ahead of the September 11 attacks."[10]

Another dimension to this story is that investigators found that Deutsche Bank, through which many of the put options on United Airlines were purchased, had been headed until 1998 by A.B. "Buzzy" Krongard. This was a source of great potential embarrassment because Krongard, after leaving this position, went to work for the CIA. In March 2001, in fact, President Bush made him the CIA's executive director. A possible implication, of course, is that Krongard's connection to both Deutsche Bank and the CIA might point to the largest and most malevolent case of insider trading in history.[11]

For our present purposes, in any case, an even more important implication is that intelligence agencies, which monitor such trades,[12] would have had good reason to believe that in the near future, American and United airplanes were going to be used in attacks on the World Trade Center. The intelligence agencies, therefore, would have had highly specific advance information about the attacks. The Commission responded to this report, but did so only in an endnote.

The more important fact about the Commission's response, however, is how it dealt with the problem. Stating its conclusion in advance, it says: "Some unusual trading did in fact occur, but each such trade proved to have an innocuous explanation." The Commission's prime example involved United Airlines. The surge in the volume of put options on this stock on September 6, the Commission says, was "highly suspicious trading on its face." However, the Commission adds, "further investigation has revealed that the trading had no connection with 9/11."

What was the Commission's basis for this conclusion? It was, in the first place, the discovery that "[a] single U.S.-based institutional investor with no conceivable ties to al Qaeda purchased 95 percent of the UAL puts" (499n130). The implicit syllogism behind this conclusion seems to run thus:

1. The attacks of 9/11 were planned and executed solely by al-Qaeda.
2. No other person or agency had any role in, or even advance knowledge of, the attacks.
3. The purchaser of the put options on United Airlines stock had no connection with al-Qaeda.
4. Therefore the purchaser could not have had any advance knowledge of the attacks.

We have here a perfect example of the way the Kean–Zelikow Commission's work was entirely under the control of its unquestioned assumption—that the attacks were masterminded and executed solely by al-Qaeda, with no help from US officials or anyone else. Accordingly, if purchasers did not get advance information about the attacks directly from al-Qaeda, they did not get advance information, period.

We could perhaps accept this logic as satisfactory if the Commission had proved to us that (1) al-Qaeda was indeed the sole actor behind the attacks of 9/11 and that (2) no other groups or individuals knew of their plans. But the Commission, rather than providing any evidence for this hypothesis, simply assumes its truth.

This assumption is, in fact, treated as so unquestionable that it can even be used to block possible lines of research that might have refuted it.

That is, let us assume that one of the staff members suggested that they should find out if the purchaser of the United Airlines put options obtained information about the attacks from someone in the Saudi, Pakistani, or US intelligence agencies, someone at United Airlines, or someone connected with the World Trade Center. Given the Commission's unquestionable assumption, that line of research would have been dismissed as a waste of time.

The Commission, in any case, fortifies its case with a second reason to support its conclusion that this purchase was innocuous. Besides having no conceivable ties to al-Qaeda, we are told, this institutional investor purchased the United Airlines put options on September 6 "as part of a trading strategy that also included buying 115,000 shares of American on September 10" (499n130). The implicit argument here is that on the basis of inside information, this purchaser would not have bought shares (instead of put options) in American. But that does not follow, for more than one possible reason. First, it is possible that this agency had information only that an incident was about to happen that would cause United stock to plummet. If so, buying American shares might have seemed another good way to make money. Second, we are not told how the profits and losses in the two transactions compared. We are not informed, in other words, whether the losses this investor suffered from purchasing American shares came anywhere close to balancing out the profits made off the United put options. Without this knowledge, we might suspect that the purchase of the American shares was actually a clever way to provide the basis for precisely the type of defense the Commission is now giving.

Besides its faulty logic, this second argument is problematic in another way. It does not tell us who this "institutional investor" was. If the entire transaction was innocuous, why not tell us who made it? For one thing, if the Commission is confident of its position, it would presumably be happy to have independent investigators confirm the truth of its claims. In this way, this part of the allegations about advance knowledge could finally be dismissed. But because the Commission chose not to reveal the name of this investor—or any of the others—its treatment here, far from quelling the suspicions, will likely increase them.

The Commission then gives a third argument in support of its conclusion that all these purchases were innocuous, which is that much of the seemingly suspicious trading in American on September 10 was traced to a specific U.S.-based options trading newsletter, faxed to its subscribers on Sunday, September 9, which recommended these trades. (499n130)

There are several problems here. First, the fact that someone put this recommendation in a trading newsletter would not prove that it was not based on inside information. Second, we are given no idea how much is "much," so we are left in the dark about the other (perhaps 65 percent?) of the American put option purchases. Third, we are not given the name of this newsletter so that we can check out the information for ourselves.

In any case, the Commission then, on the basis of these examples, says: "These examples typify the evidence examined by the investigation" (499n130). This claim is doubly problematic. On the one hand, even if we assume that the claim is true, it does not assure us that all or even most of the put option purchases were innocuous, due to the various problems in these examples, which we have just examined. On the other hand, if we assume that the purchases that the Commission chose to use as examples truly were innocuous, what basis do we have for believing that they were truly typical? Only the word of the Commission. That might be sufficient if the remainder of the Commission's report gave us good reason to trust its word. But as we have seen, and will see even more clearly in subsequent chapters, the Commission simply has, to put it mildly, not proved its trustworthiness. So whenever its argument for some claim finally comes down to "Trust us," we have reason to be suspicious of the claim in question.

The Commission, to be sure, rests its case not simply on its own word but on the investigations of two federal agencies. It says:

> The SEC and the FBI, aided by other agencies and the securities industry, devoted enormous resources to investigating this issue, including securing the cooperation of many foreign governments. These investigators have found that the apparently suspicious consistently proved innocuous. (499 n30)

However, to support this claim the Commission simply cites a number of interviews plus an SEC memo and an FBI briefing.[13] As usual, these are references to which we have no access. So we simply have to take the word of the Commission about what the SEC and the FBI discovered. The Commission should have had the SEC studies released, so that they could have been widely examined. Reports elsewhere in the present book—especially in Chapter 8 and the Conclusion but also here and there throughout—provide ample reason to be extremely suspicious of the FBI with regard to anything having to do with 9/11. So even if the Commission is reporting faithfully what it was told by the FBI, we have little basis for trusting the content of the report.

The Commission's extremely brief treatment of this huge problem is even more problematic because of other reports it does not even mention. For example, although the suspicions about A.B. "Buzzy" Krongard, mentioned above, are very well known, the Commission fails to report whether it investigated his role in the purchases. Also, although Dr. Philip Zelikow is part of the academic world, his staff's note fails to cite any academic studies of the issue, such as Allen Poteshman's, cited above. Because of all these problems, the 9/11 Commission cannot be said to have put down the allegations that the unusual put option purchases prior to 9/11 involved insider trading.

MAYOR WILLIE BROWN AND PENTAGON OFFICIALS

There were still other stories suggesting that some people had advance knowledge. One of these was the report that eight hours prior to the attacks, San Francisco Mayor Willie Brown, who was planning to fly to New York, received a warning from airport security personnel advising him to be cautious in traveling.[14] Whatever the truth about this story is, it has been widely reported, so the Commission should have looked into it and provided the results of its investigation. But the Commission's report contains no reference to Willie Brown.

Another incident suggesting foreknowledge is also widely known because it was reported by *Newsweek* two weeks after the attacks. On September 10, according to this report, "a group of top Pentagon officials suddenly canceled travel plans for the next morning, apparently because of security concerns."[15] I could find no evidence in the report that the 9/11 Commission had investigated this story.

THE SEPTEMBER 10TH INTERCEPT FROM KSM TO MOHAMED ATTA

The stories suggesting that both Willie Brown and some Pentagon officials received warnings on September 10 are especially interesting in light of a message that was intercepted that same day by the National Security Agency (NSA). The NSA "intercepts and analyzes foreign communications and breaks codes," the Commission reminds us, "listen[ing] to conversations between foreigners not meant for them" (86, 87). In the intercept of September 10, Mohamed Atta reportedly received final approval from Khalid Shaikh Mohammed (KSM), the supposed mastermind for the attacks of 9/11, to go ahead with the attacks the next day.

According to a story in the *Independent* four days after 9/11, the NSA had not yet revealed the date on which it translated this intercept.[16] The Joint Inquiry into 9/11, which was carried out in 2002 by the intelligence committees of the US Senate and House of Representatives, said: "In the period from September 8 to September 10, 2001, NSA intercepted, but did not translate or disseminate until after September 11, some communications that indicated possible impending terrorist activity."[17]

It appears, however, that this conclusion was reached simply by taking the word of NSA officials. It would seem odd, moreover, that the NSA would not have been translating intercepts from KSM immediately, given the fact that in June 2001, the Joint Inquiry told us, US intelligence had learned that KSM was interested in "sending terrorists to the United States."[18] Would there not have been an order within the NSA to translate all intercepts from KSM immediately?

Given the fact that the 9/11 Commission was intended to do a much more thorough investigation than was possible for the Joint Inquiry, readers who knew about this issue had reason to expect to find out more about it by reading the Commission's final report. They perhaps assumed that the Commission would have had NSA officials testify not only under oath, but also while hooked up to lie detectors, that this intercept had not been translated until after 9/11. However, although the Kean–Zelikow Report contains 272 paragraphs with references to KSM, not one of them mentions this crucial intercept.[19]

As this chapter has shown, the Kean–Zelikow Commission has supported the contention by the Bush administration and its intelligence agencies that they had no specific warnings about the attacks of 9/11. But it appears to have provided this support by simply ignoring all evidence to the contrary or dismissing any such evidence on the basis of the Commission's unquestioned and unquestionable assumption, thereby begging the question.

CHAPTER SIX

Osama, the bin Ladens, and the
Saudi Royal Family

Some of the doubts that have been raised about the official account
of 9/11 involve the possibility of hidden connections and special
arrangements between the Bush administration, the Saudi royal
family, and the bin Laden family—including Osama bin Laden (OBL)
himself. Some (but not all) of these doubts have become widely known
through the publication of the aforementioned book by Craig Unger,
House of Bush, House of Saud, and Michael Moore's movie *Fahrenheit
9/11*, which popularized some of Unger's claims. One question about *The
9/11 Commission Report* that should be of interest to a large number of
people, therefore, is the Commission's findings about these allegations.

THE HUNT FOR OSAMA BIN LADEN

One of these doubts about the official account is based on stories that
appear to conflict with America's "Hunt for bin Laden." One such story
was about events said to have occurred in July 2001. At that time, OBL
was already America's "most wanted" criminal, with a $5 million bounty
on his head. And yet Richard Labeviere, a highly respected investigative
reporter from Switzerland, later provided evidence that OBL had spent
two weeks in the American Hospital in Dubai (in the United Arab
Emirates). This story, mainly unreported in the US press, was supported
by several European news agencies. While at the hospital, OBL was
reportedly treated by an American surgeon, Dr. Terry Callaway, and visited
by the local CIA agent, Larry Mitchell. Not surprisingly, this claim was
denied by the CIA, the hospital, and OBL himself. But the European news
agencies stood by their story, while Dr. Callaway simply refused to
comment.[1] The 9/11 Commission presumably could have cleared up this
controversy by using its subpoena power to call Dr. Callaway to testify
under oath. But the Commission's report gives no indication that it did
this. Indeed, a search of the report turns up no mention of Callaway,
Labeviere, or Mitchell.

In addition to this story, which suggests that the US government was less anxious to capture OBL prior to 9/11 than it said, there are also stories suggesting something similar even after 9/11, in spite of the fact that President Bush had famously spoken of wanting OBL "dead or alive." As I pointed out in *The New Pearl Harbor*, there were several articles in mainstream sources, including *Newsweek*, suggesting that the US military let OBL and his al-Qaeda forces escape on four occasions, ultimately from the Tora Bora Mountains. General Richard Myers, furthermore, said that "the goal has never been to get bin Laden."[2] One American official even reportedly warned of "a premature collapse of the international effort if by some lucky chance bin Laden was captured."[3] These actions and statements have led some critics to suspect that the US military deliberately allowed OBL and his al-Qaeda cohorts to escape, so that "the hunt for bin Laden and al-Qaeda" could be used as a pretext to achieve other US goals. An article in the *Telegraph*, in fact, said: "In retrospect, and with the benefit of dozens of accounts from the participants, the battle for Tora Bora looks more like a grand charade."[4]

The 9/11 Commission might have performed a valuable service by asking General Myers and other military leaders about these reports and statements, then informing the rest of us of their explanations. But there is no mention of any of this in the Kean–Zelikow Report.

OSAMA, THE BIN LADEN FAMILY, AND THE SAUDI GOVERNMENT

Another topic not discussed is whether the official portrait of OBL as the disowned "black sheep" of the bin Laden family is correct. According to Labeviere, while OBL was in the hospital in Dubai, he also received visits "from many members of his family as well as prominent Saudis and Emirates."[5] The idea that OBL had not really been rejected and disowned is also supported by other evidence. Unger, for example, reports that "[d]uring the summer of 2001, just a few months before 9/11, several of the bin Ladens attended the wedding of Osama's son in Afghanistan, where Osama himself was present."[6] But the 9/11 Commission does not discuss any of these reports.

A related question involves OBL's relationship to the Saudi government. The official story is that all positive ties were severed many years before 9/11. According to Prince Faisal bin Salman, "Osama bin

Laden is the arch enemy of the Saudi regime. He was kicked out of the country 10 years ago. His citizenship was revoked."[7] But one of many reports in apparent tension with this story is Labeviere's, which said that OBL's visitors at the Dubai hospital included the head of Saudi intelligence, which would have been Prince Turki (to be discussed below).[8] Again, the 9/11 Commission might have been able to get information about this by forcing Dr. Callaway to testify, but clearing up this issue was evidently not a priority.

SAUDI ADVANCE KNOWLEDGE OF ATTACKS ON AMERICA?

Another related—even more explosive—question is whether there was any relationship between the Saudi royal family and 9/11. A story suggesting that there was has been published by Gerald Posner.[9] Posner's story is about the interrogation of a major al-Qaeda operative, Abu Zubaydah, who was captured in March 2002. I will here summarize Posner's account of what happened next, only asking later whether we should accept this account.

Posner says that Zubaydah was being interrogated by two Arab-American agents who were pretending to be, like himself, from Saudi Arabia. Believing he was talking with fellow Saudis, Posner says, Zubaydah told them that he had been working on behalf of senior Saudi officials. Then Zubaydah, encouraging his interrogators to confirm his claim, gave them from memory the telephone numbers of one of King Fahd's nephews, Prince Ahmed bin Salman (founder of the Thoroughbred Corporation, which owned Point Given, the 2001 Horse of the Year, and War Emblem, the winner of the Kentucky Derby and the Preakness in 2002). Prince Ahmed, Zubaydah said, served as an intermediary between al-Qaeda and the Saudis. The prince, Zubaydah assured his interrogators, would confirm his statements.

These interrogators, however, replied that even if that was true, 9/11 would have surely changed everything, so that Prince Ahmed would no longer be supportive of al-Qaeda. But Zubaydah replied that nothing would have changed, because Prince Ahmed had known in advance that America would be attacked on 9/11. To be precise, Prince Ahmed, according to Zubaydah, "knew beforehand that an attack was scheduled for American soil for that day" but "didn't know what it would be."[10]

Posner also says that Zubaydah, seeking to give more support for his claims, gave from memory the phone numbers of two other relatives of King Fahd's: Prince Sultan bin Faisal and Prince Fahd bin Turki. Zubaydah said that they, also serving as intermediaries between the Saudi government and al-Qaeda, could likewise confirm his claims.[11]

Posner says that his confidence in the truth of this account is strengthened by three facts. First, the story was provided to him separately by two informants within the US government. Second, another source confirmed that the interrogation techniques were accurately described.[12]

Third, and most important, not long after CIA officials told their counterparts in Saudi Arabia about Zubaydah's claims, evidently in May of that same year (2002), all three of the named Saudis died within an eight-day period near the end of July, with the reported cause of death being surprising in each case: Prince Ahmed reportedly died of a heart attack in his sleep, although he was only 41; Prince Sultan reportedly died on the way to Ahmed's funeral in a single-car accident; and Prince Fahd, who was 21, reportedly died of thirst in the desert.[13]

Additional reason to accept the truth of Posner's account is provided by an additional surprising development involving Prince Ahmed. This additional development has been reported not by Posner but by Craig Unger, who relates and accepts Posner's account of Zubaydah's testimony to the pseudo-Saudi interrogators.[14] What happened was that a month and a half before the death of Prince Ahmed on July 22, he failed to show up for the Belmont Stakes, although he had earlier indicated that virtually nothing was more important to him than winning this race. His horse Point Given had come in fifth in the Kentucky Derby in 2001, leaving the prince devastated (although this horse did win the two other legs of racing's Triple Crown that year, the Preakness and the Belmont Stakes). In April 2002, Prince Ahmed saw another way to realize his dream. Having watched War Emblem win the Illinois Derby by six lengths, he used his enormous wealth to buy this horse "for an astonishing $910,000,"[15] being convinced that it could win the Kentucky Derby. And on May 7, it did, making Ahmed proud, he said, "to be the first Arab to win the Kentucky Derby." Then two weeks later, War Emblem won the Preakness Stakes. Ahmed was thereby only one leg away from being the first Triple Crown winner since 1977. When a reporter asked the prince how badly he wanted to win it, he replied: "As badly as I want my son and daughter to get married. . . . To win the Triple Crown would really knock me out."[16]

But on June 8—which was, according to Posner, after CIA agents had informed their counterparts in Saudi intelligence about Zubaydah's claims—Ahmed did not even show up for the Belmont Stakes, citing "family obligations."[17] And on July 22, he was dead. The official explanation—that his heart attack at such a young age could be explained by his lifestyle and genetic inheritance[18]—would surely be more believable if the two other men named by Zubaydah had not died, also under mysterious circumstances, immediately thereafter.

Posner's report should certainly be disturbing to all those who accept the official account of 9/11, especially the 9/11 Commissioners, whose assignment it was to find out all the "facts and circumstances" surrounding 9/11. If some members of the Saudi royal family knew about the 9/11 attacks in advance, that would certainly be an important part of these facts and circumstances. The Commissioners, moreover, should have had no *a priori* reason to distrust Posner, because he on most issues supports the official view, including the Commission's view that the attacks were able to succeed because of various kinds of breakdowns and bureaucratic impediments, especially the failures of agencies to share information.[19] And yet the Commission does not even mention Posner's book.

Nor does the Commission otherwise mention the claims reportedly made by Abu Zubaydah. This omission is certainly not because of any unfamiliarity with Zubaydah. He is one of the major characters in the Commission's narrative, being mentioned in 39 paragraphs. And yet not one of those paragraphs discusses his reported claim that at least three members of the Saudi royal family had foreknowledge about the attacks of 9/11. (Indeed, although Prince Ahmed was one of the best-known Saudis in America, his name is not to be found in the Commission's report.) Perhaps the Kean–Zelikow Commission felt that even to report such claims might be damaging to US–Saudi relations. But presumably the reason for having an *independent* Commission was so that it could discover and report the relevant facts without regard to possible political consequences.

As I have just indicated, my concern with Posner's story is the fact that although it made claims that, if true, were extremely germane to the work of the 9/11 Commission, the Commission did not deal with them, even to refute them. A secondary question, from the perspective of the present book, is whether Posner's story is credible. Although this *is* a secondary matter, I will discuss it briefly, pointing out that there are grounds for either view.

Doubt about the story's truth could be based on one or more of a number of reasons. First, questions about Posner's scholarship and even honesty have been raised in the past. Second, Posner's discussion of Zubaydah is the only part of his book that is in conflict with the official conspiracy theory about 9/11. Third, Posner in the past has supported the official view on controversial stories, probably most famously—or notoriously—in his *Case Closed*, in which he supported the view that President Kennedy was assassinated by Lee Harvey Oswald working entirely alone.[20] Taking into account these considerations, some people may suspect that Posner is part of a plot to prepare the American public for a possible invasion of Saudi Arabia at some time in the future (in order to gain control of the world's richest oil reserves). By adding Posner's Zubaydah story to the claim that 15 of the hijackers were Saudi nationals, the US government could argue, if and when it became convenient, that it had learned that the attacks of 9/11 had been planned and funded by the Saudi government.

This scenario could be believed, furthermore, even apart from any doubts about Posner's sincerity in telling his story about Zubaydah. That is because all of Posner's information about Zubaydah, as he reports, came from informants within the US government. One could suppose that the US government, or at least some faction within it, used Posner to spread inflammatory disinformation about the Saudi princes.

On the other hand, there is much to support Posner's account. First, it is a fact that the three Saudi princes died shortly after Zubaydah was captured (and that, as will be mentioned in Chapter 9, a Pakistani officer named by Zubaydah also died in a surprising accident not long afterwards). Second, it is also a fact that Prince Ahmed did not show up for the Belmont Stakes, in spite of his great passion for winning the triple crown (a fact that Posner perhaps did not know). Third, Zubaydah's alleged account, according to which the actual relationship of the Saudi royal family to al-Qaeda is very different from what both the Saudi and the American governments publicly claim it to be, is supported by further reports by Craig Unger, Josh Meyer, and Senator Bob Graham, discussed below.

Of course, from the perspective of those who believe that Posner's story is part of a grand plan to prepare the American public for an invasion of Saudi Arabia, the same could be true of these other stories, at least those reported by Meyer and Graham. I myself, in any case, have no basis for determining the truth of this matter—along with many other matters related to 9/11. This is one reason that in the present book, as in *The New Pearl Harbor*, I do not try to explain "what really happened." My focus is on problems in the official accounts. Just as in the previous book I concentrated on problems in the official account of 9/11 itself, in the present book I focus on problems in the 9/11 Commission's attempt to defend that official account.

One of these problems is that even though Posner's story is now in the public domain, the Commission fails to mention it.

THE QUESTION OF SAUDI FUNDING OF AL-QAEDA

While Zubaydah was making his claim about having served as an intermediary between al-Qaeda and the Saudis, Posner says, he also claimed that the Saudis regularly sent money to al-Qaeda.[21] The Commission fails to mention this reported claim. Indeed, the Commission explicitly denies having found any evidence of Saudi funding. It was not clear from Posner's account of Zubaydah's claim, incidentally, whether it referred to funding from the Saudi government as such or only from members of the royal family as individuals. In either case, however, it would be covered by the Commission's denial, which says:

> Saudi Arabia has long been considered the primary source of al Qaeda funding, but we have found no evidence that the Saudi government as an institution or senior Saudi officials individually funded the organization. (This conclusion does not exclude the likelihood that charities with significant Saudi government sponsorship diverted funds to al Qaeda.) (171)

The parenthetical caveat at the end allows the Commission to acknowledge that Saudi-sponsored "charities" may have given money to al-Qaeda. But this acknowledgment is consistent with the Commission's main point—that it "found no evidence" that the Saudi government or members of the Saudi royal family intentionally provided funds for al-Qaeda.

The note for this point does not, of course, mention Posner's book. It mentions, in fact, only an interview with a David Aufhauser (498n122). Again, this is a very strange way to illustrate "exacting investigative work." It seems hard to resist the conclusion that the

Kean–Zelikow Commission's "research" on this issue was aimed less at discovering the relevant evidence than at supporting a particular conclusion—in this case, one that would be good for US–Saudi relations. The Saudi government, in any event, obviously appreciated it: A Saudi public relations ad recently released in the United States quotes the Commission's statement that it "found no evidence that the Saudi government as an institution or senior Saudi officials individually funded the organization." Again, however, the Commission's task was to provide "the fullest possible account of the events surrounding 9/11," not necessarily the account that would have the best political consequences for America's relationships with oil-rich countries.

Thanks to a story by Josh Meyer of the *Los Angeles Times*, furthermore, we have evidence from inside the Commission itself that its statement about this issue was politically motivated. Meyer's story, titled "2 Allies Aided Bin Laden, Say Panel Members," was based on interviews with "several senior members" of the 9/11 Commission, only one of whom, Bob Kerrey, is named. The occasion for this story, published June 20, 2004—about a month before the publication of *The 9/11 Commission Report*—was the appearance earlier that month of a report issued by the 9/11 Commission's staff during a hearing on the origins of al-Qaeda and the 9/11 plot. This report alluded to the staff's discoveries about the roles played by both Saudi Arabia and Pakistan in the growth of al-Qaeda. In interviews, Meyer reported, senior members of the Commission said that its investigation "had uncovered more extensive evidence than the report suggested." It in particular had uncovered evidence that "Saudi Arabia provided funds and equipment to the Taliban and probably directly to Bin Laden."[22]

The Commission, in other words, had discovered evidence similar to that found by Posner. But the Commission's first concern was evidently not to provide "the fullest possible account," regardless of political consequences. "Now," wrote Meyer, "the bipartisan commission is wrestling with how to characterize such politically sensitive information in its final report, and even whether to include it."[23]

To see which concern—eliminating "politically sensitive information" or providing "the fullest possible account"—won out in the Commission's "wrestling" with this issue, we need only to look at the Commission's statement in its final report: "[W]e have found no evidence that the Saudi government as an institution or senior Saudi officials individually funded the organization." If Meyer's story is accurate, it is hard to characterize that statement as anything other than a lie. What the Commission might have truthfully said—given Meyer's use of the word probably—is that "no conclusive proof" of such funding had been found. But the denial that any evidence whatsoever had been found is surely false.

According to Senator Bob Graham, moreover, to speak truthfully the Commission would have needed to talk of conclusive proof. In his recent book, *Intelligence Matters*, he reveals details about Saudi funding of al-Qaeda that he learned as co-chair of the Joint Inquiry into the 9/11 attacks carried out by the intelligence committees of the US Senate and House of Representatives. Although the Inquiry's public (unclassified) report was published in July of 2003, much of the material was blacked out by the CIA, the FBI, and the NSA, with the blessing of the White House. Graham's book deals with a 27-page section of this blacked-out material that dealt with "the Saudi government and the assistance that government gave to some and possibly all of the September 11 terrorists."[24]

At the center of Graham's narrative is Omar al-Bayoumi, to whom I devoted merely one paragraph in *The New Pearl Harbor*. The main facts of his case were the following: In 1999, while living in San Diego, he picked up two of the (alleged) hijackers—Nawaf Alhazmi and Khalid Almihdhar—at the Los Angeles airport, set them up in an apartment near his place, and helped them locate flight schools. He was thought by an FBI informer to be a Saudi intelligence officer. After 9/11, he was arrested by agents in England, where he had moved two months earlier; but the FBI, saying that it believed his story that he had met Alhazmi and Almihdhar by chance, had him released.[25] Graham fills in many details not provided in earlier reports about al-Bayoumi.

Besides showing that al-Bayoumi's meeting with the two al-Qaeda operatives did not occur by chance, Graham points out that just before picking them up, he met with a man at the Saudi consulate in Los Angeles suspected of terrorist connections.[26] Graham also reveals that not only did al-Bayoumi have a "ghost job"—meaning he did no work—for which he was paid, at the insistence of the Saudi government, over $3,000 a month, but also that these payments went up to $6,500 a month while Alhazmi and Almihdhar were with him.[27] Furthermore, Graham points out that al-Bayoumi, besides making an extraordinary number of calls to Saudi officials, also had the contact number for someone in the Saudi embassy in his possession when he was arrested in

England.[28] Finally, Graham quotes a CIA memo from August 2002 calling him an "agent" and speaking of "incontrovertible evidence that there is support for these terrorists [al-Bayoumi and Osama Basnan, to be discussed below] within the Saudi government."[29]

In spite of all this evidence, however, Graham reports, the FBI closed its case on al-Bayoumi, claiming that he had only "briefly lent money to two of the 19 hijackers" and that all his assistance to them was "in compliance with the Muslim custom of being kind to strangers [rather] than out of some relationship with Saudi Intelligence."[30] Graham, amazed by this conclusion, asked to interview the FBI agents who made this report, but FBI Director Robert Mueller refused to allow this.[31] Although Graham realizes that this refusal could simply reflect the FBI's attempt to avoid embarrassment, he also muses about a "far more damning possibility," namely, "that perhaps the informant did know something about the plot that would be even more damaging were it revealed, and that this is what the FBI is trying to conceal."[32]

Graham's criticism is, however, not finally directed at the FBI but at the administration from which it takes its orders. During the course of his investigations, he found not only that "the White House was directing the cover-up" but that it was doing so "for reasons other than national security."[33] His evidence suggests in particular, he says, that the White House orchestrated the cover-up "to protect not only the agencies that had failed but also America's relationship with the Kingdom of Saudi Arabia."[34]

To see the full implications of Graham's revelations for the 9/11 Commission's report, we need only to recall that the Commission began with the information that was in the final report of the Joint Inquiry. We need not wonder, therefore, whether the 9/11 Commission's staff perhaps failed to come across the matters contained in Graham's book. The 9/11 Commission had this information in hand when it began its work. With this in mind, how can we interpret the Commission's published statement—"we have found no evidence that the Saudi government as an institution or senior Saudi officials individually funded the [al-Qaeda] organization"—as anything other than a flat-out lie?

There is, moreover, yet another dimension to the Commission's cover-up of information about Saudi financial support for al-Qaeda through Omar al-Bayoumi.

DID PRINCE BANDAR AND PRINCESS HAIFA HELP AL-QAEDA?

The most publicized story about money going from the family of a Saudi official to al-Qaeda operatives involved none other than Prince Bandar bin Sultan, the Saudi ambassador to the United States, and his wife, Princess Haifa. According to both Unger and Graham, over $100,000 was sent by the two of them—most of it from Princess Haifa—to the wife of Osama Basnan, who was a friend of al-Bayoumi. The money was originally for Basnan's wife's thyroid condition. But beginning in 2000, Basnan's wife began signing over her checks to al-Bayoumi's wife. At least some of this money was then turned over to Nawaf Alhazmi and Khalid Almihdhar. That Basnan knew what was going on became clear when he later bragged to FBI agents that he had done more for the hijackers than had al-Bayoumi.[35] Unger concludes: "What had happened was undeniable: funds from Prince Bandar's wife had indirectly ended up in the hands of the hijackers."[36]

How did the Commission treat this "undeniable" story? Very briefly. It says in a note: "We have found no evidence that Saudi Princess Haifa al Faisal provided any funds to the conspiracy, either directly or indirectly." (For support evidence, it merely says [498n122]: "See Adam Drucker interview [May 19, 2004]," without telling us how we might "see" it.) The Commission does not even qualify its statement by suggesting, as Unger does, that Princess Haifa did not provide the funds "intentionally." It simply says that it found no evidence that she provided any funds—even indirectly—period.

The Commission, therefore, seems to be denying either the truth or its knowledge of the story summarized by Unger. But this story is based on articles by other reporters, including Michael Isikoff of *Newsweek*. Also, as we have seen, it would have known about this evidence through the final report of the Joint Inquiry. Perhaps in this case the Kean–Zelikow Commission, in repeating its mantra—"we have found no evidence"—implicitly meant: "We did not need to 'find' it. It was handed to us by the Joint Inquiry."

The Commission, in any case, does not even mention Prince Bandar bin Sultan in this connection. Unger does. Having pointed out that at least some of the money came from Bandar himself, Unger says that there had been "charges that Prince Sultan had knowingly funded terrorists."[37] Unger does not himself support this charge, but he does report that it was made. Not so the Kean–Zelikow Commission.

With regard to this part of the Commission's report, we have, to my knowledge, no peephole into its deliberations. But in light of Josh Meyer's story, from which we can conclude that the Commission simply decided not to include its evidence pointing to Saudi funding of al-Qaeda, we can suspect that political considerations again trumped the desire to provide the fullest possible account.

CHAPTER SEVEN

The Saudi Flights

One episode raising questions about the relations between the Bush White House, on the one hand, and the bin Laden and royal families, on the other, requires a chapter unto itself. This episode involved numerous airplane flights through which many Saudi nationals, including members of the bin Laden and royal families, were able to leave the country shortly after 9/11. These Saudi flights became a subject of public discussion because of three allegations about the flights. According to these allegations: (1) On September 13, an exception was made in order to allow a private flight to take Saudis from Tampa to Lexington. (2) Between September 14 and 24, flights carrying Saudis were allowed to leave the country without thorough investigations of the passengers. (3) These flights could have been made possible only through political intervention from the White House. *The 9/11 Commission Report* seeks to refute all three allegations.

THE TAMPA–LEXINGTON FLIGHT ON SEPTEMBER 13

In response to the first allegation, the Commission says that it "found no evidence that any flights of Saudi nationals, domestic or international, took place before the reopening of national airspace on the morning of September 13, 2001" (329). Does that refute the allegation? Readers previously unfamiliar with this controversy would find it difficult to tell because, as usual, the Commission does not tell us where or by whom the allegation had been made.

In this case, the charge was made primarily by investigative journalist Craig Unger, whose book *House of Bush, House of Saud* was mentioned earlier. The charge was that on September 13, while the ban on flights by private planes was still in effect, a private flight was allowed to take three young Saudis from Tampa to Lexington. Because this ban was still in effect, Unger concluded, "[t]he flight could not have taken place without White House approval."[1]

This flight had first been reported in the *Tampa Tribune* on October 5, 2001,[2] but it had been denied, Unger says, by the FBI, the FAA, and the White House. Unger, however, had confirmed the story through interviews with "sources who helped orchestrate the flights" and two security guards—one of whom was a former FBI agent—who accompanied the Saudis on the flight.[3] The Commission surely knew about Unger's charge, because it had been repeated in an article by Unger in the *Boston Globe* that was explicitly directed to the 9/11 Commission.[4]

The Commission, in fact, played a role in bringing out the truth about this flight. In June 2004, Tampa International Airport, after prodding by the Commission, confirmed that the flight had indeed occurred.[5]

But did the Commission then conclude that the FBI, the FAA, and the White House had been lying? No, the Commission says, it was all a mistake, a fuss over nothing. The Commission, in fact, implies that the FBI had never really denied the existence of the flight, saying:

> The FBI is alleged to have had no record of the flight and denied that it occurred, hence contributing to the story of a "phantom flight."[6] This is another misunderstanding. The FBI was initially misinformed about how the Saudis got to Lexington by a local police officer in Lexington who did not have firsthand knowledge of the matter. The Bureau subsequently learned about the flight. (557n25)

This is less than helpful. For one thing, we are not given the name of the "local police officer," and the sole support cited for the Commission's claim about what really happened is an interview on June 18, 2004, with "James M." How would any journalists check out for themselves the claim that the FBI was initially misinformed? The Commission also does not tell us when the Bureau "subsequently learned about the flight," so we do not know whether the Commission means to be contradicting Unger's allegation that the FBI had continued to deny the existence of the flight well into 2004. Because we are not told how long the FBI remained "misinformed," furthermore, we do not know whether we are being asked to believe that the FBI continued to rely on faulty information it had received from a Lexington police officer for a long period, perhaps the three years that, according to Unger, it was denying that the flight took place. If so, are we expected to believe that the FBI would not have checked with Tampa International Airport during this period? Are we to believe that the FBI had no way to learn that one of the security guards on the flight was a former member of the FBI? But the Commission's claim is so vague that we do not know what we are being asked to believe.

Another problem with this defense, in any case, is that it refers only to the FBI. The Commission does not respond to Unger's report that a spokesman for the FAA, Chris White, had told the *Tampa Tribune*, "It's not in our logs. . . . It didn't occur,"[7] and that the White House told Unger that it was "absolutely confident" that the alleged flight did not take place.[8]

The Commission also implies that there would have been no reason for these agencies to have lied, because there was nothing extraordinary about the flight. The heart of the Commission's defense, in fact, is that the flight did not take off until many hours after "the reopening of national airspace on the morning of September 13, 2001." The Kean–Zelikow Commission, appearing to be very precise, says: "The Department of Transportation reopened the national airspace to US carriers effective 11:00 AM on September 13, 2001," whereas the Saudi plane "took off at 4:37 PM, after national airspace was open, more than five hours after the Tampa airport had reopened, and after other flights had arrived at and departed from that airport" (329, 556n25). Reinforcing its point that nothing extraordinary happened here— nothing that would have required White House intervention—the Commission says: "The plane's pilot told us there was 'nothing unusual whatsoever' about the flight other than there were few airplanes in the sky" (556n25).

But if that gave us the whole picture, why would Craig Unger have oriented his entire book around this flight (along with the flights that soon left the country, to be discussed below), making it the key episode of the first and final chapters? A hint as to the answer is provided in the pilot's statement, just quoted, that "there were few airplanes in the sky." Is that not strange? All civilian flights in the country had been grounded since September 11, so there were surely thousands of flights, with millions of passengers, chomping at the bit to take off. And yet after 4:30 on September 13, almost six hours after US airspace had finally been reopened, there were still only a few planes in the sky? Why would that be?

The answer involves a crucial distinction, which was ignored by the Commission, even though it had been emphasized by Unger. His point, as I stated earlier, was that the Tampa–Lexington flight was allowed "while the ban on flights by private planes was still in effect." The Commission simply says that the authorities had at 11:00 AM "reopened the national airspace to U.S. carriers," ignoring the crucial distinction between commercial and private carriers. But Unger had emphasized this distinction, saying:

> Commercial flights had slowly began to resume, but at 10:57 AM, the FAA had issued another NOTAM [notice to airmen], a reminder that private aviation was still prohibited. Three private planes violated the ban that day, in Maryland, West Virginia, and Texas, and in each case a pair of jet fighters quickly forced the aircraft down. As far as private planes were concerned, America was still grounded.[9]

It was, Unger emphasized, not until the next day—Friday, September 14—that "private planes were cleared to fly."[10] And yet the Kean–Zelikow Commission failed to point out this distinction.

This failure is especially troublesome, in light of the fact that Unger himself, over a month and a half before *The 9/11 Commission Report* appeared, explicitly corrected it in advance in an Op-Ed piece in the *New York Times*. Pointing out that the 9/11 Commission's investigative panel had already concluded that there is "no credible evidence that any chartered flights of Saudi Arabian nationals departed the United States before the reopening of national airspace," Unger replied that "the real point is that there were still some restrictions on American airspace when the Saudi flights began."

How do we account for the Commission's failure to point out the distinction between commercial and private flights? Was the Commission deliberately trying to deceive readers? Or was its staff's allegedly "exacting investigative work" in fact incredibly incompetent? Whichever answer we choose, the implications are disturbing, eroding whatever basis we may have had for assuming that we can trust the Commission's statements as to the definitive "facts and circumstances" surrounding 9/11.

Those who suspect that the Commission's distortion was due more to design than to incompetence will find this suspicion reinforced by the Commission's use of the pilot's statement—that there was "nothing unusual whatsoever" about the flight. That statement may well have been true of the flight as such. But the question remains whether the very fact that this plane was allowed to fly on September 13 was considered unusual. And here we see again that the 9/11 Commission simply omitted crucial information. Unger had reported that one of the security guards on the flight said: "Flight restrictions had not been lifted yet." This was Dan Grossi, who had recently retired after serving 20 years on the Tampa Police Department. He added: "I was told it would take White House approval. I thought [the flight] was not going to happen." Unger had also quoted the other security guard—Manuel ("Manny") Perez, the former FBI agent—as saying: "They got the approval from somewhere. It must have come from the highest levels of government."[11]

This is a very different picture from the one we get from the Kean–Zelikow Report, which gives us only the pilot's statement, quoted above, and a statement by the airplane company's owner, who said that the flight "was just a routine little trip for us," adding that if there had been anything unusual about it, he would have heard about it (556–57n25). From the endnotes we learn that the Commission interviewed Dan Grossi and Manuel Perez. But the Commission makes no mention of their surprise, expressed to Unger, that the plane was allowed to take off. Had the staff, while doing its "exacting investigative work," failed to read Unger's book? Did the Commission's interview fail to evoke this information from Grossi and Perez? Or did the Commission simply choose to omit this part of their testimony? Again, either answer would be disturbing.

The Commission also tells us that the pilot said he followed standard procedures, filing his flight plan with the FAA prior to the flight. The Commission then adds that "FAA records confirm this account" (557n25). This would seem to imply that if back in 2001 the FAA's Chris White said of this flight, "It's not in our logs. . . . It didn't occur," he lied or at least was seriously confused. But the Commission, having not informed its readers that any FAA spokesperson ever reportedly made such a comment, did not seek to reconcile these conflicting testimonies. Although Unger's book, published early in 2004, reported that the FAA was still denying the existence of this flight, the Commission gives readers the impression that the FAA, having had the flight in its records, would never have denied its existence.

To conclude: The Kean–Zelikow Commission has been able to give readers the impression that the first allegation is unfounded only by ignoring the crucial distinction between commercial and private flights and otherwise giving a very incomplete and distorted account.[12] For readers who have the fuller picture, the Commission has done nothing to undermine the contention that the Tampa–Lexington flight on September 13 would have required authorization from the White House. I turn now to the Commission's treatment of the second allegation.

THE FLIGHTS CARRYING SAUDIS OUT OF THE COUNTRY

The second allegation is that between September 14 and 24, flights carrying Saudis were allowed to leave the country without adequate investigations and interrogations of the passengers. The Commission again argues that nothing improper was done, certainly nothing sufficiently unusual to have required White House intervention. The Commission says:

> [W]e believe that the FBI conducted a satisfactory screening of Saudi nationals who left the United States on charter flights. . . . The FBI interviewed all persons of interest on these flights prior to their departures. They concluded that none of the passengers was connected to the 9/11 attacks and have since found no evidence to change that conclusion. Our own independent review of the Saudi nationals involved confirms that no one with known links to terrorism departed on these flights. (329–30)

A problematic aspect of this statement is that it seems to confuse two very different issues: having no *known* links to terrorism and being unconnected to the 9/11 attacks. Nevertheless, readers who have full confidence in the Commission's judgment may be inclined to accept this statement, made in the text, as sufficient to settle the matter. But for readers who decide to see how well founded the Commission's conclusions are, some disturbing facts can be found, both in the Commission's notes and in Unger's writings.

In its notes, the Commission gives special attention to "the so-called Bin Ladin flight," which left the country on September 20 with "26 passengers, most of them relatives of Usama Bin Ladin."[13] The Commission seems pleased to report that "22 of the 26 people on the Bin Ladin flight were interviewed by the FBI. Many were asked detailed questions" (557n28). But this statement implies that some of the people who were interviewed were *not* asked detailed questions. It also implies that four of the passengers were not interviewed at all. Evidently not disturbed by these implications, the Commission goes on to support the FBI's conclusion—that "none of the passengers was connected to the 9/11 attacks"—by saying: "None of the passengers stated that they had any recent contact with Usama Bin Ladin or knew anything about terrorist activity" (557n28). The Kean–Zelikow Commission evidently assumed that if any of the other bin Ladens had recently been in contact with Osama or did know anything about terrorist activity, they would have spoken right up. We can only wonder if the Commission would recommend this approach to police officers in charge of interrogating suspects in criminal cases.

The Commission's apparently casual attitude to this issue is especially surprising given the fact that Unger's well-publicized book had reported, as mentioned earlier, that there were reasons to doubt the claim that the bin Laden family had "cut off ties with their errant terrorist sibling." Developing this point more fully, Unger says:

> According to Carmen bin Laden, an estranged sister-in-law of Osama's, several members of the family may have continued to give money to Osama. At least one member of the family, Osama's brother-in-law Mohammed Jamal Khalifa, was a central figure in Al Qaeda and was widely reported to be linked to the 1993 World Trade Center bombing. . . .
>
> Two other relatives were key figures in a charitable foundation linked to Osama. The American branch of the World Assembly of Muslim Youth (WAMY) was directed by Abdullah bin Laden. . . . His brother Omar bin Laden was also on WAMY's board. . . . "WAMY was involved in terrorist support activities," says a security official who served under George W. Bush. . . . FBI documents marked "Secret" and coded "199," indicating a national security case, show that Abdullah bin Laden and Omar bin Laden were under investigation by the FBI for nine months in 1996 and that the file was reopened on September 19, 2001, eight days after the 9/11 attacks.[14]

Should not Unger's information, which was available to the Commissioners, have made them more concerned about the fact that all the bin Ladens were allowed to depart so quickly?

Another disturbing fact in the Commission's notes is that the FBI's investigation of the bin Laden flight was evidently quite rigorous by comparison with its investigation of the other flights, because on those flights, "most of the passengers were not interviewed" (557n28).

The 9/11 Commission, nevertheless, conveys the impression that the evacuation flights were handled in a very orderly way. It assures us that "no inappropriate actions were taken to allow those flights to depart" (556n25). It also assures us that all the flights—or at least all the ones it examined—"were screened in accordance with policies set by FBI headquarters and coordinated through working-level interagency processes" (557n28). One would assume that the flights left in accordance with general, long-standing FBI policies (as opposed to ones manufactured on the spot) and that the local FBI agents had all the time they needed to implement these policies, especially by having extensive interviews with all passengers it considered "persons of interest."

Unger, however, suggests that the actual situation was quite different. One of the flights left Las Vegas for Geneva on September 16, carrying 46 passengers, several of whom were members of the Saudi royal family. Unger reports that one of his sources, who participated in this operation, described it as a "nightmare," explaining in these words:

> The manifest was submitted the day before. It was obvious that someone in Washington had said okay, but the [local] FBI didn't want to say they could go, so it was really tense. In the end, nobody was interrogated.

Unger then added:

> The FBI did not even get the manifest until about two hours before departure. Even if it had wanted to interview the passengers—and the bureau had shown little inclination to do so—there would not have been enough time.[15]

According to Unger, this flight, at least, did not illustrate the orderly process portrayed by the Commission. We can believe that all "persons of interest" were interviewed, moreover, only if we can assume that the FBI was able to determine within those two hours that not one of these 46 passengers was such a person.

Another flight departed from Logan Airport in Boston on September 19. That morning, Unger reports, Logan learned that a private jet was arriving from Saudi Arabia to pick up over ten members of the bin Laden family. The director of aviation—being incredulous that after Osama bin

Laden had orchestrated "the worst terrorist act in history," members of the bin Laden family were being evacuated—said that nothing was to happen without word from Washington. But when the word came, it was, as it was for all the Saudi flights, "Let them leave." The plane left that night, reports Unger, without any of the passengers being interviewed by the FBI.[16]

Unger portrays these two flights as illustrative of, rather than as exceptions to, the general pattern. The FBI did insist, he says, that no flights be allowed to leave until the FBI at least knew the names of the people on them. But "the FBI repeatedly declined to interrogate or conduct extended interviews with the Saudis."[17] The FBI agents to whom he talked, Unger reports, said that "they identified the passengers boarding the flights but did not have lengthy interviews with them."[18]

If it is read carefully, the Commission's account, which admits that "most of the passengers were not interviewed," does not differ substantially from Unger's. The Commission does, however, try to put a better face on what occurred, stating that the FBI had interviewed all "persons of interest." But even if this statement is true, which is probably debatable, it would leave open the question of whether the FBI had sufficient grounds for its judgments. The Commission seems simply to infer that if a particular person was not interrogated by the FBI, there is no reason to believe that this person should have been interrogated.

The questionableness of this inference is shown by Unger's most disturbing information, which involves a flight that left from Lexington on September 16. Unger, having obtained the passenger list, was astonished to find that one of the Saudis who left the country on this flight was none other than Prince Ahmed bin Salman.[19] Prince Ahmed, it will be recalled, was the owner of the Thoroughbred Corporation (which accounts for his presence in Lexington—he had just, on the day after 9/11, bought two horses for $1.2 million[20]). Prince Ahmed was also—in Gerald Posner's narrative—said by Abu Zubaydah to have been an intermediary between al-Qaeda and the Saudi rulers. We now learn from Unger that the FBI had an opportunity to interview him just five days after the attacks. But, Unger reports, "[Prince Ahmed] had been identified by FBI officials, but not seriously interrogated."[21] The FBI evidently did not consider Prince Ahmed a "person of interest." If Posner's narrative about Zubaydah is accurate, however, the prince had known that there were to be attacks on America by al-Qaeda on September 11.

The Commissioners could reply, of course, that there was no way for the FBI to have known on September 16, 2001, about Zubaydah's revelations in 2002. The point, however, is that the Commission could not justifiably infer that none of the passengers were connected to 9/11 from the mere fact that the FBI concluded—or at least said that it concluded—that none of them were. Prince Ahmed was reportedly said by Zubaydah to have been sufficiently "connected to the 9/11 attacks" to know of them in advance. Unger, writing in April of 2004, said: "The commission should ask [FBI Director Robert] Mueller about Zubaydah's interrogation. They should also ask whether the FBI interrogated Prince Ahmed before his departure."[22] The Kean–Zelikow Report, however, gives no indication that Mueller was asked either of these questions.

Unger points out, furthermore, that even before Zubaydah's reported revelations in April of 2002, there were sufficient grounds for not allowing Prince Ahmed to leave the country immediately after 9/11, at least without a rigorous investigation. Unger reports that Prince Ahmed's father, Prince Salman bin Abdul Aziz, had "worked closely with Osama bin Laden and his Afghan Arabs during the Afghanistan War in the eighties."[23] It surely would not have involved undue suspicion on the FBI's part if it had wondered whether Prince Salman's son might have had a continuing relationship with OBL (as Zubaydah reportedly said he did).

In any case, whatever we may think the FBI should have done, the 9/11 Commission, doing most of its work after Posner published his account of Zubaydah's interrogation, surely had available to it sufficient grounds to explore this question. But we are given no sign that it did. The Commission, evidently not finding Prince Ahmed bin Salman a person of interest, has not a single reference to him in its report.

Unger, besides revealing that Prince Ahmed was one of the Saudis who departed without being seriously interrogated, later reported that far more flights carrying Saudis left the country right after 9/11 than the Commission's report indicates. Although the Commission's report, published on July 22, 2004, does not say exactly how many Saudis left the country in this exodus, it speaks of ten flights—one Saudi government flight plus nine chartered flights—"with 160 people, mostly Saudi nationals, [who] departed the United States between September 14 and 24" (556n25). This statement is compatible with the figure of 142 Saudis, which had been given in Unger's book. On June 1, however, Unger reported that a document released by Judicial Watch—which Judicial

Watch had obtained from the Department of Homeland Security under the Freedom of Information Act—showed that between September 11 and 15, another 160 Saudis left the country on 55 flights, most of which were commercial flights, originating from over 20 cities. This new information, Unger points out, means that "a total of about 300 people . . . left with the apparent approval of the Bush administration."[24]

This revelation raises another serious question about the 9/11 Commission's report. Did the Commission not know about these other flights? That ignorance would have disturbing implications for the thoroughness of the Commission's research. If Judicial Watch was able to obtain this information, why could Philip Zelikow's research staff not have done the same? Even if the staff did not learn about this information on its own, it would seem that it would have learned about it through the article by Unger appearing on June 1. Zelikow's staff would have thereby learned about it in time to include a reference to it. (The notes in the Kean–Zelikow Report contain references to interviews carried out as late as July 2004.) Or did the Commission know about this information in plenty of time and yet fail to mention it?

Mentioning this new information would, to be sure, have threatened the Commission's conclusion that no Saudi nationals were allowed to leave the country without being adequately interrogated. For the Commission would have then needed to argue that these additional 160 Saudis, including 48 who left on September 13, were adequately vetted. However, if the Commission did know about these flights, then it was its duty either to present evidence that all these individuals were indeed sufficiently interrogated or else to revise its conclusion. Given the Commission's treatment of this matter, one could infer that it deliberately hid this information in order to avoid the need to revise its conclusion.

Assuming the Commission did know about these additional 160 Saudis, the Commission had two more duties, if it was honestly to maintain its conclusion that nothing improper was done. First, given the Commission's emphasis on the fact that American air space was opened to commercial flights at 11:00 AM on September 13, it should have made sure, on our behalf, that the commercial flight that left the country that day carrying 48 Saudis did not leave until after 11:00 AM. Second, it should have made sure, on our behalf, that the flight leaving on September 11 with a Saudi passenger departed before US airspace was closed to all flights, both commercial and private.

Although the Commission does not refer to these additional 55 flights carrying 160 Saudis, most of which were commercial flights, it does seek to refute the allegations of journalists that some commercial flights left the country containing suspect Saudi nationals. The Commission, stating that it had "the names of Saudi nationals on commercial flights" (as well as the names of all the passengers believed to be on the ten aforementioned flights) checked against the TIPOFF terrorist watchlist, reports: "There were no matches" (558n31).

But surely, as the case of Prince Ahmed shows, the fact that a person's name was not on this list does not prove that this person had no relevant information about the attacks of 9/11.

This point could also be illustrated by means of other passengers. Unger learned that the passenger list for the September 19 flight from Boston included the name of Omar bin Laden,[25] whose FBI file, as we saw earlier, was reopened on that very day. When Omar departed that night, therefore, he was definitely, from the FBI's point of view, a "person of interest." And yet, Unger told us, that flight left without any of the passengers being interviewed.

I conclude that the Kean–Zelikow Report has not successfully undermined the second allegation—that the evacuation of Saudis from the United States was carried out in a way that precluded rigorous investigations of people who may have been able to provide vital information about the attacks of 9/11.

THE QUESTION OF WHITE HOUSE AUTHORIZATION

The Commission's failure to undermine the first two allegations brings us to the third one—that the Saudi evacuation flights occurred through political intervention by the White House. This is an explosive allegation, of course, because it suggests that the White House helped expedite the rapid departure of, in Unger's words, "many Saudis who may have been able to shed light on the greatest crime in American history" and "thereby interfere[d] in an investigation into the murder of nearly 3,000 people."[26] The reference to the "White House" here is a reference, ultimately, to the president.

With regard to this third allegation, the final report of the 9/11 Commission says:

[W]e found no evidence of political intervention. We found no evidence that anyone at the White House above the level of Richard Clarke participated in a decision on the departure of Saudi nationals. . . . White House Chief of Staff Andrew Card . . . said he . . . did not ask anyone to do anything about [the Saudi request]. The President and Vice President told us they were not aware of the issue at all until it surfaced much later in the media. (329)

The Commission evidently meant for us to conclude from its statement—that it found no evidence of political intervention from anyone at the White House above Richard Clarke's level—that no such intervention occurred. The question before us is whether the Commission provides any good reason for us to accept this conclusion. We can begin with the question of whether we can believe—as the Commission evidently does—that President Bush was not aware of the issue until much later.

On September 13, 2001, the president kept an appointment, arranged prior to 9/11, to see Prince Bandar bin Sultan.[27] Besides being the Saudi ambassador to the United States, Prince Bandar, Unger points out, is "the nephew of King Fahd . . . and the grandson of the late king Abdul Aziz, the founder of modern Saudi Arabia." By 2001, the Bush and Saud families, Unger adds,

had a history dating back more than twenty years. Not just business partners and personal friends, the Bushes and the Saudis had pulled off elaborate covert operations and gone to war together. They had shared secrets that involved unimaginable personal wealth, spectacular military might, [and] the richest energy resources in the world.[28]

With regard to the friendship, Unger points out that since 1990, the Bush family had been thinking of Prince Bandar as almost part of their family, even calling him "Bandar Bush."[29]

On September 13, Prince Bandar, in his role as the Saudi ambassador, may have been especially glad to have a friend in the White House, because he had been working for two days to orchestrate the Saudi exodus.[30] In any case, when he arrived at the White House,

he and President Bush retreated to the Truman Balcony, a casual outdoor spot . . . that also provided a bit of privacy. . . . [T]he two men each lit up a Cohiba [cigar] and began to discuss how they would work together on the war on terror. . . . Only Bush and Bandar know what transpired that day on the Truman Balcony. But the ties between the two families were so strong that allowing the Saudis to leave America would not have been difficult for Bush. . . . A spokesman for the Saudi embassy later said he did not know whether repatriation was a topic of discussion.[31]

It is true that we cannot know that it was a topic. But this issue was surely one of the main things on the ambassador's mind when he met with the president. Are we expected to believe that when George and Bandar Bush were by themselves, smoking cigars, Bandar did not bring up the issue? Can we believe George Bush's statement that he had not even heard of the issue until later? Are we to suppose that it was just a coincidence that later the same day, private planes carrying Saudi passengers were allowed to fly?[32]

It is not even necessary, furthermore, to think that authorization from the White House, including the president himself, had to wait for this face-to-face meeting. "For the 48 hours after the attacks," Unger tells us, Prince Bandar "stayed in constant contact with Secretary of State Colin Powell and National Security Adviser Condoleezza Rice."[33] Rice, furthermore, was surely in rather constant contact with the president during those days.

The Kean–Zelikow Commission, however, does not tell us about the Bandar–Rice contact as background for its assertion that, as far as it could discover, no one in the White House above Richard Clarke participated in the decision to allow Saudis to depart. In spite of Unger's report about this contact, the Commissioners do not tell us if they asked Rice whether, in her many conversations with Prince Bandar from September 11 to 13, the issue came up. They merely say, "None of the officials we interviewed recalled any intervention or direction on this matter from any political appointee" (329), then indicate in a note that Rice was one of the people they interviewed (557n27). As is often the case, the Commission's "research" seemed to consist primarily of asking people questions and writing down their answers, no matter how implausible.

One thing the Commission evidently wrote down from one or more interviews was a view about how the flights got arranged that differs significantly from Unger's account. The matter was really handled, the Commission asserts, in the following way:

Within days of September 11, fearing reprisals against Saudi nationals, Rihab Massoud, the deputy chief of mission at the Saudi embassy in Washington, DC, called Dale Watson, the FBI's director for counterterrorism, and asked for help in getting some of its citizens out of the country. (557n27)

The only evidence cited for this account is an interview with Rihab Massoud himself. And there are other reasons for being suspicious of this account, one of which is that it—conveniently for the Commission's thesis about the president's noninvolvement—leaves Prince Bandar, the very close friend of the Bush family, out of the picture.

In any case, the most important question is whether—assuming that Prince Bandar did ask—the White House granted the favor. Events that followed suggest, Unger clearly believes, that a deal was struck. On the one hand, "the repatriation of the bin Ladens," states Unger, "could not have taken place without approval at the highest levels of the executive branch,"[33] and the flights to evacuate Saudis, including many members of the bin Laden family, were approved. On the other hand, Ambassador Bandar promised "that Saudi Arabia would help stabilize the world oil markets" and this promise was kept: "In a breathtaking display of their command over the oil markets, the Saudis dispatched 9 million barrels of oil to the United States. As a consequence, the price instantly dropped from $28 to $22 per barrel."[35]

Unger has, accordingly, shown the existence of strong circumstantial evidence for presidential intervention. The Kean–Zelikow Commission, however, failed to mention any of this circumstantial evidence. If the Commission had mentioned it, would it still have been able to claim that it found no evidence for political intervention? Although circumstantial evidence is by definition not direct evidence, it is evidence.

Unger in addition provides verbal testimony from the Saudi side that there was indeed intervention from the presidential level. In an interview with Nail al-Jubeir, a spokesman for the Saudi embassy, Unger was told that the flights were approved by "the highest level of the US government,"[36] an expression that would seem to point to the president himself. The 9/11 Commission also fails to mention this statement.

Furthermore, although the FBI for a long time, according to Unger, denied that it was involved in facilitating the flights, the evidence that it was involved is, as we have seen, strong. We again have verbal testimony from the Saudi side: Prince Bandar, speaking on CNN, said that a critical role in the evacuation was played by the FBI.[37] He later, when asked on *Meet the Press* whose permission he asked, replied: "The FBI."[38] Although some people might be tempted to use this statement to say that the flights were authorized by the FBI instead of by the president, surely the 9/11 Commission would not contend that the FBI would have played this role without presidential authorization. (Certainly there is no sign in the Commission's report that it confronted Director Mueller or any other FBI officials about whether they were guilty of such an egregious usurpation of authority.) The FBI's role provides, therefore, further indirect evidence of authorization from the president.

Of course, there is now agreement, in one sense, that the evacuation flights were authorized by "the White House." But the official story, endorsed by the 9/11 Commission, is that this authorization did not come from President Bush, Vice President Cheney, or even National Security Advisor Condoleezza Rice. Rather, as we saw, the Commission says that it saw no reason to believe that "anyone at the White House above the level of Richard Clarke participated in a decision on the departure of Saudi nationals."

However, Clarke himself, in an interview with Unger, reportedly said: "Somebody brought to us for approval the decision to let an airplane filled with Saudis, including members of the bin Laden family, leave the country."[39] Clarke even made a similar statement in his testimony to the Commission, saying: "I would love to be able to tell you who did it, who brought this proposal to me, but I don't know" (557n27).

How could the Commission go from this statement to its apparent conclusion that no one above Clarke in the White House was involved in the decision? The Commission seems to rest this conclusion partly on a statement in which Clarke said, "I have no recollection of clearing [the decision] with anybody at the White House" (329). But if Clarke already knew that his superiors wanted the evacuation to go forward, he of course would have felt no need to clear it with them.

REFLECTIONS

The 9/11 Commission's attempt to defend the Bush administration against the third allegation—that it intervened to make possible the rapid departure, without proper interrogation, of Saudi nationals—seems as fully unsuccessful as its attempt to refute the first two allegations.

If readers who accept the official account of 9/11 agree that this attempt by the Commission is unsuccessful, this failure should be very disturbing. For according to the official account, the attacks were carried out by a group of men, mainly Saudis, who were organized by Osama bin Laden, a member of one of Saudi Arabia's most prominent families. Although OBL was said to have been disowned by his own family, at least some of the family members had evidently remained in contact. Another part of the overall picture that should be disturbing is that two of OBL's relatives living in the USA—Omar and Abdullah bin Laden—were leaders of an organization that was said by US officials to be supporting terrorism.

Furthermore, although OBL was also said to have been denounced and banished by the royal family, there have been reports of continuing contact between him and some of the royals. According to Posner's account, moreover, Abu Zubaydah said that the Saudis had continued to support al-Qaeda financially, and this claim has now been supported by Bob Graham of the Senate Intelligence Committee.

Abu Zubaydah also reportedly said that in 1998 he was present at a meeting between OBL and Prince Turki bin Faisal, the chief of Saudi intelligence, in which a deal was worked out.[40] This story is given added credibility by Richard Labeviere's account of OBL's stay in the hospital in Dubai, according to which this chief of Saudi intelligence was still in touch with OBL as late as July 2001.[41] A fact adding interest to these reports about Prince Turki is that, having long been the head of Saudi intelligence, he was dismissed only ten days before 9/11 (after which he was appointed the Saudi ambassador to Great Britain).[42]

Given all these reports and facts, how could the 9/11 Commission treat so cavalierly the possibility that members of the royal and bin Laden families were allowed to depart the country immediately after 9/11? Why does the Commission not show signs of being outraged at the president? Whoever authorized the flights obstructed a criminal investigation of the greatest terrorist attack in US history, and there are only three possibilities: The president directly authorized the flights; he knowingly allowed them to be authorized by subordinates; or he was inexcusably ignorant of the fact that subordinates authorized them. Whichever possibility is the truth, the president was responsible for an exodus that obstructed an investigation into a massive crime. But the Kean–Zelikow Report here, as with most other issues, seemed more concerned with defending the White House than in giving the American people "the fullest possible account of the events surrounding 9/11."

CHAPTER EIGHT

Allegations about FBI Headquarters

There have been several allegations by FBI agents that FBI headquarters blocked 9/11-related investigations. Some of these allegations involved pre-9/11 leads that, had they been vigorously investigated, could have led to discoveries through which the attacks might have been prevented. Other allegations involved post-9/11 decisions that may have prevented learning information about the perpetrators of the attacks. One of the questions to ask about *The 9/11 Commission Report*, accordingly, is how it treated these allegations about FBI headquarters. We will look first at the Commission's response to well-known allegations related to Phoenix, Chicago, and Minneapolis, all of which involved pre-9/11 leads through which the plans might have been discovered. We will then look at the Commission's response to allegations by former FBI translator Sibel Edmonds about serious problems within the translation program of the FBI's counterterrorism division.

THE PHOENIX MEMO FROM KENNETH WILLIAMS

In July 2001, Kenneth Williams, an FBI agent in Phoenix, sent a memorandum to FBI headquarters. Warning that Osama bin Laden's followers might be taking flying lessons for terrorist purposes, Williams recommended that the FBI begin a national program to track suspicious flight-school students. Such a program was never instituted.[1]

The 9/11 Commission Report offers us an explanation as to why this program was not instituted:

> Managers of the Usama Bin Ladin unit and the Radical Fundamentalist unit at FBI headquarters were addressees, but they did not even see the memo until after September 11. No managers at headquarters saw the memo before September 11. (272)

The implication is clearly that people at FBI headquarters were not blameworthy for not instituting the program suggested by Williams because they did not know about his suggestion.

How did the Commission reach this conclusion? It evidently did no research on this issue itself, because it simply refers the interested reader to an investigation carried out by the Congressional Joint Inquiry and a report issued July 2, 2004, by the Department of Justice's Inspector General (540nn86,88). The Commission does not tell us how these previous reports reached the conclusion that "[n]o managers at headquarters saw the memo before September 11." Did they have any evidence for this assertion, or did they simply take the word of those managers themselves?

An answer to this question would be especially important to readers who know about the case involving Zacarias Moussaoui and Minneapolis FBI agent Coleen Rowley (to be discussed below), because reports about this case do not inspire confidence in the integrity of the manager of the Radical Fundamentalist Unit, David Frasca. Indeed, in a 13-page letter written to Direct Robert Mueller and the Senate Intelligence Committee, most of which was posted on the *Time* magazine website, Rowley indicated that Frasca had been "privy" to the Williams memo, had been "warned" by it, but then "never disclosed" the existence of this warning to the Minneapolis agents while he was thwarting their efforts to examine Moussaoui's computer. She certainly did not believe he had failed to warn them only because the Phoenix memo somehow never came to his attention.[2]

The Commission, however, simply assures us, without mentioning Rowley's well-known claim to the contrary, that Frasca did not see this memo before September 11. Perhaps the Commission determined that Rowley was wrong. But if so, why does the Commission not tell us how this was determined? Should not the 9/11 Commission, realizing that it was very convenient for Frasca to deny having seen the report, engaged in some of its "exacting investigative work" to see if this claim could hold up under close scrutiny? A reference to the report of the Joint Inquiry should especially not have been used in lieu of its own investigative work in a matter involving the FBI, given reports suggesting that members of the committees carrying out this inquiry had been intimidated by the FBI.[3] But this was evidently not a question the Zelikow-led staff considered a worthwhile use of its time.

THE CHARGE BY CHICAGO FBI AGENT ROBERT WRIGHT

In the case of the Phoenix memo, the allegations about FBI headquarters were made by others rather than by Williams himself. But in another case reported in *The New Pearl Harbor*, Chicago FBI agent Robert Wright leveled very direct charges against FBI headquarters. I summarized his case in the following words:

> In 1998, FBI agent Robert Wright had begun tracking a terrorist cell in Chicago, suspecting that money used for the 1998 bombings of US embassies came from a Saudi multimillionaire living in Chicago. In January of 2001, in spite of his belief that his case was growing stronger, he was told that it was being closed. In June, he wrote an internal memo charging that the FBI, rather than trying to prevent a terrorist attack, "was merely gathering intelligence so they would know who to arrest when a terrorist attack occurred." In May of 2002, Wright announced that he was suing the FBI for refusing to allow him to publish a book he had written about the affair. Included in his description of the actions of his superiors in curtailing his investigations were words such as "prevented," "thwarted," "obstructed," "threatened," "intimidated," and "retaliation." In a later interview, . . . he said: "September the 11th is a direct result of the incompetence of the FBI's International Terrorism Unit."[4]

Given the nature of Wright's charges, we would assume that the 9/11 Commission would have been very interested to learn more about what he had to say. Given the fact that Wright's charges had been reported by such mainline sources as UPI, ABC News, and the *LA Weekly*, the Commission would surely have known about his case.[5] But the Commission's report contains no evidence that it interviewed him. Even if there was some good reason why Wright could not be interviewed, the Commission should have asked FBI Director Mueller about Wright's charge that he was being intimidated by FBI headquarters. But although there was plenty of time to ask Mueller about this, Robert Wright's name is nowhere to be found in the Commission's report.

THE COLEEN ROWLEY–ZACARIAS MOUSSAOUI CASE

Most readers will not notice the fact that the case of Robert Wright is omitted from the Commission's report, because it received only a little publicity. The case involving Coleen Rowley and Zacarias Moussaoui, however, received enormous publicity. Rowley was even named one of three "Persons of the Year" by *Time* magazine in 2002.[6] In preparation for looking at the Commission's treatment of this case, I will quote from my summary in *The New Pearl Harbor*.

In mid-August of 2001, the staff at a flight school in Minneapolis called the local FBI to report their suspicion that Zacarias Moussaoui, who had paid to train on a Boeing 747 simulator, was planning to use a real 747 "as a weapon." After the Minneapolis FBI agents arrested Moussaoui and discovered many suspicious things about him, they asked FBI headquarters for a warrant to search his laptop computer and other possessions. However, even though FBI headquarters received additional information about Moussaoui from France—which according to French officials clearly showed that he posed a threat—senior FBI officials said that the information "was too sketchy to justify a search warrant for his computer." But the Minneapolis agents, having seen the French intelligence report, were "in a frenzy," with one agent speculating that Moussaoui might "fly something into the World Trade Center." Becoming "desperate to search the computer lap top," the Minneapolis agents sent a request through FBI headquarters for a search warrant under the Foreign Intelligence Surveillance Act (FISA), which would be certain to grant it, because in the past its officials had granted virtually all requests.

At FBI headquarters, however, the request was given to the Radical Fundamentalist Unit (RFU) . . . . The Minneapolis request was then given to RFU agent Marion "Spike" Bowman, who lived up to his nickname by proceeding to remove the evidence that Moussaoui was connected to al-Qaeda through a rebel group in Chechnya. Then the FBI Deputy General Counsel, on the basis of this edited request, said that there was insufficient connection to al-Qaeda for a search warrant and did not even forward the request to FISA. Minneapolis FBI legal officer Coleen Rowley asked: "Why would an FBI agent deliberately sabotage a case?"

. . . . [L]ater, Rowley released a long memo she had written about the FBI's handling of the Moussaoui case, which *Time* magazine called a "colossal indictment of our chief law-enforcement agency's neglect."

. . . . Marion "Spike" Bowman . . . was in December of 2002 given an FBI award for "exceptional performance." This award came, furthermore, after a congressional report said that Bowman's RFU unit had given Minneapolis FBI agents "inexcusably confused and inaccurate information" that was "patently false."[7]

Although *The 9/11 Commission Report* discusses this case, it omits crucial details. One of these is Marion "Spike" Bowman's removal of the evidence of Moussaoui's connection to al-Qaeda through the Chechen group. The Commission's report simply says:

> [There was a difference of opinion] whether the Chechen rebels and [their leader] Kattab were sufficiently associated with a terrorist organization to constitute a "foreign power" for purposes of the FISA statute. FBI headquarters did not believe this was good enough, and its National Security Law Unit declined to submit a FISA application.

According to this account, the person at FBI headquarters who refused to submit the FISA application did so merely because of a difference of opinion. There is no reference to the fact that this person did not see the request as written in Minneapolis but only the request as modified by Bowman, who removed the information about Moussaoui's connection to the group in Chechnya. Given the fact that the Commission omitted this part of the story, it is not surprising to find that it also omitted Coleen Rowley's query as to why an FBI agent would "deliberately sabotage a case." In the Commission's world, there is no deliberate sabotage, only honest differences of opinion. Finally, the Commission, having left out "Spike" Bowman's role, had no occasion to mention the irony in the fact that he subsequently received an FBI award for "exceptional performance," even though Bowman 's unit (under Dave Frasca's leadership) had provided "inexcusably confused and inaccurate information."

It must be wondered how the Commission could have failed to learn about these details. Surely its staff, with its "exacting investigative work," read the reports in *Time*. Surely Coleen Rowley, given an opportunity to testify before the Commission, would have provided all these details. And surely, given the fact that she was named one of *Time* magazine's "persons of the year" for her confrontation with FBI headquarters over this matter, she would have been invited to testify before the Commission. Apparently, however, she was not interviewed. There is, in fact, only one reference to Coleen Rowley in the entire document, and this reference—to an interview of her by the Department of Justice's Inspector General in July 2002—contains nothing about her difficulties with FBI headquarters (540n94).

The 9/11 Commission evidently did not consider the flap involving Coleen Rowley and FBI headquarters worth mentioning, even though *Time* magazine had portrayed it one of the most important stories of the year. One possible explanation of this omission is that the Commission's proviso was again operating—the proviso that its "fullest possible account of the events surrounding 9/11" be consistent with the government's official story about 9/11. Given the Commission's account, there is nothing that would provide the slightest hint that FBI headquarters might not have wanted investigations to discover the plans for the attacks of 9/11.

SIBEL EDMONDS VS. THE FBI AND THE ATTORNEY GENERAL
In addition to the above cases, which involve allegations about questionable conduct on the part of FBI headquarters prior to 9/11, there have been allegations about such conduct after 9/11. The most well-publicized of these allegations have been leveled by Sibel Edmonds, a Turkish-American citizen hired by the FBI shortly after 9/11 to do translation. She soon reported to her superiors that another woman hired at the same time, Melek Can Dickerson, was mistranslating, or failing to translate altogether, certain documents about a foreign organization for which she had worked. Edmonds reported, furthermore, that Dickerson was still working for this organization as a spy and had tried to persuade Edmonds to join her in this espionage.

Failing to get a response from her superiors at the FBI, Edmonds then wrote a letter to the Department of Justice, after which she was fired.[8] She then sued under the whistleblowers protection act, but Attorney General John Ashcroft asked the court to throw out the suit "to protect the foreign policy and national security interests of the United States." Ashcroft also used the rarely used appeal to the "state secrets" privilege to obtain a gag order that prevents Edmonds from revealing any details about information she acquired while working for the FBI. Edmonds' case, with the above facts, was discussed briefly in the first edition of *The New Pearl Harbor*.[9]

I then discussed later developments in her case in the Afterword to the second edition.[10] This discussion of later developments revolved partly around the attempt by Edmonds to get the gag order lifted by challenging the Justice Department's use of the state secrets privilege. At the time of that writing, Judge Reggie Walton had just called off the hearing about this matter for the fourth time, giving no reason.

Shortly thereafter, on July 6, Judge Walton—an appointee of President George W. Bush—ruled in favor of the Justice Department's request that Edmunds' suit be thrown out. In response, Edmonds wrote:

> John Ashcroft's relentless fight against me, my information, and my case. . . has been taking place under his attempt at a vague justification titled "Protecting Certain Foreign and Diplomatic Relations for National Security." On September 11, 2001, 3,000 lives were lost. Yet this administration has hindered all past and ongoing investigations into the causes of that horrific day for the sake of this vague notion of protecting "certain diplomatic and foreign relations."[11]

My discussion of "later developments" in the Afterword also dealt with Edmonds' statements about her 3.5-hour testimony "behind closed doors" to the staff of the 9/11 Commission. In reporting on her decision to begin speaking out (in general terms) about the kinds of things that were included in her testimony, I mentioned that she, comparing "behind closed doors" to "a black hole," predicted that the information she had provided behind those closed doors "will stay there and will never get out."

Now that this document has appeared, we can see that her prediction was accurate. The Kean–Zelikow Report contains only one reference to her testimony. And this reference, in an endnote, is merely one of four references given in support of a bland, general statement about the need for the FBI's translation program to "maintain rigorous security and proficiency standards" and to "ensure compliance with its quality control program" (473n25). There is no discussion of her long-term battle with the FBI and the Department of Justice, except for the title of one of the other references—"A Review of the FBI's Actions in Connection with Allegations Raised by Contract Linguist Sibel Edmonds," issued by the Justice Department's Inspector General. There is no hint as to what those allegations were or the FBI's response to them. Most important for our present purposes, there is no hint, aside from the innocuous recommendations mentioned above, as to what she might have spent her 3.5 hours talking about.

However, Sibel Edmonds herself, seeing this huge omission in the

Commission's report, decided to let the world know what she talked about by means of an open letter to Thomas Kean, as chairman of the Commission. Pointing out in her opening paragraph that Kean was now asking Americans to support his report's recommendations, she stated her overall complaint:

> Unfortunately, I find your report seriously flawed in its failure to address serious intelligence issues that I am aware of, which have been confirmed, and which as a witness to the commission, I made you aware of. Thus, I must assume that other serious issues that I am not aware of were in the same manner omitted from your report. These omissions cast doubt on the validity of your report and therefore on its conclusions and recommendations.[12]

Having offered this general critique, Edmonds then reminded Kean of eight points she had made to his staff. I will summarize four of these points, for the most part using Edmonds' own words.

One of Edmonds' points discusses Melek Can Dickerson, with whom the whole story began. Repeating what she had told the Commission's staff, Edmonds wrote:

> For months Melek Can Dickerson blocked all-important information related to . . . semi-legit organizations and the individuals she and her husband associated with. She stamped hundreds, if not thousands, of documents related to these targets as "Not Pertinent." . . . Melek Can Dickerson, with the assistance of her direct supervisor, Mike Feghali, took hundreds of pages of top-secret sensitive intelligence documents outside the FBI to unknown recipients. Melek Can Dickerson, with the assistance of her direct supervisor, forged signatures on top-secret documents related to certain 9/11 detainees. After all these incidents were confirmed and reported to FBI management, Melek Can Dickerson was allowed to remain in her position, to continue the translation of sensitive intelligence received by the FBI, and to maintain her Top Secret clearance. . . . I provided your investigators with a detailed and specific account of this issue, the names of other witnesses willing to corroborate this, and additional documents. (Please refer to tape-recorded 3.5 hours testimony by Sibel Edmonds, provided to your investigators on February 11, 2004.)

Today, more than two years since the Dickerson incident was reported to the FBI, and more than two years since this information was confirmed by the United States Congress and reported by the press, these administrators in charge of FBI personnel security and language departments in the FBI remain in their positions and in charge of translation quality and translation departments' security. Melek Can Dickerson and several FBI targets of investigation hastily left the United States in 2002, and the case still remains uninvestigated criminally. Not only does the supervisor facilitating these criminal conducts remain in a supervisory position, he has been promoted to supervising Arabic language units of the FBI's Counterterrorism and Counterintelligence investigations. . . . Why did your report choose to exclude this information and these serious issues despite the evidence and briefings you received?[13]

In another point, Edmonds discussed "a long-term FBI informant/ asset who had been providing the bureau with information since 1990." More than four months prior to 9/11, she said, this informant, who "was previously a high-level intelligence officer in Iran in charge of intelligence from Afghanistan," informed two FBI agents and a translator that Osama bin Laden was planning a major terrorist attack, involving airplanes, in the United States in the next few months. She then continued:

The agents who received this information reported it to their superior, Special Agent in Charge of Counterterrorism, Thomas Friells, at the FBI Washington Field Office. . . . No action was taken by the Special Agent in Charge, and after 9/11 the agents and the translators were told to "keep quiet" regarding this issue. The translator who was present during the session with the FBI informant, Mr. Behrooz Sarshar, reported this incident to Director Mueller in writing, and later to the Department of Justice Inspector General. The . . . report in the *Chicago Tribune* on July 21, 2004 stated that FBI officials had confirmed that information was received in April 2001, and further, the *Chicago Tribune* quoted an aide to Director Mueller that he (Mueller) was surprised that the Commission never raised this particular issue with him during the hearing. . . . Mr. Sarshar reported this issue to your investigators on February 12, 2004, and provided them with specific dates, location, witness names, and the contact information for that particular Iranian asset and the two special agents who received the information (Please refer to the tape-recorded testimony provided to your investigators during a 2.5 hours testimony by Mr. Sarshar on February 12, 2004). . . . Why did your report choose to exclude the information regarding the Iranian asset and Behrooz Sarshar from its timeline of missed opportunities? . . . Why did you surprise even Director Mueller by refraining from asking him questions regarding this significant incident and lapse during your hearing? (Please remember that you ran out of questions during your hearings with Director Mueller and AG John Ashcroft, so please do not cite a "time limit" excuse.)[14]

A third episode discussed by Edmonds began about a month after 9/11 when a Special Agent from an FBI field office, believing that the translation of a particular document might have missed some valuable information about a target of investigation, sent the document back to the FBI Washington Field Office for retranslation. The retranslation, Edmonds said, proved the field agent's hunch to be correct. But then,

> after the re-translation was completed and the new significant information was revealed, the unit supervisor in charge of certain Middle Eastern languages, Mike Feghali, decided NOT to send the re-translated information to the Special Agent who had requested it. Instead, this supervisor decided to send this agent a note stating that the translation was reviewed and that the original translation was accurate. . . . I provided your investigators with a detailed and specific account of this issue, the name and date of this particular investigation, and the names of other witnesses willing to corroborate this. . . . The supervisor involved in this incident, Mike Feghali, . . . had a record of previous misconducts. After this supervisor's several severe misconducts were reported to the FBI's higher-level management, after his conducts were reported to the Inspector General's Office, to the United States Congress, and to the 9/11 Commission, he was promoted to include the FBI's Arabic language unit under his supervision. Today this supervisor, Mike Feghali, remains in the FBI Washington Field Office and is in charge of a language unit receiving those chitchats that our color-coded threat system is based upon. Yet your report contains zero information regarding these systemic problems . . . . Why does your report choose to exclude this information and these serious issues despite all the evidence and briefings you received?

Edmonds began another point, surely her most important, by saying that although "the latest buzz topic regarding intelligence is the problem of sharing information/intelligence within intelligence agencies and between intelligence agencies," the more serious problem is "intentional blocking of intelligence." Becoming more specific, she says:

> If Counterintelligence receives information that contains money laundering, illegal arms sales, and illegal drug activities, directly linked to terrorist activities; and if that information involves certain nations, certain semi-legit organizations, and ties to certain lucrative or political relations in this country, then, that information is not shared with Counterterrorism, regardless of the possible severe consequences. In certain cases, frustrated FBI agents cited "direct pressure by the State Department" . . . . I provided your investigators with a detailed and specific account of this issue, the names of other witnesses willing to corroborate this, and the names of certain US officials involved in these transactions and activities . . . . After almost three years the . . . victims' family members still do not realize that information and answers they have sought relentlessly for over two years has been blocked due to the unspoken decisions made and disguised under "safeguarding certain diplomatic relations." Your report did not even attempt to address these unspoken practices, although, unlike me, you were not placed under any gag. [16]

Having made these (and still more) points, Edmonds said in her penultimate paragraph:

> As you are fully aware, the facts, incidents, and problems cited in this letter are by NO means based upon personal opinion or un-verified allegations. . . . As you know, according to officials with direct knowledge of the Department of Justice Inspector General's report on my allegations, "none of my allegations were disproved." As you are fully aware, even FBI officials "confirmed all my allegations and denied none" during their unclassified meetings with the Senate Judiciary staff over two years ago. However, neither your commission's hearings, nor your commission's 567-page report, nor your recommendations include these serious issues, major incidents, and systemic problems. Your report's coverage of FBI translation problems consists of a brief microscopic footnote. . . . Yet, your commission is geared to start aggressively pressuring our government

to hastily implement your measures and recommendations based upon your incomplete and deficient report. [17]

Assuming that Sibel Edmonds, in her letter to Chairman Kean, has reported truthfully about her testimony to the 9/11 Commission's staff—and it is hard to see how anyone could doubt this, since her testimony was recorded, so that Kean could easily disconfirm any false statements—her letter constitutes one of the strongest possible indictments of the Commission's work and its report. To mention only the most obvious questions raised by her revelations about her testimony: Given her extremely serious charges against Mike Feghali—that he "took hundreds of pages of top-secret sensitive intelligence documents outside the FBI to unknown recipients" and lied to a diligent agent about the accuracy of a translation—we would assume that the Commission would have summoned Mr. Feghali to ask him about these charges. But a search for Feghali's name in *The 9/11 Commission Report* comes up empty. Given her charge that Thomas Frields took no action on information from a long-term FBI informant from Iran that Osama bin Laden was planning a major terrorist attack, involving airplanes, in the United States in the next few months, then later told the FBI agents and translators to "keep quiet" about the fact that this information was received, we would assume that the Commission would have interviewed Mr. Frields about this two-fold charge. But the name of Thomas Frields is nowhere to be found in the Kean–Zelikow Report.

One might reply, of course, that the Commission had limited time and a limited budget. It simply could not interview everyone who claimed to have something of relevance to report. This excuse would, however, be difficult to accept with regard to Feghali and Frields, given the seriousness of the charges leveled against them. But even if we could accept it, we would at least expect the Commission to have queried FBI Director Mueller about them and also about his own decision to promote Feghali instead of firing him. But, as Edmonds mentioned, there were no questions about these matters in the public interview with Mueller—who was himself reportedly surprised that he has not asked about the case involving Frields and the Iranian informant.

Of course, the Commission's staff had, Edmonds pointed out, heard about the Frields episode directly from one of the translators involved, Behrooz Sarshar. The curious reader might suspect, therefore, that the place to find some reference to this episode would be in the Commission's notes about its interview with Sarshar. But a search reveals that the Kean–Zelikow Report contains no mention of this interview—in spite of Edmonds' statement that Sarshar had given testimony for 2.5 hours.

So, the result of six hours of testimony from these two FBI employees, who reported extremely serious misconduct within the division of the FBI for which they worked, was a single reference to Sibel Edmonds as one of four interviewees who said that the FBI translation program needed to "maintain rigorous security and proficiency standards" and to "ensure compliance with its quality control program." She certainly was saying that. But without her open letter to Chairman Kean, the reader of *The 9/11 Commission Report* would have no idea of the very specific and enormous violations she had described—violations that could be read by more suspicious minds as suggesting that the FBI was actually engaged in covering up, rather than discovering, the forces behind 9/11.

In the meantime, Edmonds has joined with 24 other former employees of the FBI and other governmental agencies to send the letter to the US Congress that is quoted in the Introduction. All 25 of these people signed as people "with direct knowledge" of serious incidents and problems within those agencies who had "duly reported" those matters to the 9/11 Commission but then found them unmentioned in the final report. All of them presumably share the inference that Edmonds herself draws. That is, having emphasized to Kean that she knew of the omissions about which she reported only because she had personally informed the Commission about the issues in question, she concluded: "I must assume that other serious issues that I am not aware of were in the same manner omitted from your report."

The present book shows that this assumption was entirely reasonable.

CHAPTER NINE

Pakistan and Its ISI

onsiderable evidence has surfaced of involvement in 9/11 by
Pakistan, in particular its ISI (Inter-Services Intelligence). The
ISI is Pakistan's equivalent of America's CIA. The two
organizations have, in fact, worked closely together.[1] One more
question to raise about *The 9/11 Commission Report*, accordingly, is how
it deals with evidence suggestive of complicity by the ISI in the attacks
of 9/11. Such evidence would, of course, be threatening to the
Commission's narrative, according to which al-Qaeda alone planned
and executed the attacks. Such evidence would also be threatening to
the Commission's recommendation, near the end of its report, that the
United States should sustain "the current scale of aid to Pakistan" (369).
Given what we have seen already about the Commission's treatment of
controversial material, we might predict that it would simply ignore all
evidence suggesting ISI involvement. But let us see. I will discuss the
Commission's treatment of seven types of evidence for ISI involvement
in the attacks of 9/11.

ISI CHIEF MAHMOUD AHMAD IN WASHINGTON

The head of Pakistan's ISI, General Mahmoud Ahmad, was in
Washington from September 4, 2001, until several days after 9/11. He
reportedly was meeting with George Tenet, the head of the CIA, from
September 4 through September 9, after which he met with officials in
the Pentagon, the National Security Council, and the State Department.
Immediately after 9/11, Pakistan became one of America's chief allies in
the so-called war on terror. It was rather a remarkable coincidence,
therefore, that the head of Pakistan's intelligence agency was in
Washington, having a week-long meeting with the head of American
intelligence. It was, indeed, treated as a mere coincidence by the
American press, with the *New York Times* saying that General Ahmad
"happened to be [in Washington] on a regular visit."[2]

However, even if it was merely coincidental, it was a noteworthy fact.

One might assume, therefore, that there would be some mention of Ahmad's presence in Washington that week in the Commission's report, given its effort to provide "the fullest possible account of the events surrounding 9/11." However, this report makes no mention of the fact that Ahmad had been in town since September 4, meeting much of that time with the head of the CIA. Nor is there any mention of his other meetings. For example, Senator Bob Graham begins his recent book, *Intelligence Matters*, with an account of the breakfast meeting he, Porter Goss, and other personnel of the congressional intelligence committees were having with General Ahmad on the morning of 9/11 until it was interrupted by word of the attacks.[3] One would assume that Graham and Goss—in the meantime made the new head of the CIA—would have told the Commission about this meeting. And yet the closest the Commission came to reporting General Ahmad's remarkable presence in Washington on that remarkable week was to mention that on September 13, Deputy Secretary of State Richard Armitage met with "the visiting head of Pakistan's military intelligence service, Mahmud Ahmed" (331; the Commission's spelling). For all the reader would know, General Ahmad had come to Washington only after 9/11, perhaps to offer help. Indeed, the Commission gives this impression by then saying that Armitage told General Ahmad and the Pakistani ambassador that "the United States wanted Pakistan to take seven steps" and that Pakistan had agreed by that afternoon (331).

To be sure, even though Pakistan did become one of America's leading allies in its "war on terror" immediately after 9/11, we might dismiss this failure to mention the ISI chief's presence in Washington prior to 9/11 as of no particular significance, explainable perhaps by the fact that he stepped down from his post shortly after 9/11. There were further reports, however, that make this omission even more noteworthy.

THE REPORT THAT ISI CHIEF AHMAD ORDERED MONEY SENT TO ATTA

One of those reports was that an ISI agent, Saeed Sheikh, had wired $100,000 to Mohamed Atta, considered the ringleader of the 9/11 hijackers. That report by itself, if it had become widely known, would have had explosive implications for the prospect of positive relations between Pakistan and the United States after 9/11. But even more potentially explosive was the report that Saeed Sheikh had wired this money at the instruction of none other than ISI chief Mahmoud Ahmad.[4] This "damning link," as Agence France Presse called it, had explosive implications not only for US-Pakistani relations but also—given the close relations between the CIA and the ISI—for the question of possible CIA involvement in the attacks.[5]

It is not surprising to learn, therefore, that the Bush administration evidently tried to keep any possible links between the ISI and 9/11 hidden. One example: When Attorney General Ashcroft later announced a criminal indictment against Saeed Sheikh, it was only for his role in the kidnapping and murder of *Wall Street Journal* reporter Daniel Pearl (to be discussed below). Ashcroft made no mention of Saeed's role in financing the 9/11 attacks or his connection to the ISI.[6]

The Bush administration also evidently attempted to conceal the fact that General Ahmad was in Washington the week of 9/11. Michel Chossudovsky, a Canadian expert on the global economy, has drawn attention to a White House transcript that suggests such an attempt. During Condoleezza Rice's press conference on May 16, 2002, the following interchange occurred between Rice and a reporter:

QUESTION: Are you aware of the reports at the time that the ISI chief was in Washington on September 11th, and on September 10th, $100,000 was wired from Pakistan to these groups in this area? And why he was here? Was he meeting with you or anybody in the administration?

MS. RICE: I have not seen that report, and he was certainly not meeting with me.

This transcript of the press conference was issued by the Federal News Service. However, the White House version of this transcript begins thus:

QUESTION: Dr. Rice, are you aware of the reports at the time that (inaudible) was in Washington on September 11th. . . ?

This version of the transcript, which does not contain the information that the person being discussed was "the ISI chief," was the version provided by the White House to the news media—it was, for example, the one reported on the CNN show *Inside Politics* later that day.[7]

This effort by the White House was evidently quite successful, because to this day few Americans seem to realize either that General Ahmad was present in Washington the week of 9/11 or that he reportedly ordered $100,000 wired to Mohamed Atta. To realize how strange this lack of awareness is, we can try to imagine what the US reaction would have been to a report that this money had been sent to the 9/11 ringleader by Saddam Hussein. This report would have provided the headline for virtually every newspaper in the country. This story would have dominated the TV news shows for weeks. The Bush administration would not have needed reports of weapons of mass destruction or anything else to justify its attack on Iraq. Indeed, the attack on Iraq might well have preceded the attack on Afghanistan.

The Bush administration's behavior here—trumpeting invented links between 9/11 and Iraq while covering up actual links involving Pakistan—is simply an extreme version of the kind of distortion that we, unfortunately, have come to expect from politicians and ideologues. But the 9/11 Commission was explicitly created as a nonpolitical, nonpartisan investigating body. The Republicans would keep the Democrats honest, and the Democrats would keep the Republicans honest. We should have been able to expect, therefore, that regardless of any possible embarrassment to the Bush administration resulting from the exposure of these two stories about the ISI chief—that he was meeting with the CIA director the week prior to 9/11 and that he ordered money sent to Atta— the 9/11 would have discussed them, if only to refute them. But the Kean–Zelikow Commission does not even mention them.

The Commission even denies knowledge of any evidence that Pakistan's ISI provided funding for the hijackers through Atta. In its paragraph on "The Funding of the 9/11 Plot," the Commission says:

> [T]he 9/11 plotters spent somewhere between $400,000 and $500,000 to plan and conduct their attack. The available evidence indicates that the 19 operatives were funded by al Qaeda. . . . [W]e have seen no evidence that any foreign government—or foreign government official—supplied any funding. (172)

This would seem to mean that the Commission, in spite of the "exacting investigative work" of its staff, did not learn about the story in the *Times of India*, entitled "India Helped FBI Trace ISI-Terrorist Links," which reported on General Ahmad's order to have money sent to Atta.[8]

If the staff did not know about this story, it must have failed to discover Michel Chossudovsky's 2002 book, *War and Globalisation: The Truth Behind September 11*. But is it really believable that the Commission's research staff would not have immediately done a search for all books with "9/11" or "September 11" in the title? Surely Dr. Philip Zelikow, who has produced several scholarly books, would have given the directive for such a search. In this light, can we really believe the Commission's statement that it had seen "no evidence that any foreign government—or foreign government official—supplied any funding"? Note that this statement does not even give the Commissioners a loophole by limiting the claim to credible evidence. It says that they have seen no evidence, period. This is either a falsehood or it implies that the Commission based its report on research that failed to carry out one of the first standard steps.

In light of Josh Meyer's story, discussed in Chapter Six,[9] we can reasonably suspect that the failure here was not on the part of the investigative work carried out by the Commission's staff. The omission more likely resulted from the political filters in the minds of those in charge of determining what would be included in the final report.

Be that as it may, the Commission, in ignoring evidence of funding from Pakistan, may have missed more of the truth about the funding for the 9/11 attacks than already suggested. As I reported previously the ISI may have transferred as much as $325,000 to Atta.[10] So, it would mean that Pakistan—America's major Asian ally in the war on terror—provided most of the money that the Commission believes the 9/11 operation required. The Commission itself evidently would not care, having declared the question of "the origin of the money used for the 9/11 attacks...of little practical importance" (172). But most of us would surely disagree.

THE DISMISSAL OF GENERAL AHMAD

There is yet another dimension to this story. As mentioned earlier, General Mahmoud Ahmad stepped down from his position as head of the ISI. This resignation occurred on October 8, less than a month after 9/11. The official announcement said he simply decided it was time to retire. Is it not strange, however, that he would have spent over a week in meetings with officials in Washington if he had been planning to retire? We need not, furthermore, rely solely on such *a priori* reasoning.

The *Times of India*, having reported the official story about Ahmad's sudden decision to retire, said that "the truth is more shocking." This more shocking truth was that after Indian intelligence had given US officials evidence of the money transfer ordered by Ahmad, he had been quietly dismissed after "US authorities sought his removal."[11]

If Mahmoud Ahmad really was dismissed by Pakistan's ruler, General Pervez Musharraf, because of US pressure, it surely would have taken more than minor pressure. For, as Steve Coll points out in *Ghost Wars*, General Musharraf owed his own position to General Ahmad. It was primarily thanks to Ahmad's actions that the coup of October 1999 against Nawar Sharif was successful. Ahmad then stood aside to allow Musharraf to take power. Musharraf rewarded Ahmad by making him the new director-general of ISI.[12] Given that background, it must have taken great pressure to convince Musharraf to force Ahmad to step down only two years later. If so, the Bush administration must have considered the removal of Mahmoud Ahmad from this position a matter of the utmost importance.

If this is what really happened, would it not suggest a cover-up? Nafeez Mosaddeq Ahmed, the author of one of the first books about 9/11, certainly thought so. Although one might think the United States "would be spearheading a full-scale investigation into the role of the ISI," Ahmed wrote, it "actually prevented one from going ahead by asking from behind the scenes for the ISI chief . . . to quietly resign." Explaining his point, Ahmed continued:

> By pressuring the then ISI Director-General to resign without scandal on the pretext of reshuffling, while avoiding any publicity with respect to his siphoning of funds to alleged lead hijacker Mohamed Atta, the US had effectively blocked any sort of investigation into the matter. It prevented wide publicity of these facts, and allowed the ISI chief, who was clearly complicit in the terrorist attacks of 11th September, to walk away free.[13]

If this is all true—that General Mahmoud Ahmad was forced out because of pressure from the United States and that the United States exerted this pressure in order to avoid publicity about the financial connection between the ISI and the hijackers—we can imagine various reasons why the Bush administration would want to cover up these facts. Should we expect the same of the "independent and impartial" 9/11

Commission? With allegations in the public record that the United States pressured Pakistan to force General Ahmad to resign in order to cover up the fact that he had ordered ISI money transferred to the supposed ringleader of the hijackers, wouldn't we expect the 9/11 Commission to investigate this story?

Again, however, our expectation would be disappointed. There is no mention of General Mahmoud Ahmad's "retirement." Nor is there any mention of the story in the *Times of India* or any mention of the book by Nafeez Mosaddeq Ahmed, with its suggestion as to why General Ahmad suddenly retired. To find this story, furthermore, the Commission's staff would not have had to locate that book or the *Times of India*, because the story from the latter was partly quoted in a *Wall Street Journal* editorial. Titled "Our Friends the Pakistanis," this editorial quoted the following passage:

> Top sources confirmed here on Tuesday, that the general lost his job because of the "evidence" India produced to show his links to one of the suicide bombers that wrecked the World Trade Centre. The US authorities sought his removal after confirming the fact that $100,000 were wired to WTC hijacker Mohammed [sic] Atta from Pakistan by Ahmad Umar Sheikh [sic] at the instance of Gen. Mahmud [sic].

The editorial then added: "Senior government sources have confirmed that India contributed significantly to establishing the link between the money transfer and the role played by the dismissed ISI chief."[14]

Accordingly, two parts of this embarrassing story—that General Mahmoud Ahmad ordered the money wired to Atta and that he was then forced out under US pressure—were confirmed by the *Wall Street Journal*. But the 9/11 Commission's report kept silent about the whole episode. For those with eyes to see, to be sure, there is an allusion to it in the Appendix listing the major figures discussed in the report. "Mahmud Ahmed" is identified as "Director General of Pakistan's Inter-Services Intelligence Directorate, 1999–2001" (433). But there is no mention here or elsewhere that his tenure in this post was so brief because the United States had him forced out. The Kean–Zelikow Report, rather than trying to give the American people the fullest possible account of events surrounding 9/11, has instead aided the Bush administration's effort to keep a lid on this story.

THE ASSASSINATION OF AHMAD SHAH MASOOD

Another dimension of this episode involves the assassination of Ahmad Shah Masood,[15] the leader of the Northern Alliance in Afghanistan. This assassination occurred on September 9, just two days before 9/11 and just after the week-long meeting between the ISI and CIA chiefs. Was this merely a coincidence? We might assume so, as long as we could not imagine that the demise of Masood would have served the interests of the US government.

Chossudovsky, however, suggested that the death of Masood did serve US interests. After Masood was dead, Chossudovsky wrote, "the Northern Alliance became fragmented into different factions. Had Masood not been assassinated, he would have become the head of the post-Taliban government formed in the wake of the US bombings of Afghanistan."[16] The United States, however, wanted a government headed by someone who would more faithfully serve US interests in Afghanistan (see the next chapter). The elimination of Masood meant that the Northern Alliance, once it had helped US forces defeat the Taliban, would not have a natural leader to put in charge of the country. The plausibility of Chossudovsky's suggestion is increased if we know that Masood, known as "the Lion of Panjshir," was not only "Afghanistan's most formidable military leader" but also "a charismatic popular leader." Indeed, Masood was so important that the Prologue of Steve Coll's recent book on Afghanistan—from which those quotations about Masood were taken[17]—focuses almost entirely on him.

Another factor with possible relevance involved a competition to build an oil-and-gas pipeline through Afghanistan (to be discussed in the next chapter). America supported Unocal, whereas Masood, as Coll writes, "had signed an agreement with Unocal's Argentine rival," leading Masood's people to fear that "they had been branded as Unocal's—and therefore America's—enemies."[18]

Nevertheless, one might reply, even if the United States may have wanted Masood eliminated, the mere fact the CIA and ISI chiefs had been meeting for several days prior to his assassination is irrelevant, because Masood was assassinated by al-Qaeda, not by the ISI. This is the position of *The 9/11 Commission Report*, which says that the two men who got into position to kill Masood by posing as Arab journalists were "actually al Qaeda assassins" (214). In a note, the Commission refers to the discussion of the assassination in Coll's book, which indeed provides good evidence that the assassins were sent by al-Qaeda.[19]

The Commission omits, however, any discussion of the possibility that the ISI was also behind the plot. Insofar as the Commission was implicitly denying ISI involvement, its argument would seem to be: It was al-Qaeda, therefore it was not the ISI. The problem with this logic is that it ignores the possibility that al-Qaeda and the ISI were working together on this operation—even though this is exactly what the Northern Alliance asserted. On September 14, the Northern Alliance released an official statement saying that a "Pakistani ISI–Osama–Taliban axis" was responsible for plotting the assassination. "We believe that this is a triangle between Osama bin Laden, ISI, which is the intelligence section of the Pakistani army, and the Taliban."[20] Why did the Commission not mention this claim? We must assume that the Commission was aware of this press release, which was carried by Reuters News Service and was later published in Chossudovsky's *War and Globalisation*. But if so, why did the Commission's report contain no mention of it?

A defender of the Commission's omission might say that the Northern Alliance's charge is simply too implausible to be worthy of mention. However, Coll's book, cited by the Commission to support its claim that the assassins were from al-Qaeda, also says that by 1998 the CIA and other US intelligence agencies had "documented many links between ISI, the Taliban, [and] bin Laden." Coll even says that in 1999 "bin Laden and al Qaeda . . . thrived on their links to Pakistani intelligence."[21]

Still, one might argue, these connections do not provide support for Chossudovsky's suspicion that the CIA was involved in planning the assassination. That theory—assuming the truth of the claim that the ISI and al-Qaeda worked together on this operation—would imply that the United States was, at least implicitly, working in conjunction with al-Qaeda, and that, defenders of the Commission might say, would be absurd. In Chapters Six and Seven, however, we saw reasons to suspect that the relation between OBL and the United States, especially under the Bush administration, was in reality somewhat different from the relation as portrayed in the official account.

So, given the long-standing relations between the CIA and the ISI, the long-standing relations between the ISI and OBL, the possibility that the long-standing relations between the United States and OBL had not been fully severed, the reasons why the United States might have wanted to have Masood out of the way before the battle to remove the Taliban began, and the fact that his assassination followed directly upon a week-long meeting between the ISI and CIA directors, we would think that the 9/11 Commission would have at least mentioned the possibility that the CIA was involved in the planning for the assassination of Ahmad Shah Masood. But it again seems as if the Commission's desire to give a full account was overridden by its desire to include only those "facts and circumstances" that are consistent with the official story told by the Bush administration.

KSM (KHALID SHAIKH MOHAMMED) AND THE ISI

Khalid Shaikh Mohammed, generally referred to in the Commission's report as "KSM," is central to its narrative. He is called the mastermind behind 9/11. He was reportedly captured by American forces in 2003. There are 272 paragraphs in which he is mentioned. These paragraphs provide many types of information about KSM. Not one of them, however, mentions the possibility that he was connected not only to al-Qaeda but also to the ISI.

There would, of course, be no occasion for such a mention if no credible source had ever connected KSM and the ISI. However, as I reported in *The New Pearl Harbor*, Josef Bodansky stated in 2002 that KSM was related to the ISI, which had acted to shield him.[22] And Bodansky, having been the director of the Congressional Task Force on Terrorism and Unconventional Warfare, should be considered a credible source.

If Bodansky was right, the implications would be considerable, especially given the report, mentioned in Chapter 5, that KSM telephoned Mohamed Atta the day before 9/11 to give him final authorization for the hijackings. Putting this together with other reports, the preparation for 9/11 may have included these elements:

1. One ISI agent, Saeed Sheikh, wired a large sum of money to the man described as the ringleader of the 9/11 hijackers, Mohamed Atta.

2. Saeed was ordered to send this money by General Mahmoud Ahmad, the director of the ISI.

3. Mohamed Atta was given final authorization for the hijacking mission by the mastermind of the hijacking plot, KSM, who was also

connected to the ISI. It would seem, therefore, that the possibility that KSM worked on behalf of the ISI should at least have been mentioned.

DANIEL PEARL, KSM, AND THE ISI

Wall Street Journal reporter Daniel Pearl was kidnapped in Pakistan in January 2002. He was evidently there to investigate links between Richard Reid (the "shoe bomber") and Pakistani extremists. The day Pearl was kidnapped, he was reportedly going to see a religious leader with connections to both Saeed Sheikh and the ISI. As the Washington Post put it, "Pearl may have strayed into areas involving Pakistan's secret intelligence organizations."[23] UPI made an even stronger statement, reporting that US intelligence believed the kidnappers to be connected to the ISI. After Pearl was murdered, it was learned that ISI agent Saeed Sheikh had been involved in the kidnapping. Soon thereafter, under circumstances suggesting that Saeed may have been tricked into confessing, he was charged with Pearl's murder.[24] According to later reports, US authorities concluded that Pearl's murder was ordered, and perhaps even carried out, by KSM.[25]

At this time, stories in the US press were no longer mentioning the possible connection between the ISI and Pearl's kidnapping. But if Saeed and KSM were both connected to the ISI, there is reason to believe that both the kidnapping and the murder of Daniel Pearl were ordered by the ISI. A possible motive might have been concern that his investigations were bringing him too close to the truth about 9/11.

The US government clearly did not want any discussion of this possibility. Secretary of State Powell declared that there were no links between Pearl's murder and "elements of the ISI." The Guardian, in light of the overwhelming evidence that Saeed Sheikh worked for the ISI, called Powell's denial "shocking."[26] Unfortunately we have learned not to be shocked by the fact that our national political leaders, in pursuit of their agendas, tell blatant lies.

The 9/11 Commission, however, was ostensibly created to discover the truth about 9/11, not to promote some agenda. It appears, nevertheless, to have participated in the Bush administration's effort to prevent any discussion of the possible relation between the ISI and Pearl's murder. Indeed, the name of Daniel Pearl is one of those many names that the Kean–Zelikow Report does not even mention.

ABU ZUBAYDAH, MUSHAF ALI MIR, AND ISI AGENT RAJAA GULUM ABBAS

The first of two final examples of a possible ISI connection to 9/11 brings us back to the testimony of al-Qaeda operative Abu Zubaydah as reported by Gerald Posner. "According to Zubaydah," says Posner,

> he was present in 1996, in Pakistan, when bin Laden struck a deal with Mushaf Ali Mir, a highly placed military officer with close ties to some of the most pro-Islamist elements in ISI. It was a relationship that was still active and provided bin Laden and al Qaeda protection, arms, and supplies.

Zubaydah also reportedly said that Mir, like the three Saudis he named, knew that an al-Qaeda attack was scheduled to occur on American soil on September 11, 2001. Posner then reports that another seven months after the three Saudis died in surprising ways, Mir's recently inspected air force plane went down in good weather, killing him, his wife, and several confidants.[27] As with the Saudis, Mir's death gave added credibility to Zubaydah's reported claims—that Mir was closely related to the ISI as well as to al-Qaeda and that he knew that al-Qaeda attacks were to occur in the United States on 9/11.

The idea that there was foreknowledge of the 9/11 attacks within Pakistan's ISI is given additional support by a story involving a US government informant, Randy Glass. In July 1999, Glass recorded a conversation with an ISI agent named Rajaa Gulum Abbas and some illegal arms dealers. This conversation occurred at a restaurant from which they could see the WTC. After saying that he wanted to buy some stolen US military weapons to give to bin Laden, Abbas reportedly pointed to the WTC and said: "Those towers are coming down."[28]

These last two stories, it would seem, provide such strong evidence of foreknowledge about 9/11 within Pakistan's ISI that the 9/11 Commission, if it wanted to make even a gesture towards giving a full accounting of the "facts and circumstances" surrounding 9/11, would simply have had to mention them. By now, however, the reader will probably not be surprised to learn that the names of Mushaf Ali Mir, Randy Glass, and Rajaa Gulum Abbas are all absent from the Kean–Zelikow Report.

CHAPTER TEN

Possible Motives of the Bush Administration

The 9/11 Commission understood that its mandate, as we have seen, was to provide "the fullest possible account" of the "facts and circumstances" surrounding 9/11. Included in those facts and circumstances are ones that, according to some critics of the official account of 9/11, provide evidence that the Bush administration intentionally allowed the attacks of 9/11. Some critics have even suggested that the Bush administration actively helped the attacks succeed. In light of the fact that several books have been written propounding such views, including some in English, the Commission's staff, given its "exacting investigative work," would surely have discovered such books. Or if not, the staff would at least have known about a front-page story on this topic in the *Wall Street Journal.* Readers of this story learned not only that a poll showed that 20 percent of the German population believed "the U.S. government ordered the attacks itself" but also that similar views were held in some other European countries.[1] Also, as we saw in the Introduction, polls show that significant percentages of Americans and Canadians believe that the US government deliberately allowed the attacks to happen, with some of those believing the Bush administration actually planned the attacks. Knowing that such information is available and such views are held, the Commission, we would assume, would have felt called upon to respond to these suspicions.

An adequate response would contain at least the following elements: (1) an acknowledgment that these suspicions exist; (2) a summary of the main kinds of reports and alleged facts cited as evidence by those who have promoted these suspicions; and (3) an explanation of why these reports and alleged facts do not really constitute evidence for complicity by the Bush administration.

Finally, the persistence and widespread documentation of these allegations means that an adequate response would need to consider (if only to debunk) the motives that some critics have alleged the Bush administration would have had for facilitating the 9/11 attacks—just as the Commission properly looked at motives that Osama bin Laden and his al-Qaeda organization may have had for planning the attacks. For many Americans, of course, even considering the possibility that their own government might have had motives for facilitating such attacks would not be pleasant. But an account, if it is to be the fullest possible account, cannot decide in advance to restrict itself to ideas that are pleasant.

In this chapter, accordingly, we will look at *The 9/11 Commission Report* from this perspective, asking how it has responded to the fact that some critics of the official account have alleged that the Bush administration would have had several motives for allowing the attacks and even helping them succeed.

THE 9/11 ATTACKS AS "OPPORTUNITIES"

One way to approach this question would be to ask whether these attacks brought benefits to this administration that could reasonably have been anticipated.

There is no doubt that the attacks brought benefits. Indeed, several members of the Bush administration publicly said so. The president himself declared that the attacks provided "a great opportunity."[2] Donald Rumsfeld stated that 9/11 created "the kind of opportunities that World War II offered, to refashion the world." Condoleezza Rice had the same thing in mind, telling senior members of the National Security Council to "think about 'how do you capitalize on these opportunities' to fundamentally change . . . the shape of the world."[3] The National Security Strategy of the United States of America, issued by the Bush administration in September 2002, said: "The events of September 11, 2001 opened vast, new opportunities."[4]

Of course, the fact that these members of the Bush administration described attacks as opportunities after the fact does not necessarily mean that they could have anticipated in advance that attacks of this nature would bring such opportunities. However, all of these statements, except for the last one, were made shortly after 9/11. If the benefits could be seen so soon after the attacks, we can assume that, if these people were thinking about such attacks ahead of time, they could have anticipated that they would create these opportunities.

It would seem, therefore, that the Bush administration's description of the attacks as providing opportunities, along with the fact that at least some of these opportunities could have been anticipated, were important parts of the "events surrounding 9/11" that "the fullest possible account" would have included. These descriptions of the attacks of 9/11 as opportunities, however, are not mentioned in *The 9/11 Commission Report.*[5]

In any case, the idea that members of the Bush administration could have anticipated benefits from catastrophic attacks of the type that occurred on 9/11 does not rest entirely on inference from fact that the attacks were seen as opportunities immediately after 9/11. Critics have referred to a pre-9/11 document that speaks of benefits that could accrue from catastrophic attacks. We need to see how the Commission responded to this part of the facts and circumstances surrounding 9/11.

"A NEW PEARL HARBOR" TO ADVANCE THE PAX AMERICANA

In the fall of 2000, a year before 9/11, a document entitled *Rebuilding America's Defenses* was published by an organization calling itself the Project for the New American Century (PNAC).[6] This organization was formed by individuals who were members or at least supporters of the Reagan and Bush I administrations, some of whom would go on to be central figures in the Bush II administration. These individuals include Richard Armitage, John Bolton, Dick Cheney, Zalmay Khalilzad (closely associated with Paul Wolfowitz[7]), Lewis "Scooter" Libby, Richard Perle, Donald Rumsfeld, Paul Wolfowitz, and James Woolsey. Libby (now Cheney's chief of staff) and Wolfowitz (now Rumsfeld's deputy) are listed as having participated directly in the project to produce *Rebuilding America's Defenses*. Interestingly, John Lehman, a member of the 9/11 Commission, has been a member of PNAC or at least publicly aligned with it.[8]

This PNAC document, after bemoaning the fact that spending for military purposes no longer captured as much of the US budget as it once did, argues that it is necessary for defense spending to be greatly increased if the "American peace is to be maintained, and expanded," because this Pax Americana "must have a secure foundation on unquestioned U.S. military preeminence." The way to acquire and retain such military preeminence is to take full advantage of the "revolution in military affairs" made possible by technological advances. Bringing about this transformation of US military forces will, however, probably be a long, slow process, partly because it will be very expensive. However, the document suggests, the process could occur more quickly if America suffered "some catastrophic and catalyzing event—like a new Pearl Harbor."[9] This statement, we would think, should have gotten the attention of some members of the 9/11 Commission.

After the 9/11 attacks came, moreover, the idea that they constituted a new Pearl Harbor was expressed by the president and some of his supporters. At the end of that very day, President Bush reportedly wrote in his diary: "The Pearl Harbor of the 21st century took place today."[10] Also, minutes after the president's address to the nation earlier that day, Henry Kissinger posted an online article in which he said: "The government should be charged with a systematic response that, one hopes, will end the way that the attack on Pearl Harbor ended—with the destruction of the system that is responsible for it."[11]

One might think that the existence of these statements would have been perceived by the 9/11 Commission as part of the relevant "events surrounding 9/11" that should be included in "the fullest possible account." But there is no mention of any of these statements on any of the 567 pages of the Kean–Zelikow Report.

Those pages are largely filled—in line with the Commission's unquestioned assumption—with discussions of Osama bin Laden, al-Qaeda, Islamic terrorism more generally, and American responses thereto. Then, after the Commission had disbanded, its staff released another 155-page report on al-Qaeda financing.[12] These matters were obviously considered essential for understanding the "facts and circumstances relating to the terrorist attacks of September 11, 2001."

But the fact that individuals who are central members and supporters of the Bush–Cheney administration endorsed a document indicating that "a new Pearl Harbor" would be helpful for furthering its aims; that some supporters of this administration and even the president himself then compared the 9/11 attacks to the Pearl Harbor attacks; and that several members of this administration said that 9/11 provided "opportunities"—this complex fact was not thought worthy of a single sentence in the Commission's "fullest possible account." Indeed, the Commission's report does not even mention the Project for the New American Century.

GENERATING FUNDS FOR THE US SPACE COMMAND

One dimension of the "revolution in military affairs" discussed in the PNAC document is so important as to deserve separate treatment. This dimension is the militarization of space, which is now the province of a new branch of the American military, the US Space Command.

The purpose of this branch is to bring about "full spectrum dominance." The idea is that the US military, with its air force, army, and navy, is already dominant in the air and on land and sea. The US Space Command will now ensure dominance in space. "Vision for 2020," a document published by the US Space Command, puts it thus: "The emerging synergy of space superiority with land, sea, and air superiority, will lead to Full Spectrum Dominance."[13]

The government's description of spending for the US Space Command as spending for "missile defense" makes its mission sound purely defensive—augmenting "homeland security" by defending the United States from missile attacks. The mission statement in "Vision for 2020," however, states: "U.S. Space Command—dominating the space dimension of military operations to protect US interests and investment."[14] Its primary purpose, in other words, is not to protect the American homeland but to protect American investments abroad. Such protection will be needed, it says, because "[t]he globalization of the world economy will continue with a widening between 'haves' and 'have-nots.'" The mission of the US Space Command, it is clear, is to protect the American "haves" from the world's "have-nots," as American-led globalization leaves these "have-nots" with even less.

The 9/11 Commission, however, makes no mention of the US Space Command's program and mission. To understand the full significance of this omission, it is necessary to understand that its program involves three parts. The first part involves space-based surveillance technology, through which US military leaders can identify enemies of US forces anywhere on the planet.[15]

The second part involves putting up space weapons, such as laser cannons, with which the United States will be able to destroy the satellites of other countries. "Vision for 2020" frankly states its desire to be able "to deny others the use of space."[16]

The third part of the program is usually called the "missile defense shield," but its purpose, like that of the first two parts, is offensive.

As *Rebuilding America's Defenses* said (in a passage called "a remarkable admission" by Rahul Mahajan):

> In the post-Cold-War era, America and its allies . . . have become the primary objects of deterrence and it is states like Iraq, Iran and North Korea who most wish to develop deterrent capabilities. Projecting conventional military forces . . . will be far more complex and constrained when the American homeland . . . is subject to attack by otherwise weak rogue regimes capable of cobbling together a minuscule ballistic missile force. Building an effective . . . system of missile defenses is a prerequisite for maintaining American preeminence.[17]

The purpose of the "missile defense shield," in other words, is not to deter other countries from launching a first strike against the United States. Its purpose is to prevent other countries from being able to deter the United States from launching a first strike against them.[18]

The major impediment to making this program operational is that it will be extremely expensive. According to one expert, it will require over $1 trillion from American taxpayers.[19] The difficulty of getting Congress and the American people to pony up was the main reason for the PNAC document's statement that the desired transformation will take a long time "absent some catastrophic and catalyzing event—like a new Pearl Harbor."[20]

In omitting any mention of this project for achieving global domination, therefore, the 9/11 Commission omitted a project so big that some of its backers, we can imagine, may have been able to rationalize an attack taking a few thousand American lives, if such an attack seemed necessary to get adequate funding for this project.

Donald Rumsfeld, as we saw, was a member of PNAC when it produced its document. He was also the chairman of the Commission to Assess US National Security Space Management and Organization.[21] The task of this commission—commonly known as the "Rumsfeld Commission"—was to make proposals with regard to the US Space Command. After making various proposals that would "increase the asymmetry between U.S. forces and those of other military powers," the Rumsfeld Commission Report said that, because its proposals would cost a lot of money and involve significant reorganization, they would probably encounter strong resistance. But, the report—which was issued January 7, 2001—said:

The question is whether the U.S. will be wise enough to act responsibly and soon enough to reduce U.S. space vulnerability. Or whether, as in the past, a disabling attack against the country and its people—a "Space Pearl Harbor"—will be the only event able to galvanize the nation and cause the U.S. Government to act.[22]

In speaking of a "Space Pearl Harbor," the report meant an attack on its military satellites in space. The 9/11 attacks were obviously not of this nature. It is interesting, nevertheless, that only a few months after PNAC had issued its statement about "a new Pearl Harbor," the Rumsfeld Commission also pointed out that a Pearl Harbor type of attack might be needed to "galvanize the nation."

When the new Pearl Harbor came, Rumsfeld, having been made secretary of defense, was in position to use it to get more money for the US Space Command. Before TV cameras on the evening of 9/11 itself, Rumsfeld said to Senator Carl Levin, then chairman of the Senate Armed Services Committee:

Senator Levin, you and other Democrats in Congress have voiced fear that you simply don't have enough money for the large increase in defense that the Pentagon is seeking, especially for missile defense. . . . Does this sort of thing convince you that an emergency exists in this country to increase defense spending, to dip into Social Security, if necessary, to pay for defense spending—increase defense spending?[23]

Earlier that day, the Pentagon, which by then had been under Rumsfeld's leadership for almost seven months, failed to prevent airplane attacks on the World Trade Center and the Pentagon itself. Now that very evening Rumsfeld was using the success of those attacks to get more money from Congress for the Pentagon and, in particular, for the US Space Command. One might think that this rather remarkable coincidence would have gotten the attention of the 9/11 Commission, because it suggests that the secretary of defense may not have wanted to prevent this "new Pearl Harbor." But the Commission's report, focusing exclusively on al-Qaeda terrorists, makes no mention of this possible motive.

Rumsfeld was, moreover, not the only person highly committed to promoting the US Space Command who was in charge of military affairs on 9/11. Another was General Ralph E. Eberhart, the current head of the

US Space Command, who is also the commander of NORAD.[24] General Richard Myers, the former head of the US Space Command, was on 9/11 the Acting Chairman of the Joint Chiefs of Staff.

A truly "independent" and "impartial" commission would surely comment on this remarkable coincidence—that three of the men in charge of the US military response on 9/11 were outspoken advocates of the US Space Command, that the US military under their control failed to prevent the attacks, and that one of these men then used the success of the attacks to obtain billions of dollars more for this branch of the military.

Coincidence does not, of course, prove complicity. Sometimes when events coincide in an improbable way, the coincidence is exactly what the term has generally come to mean: *simply* coincidental. It is well known, however, that after a crime the first question to be asked is *cui bono?*— who benefits? A truly independent commission would at least have proceeded on the assumption that Rumsfeld, Myers, and Eberhart had to be regarded as possible suspects, whose actions that day were to be rigorously investigated. Instead, the testimonies of these three men were treated as unquestionable sources of truth as to what really happened— despite, as we will see later, the contradictions in their stories.[25]

THE PLAN TO ATTACK AFGHANISTAN

Critics have alleged that another possible motive on the part of the Bush administration was its desire to attack Afghanistan so as to replace the Taliban with a US-friendly government in order to further US economic and geopolitical aims.

The 9/11 Commission does recognize that the US war in Afghanistan—which began on October 7, less than a month after 9/11— was a war to produce "regime change" (203). According to the Commission, however, the United States wanted to change the regime because the Taliban, besides being incapable of providing peace by ending the civil war, was perpetrating human rights abuses and providing a "safe haven" for al-Qaeda (111, 203, 337). In limiting the US motives to these, however, the Commission ignored abundant evidence that the motives were more complex, more self-interested, and more ambitious.

At the center of these motives was the desire to enable the building of a multibillion dollar pipeline route by a consortium known as CentGas (Central Asia Gas Pipeline), which was formed by US oil giant Unocal.

The planned route would bring oil and gas from the land-locked Caspian region, with its enormous reserves, to the sea through Afghanistan and Pakistan. By 2001, the Taliban had come to be perceived as an obstacle to this project.

The Taliban was originally supported by the United States, working together with Pakistan's ISI. The pipeline project had become the crucial issue in what Ahmed Rashid in 1997 dubbed "The New Great Game."[26] One issue in this game was who would construct the pipeline route—the Unocal-dominated CentGas Consortium or Argentina's Bridas Corporation. The other issue was which countries the route would go through. The United States promoted Unocal and backed its plan to build the route through Afghanistan and Pakistan, since this route would avoid both Iran and Russia.[27] The main obstacle to this plan was the civil war that had been going on in Afghanistan since the withdrawal of the Soviet Union in 1989. The US government supported the Taliban in the late 1990s on the basis of hope that it would be able to unify the country through its military strength and then provide a stable government.

The centrality of this issue is shown by the title Rashid gave to two of his chapters: "Romancing the Taliban: The Battle for Pipelines."[28] With regard to the United States in particular, Rashid says that "the strategy over pipelines had become the driving force behind Washington's interest in the Taliban."[29] However, although the Kean–Zelikow Commission cites Rashid's well-known book several times, it makes no reference to his discussion of the centrality of the pipelines to Washington's perspective.

From reading the Commission's report, in fact, one would never suspect that the "pipeline war" (as it became called) was a major US concern. The pipeline project in general and Unocal in particular are mentioned in only one paragraph (along with its accompanying note). And the Commission here suggests that the US State Department was interested in Unocal's pipeline project only insofar as "the prospect of shared pipeline profits might lure faction leaders to a conference table" (111). The United States, in other words, regarded the pipeline project only as a means to peace. That may indeed have been the view of some of the American participants. But the dominant hope within Unocal and the US government was that the Taliban would bring peace by defeating its opponents, primarily Ahmad Shah Masood—after which the US government and the United Nations would recognize the Taliban as the government of Afghanistan, which in turn would allow Unocal to get the loans it would need to finance the project.[30]

The Commission's report, by contrast, suggests that neither the US government nor Unocal took the side of the Taliban in the civil war. The Commission tells us that Marty Miller, who had been in charge of the pipeline project for Unocal, "denied working exclusively with the Taliban and told us that his company sought to work with all Afghan factions to bring about the necessary stability to proceed with the project" (480n14). As is often the case, the Commission's "exacting investigative work" consisted primarily of interviewing people and recording their answers. Had the Commission consulted Steve Coll's *Ghost Wars*, which the Commission quotes elsewhere, it could have learned that although "Marty Miller insisted publicly that Unocal remained 'fanatically neutral' about Afghan politics," in reality "Marty Miller and his colleagues hoped the Taliban takeover of Kabul would speed their pipeline negotiations."[31] Coll is here referring to September 1996, when the Taliban, heavily financed by Pakistan and Saudi Arabia, took over Kabul, the capital, by forcing Masood to flee. As soon as this occurred, Rashid reports, a Unocal executive "told wire agencies that the pipeline project would be easier to implement now that the Taliban had captured Kabul."[32] We are again left wondering if the Kean–Zelikow's Commission's research was simply inadequate or if it deliberately left out information that did not fit its narrative.

There is a similar problem with the Commission's statement about US neutrality. The Commission says flatly: "U.S. diplomats did not favor the Taliban over the rival factions but were simply willing to 'give the Taliban a chance'" (111). Interviews are again the only support offered. Had the Commission consulted Rashid's book on this issue, it would have read that the United States "accepted the ISI's analysis . . . that a Taliban victory in Afghanistan would make Unocal's job much easier."[33] Rashid also reports that "within hours of Kabul's capture by the Taliban"—when much of the country still remained under the control of other factions—"the US State Department announced it would establish diplomatic relations with the Taliban."[34] The lack of US neutrality is likewise shown by Steve Coll, who says: "[T]he State Department had taken up Unocal's agenda as its own"— which meant, of course, support for the Taliban.[35]

Rashid, summarizing the situation, says that "the US–Unocal partnership was backing the Taliban and wanted an all-out Taliban victory—even as the US and Unocal claimed they had no favourites in Afghanistan."[36] The Kean–Zelikow Commission, by contrast, simply gives us the public relations statements of some of the US and Unocal actors, repeated in recent interviews, as actual history.

Why is it important to point out this distortion? Because the Commission's portrayal of US interests in Afghanistan suggests that the United States had no imperialistic or crass material interests in the area— the kind of interests that might lead a government to devise a pretext for going to war. This issue becomes more important as we move to the point in the story at which the United States comes to think of the Taliban as an obstacle rather than a vehicle of the Unocal (CentGas) pipeline project.

In July 1998, the Taliban, after having failed in 1997 to take the northern city of Mazar-i-Sharif, finally succeeded, giving it control of most of Afghanistan, including the entire pipeline route. After this victory, CentGas immediately announced that it was "ready to proceed."[37] Shortly thereafter, however, the US embassies in Kenya and Tanzania were blown up, leading the United States to launch cruise missile strikes against OBL's camps in Afghanistan. These and related developments led Unocal to withdraw from CentGas, convinced that Afghanistan under the Taliban would never have the peace and stability needed for the pipeline project.[38] Rashid, finishing his book in mid-1999, wrote that the Clinton administration had shifted its support to the pipeline route from Azerbaijan through Georgia to Turkey, adding that "by now nobody wanted to touch Afghanistan and the Taliban."[39]

When the Bush administration came to power, however, it decided to give the Taliban one last chance. This last chance occurred at a four-day meeting in Berlin in July 2001, which would need to be mentioned in any realistic account of how the US war in Afghanistan came about. According to the Pakistani representative at this meeting, Niaz Naik, US representatives, trying to convince the Taliban to share power with US-friendly factions, said: "Either you accept our offer of a carpet of gold, or we bury you under a carpet of bombs."[40] Naik said that he was told by Americans that "military action against Afghanistan would go ahead . . . before the snows started falling in Afghanistan, by the middle of October at the latest."[41] The US attack on Afghanistan began, in fact, on October 7, which was as soon as the US military could get ready after 9/11.[42]

The 9/11 Commission's discussion of what transpired in July is much milder. Some members of the Bush administration, we are told, were "moving toward agreement that some last effort should be made to convince the Taliban to shift position and then, if that failed, . . . the United States would try covert action to topple the Taliban's leadership from within" (206). There is no mention of Niaz Naik or the meeting in Berlin. The Commission's reference to the fact that the United States wanted the Taliban to "shift position" does not mention that this shift involved not simply turning over OBL but joining a "unity government" that would allow Unocal's pipeline project to go forward. Nor does the Commission mention the statement by US officials that if the Taliban refused, the United States would use military force (not merely covert action). And yet all this information was available in books and newspapers articles that the Commission's staff should have been able to locate.

In any case, there was still further evidence, ignored by the Commission, that the US war against the Taliban was related more to the pipeline project than to 9/11. For one thing, President Bush's special envoy to Afghanistan, Zalmay Khalilzad (mentioned previously as a member of PNAC), and the new Prime Minister, Hamid Karzai, were previously on Unocal's payroll. As Chalmers Johnson wrote: "The continued collaboration of Khalilzad and Karzai in post-9/11 Afghanistan strongly suggests that the Bush administration was and remains as interested in oil as in terrorism in that region."[43] As early as October 10, moreover, the US Department of State had informed the Pakistani Minister of Oil that "in view of recent geopolitical developments," Unocal was again ready to go ahead with the pipeline project.[44] Finally, as one Israeli writer put it: "If one looks at the map of the big American bases created, one is struck by the fact that they are completely identical to the route of the projected oil pipeline to the Indian Ocean."[45]

There is considerable evidence, therefore, that, in Chalmers Johnson's words, "Support for [the dual oil and gas pipelines from Turkmenistan south through Afghanistan to the Arabian Sea coast of Pakistan] appears to have been a major consideration in the Bush administration's decision to attack Afghanistan on October 7, 2001"—a point that Johnson makes apart from any allegation that the Bush administration orchestrated the attacks of 9/11.[46] But the 9/11 Commission does not even mention the fact that many people share Johnson's view, according to which the US war in Afghanistan was motivated by a concern much larger than those mentioned by the Commission.

This larger concern, furthermore, "was not just to make money," suggests Johnson, "but to establish an American presence in Central Asia." Evidence for this view is provided by the fact that the United States, besides establishing long-term bases in Afghanistan, had within a month after 9/11 arranged for long-term bases in Pakistan, Kyrgyzstan, and Uzbekistan.[47] The United States could thereby be seen to be carrying out the prescription of Zbigniew Brzezinski in his 1997 book, *The Grand Chessboard: American Primacy and Its Geostrategic Imperatives*, in which he portrayed Central Asia, with its vast oil reserves, as the key to world power. Brzezinski, who had been the National Security Advisor in the Carter administration, argued that America, to ensure its continued "primacy," must get control of this region. The Bush administration's use of 9/11 to establish bases in several countries in this region provided an essential step in that direction. In *The 9/11 Commission Report*, however, there is no hint of this development. The United States simply wanted to stop the war, bring an end to the Taliban's human rights abuses, and prevent Afghanistan from being used as a haven for terrorists (111, 203). In the world of the Kean–Zelikow Commission, the United States had no larger ambitions.

The omission of Brzezinski's book means, furthermore, the omission of an earlier suggestion that a new Pearl Harbor could be helpful. Brzezinski, having argued that the present "window of historical opportunity for America's constructive exploitation of its global power could prove to be relatively brief,"[48] bemoans the fact that the American public might be unwilling to use its power for imperial purposes. The problem, according to Brzezinski's analysis, is that

> America is too democratic at home to be autocratic abroad. This limits the use of America's power, especially its capacity for military intimidation. . . . The economic self-denial (that is, defense spending) and the human sacrifice (casualties even among professional soldiers) required in the effort are uncongenial to democratic instincts. Democracy is inimical to imperial mobilization.[49]

Brzezinski suggests, however, that this weakness in democracy can be overcome. Having said that "the pursuit of power is not a goal that commands popular passion," he then adds: "except in conditions of a sudden threat or challenge to the public's sense of domestic well being."[50]

What would make the American public willing to make the economic and human sacrifices needed for "imperial mobilization," he suggests, would be "a truly massive and widely perceived direct external threat." This passage, near the end of the book, is parallel to an earlier passage, in which Brzezinski said that the public was willing to support "America's engagement in World War II largely because of the shock effect of the Japanese attack on Pearl Harbor."[51] A new Pearl Harbor would, accordingly, allow America to ensure its continued primacy by gaining control of Central Asia.

In deciding which events belonged to the category of "events surrounding 9/11"—meaning events relevant to understanding why and how the attacks of 9/11 occurred—the Commission chose to include OBL's 1998 statement that Muslims should kill Americans (47). That was considered obviously relevant. But the 9/11 Commission did not include Brzezinski's 1997 suggestion that a new Pearl Harbor would prod Americans to support the increased money for the military needed to support imperial mobilization—even though the Commission points out that 9/11 had exactly the result that Brzezinski predicted, saying:

> The nation has committed enormous resources to national security and to countering terrorism. Between fiscal year 2001, the last budget adopted before 9/11, and the present fiscal year 2004, total federal spending on defense (including expenditures on both Iraq and Afghanistan), homeland security, and international affairs rose more than 50 percent, from $345 billion to about $547 billion. The United States has not experienced such a rapid surge in national security spending since the Korean War. (361)

But the Commissioners evidently thought it too much of a stretch to ask whether motive might be inferred from effect.

We see again how the Commission's unquestioned assumption—that the 9/11 attacks were planned and executed entirely by al-Qaeda under the guidance of Osama bin Laden—determined in advance its selection of which events constituted "events surrounding 9/11." In line with this assumption, the 9/11 Commission has given us an extremely simplistic picture of US motivations behind the attack on Afghanistan. The Commission has, in particular, omitted all those facts suggesting that 9/11 was more the pretext than the basis for the war in Afghanistan.

THE PLAN TO ATTACK IRAQ

The Bush administration's attack on Iraq in 2003 is probably the issue on which the 9/11 Commission has been regarded as the most critical, stating that it found no evidence of "collaborative operational relationship" between OBL and Saddam Hussein's Iraq and no evidence, in particular, "that Iraq cooperated with al Qaeda in developing or carrying out any attacks against the United States" (66). This statement, released in a staff report about a month before the publication of the final report, created much discussion in the press. The quantity and the intensity of this discussion was increased by the fact that the president and especially the vice president reacted strongly, with the latter calling "outrageous" a front-page story in the *New York Times* headed "Panel Finds No Qaeda–Iraq Tie."[52] The resulting commentary ranged from William Safire's column, in which he lashed out at the Commission's chairman and vice chairman for letting themselves be "jerked around by a manipulative staff," to a *New York Times* story headed "Political Uproar: 9/11 Panel Members Debate Qaeda–Iraq 'Tie,'" to Joe Conason's article entitled "9/11 Panel Becomes Cheney's Nightmare."[53]

This commentary gave the appearance that the 9/11 Commission, perhaps especially its staff, was truly independent, telling the truth no matter how embarrassing it might be to the White House. That, of course, was *mere* appearance. Nevertheless, given the fact that Bush and Cheney continued to insist on the existence of ties between Iraq and al-Qaeda, the Commission did in this case report something contrary to the public position of the White House.

The Commission was, furthermore, forthcoming about the extent to which certain members of the Bush administration pushed for attacking Iraq immediately after 9/11. It pointed out that Secretary of Defense Rumsfeld instructed General Myers to find out as much as he could about Saddam Hussein's possible responsibility for 9/11. It also cited a report according to which, at the first session at Camp David after 9/11, Rumsfeld began by asking what should be done about Iraq (334–35). The Commission even portrayed Rumsfeld's deputy, Paul Wolfowitz, as arguing that Saddam should be attacked even if there were only a 10 percent chance that he was behind the 9/11 attacks (335–36).[54] Finally, the Commission reported Richard Clarke's statement that the president told him the day after 9/11 to see if Saddam was linked to the attacks in any way (334). The Commission was, therefore, quite frank about the fact that some leaders of the Bush administration were ready from the outset to attack Iraq because of its possible connections to 9/11 or at least al-Qaeda—connections for which the Commission said that it could find no credible evidence.

The Commission has, nevertheless, omitted facts about the decision to attack Iraq that should have been included in a "fullest possible account." These facts are important because their omission means that readers of *The 9/11 Commission Report* are shielded from evidence about how deep and long-standing the desire to attack Iraq had been among some members of the Bush administration.

Some of these omitted facts support the claim that the plan to attack Iraq had, in Chalmers Johnson's words, "been in the works for at least a decade."[55] In pushing it back that far, Johnson is referring to the fact that after the Gulf War of 1991, several individuals in the White House and the Pentagon believed that the United States should have gone to Baghdad and taken out Saddam Hussein, as they indicated "in reports written for then Secretary of Defense Cheney."[56] In 1996, a document entitled "A Clean Break" was produced by a study group led by Richard Perle (who would the following year become a founding member of PNAC). Recommending that Israel adopt a policy of "preemption," Perle and his colleagues suggested that Israel begin "rolling back Syria," an effort that should "focus on removing Saddam Hussein from power in Iraq." Advocating that Israel invade Lebanon and then Syria, this document included texts to be used for speeches justifying the action in a way that would win sympathy in America. Besides "drawing attention to [Syria's] weapons of mass destruction," Israel should say:

> Negotiations with repressive regimes like Syria's require cautious realism. . . . It is dangerous for Israel to deal naively with a regime murderous of its own people, openly aggressive toward its neighbors, . . . and supportive of the most deadly terrorist organizations.[57]

As James Bamford points out in *A Pretext for War*, these justifications were very similar to those that would be used in later years to justify America's attack on Iraq.[58]

The argument for this American attack on Iraq became more visible the following year, after PNAC was formed. In December 1997, Paul

Wolfowitz and Zalmay Khalilzad published an article in the *Weekly Standard*—which is edited by the chairman of PNAC, William Kristol—entitled "Saddam Must Go."[59] A month later, these three and fifteen other members of PNAC—including Donald Rumsfeld, John Bolton, and Richard Perle—sent a letter to President Clinton urging him to use military force to "remov[e] Saddam Hussein and his regime from power" and thereby "to protect our vital interests in the Gulf." In May 1997, they sent a letter to Newt Gingrich and Trent Lott—the Speaker of the House and the Senate majority leader, respectively. Complaining that Clinton had not listened to them, these letter-writers said that the United States "should establish and maintain a strong U.S. military presence in the region, and be prepared to use that force to protect our vital interests in the Gulf—and, if necessary, to help remove Saddam from power."[60] Finally, *Rebuilding America's Defenses*, published by PNAC in September 2000, emphasized that Iraq under Saddam Hussein was a threat to American interests in the region.[61]

When the Bush administration took office in 2001, Chalmers Johnson points out, "ten of the eighteen signers of the letters to Clinton and Republican congressional leaders became members of the administration."[62] It was no mere coincidence, therefore, that—as both Paul O'Neill and Richard Clarke have emphasized—the Bush administration was already intent on removing Saddam Hussein when it took office.[63] And it is also not surprising to learn that immediately after the 9/11 attacks, some members of the Bush administration wanted to use those attacks as the basis for their long-desired invasion to bring about regime change in Iraq.

But the Kean–Zelikow Commission, having left out that background, provides no context for readers to understand why and how strongly some members of the Bush administration wanted to attack Iraq. Indeed, the Commission fails to make clear just how ready some of them were to go to war against Iraq even if there was no evidence of its complicity in the attacks. A crucial omission in this respect is the failure to quote notes of Rumsfeld's conversations on 9/11 that were jotted down by an aide. These notes, which were later revealed by CBS News, indicate that Rumsfeld wanted the "best info fast. Judge whether good enough hit S.H. [Saddam Hussein] at same time. Not only UBL [Usama bin Laden]. Go massive. Sweep it all up. Things related and not."[64] James Bamford, after quoting these notes, says: "From the notes it was clear that the attacks would be used as a pretext for war against Saddam Hussein."[65]

The Commission, by contrast, merely tells us that notes from that day indicate that "Secretary Rumsfeld instructed Myers to obtain quickly as much information as possible" and to consider "a wide range of options and possibilities" (334–35). The Commission then adds:

> The secretary said his instinct was to hit Saddam Hussein at the same time—not only Bin Ladin. Secretary Rumsfeld later explained that at the time, he had been considering either one of them, or perhaps someone else, as the responsible party. (335)

From the Commission's account alone, we would assume that Rumsfeld was thinking of hitting Saddam if and only if there was good evidence that he was "the responsible party." As the notes quoted by CBS and Bamford show, however, Rumsfeld wanted to use 9/11 as the basis for a "massive" response that would take care of many threats to American interests ("Sweep it all up"), especially Saddam Hussein, whether he was responsible or not ("Things related and not"). The Kean–Zelikow Commission, with its omissions and distortions, hides this fact from us.

Furthermore, just as the Commission failed to point out the centrality of oil and military bases in the Bush administration's interest in Afghanistan, it does the same in relation to Iraq—even though this country has the second largest known oil reserves in the world. The Commission does say that at a National Security Council meeting on September 17, "President Bush ordered the Defense Department to be ready to deal with Iraq if Baghdad acted against U.S. interests, with plans to include possibly occupying Iraqi oil fields" (335). But this is the sole hint in the Kean–Zelikow Report that the Bush administration might have had an interest in getting control of Iraqi oil.

Even this statement, moreover, is doubly qualified. Far from suggesting that Rumsfeld, Wolfowitz, and other members of the Bush administration were chomping at the bit to attack Iraq, as the PNAC letters reveal, the Commission suggests that the Bush administration would have thought of acting against Saddam only if he "acted against U.S. interests." And far from suggesting that getting control of Iraq's oil would be a central motivation, the Commission suggests that the plans for the attack might only "possibly" include occupying Iraqi oil fields.

From other sources, however, we get a quite different picture. Within months after 9/11, Paul O'Neill reports, the Defense

Intelligence Agency, which works for Rumsfeld, had begun mapping Iraq's oil fields. It also provided a document, entitled "Foreign Suitors for Iraqi Oilfield Contracts," which suggested how Iraq's huge reserves might be divided up.[66] The centrality of oil was also pointed out by Stephen Gowans, who wrote:

> [T]he top item on the Pentagon's agenda, once it gave the order for jackboots to begin marching on Baghdad, was to secure the oil fields in southern Iraq. And when chaos broke out in Baghdad, US forces let gangs of looters and arsonists run riot through "the Ministry of Planning, the Ministry of Education, the Ministry of Irrigation, the Ministry of Trade, the Ministry of Industry, the Ministry of Foreign Affairs, the Ministry of Culture and the Ministry of Information."
> . . . But at the Ministry of Oil, where archives and files related to all the oil wealth Washington has been itching to get its hands on, all was calm, for ringing the Ministry was a phalanx of tanks and armoured personnel carriers.[67]

These accounts reveal the distorted picture provided by 9/11 Commissioners, whose solitary mention of Iraq's oil suggests that US troops, if they attacked Iraq, might or might not occupy the oil fields.

A more realistic account is also given by Chalmers Johnson, who emphasizes that in relation to oil-rich regions, the US interest in oil and its interest in bases go hand in hand.

> [The] renewed interest in Central, South, and Southwest Asia included the opening of military-to-military ties with the independent Central Asian republics of Kyrgyzstan and Uzbekistan and support for a Taliban government in Afghanistan as a way to obtain gas and oil pipeline rights for an American-led consortium. But the jewel in the crown of this grand strategy was a plan to replace the Ba'ath regime in Iraq with a pro-American puppet government and build permanent military bases there.[68]

Johnson's emphasis on the motivation to establish more military bases is supported by PNAC itself, which said in its 2000 document:

> [T]he United States has for decades sought to play a more permanent role in Gulf regional security. While the unresolved conflict with Iraq provides the immediate justification, the need for a substantial American force presence in the Gulf transcends the issue of the regime of Saddam Hussein.[69]

As this statement indicates, the plan was for the American military to remain in Iraq long after Saddam Hussein was deposed—perhaps until the exhaustion of the Iraqi oil reserves.

If we move beyond the 9/11 Commission's simplistic and noncontextual account of the Bush administration's reasons for attacking Iraq, we can see that the stakes were immense, involving not only trillions of dollars but also global geopolitical control. (For example, even if the United States will not need Iraqi oil in the near future, East Asia and Europe will, so that the United States, by controlling their oil supply, will be able to exert strong influence over their political-economic life.) Accordingly, we can see that the desire to attack and occupy Iraq, expressed by the same people who suggested that a "new Pearl Harbor" could be helpful, might have provided a motive for facilitating the attacks of 9/11.

The 9/11 Commission Report, however, omits all the parts of the story that might lead to this thought. We receive no idea that Iraq might have been "the jewel in the crown" of the US master plan. In the world of the Kean–Zelikow Report, in fact, America has no imperialistic master plan. It is simply an altruistic nation struggling to defend itself against enemies who hate its freedoms.

SUMMARY

As I pointed out in the Introduction, *The 9/11 Commission Report* endorses the official conspiracy theory, according to which the attacks of 9/11 were carried out solely by al-Qaeda, under the direction of Osama bin Laden. I am looking at this report from the perspective of the alternative conspiracy theory, according to which officials of the US government were involved. Although the Commission did not mention this alternative hypothesis, it was clearly seeking to undermine its plausibility. One way to do this would be to show that, contrary to those who hold this hypothesis, the Bush administration did not have any interests or plans that could have provided a sufficient motive for arranging or at least allowing such murderous attacks on its own citizens. The Commission did not do this directly, by explicitly addressing the motives alleged by those who endorse the alternative hypothesis. But it did do it indirectly, by portraying the Bush administration, and the US government more generally, as devoid of the motives in question.

The Kean–Zelikow Commission, however, could provide this portrayal only by means of numerous omissions and distortions. Besides omitting the Bush administration's reference to the 9/11 attacks as "opportunities," it omitted any discussion of the US Space Command, with its mission to solidify global dominance, and of the PNAC document, with its suggestion that a new Pearl Harbor would be helpful. It omitted historical facts showing that the Bush administration had plans to attack both Afghanistan and Iraq before 9/11, so that the attacks served as pretext rather than cause. And the Commission distorted US motives in those attacks, portraying US leaders as interested only in self-defense, human rights, and peace, not oil, bases, and geopolitical primacy.

PART TWO

The Commission's Defense of the US Military

CHAPTER ELEVEN

Problems in Earlier Accounts of the Flights

The central charge by critics of the official account is that if standard operating procedures for responding to hijacked airplanes had been followed on 9/11, jet fighters should have intercepted Flights 11, 175, and 77 long before the North Tower, the South Tower, and the Pentagon were struck, and fighters should have intercepted Flight 93 long before it crashed. The standard procedures in question are those of the FAA (the Federal Aviation Administration) and the US military.

The "US military" here means, in particular, the NMCC (National Military Command Center), located in the Pentagon, and NORAD (the North American Aerospace Defense Command), with its headquarters in Colorado Springs. NORAD is divided into various sectors, only one of which was involved on 9/11: the Northeast Air Defense Sector, known as NEADS.

In this chapter, I discuss the standard procedures and their apparent violation on 9/11. In the following chapters, I will examine the 9/11 Commission's attempt to show that the US military did not violate these procedures.

STANDARD PROCEDURES FOR RESPONDING TO HIJACKED AIRPLANES

According to standard operating procedures, the FAA is supposed to contact the NMCC whenever it suspects that an airplane has been hijacked. There are three major signs that a plane may have been hijacked: (1) if it deviates seriously from its flight plan; (2) if radio contact is lost; or (3) if its transponder goes off. (The transponder is an electronic device that identifies the plane on the controller's screen and gives its exact location and altitude. It also can be used to send a four-digit emergency hijack code.) If any of these things happen, the flight controller is to try to contact the pilot to get the problem fixed. If the pilot does not respond appropriately, or if radio contact cannot be quickly restored, the FAA is to contact the NMCC to request assistance.

Note that it is not the FAA's task to determine whether a hijacking has actually occurred. Rather, FAA traffic controllers are given the following instruction: "If . . . you are in doubt that a situation constitutes an emergency or potential emergency, handle it as though it were an emergency."[1] In other words, treat a possible hijacking as an actual hijacking.

Military regulations say: "In the event of a hijacking, the NMCC will be notified by the most expeditious means by the FAA."[2] The NMCC then tells NORAD to have jets sent up—"scrambled"—from the nearest Air Force base with jets on alert. Typically one or two jet fighters will be sent to intercept the suspect airplane. *Boston Globe* writer Glen Johnson, reporting what he was told immediately after 9/11 by Major Mike Snyder—"a spokesman for NORAD headquarters in Colorado Springs"—explained what happens next:

> When planes are intercepted, they typically are handled with graduated response. The approaching fighter may rock its wingtips to attract the pilot's attention, or make a pass in front of the aircraft. Eventually, it can fire tracer rounds in the airplane's path, or, under certain circumstances, down it with a missile.[3]

Shooting down an aircraft would, of course, be a very serious matter, and it can be done only if the pilot has authorization from the Pentagon. But it is necessary to distinguish shooting down from interception, which is carried out, as Major Snyder reported, "routinely."[4] Interceptions evidently occur, in fact, about 100 times a year. The FAA reported, for example, that there were 67 interceptions between September 2000 and June 2001.[5]

Interception also occurs quickly. As General Ralph Eberhart, the head of NORAD, reported in October 2002: From the time the FAA senses that something is wrong, "it takes about one minute" for it to contact NORAD, after which NORAD can scramble fighter jets "within a matter of minutes to anywhere in the United States."[6] Part of the reason they can get anywhere within a matter of minutes is that, according to the US Air Force website, an F-15 routinely "goes from 'scramble order' to 29,000 feet in only 2.5 minutes," after which it can fly 1,850 miles per hour.[7]

For the sake of accuracy, however, I need to point out that Eberhart's statement was preceded by the word "now," so he was saying that it *now* takes the FAA only about a minute to contact NORAD and that *now* NORAD can scramble jets to anywhere in the USA within a matter of minutes. Eberhart was thereby implying that procedures had been speeded up after 9/11. But if this is true, it could be easily supported by comparing NORAD's response times for interceptions prior to 9/11 with those afterward.

I know of no such comparison. *The 9/11 Commission Report* does not mention any comparison and reflects no probing about any such speed-up of procedures. My own assumption is that no such change was made. One piece of support for this belief is a 1998 document warning pilots that any airplanes persisting in unusual behavior "will likely find two [jet fighters] on their tail within 10 or so minutes."[8]

On 9/11, however, this did not happen. The first hijacked airliner, Flight 11, showed clear signs of a possible hijacking at 8:14 that morning, and yet when it crashed into the North Tower of the World Trade Center 32 minutes later, no Air Force jets had even been scrambled. The other three hijacked flights also provided signs of their hijacking in plenty of time to have been intercepted. Standard procedures had clearly been violated. Critics charged that "stand-down orders," suspending standard procedures, must have been issued.

THE MILITARY'S ACCOUNT OF 9/11: VERSIONS 1 AND 2

In the first few days after 9/11, statements by spokesmen for the US military appeared to lend credence to the stand-down charge. On September 13, General Richard Myers, who on 9/11 had been Acting Chairman of the Joint Chiefs of Staff, was asked whether the order to scramble fighter aircraft was given "before or after the Pentagon was struck." He replied: "That order, to the best of my knowledge, was after the Pentagon was struck."[9]

The same message was conveyed by NORAD spokesman Mike Snyder in the interview for the previously mentioned story by *Boston Globe* reporter Glen Johnson. Snyder, wrote Johnson,

> said the fighters were not scrambled for more than an hour after the first hijacking was reported, by which time the three buildings were struck and a fourth hijacked plane was over Pennsylvania on a course towards Washington.[10]

By the time of the interview, CBS News had, on September 14, given a different account, saying that "contrary to early reports, US Air Force jets did get into the air on Tuesday while the attacks were under way." This report said that fighter jets were scrambled to both New York City and Washington, although they arrived too late to prevent the attacks.[11] "But Snyder," wrote Johnson,

> had a different version. He said the command [NORAD] did not immediately scramble any fighters even though it was alerted to a hijacking 10 minutes before the first plane . . . slammed into the first World Trade Center tower. . . . The spokesman said the fighters remained on the ground until after the Pentagon was hit by American Airlines Flight 77. . . . By that time, military authorities realized the scope of the attack, Snyder said, and finally ordered the jets aloft. The delay in scrambling fighters was confirmed by Air Force General Richard B. Myers, a four-star officer who has been nominated to be the next chairman of the Joint Chiefs of Staff.[12]

According to the scenario articulated by Snyder as well as Myers, therefore, fighter jets were sent up only after 9:38, hence at least 52 minutes after the North Tower was struck and at least an hour after NORAD was notified that Flight 11 had been hijacked.

This same scenario was articulated by Matthew Wald in the *New York Times* on September 15, 2001. Wald wrote: "By 9:25 AM the FAA, in consultation with the Pentagon, had taken the radical step of banning all takeoffs around the country, but fighters still had not been dispatched."[13]

This scenario also appears to be supported by an interview contained in one of the staff reports of the 9/11 Commission itself, two months before the Commission's final report appeared. According to this staff report, New York Mayor Rudolph Giuliani said that about a minute before the South Tower began to fall—and hence at about 9:58—he telephoned the White House. Reaching Chris Henick, the president's deputy political director, Giuliani asked about getting fighter cover for his city. According to Giuliani, Henick replied: "The jets were dispatched 12 minutes ago and they should be there very shortly."[14] This would mean that the planes were sent at about 9:46. If Giuliani's report is accurate, Henick's statement would support the story—which evidently everyone was telling the first few days—that no planes were scrambled until after 9:38, when the Pentagon was hit.

Whatever we may think of Giuliani's story, there is good reason to assume the truth of the first account. General Myers, as the acting chairman of the Joint Chiefs of Staff, and Major Mike Snyder, as spokesman for NORAD headquarters in Colorado Springs, should have known what happened on 9/11. And it is hard to suppose that they would have fabricated this account, since it certainly did not make the US military look good. Indeed, had it remained the official story, it is difficult to see how the Bush administration and the Pentagon could have refuted the charge that standard procedures had been suspended on 9/11.

As already indicated, however, a second version of the official account quickly began to appear, being publicly articulated September 14 on the *CBS Evening News*.[15] Glen Johnson reported that Snyder, speaking for NORAD, would not comment on this CBS report. But on September 18, NORAD issued a news release that turned this second version—according to which planes were scrambled although they arrived too late—into the official version of what happened on 9/11. This news release consisted of a timeline providing the times at which NEADS was notified by the FAA and the times at which NEADS then issued scramble orders.[16] The implicit argument of this second version of the official story was that all the fault lay with the FAA, because it had not alerted the military quickly enough.

This second version, however, did little to allay the suspicion by critics that a stand-down order had been given. Assuming the truth of the times provided by NORAD, the FAA clearly seemed to have violated its own procedures more than once. Even with these violations, furthermore, it seemed to critics that the military's fighter jets should have intercepted the four hijacked airliners. NORAD's September 18 timeline, therefore, seemed to make both the FAA and the US military guilty. I will show why this is so with regard to each of the four flights. In these accounts, I emphasize, I am summarizing what was generally believed, prior to the 9/11 Commission's report, on the basis of news stories and NORAD's timeline of September 18, 2001. The point is to show why, on the basis of this information, critics of the official account argued that a stand-down order must have been given. Understanding why NORAD's 2001 timeline left the US military vulnerable to this charge is essential for understanding the new story told in the Kean–Zelikow Report.

VIOLATIONS OF STANDARD PROCEDURES: AA FLIGHT 11

According to NORAD's 2001 timeline and news stories related thereto, here is what happened in relation to AA Flight 11: Between 8:14 and 8:15, Flight 11 failed to respond to an FAA order to climb. It then discontinued radio contact and turned off its transponder.[17] At 8:20, the plane went radically off course. The flight controller concluded that it had probably been hijacked but did not call the military.[18] At 8:21, a flight attendant reported by telephone to American Airlines that the plane had been taken over by hijackers, who had already killed some people.[19] At 8:24, the flight controller heard a hijacker's voice tell the passengers: "We have some planes. Just stay quiet and you will be OK. We are returning to the airport."[20] The controller later reported that he "knew right then that he was working a hijack."[21] At 8:25, Boston controllers notified other FAA flight control centers that Flight 11 has been hijacked.[22] At 8:28, controllers watched the plane make a 100-degree turn south, towards New York.[23]

According to NORAD's September 18 timeline, however, the FAA did not notify NORAD (NEADS) until 8:40.[24] So, rather than notifying the military shortly after 8:14, or at least immediately after 8:20, as standard procedures would dictate, the FAA waited 20 to 24 minutes after signs that Flight 11 had been hijacked. The FAA clearly appeared to have violated standard procedures. *ABC News* said: "There doesn't seem to have been alarm bells going off, traffic controllers getting on with law enforcement or the military. There's a gap there that will have to be investigated."[25]

Another very strange part of NORAD's timeline is its implicit claim that it was not directly notified by American Airlines, although according to newspaper accounts, American Airlines had received word from a flight attendant at 8:21 that hijackers had taken over the plane and killed some people.

In any case, critics suggested that if the times provided by NORAD were correct, the FAA must have issued a stand-down order to its own personnel. The suspicion that either that was done, or that NORAD was lying about the notification time, was increased by the fact that no FAA personnel were fired or even publicly reprimanded.

This new version, furthermore, did not actually get the military off the hook. It seems that when it received word about Flight 11 at 8:40, it should have immediately issued a scramble order to nearby McGuire Air Force Base in New Jersey. Fighter jets could have been airborne by 8:42. Traveling 30 miles per minute, they could have traversed the 70-mile distance to New York City in time to intercept Flight 11 shortly before 8:46, when it crashed into the North Tower. Instead, however, NORAD, according to its own statement, did not issue a scramble order until six minutes later, at 8:46. This order, moreover, was given not to McGuire but to Otis Air Force Base in Cape Cod, Massachusetts, which is over twice as far from New York City. Finally, then, the two F-15s did not take off from Otis for another six minutes, meaning they were not airborne until 8:52—six minutes after the North Tower was hit.[26] All these factors seemed to suggest a stand-down order within the US military, in addition to the stand-down order within the FAA implied by NORAD's timeline.

VIOLATIONS OF STANDARD PROCEDURES: FLIGHT 175
Nevertheless, in spite of all the delays by the FAA, NORAD, and Otis, the F-15s still should have arrived in New York City in time to intercept Flight 175 before it hit the South Tower at 9:03. But this did not happen either. Here was the story as told by NORAD's 2001 timeline and news reports related to it.

Between 8:41 and 8:42, controllers at the Boston Center heard suspicious transmissions from Flight 175, including one saying: "Everyone stay in your seats."[27] Then at 8:42, the plane veered from its scheduled route and its transponder signal was lost.[28] In this case, the FAA contacted the military almost immediately. NORAD reported being notified only one minute later, at 8:43. This notification time was, in fact, reported prior to NORAD's September 18 statement by several news media, with the *Washington Post* reporting it on September 12.[29] This early notification meant that NORAD had a full 20 minutes before 9:03, when the South Tower was hit.

However, the jets assigned to this task were the two F-15s that were scrambled from Otis and, as we already saw, they were not airborne until 8:52. This meant that it took an astounding nine minutes for the scramble order to be given and for the pilots to lift off. NORAD's timeline contained no explanation of this enormous delay, which clearly failed to exemplify the standard protocol.

Even with that unexplained delay, however, the eleven minutes remaining should have been plenty of time for an interception to be made. Also, given the crash of the previously hijacked airliner into the North Tower, we would assume that the military would have given the pilots the authorization to shoot down Flight 175 if it did not obey orders. So, even if it is debatable whether there was time to prevent the strike on the North Tower, it seems clear that the South Tower should not have been struck. NORAD had to explain why, nevertheless, it was.

What we were told was that once the F-15s were airborne at 8:52, they headed for New York City. This report was given both by Lt. Col. Timothy Duffy, who was one of the pilots, and NORAD commander Major General Larry Arnold.[30] The F-15s then reportedly flew as fast as possible, with Duffy saying that they were going "full-blower all the way."[31] Going "full-blower" in an F-15 would mean going over 1,850 mph.[32] Since they were already airborne at 8:52, they should have traversed the distance to Manhattan within six minutes, so they would have arrived by 8:58.[33] But at 9:03 (or 9:02, which NORAD estimated), when the tower was hit, the F-15s were, NORAD said, still 71 miles away.[34] Critics, doing the math, concluded that the jets, rather than going full speed, must have been flying at considerably less than half speed.[35] Someone was clearly not telling the truth.

NORAD's new timeline had not removed the suspicion that the US military failed to intercept Flight 175 only because it did not try. *The 9/11 Commission Report* seeks to overcome the basis for this suspicion by providing a still newer timeline, thereby giving us a third version of the official account of 9/11. Before examining this new timeline, however, we need to review what we had previously been told about Flights 77 and 93.

VIOLATIONS OF STANDARD PROCEDURES: FLIGHT 77

AA Flight 77 left Dulles airport in Washington, DC, at 8:20 AM. At 8:46, it went significantly off course.[36] At 8:50, it got back on course, but then radio contact was lost.[37] A *New York Times* story said that flight controllers learned that Flight 77 had been hijacked at about this time.[38] At 8:56, the plane's transponder went off.[39] Just before that occurred, according to newspaper reports, the plane turned around over northeastern Kentucky and headed back east.[40] "By 8:57 AM," wrote the *New York Times*, "it was evident that Flight 77 was lost."[41]

According to NORAD, however, it was not notified about Flight 77 by the FAA until 9:24, at which time it was reportedly told that the plane "may" have been hijacked and appeared to be heading back towards Washington.[42] This would mean that although the FAA, according to the *New York Times*, knew the plane was hijacked by about 8:50, it waited another 34 minutes before telling the US military. Assuming the truth of the newspaper reports and the NORAD timeline, the FAA's response to Flight 77 violated standard procedures even more flagrantly than had its response to Flight 11.

Even with all this blame loaded onto the FAA, however, NORAD's timeline of September 18, 2001, did not allow it to escape criticism for its response to Flight 77. In this case, however, no criticism could be directed at it for tardiness in issuing a scramble order. NORAD reported that it issued a scramble order for Flight 77 at 9:24, which would mean that it did so within seconds of receiving the notification (a report that should be sobering to those who assume that issuing a scramble order takes several minutes).

A problem did arise, however, with regard to the base to which the scramble order was given. This was Langley Air Force Base in Virginia, which is some 130 miles from Washington. The order should have gone, critics have said, to Andrews Air Force Base in Maryland, which is only 10 miles from Washington and has the assignment to protect the nation's capital.

A second problem was that, although this scramble order was received at 9:24, the Langley F-16s were said not to have been airborne until 9:30. Why would it have taken them a full six minutes simply to take off if, as we saw earlier, a fighter jet routinely "goes from 'scramble order' to 29,000 feet in only 2.5 minutes"?

A third problem was that, even with this delay and the greater distance from Langley, the F-16s should have arrived in plenty of time to prevent the Pentagon from being struck at 9:38, the generally accepted time (or even at 9:37, the time NORAD estimated in its September 18 timeline).[43] F-16s can fly at 1,500 mph (25 miles per minute). At this rate, they could have traversed the 130 miles to Washington in slightly over five minutes, leaving them almost three minutes to intercept and, if necessary, shoot down the hijacked aircraft. But according to NORAD's September 18 timeline, the F-16s, far from getting to Washington at 9:35, were still 105 miles away at 9:38 when the Pentagon was struck.[44]

Critics who did the math could point out that NORAD's account was absurd. It entailed that during their eight-minute flight after they were airborne, the F-16s had traveled only 25 miles, which would mean they had been flying at under 200 miles per hour.[45]

Still another problem was why the Pentagon was not evacuated. Jokingly called "Ground Zero" by its staff, the Pentagon even had a snack bar of that name.[46] Why would its officials, knowing of the attacks on the WTC and knowing that Flight 77 appeared to be heading back towards Washington, not have ordered its immediate evacuation? The official answer was that Defense Secretary Rumsfeld and other Pentagon officials were wholly unaware of any danger, with one Pentagon spokesman saying: "The Pentagon was simply not aware that this aircraft was coming our way."[47] However, given NORAD's report that it had been notified at 9:24 that Flight 77 may have been hijacked and appeared to be heading back to Washington, these denials strained credulity.

As one could readily see, NORAD's September 18 story about Flight 77 needed a radical revision. The US military would use *The 9/11 Commission Report* to publish this radically revised account of its relation to Flight 77. Before looking at this revision, however, we need to review violations of standard procedures in relation to Flight 93, given what we had previously been told about it.

VIOLATIONS OF STANDARD PROCEDURES: UA FLIGHT 93

On the basis of NORAD's 2001 timeline and related stories, the generally accepted story about Flight 93 went like this: The plane left Newark at 8:42. At about 9:27, the hijackers evidently got control of the cockpit and one of them, speaking with an accent, was heard by flight controllers to say that there was a bomb on board.[48] About 9:28, the controllers heard screaming, scuffling, and men referring to "our demands" and using various non-English phrases.[49] It was clear that a hijacking was in process. It became clearer yet at 9:30, when the transponder signal was lost,[50] and still clearer at 9:34, when controllers heard a voice say: "Ladies and gentlemen, here is the captain, please sit down. Keep remaining sitting. We have a bomb aboard."[51]

During all of this, nevertheless, the FAA did not call the US military to ask for assistance, if we can believe NORAD's September 18 timeline.

After "FAA Notification to NEADS," this timeline simply has "N/A" (for Not Applicable).

However, according to a CNN report on September 17, 2001, NORAD said that the FAA had notified it about Flight 93 at 9:16. If that is correct, then the FAA followed its procedures in this case very swiftly, notifying NEADS of the hijacking on the basis of signs that have not become generally known. Of course, given the fact that these early signs have not become known, we could perhaps simply dismiss this report as the mistake of some individual. However, the idea that NORAD was notified about Flight 93 at 9:16 was evidently firmly implanted in NORAD's collective memory. In testimony to the 9/11 Commission on May 23, 2003, NORAD's General Larry Arnold repeated this story, saying that at 9:16, the FAA reported "a possible hijack of United Flight 93."[52] This statement evoked a rebuke in the 9/11 Commission's final report. Pointing out the fact that this statement had been made by "NORAD officials," the Commission proclaimed: "This statement was incorrect. There was no hijack to report at 9:16. United 93 was proceeding normally at that time" (34).

Be that as it may, the timeline provided by NORAD on September 18, 2001, which became the official account, implied that the FAA, far from acting better than it had in relation to the other flights, did even worse. For in spite of a series of signs beginning at 9:27, which provided abundant evidence that Flight 93 had been hijacked, the FAA never did contact the military.

It may seem that NORAD's September 18 timeline, by saying that it was never notified about Flight 93, had removed any possible basis for suspicion that the US military had acted improperly in relation to this flight. That, however, is not true, although the suspicion that arose in this case involved wrongdoing of a different nature. In the other cases, the suspicion is that the US military failed to shoot down airliners that it should have shot down. In this case, the suspicion is that it shot down a flight that should not have been shot down. There are several reasons for this suspicion.

First, although the time of the crash of Flight 93 is disputed, everyone agrees that the crash did not occur before 10:03.[53] Because fighter jets were finally given shoot-down orders by Vice President Cheney shortly after 9:56, according to several mainstream news sources,[54] there was time for these orders to be put into effect for Flight 93.

Second, a military aide shortly thereafter reportedly said to Vice President Cheney: "There is a plane 80 miles out. There is a fighter in the area. Should we engage?", to which Cheney responded "Yes," after which an F-16 went in pursuit of Flight 93. Then, as the fighter got nearer to Flight 93, Cheney was asked two more times to confirm that the fighter should engage, and he did.[55]

Third, CBS television reported, shortly before the crash, that two F-16 fighters were tailing Flight 93. Also a flight controller, ignoring a general order to controllers not to talk to the media, reportedly said that "an F-16 fighter closely pursued Flight 93."[56]

Fourth, Deputy Secretary of Defense Paul Wolfowitz later confirmed these reports, saying that "the Air Force was tracking the hijacked plane that crashed in Pennsylvania . . . and had been in a position to bring it down if necessary."[57]

Fifth, evidence that the plane was "holed" by a missile or two was provided by witnesses on the ground. Several people reported having heard "a loud bang" or "two loud bangs" just before the plane began to drop. The mayor of Shanksville said that he knew two people—one of whom had served in Vietnam—who reported having heard a missile.[58] Other witnesses reported finding debris, including what appeared to be human remains, as far as eight miles from the crash site.[59] Workers at a lake six miles from the site said they saw "a cloud of confetti-like debris descend on the lake and nearby farms minutes after hearing the explosion."[60] Finally, a half-ton piece of one of the engines was reportedly found at what even the FBI acknowledged to be "a considerable distance" from the crash site. One newspaper story called this fact "intriguing" because "the heat-seeking, air-to-air Sidewinder missiles aboard an F-16 would likely target one of the Boeing 757's two large engines."[61]

Sixth, telephone calls from passengers, some of which were being monitored by FBI agents,[62] indicated that some of the male passengers—among whom was a pilot[63]—were wresting control of the plane from the hijackers. Just as success seemed imminent, there were indications that the plane had been holed. For example, one woman, having earlier told her husband that the passengers were trying to break into the cockpit, exclaimed: "They're doing it! They're doing it! They're doing it!" Right after this, her husband heard screaming followed by a "whooshing sound, a sound like wind," then more screaming, after which he lost contact.[64] Another passenger, calling from a restroom, reportedly said that he heard "some sort of explosion" and saw "white smoke coming from the plane."[65]A report in the *Mirror* said: "Sources claim the last thing heard on the cockpit voice recorder is the sound of wind—suggesting the plane had been holed."[66]

Seventh, Major Daniel Nash, one of the two F-15 pilots sent to New York City, later reported that after he returned to base, he was told that a military F-16 had shot down a fourth airliner in Pennsylvania.[67]

This rumor was sufficiently widespread that during General Myers' interview with the Senate Armed Services Committee on September 13, 2001, the chairman of this committee, Senator Carl Levin, said that "there have been statements that the aircraft that crashed in Pennsylvania was shot down," then added: "Those stories continue to exist." Myers declared that "the armed forces did not shoot down any aircraft."[68]

But clearly there was strong evidence that US armed forces had shot down Flight 93 and that they did so just after it appeared that the passengers were about to gain control. To shoot down a civilian airliner in such a situation would clearly be a violation of standard procedures.

To summarize: The evidence available from each of the flights seemed to suggest that standard procedures had been severely violated on 9/11, not only by the FAA but also by the US military. So, whether critics have accepted the first or the second version of the official account, they have had strong grounds for suspecting that standard procedures were suspended on 9/11.

Chapter 1 of *The 9/11 Commission Report* is devoted primarily to an attempt to remove any grounds for this suspicion. How does the report make this attempt? By giving us nothing less than a third version of the official account. The following chapters will examine the Commission's new account of the four flights. To make it a little easier to keep the timelines of three versions of four flights straight, I will here provide an overview of the three versions of the official account of these flights.

VERSION 1 (SEPTEMBER 11–14, 2001)

1. AA Flight 11
7:59 AM Departed Boston
8:46 AM North Tower of WTC struck
No planes scrambled

2. UA Flight 175
8:14 AM Departed Boston
9:03 AM South Tower of WTC struck
No planes scrambled

3. AA Flight 77
8:20 AM Departed Dulles (Washington D.C.)
9:38 AM Pentagon struck
No planes scrambled

4. AA Flight 93
8:42 AM Departed Newark
10:03 or 10:06 AM Crashed in Pennsylvania
Planes scrambled shortly before Flight 93 crashed

VERSION 2 (SEPTEMBER 18, 2001: NORAD)[69]

1. AA Flight 11
8:40 FAA notified NEADS (NORAD)
8:46 Impact: NEADS scramble order to Otis
8:52 Otis F-15s airborne

2. UA Flight 175
8:43 FAA notified NEADS (NORAD)
8:46 NEADS scramble order (same 2 F-15s as Flight 11)
8:52 Otis F-15s airborne
9:02 (est.) Impact: F-15s 71 miles away

3. AA Flight 77
9:24 FAA notified NEADS (NORAD)
9:24 NEADS scramble order to Langley
9:30 Langley F-16s airborne
9:37 (est.) Impact: F-16s 105 miles away

4. UA Flight 93
FAA notification: N/A (Not Applicable)
Scramble order: N/A (Langley F-16s already airborne for AA 77)
10:03 (est.) Crash: F-16s 100 miles away (protecting DC)

VERSION 3 (JULY 2004:THE REPORT [32–33])
1. AA Flight 11
8:25 FAA (Boston Center) aware of hijacking
8:38 FAA (Boston) notifies NEADS (NORAD) of hijacking
8:46 NEADS scramble order to Otis
8:46:40 AA 11 strikes WTC
8:53 Otis F-15s airborne
9:16 American Airlines aware its Flight 11 struck WTC
9:21 Boston FAA (erroneously) tells NEADS: AA 11 headed to DC
9:24 NEADS scrambles Langley F-16s to stop phantom AA 11

2. UA Flight 175
8:42–8:47 Various signs that a hijacking had occurred
8:52 Flight attendant notified United Airlines of hijacking
8:55 FAA (New York Center) suspects hijacking
9:03 UA 175 strikes WTC
9:15 FAA notifies NEADS of strike (12 min. afterwards)

3. AA Flight 77
9:05 American Airlines aware of hijacking
9:24 NEADS scrambles Langley F-16s (but to go after phantom AA 11, not AA 77)
9:34 FAA notifies NEADS that AA 77 is missing (not hijacked)
9:38 AA 77 strikes Pentagon
9:38 F-16s scrambled to stop phantom AA 11 are 150 miles away from DC (had gone wrong direction)

4. UA Flight 93
9:34 FAA headquarters aware of hijacking
10:03 UA 93 crashes
10:07 FAA (Cleveland Ctr.) tells NEADS of hijacking
10:15 FAA (Washington Center) tells NEADS of crash

CHAPTER TWELVE

The Commission on Flight 11

I f we accept the third version of the official account, the 9/11 Commission's attempt to defend the US military from the suspicion that it acted too slowly is largely successful. A few problems remain, but insofar as they are mentioned, they are treated as due to poor communication, confusion, lack of prior experience with this kind of crisis, and the like, not as evidence of deliberate intent to allow the attacks to happen. The question, however, is whether we should accept this new account. I begin my answer to this question by looking at the Commission's account of how the FAA and the military responded to Flight 11.

THE COMMISSION'S PORTRAYAL OF FAA INCOMPETENCE

In its portrayal of the FAA's response to Flight 11, the Commission for the most part simply elaborates on the earlier portrayal in such a way as to intensify the point implicit in NORAD's September 18 timeline— that because FAA personnel violated standard procedures, the US military was not informed about Flight 11 in time to prevent its crash into the North Tower. I will summarize and comment on the Commission's account.

American Airlines Flight 11 took off from Boston at 7:59 AM. At 8:14, the plane failed to follow an order to climb, and radio contact was lost. Then the transponder went off (18).[1] As the 9/11 Commission's report says, "the simultaneous loss of radio and transponder signal would be a rare and alarming occurrence" (16). We are told, however, that neither the FAA controller at the Boston Center nor his supervisor suspected a hijacking (18). So, rather than notify the military, they merely asked American Airlines if it would try to contact its Flight 11. But then the controller "became even more concerned as [Flight 11's] route changed" (19). A route change, as we were told by MSNBC on the day after 9/11, is considered a "real emergency" by flight controllers, leading them to "hit the panic button."[2] But instead of reporting Flight 11 to the military, we are told, the FAA simply "began to move aircraft out of its path" (19).

Finally, at about 8:25, the controller heard two voice transmissions from Flight 11. In the first one, the voice said "we have some planes." But, we are told: "The controller only heard something unintelligible; he did not hear the specific words 'we have some planes'" (19). The idea that this phrase—which provides the title for Chapter 1 of the Commission's report—was unintelligible plays an important role in the Commission's argument, because if the controllers had understood the phrase, they would have realized immediately that more than one airplane had been hijacked. The Commission says, however, that the phrase was not rendered intelligible until another 40 minutes and not generally known throughout the FAA until some time later (19, 23, 25).[3]

In the second voice transmission, in any case, the controller heard someone on Flight 11 say: "Nobody move. . . . If you try to make any moves, you'll endanger yourself and the airplane." It was only at this point, the controller reportedly told the Commission, that he knew that it was a hijacking. (According to earlier news reports, as we saw in Chapter 11, he said that this realization came after hearing the statement "We have some planes.") He then informed his supervisor of this fact, after which: "Between 8:25 and 8:32, in accordance with the FAA protocol, Boston Center managers started notifying their chain of command that American 11 had been hijacked" (19).

One point to notice here is that, according to this account, FAA personnel did not even begin the process of contacting the military until they *knew* it was a hijacking. As we saw in Chapter 11, however, they are not supposed to wait for certainty. Rather, if they are in doubt about some situation, they are told to "handle it as though it were an emergency."

Another point to notice is that the Boston managers did not contact the NMCC or NORAD directly. Rather, they "started notifying their chain of command." The length of the chain of command in both the FAA and NORAD plays an essential role in the narrative provided by the 9/11 Commission. "As they existed on 9/11," its report says, "the protocols for the FAA to obtain military assistance from NORAD required multiple levels of notification and approval at the highest levels of government" (17). The expression "highest levels" is taken to mean the Office of the Secretary of Defense (not necessarily the Office of the President or the Vice President [18]).

Going through these multiple levels was time-consuming. With regard to the FAA, any controllers not at a regional center, such as the Boston Center, needed to call their regional center. (There are 20 regional centers in the USA.) Then this regional center would call the FAA Command Center, which is in Herndon, Virginia. Herndon would then call the hijack coordinator at FAA Headquarters in Washington. Next, this hijack coordinator would call the NMCC (17–18).

The NMCC would then seek approval from the Office of the Secretary of Defense to provide military assistance. If approval was given, the orders would be transmitted down NORAD's chain of command (18).

Given this account, getting a scramble order would take 8 or 9 telephone calls and hence 8 or 9 minutes, even if each call took only a minute. This account is very different from the protocol summarized before, according to which "it takes about one minute" for the FAA to notify NORAD and only "10 or so minutes" for the suspect airplane to be intercepted. This idea—that on 9/11 this very elaborate, time-consuming protocol was in effect—plays an essential role in the Commission's explanation of why the military was blameless on 9/11.

To return to the Commission's narrative about Flight 11: As we saw, the FAA managers at the Boston Center, rather than calling the NMCC or NORAD itself, "started notifying their chain of command." This meant that Boston, at 8:28, called the Herndon Command Center. Then Herndon, four minutes later, called FAA headquarters. Had headquarters called the NMCC at this time, 8:32, there would still have been fourteen minutes before Flight 11 was to strike the North Tower. But even getting the information to FAA headquarters, we are told, did not result in a call to the NMCC. Instead:

> The duty officer replied that security personnel at headquarters had just begun discussing the apparent hijack on a conference call with the New England regional office. FAA headquarters began to follow the hijack protocol but did not contact the NMCC to request a fighter escort. (19)

It is not clear how the Commission can say that headquarters "began to follow the hijack protocol," given the fact that the essential role played by FAA headquarters in this protocol is to contact the NMCC.

In any case, the report then praises the Boston Center for not following protocol: "Boston Center took the initiative, at 8:34, to contact the military," reaching NEADS at 8:38. The Boston Center told NEADS: "We have a hijacked aircraft headed towards New York, and we need . . . someone to scramble some F-16s or something up there" (20). NEADS, it will be recalled, is NORAD's Northeast Air Defense Sector (which is located in Rome, New York).

This part of the story introduces a discordant note in the report's picture, according to which everything must go up and down the chain of command. Here we suddenly see that the regional FAA managers could call the military themselves, without going through FAA headquarters. We also see that they did not need to go through the NMCC in the Pentagon but could call their local NORAD sector—in this case NEADS—directly.

But the report simply ignores this contradiction in favor of emphasizing its main point, namely, that "[t]his was the first notification received by the military—at any level—that American 11 had been hijacked" (20). In saying this, *The 9/11 Commission Report* simply reaffirms the position taken in NORAD's September 18 timeline. Indeed, the Commission is slightly kinder to the FAA, revising the time of notification from 8:40 to 8:38. But the basic point is the same: Very little time—the Commission says nine minutes (21)—remained until Flight 11 would crash into the WTC.

THE COMMISSION'S TREATMENT OF THE
US MILITARY RESPONSE

As we saw in Chapter 11, however, this point by itself does not let the military off the hook, because at 8:38 there was still time for the flight to be intercepted before 8:47, when, according to the Commission the North Tower of the WTC was hit.[4] The Commission realized that it needed to explain why it was not. Let us look at its attempt.

One of the charges by critics, as we saw, was that NEADS should have given the scramble order to a base closer to New York City, such as McGuire Air Force Base. The Commission's account begins by saying: "NEADS ordered to battle stations the two F-15 alert aircraft at Otis Air Force Base in Falmouth, Massachusetts, 153 miles away from New York City" (20). The Commission's implicit answer to the question about McGuire is that NORAD, after the Cold War, "was barely able to retain any alert bases," so that "by 9/11 there were only seven alert sites left in the United States, each with two fighter aircraft on alert" (352, 17). Only two of those bases, Otis in Massachusetts and Langley in Virginia, were in NORAD's Northeast Sector (17), so NEADS had to choose between them and, of these two bases, Otis was closer.

This account of the situation on 9/11 would explain why NEADS did not have jets scrambled from McGuire Air Force Base in New Jersey. It would also explain a related problem that we saw in NORAD's second version, which is why, to protect Washington, NEADS had planes scrambled from Langley, which is 130 miles from Washington, rather than from Andrews Air Force Base, which is only 10 to 12 miles away. However, although this claim would explain these apparent anomalies, we need to ask whether it is believable.

INTERLUDE: HOW MANY BASES HAD FIGHTER JETS ON ALERT?

There are many reasons to doubt the truth of this claim. One of these reasons arises simply from the nature and size of the region for which NEADS is responsible. As shown by a map in *The 9/11 Commission Report* (15), the area assigned to NEADS runs from Maine across to the middle of North Dakota, from Maine down to Virginia, and from Virginia across to western Oklahoma. This area is by far the most populated part of the country, with by far the greatest air traffic. It is also, especially by virtue of containing the nation's capital and its financial center, by far the most sensitive from a security standpoint. Are we really expected to believe that prior to 9/11, only two military bases in this entire region retained fighter jets on alert?

After 9/11, Colonel Robert Marr, the head of NEADS, reportedly said: "I have determined, of course, that with only four aircraft, we cannot defend the whole northeastern United States."[5] It was good that he said "of course," because it certainly would not have taken our military leaders the experience of 9/11 to realize that four fighters could not defend the huge area—"more than half a million square miles of airspace"[6]—assigned to NEADS. Must we not conclude, therefore, that either the claim about only four alert fighters is a lie or else our military leaders deliberately left the northeastern United States woefully unprotected?

The claim made by both the US military and the 9/11 Commission is made even more incredible by the fact that it entails that there were no alert fighters at—in the words of a *Newsday* article—"bases close to two obvious terrorist targets—Washington, DC, and New York City."[7]

Such an astounding claim should at least be supported by extensive documentation. If the remainder of the bases that had previously kept fighters on alert had been ordered to discontinue this practice after the end of the Cold War, abundant documentation to this effect should be available. Dr. Philip Zelikow, as a trained historian, surely knows the importance of providing contemporary documentation of all potentially controversial claims about past events, rather than relying solely on present-day testimony, especially from people who could be suspected of having an ax to grind. And yet the note for this claim cites only a 2004 interview with General Richard Myers (17, 458n99), who as the head of the Pentagon's Joint Chiefs of Staff is one of the main suspects of those who believe that there was a military stand-down order.[8] In any case, he can hardly be considered a disinterested source of information, and yet he is treated as such by the Kean–Zelikow Commission.

The claim that Otis and Langley were the only bases to which NEADS could have given scramble orders is also undermined by the simple fact that to make this claim is to deny that Andrews Air Force Base keeps fighters on alert at all times. This denial is, for one thing, simply implausible in light of the fact that Andrews, being about ten miles from Washington DC, has the primary responsibility to guard the nation's capital. This point was made the day after 9/11 by a story in the *San Diego Union-Tribune*. Citing a National Guard spokesman, this story said: "Air defense around Washington is provided mainly by fighter planes from Andrews Air Force Base in Maryland near the District of Columbia border."[9]

The claim that Andrews would not keep fighters on full-time alert is also rendered implausible by the fact that Andrews is the home of Air Force One. Are we expected to believe that after the Cold War, some penny-pinching president approved a plan entailing that the presidential plane would no longer be protected by alert fighters at Andrews, so that the Secret Service, to protect the president, would need to rely on fighters sent up from Langley?

This implausible claim was, to be sure, explicitly made shortly after 9/11. *USA Today* was told by Pentagon sources, it reported, that Andrews "had no fighters assigned to it."[10] Making only a slightly less implausible claim, Major General Larry Arnold—the commanding general of NORAD's Continental Region—said: "We [didn't] have any aircraft on alert at Andrews."[11]

It may be that one could technically reconcile General Arnold's statement with the realization that Andrews must always have alert fighters, which can be called on by the Secret Service, by suggesting that Arnold meant only that NORAD as such had none of its own fighters on alert at Andrews that morning. That is, all the fighters on alert were under the jurisdiction of other authorities, such as the Secret Service. This technical resolution would, however, do nothing to solve the problem, as long as there were fighters on alert that NORAD could have called on. Surely no one would seek to defend the official account by saying that the Secret Service refused to let its fighters be used by NORAD to defend the Pentagon. The only claim that could explain why fighters were not immediately sent up from Andrews is the more sweeping claim—which *was* made—that there were simply no fighters on alert at that base. And this claim is simply implausible.

My own suspicion about this was given support by a conversation that Kyle Hence, co-founder of 9/11 CitizensWatch, reported having with Donald Arias, the Chief of Public Affairs for NORAD's Continental Region. Hence, who had first met Arias at a hearing of the 9/11 Commission in 2003, called him in January 2004 to ask some questions about NORAD's response on 9/11. "Pretty soon," reports Hence, "I asked him if there were any strip alert planes available. He refused to say and insisted that Andrews was not part of NORAD." Then, Hence says, "When I pressed him on the issue of whether or not there were assets at Andrews that, though not technically part of NORAD, could have been tasked," Arias "hung up on me."[12] If Arias' only alternatives were to lie or to hang up, we should have sympathy for him. But his reaction does provide one more reason to believe that the US military has been lying about the true situation at Andrews.

In any case, besides the fact that the no-planes-on-alert-at-Andrews claim is *a priori* implausible, it is also challenged by several empirical facts. One of these is the fact, which is even mentioned in the Commission's report, that planes were scrambled from Andrews later that morning (44). And they were, as both General Myers and Major Snyder had said in the days right after 9/11, scrambled immediately after the Pentagon was hit.

"Within minutes of the attack," wrote the *Telegraph*, "F-16s from Andrews Air Force Base were in the air over Washington DC." According to a story in the *Denver Post*, "fighter jets scrambled from Andrews Air Force Base and other installations" were flying over Washington a "few moments" after the attacks.[13] A story in *Aviation Week and Space Technology* even says that fighters armed with missiles arrived from Andrews shortly after the attacks.[14]

However, this fact could be deflected by defenders of the official account by pointing out that according to that same story, Secret Service agents had called Andrews at 9:03 to notify it to have F-16s armed and ready to scramble. This story then says that when the Pentagon was hit, the missiles were still being loaded in the F-16s. Then at 9:38, just after the Pentagon was struck, the Secret Service called Andrews back and said: "Get in the air now!" With the loading virtually complete by then, the missile-carrying F-16s were able to get up and over Washington within 10 minutes.[15] This story would, therefore, provide a way to reconcile the claim that Andrews had no fighters on alert with the fact, observed by many, that Andrews was able to send up many fighters within minutes of the attack on the Pentagon.

This solution would, however, face problems. One problem is the fact that immediately after 9/11, a spokesman for the National Guard, in referring to the delay by Andrews in sending up fighters, did not try to explain this delay by appealing to this claim. I refer here to the National Guard spokesman who told the *San Diego Union-Tribune* that Washington's air defense is provided primarily by fighter planes from Andrews. The paper then quoted him as saying: "But the fighters took to the skies over Washington only after the devastating attack on the Pentagon."[16] There is no suggestion that the fighters were scrambled as soon as they could be, after they got loaded with missiles. Such a claim would, in any case, be implausible: Fighters loaded with bullets, but no missiles, could have provided considerable protection. Even fighter jets completely unloaded would be better than no fighters at all, given their ability to deter and, if all else failed, ram an airliner headed towards the Pentagon, the White House, or the Capitol.[17] In any case, the account by this spokesman for the National Guard, given on September 11 or 12, fits with the story told in those early days by General Myers and NORAD spokesman Mike Snyder—that no planes were scrambled until after the Pentagon strike.

The most important factual challenge to the claim that Andrews had no fighters on alert is the simple fact that the US military's own website at the time said otherwise. According to this website, Andrews Air Force Base was the home of the 121st Fighter Squadron of the 113th Fighter Wing. This squadron, equipped with F-16s, was said to provide "capable and ready response forces for the District of Columbia in the event of natural disaster or civil emergency." One could learn from this website that Andrews also housed the Marine Fighter Attack Squadron 321. Besides flying "the sophisticated F/A-18 Hornet," this attack squadron was supported by a reserve squadron providing "maintenance and supply functions necessary to maintain a force in readiness."[18] One could find, moreover, that Andrews also housed DCANG (the District of Columbia Air National Guard). DCANG's statement on the website said that its "mission" was "to provide combat units in the highest possible state of readiness."[19]

It would be hard to read these statements, especially DCANG's statement about combat forces in the "highest possible state of readiness," as referring to anything other than fighter jets on alert around the clock. We have reason to believe, in fact, that after 9/11 the US military realized this and found the statement embarrassing. Shortly after 9/11, researchers reported, the DCANG website was changed to say merely that it had a "vision" (rather than a "mission"). And that this vision was merely to "provide peacetime command and control and administrative mission oversight to support customers, DCANG units, and NGB in achieving the highest state of readiness." So DCANG no longer advertised that it maintained forces of its own in the "highest possible state of readiness." It merely hoped to help various groups—including DCANG units, to be sure, but also customers—in "achieving the highest state of readiness." With DCANG units put on the same level as "customers," the phrase "highest state of readiness" no longer implied being on constant alert for scramble orders.[20] Is it possible to understand this alteration as anything other than an attempted cover-up on the part of the US military?

That the Pentagon attempted after 9/11 to obfuscate the pre-9/11 situation at Andrews is also suggested by a change reported by Illarion Bykov and Jared Israel. Having found the DC Military website with the above-cited information about Andrews on September 24, 2001, they discovered a month later that the address had been changed, that the information about Andrews had been put in the smallest possible type, and that the official Andrews AFB website was "down."[21] Can we believe that the timing of these changes, especially when combined with the altered wording of the DCANG statement, was purely coincidental?

The presumption that there were DCANG fighters on alert the morning of 9/11 is also supported by a statement attributed to General Myers in an account of that morning provided by Richard Clarke, who, as we saw in Chapter 4, was the National Coordinator for Security and Counterterrorism. Clarke reports that during a teleconference he was running, General Myers reported, just after the strike on the Pentagon, that "Andrews is launching fighters from the D.C. Air National Guard."[22]

There are several points to be drawn from this discussion. One point is that, at the very least, the question of how many bases had fighter jets on alert prior to 9/11 is far more complex than one would know from merely reading the 9/11 Commission's report. A second point is that if the Commission had taken its mandate seriously, treating the crimes of 9/11 with as much seriousness as an ordinary murder is usually treated, the principals involved, such as General Myers and General Larry Arnold, would have been subjected to much more rigorous interrogation. Their testimony, moreover, would have been compared with testimony from dozens of other people—all under oath and with lie detectors—along with facts available in written documents. A third point is that there are several reasons, as we have seen, to consider untrue the claim that Andrews Air Force Base had no fighters on alert.

This third point brings us, finally, to the relevance of this excursion for the official story about Flight 11. If the claim about Andrews is a lie, what reason do we have to believe the claim about McGuire? And if McGuire did indeed have fighters on alert, the fact that the scramble order went to Otis instead provides strong evidence for the claim that officials in the US military were actively working to facilitate the success of the attacks. This evidence is even stronger if the military tried to cover up this fact by falsely claiming that McGuire had no fighters on alert. Perhaps that claim happens to be true. But given the failure of the Kean–Zelikow Commission to deal with any of the issues raised above, the mere fact that it accepts the claim gives us no basis for confidence that it is true.

THE EIGHT-MINUTE PHONE CALL TO FLORIDA

To return to our narrative about Flight 11: We would perhaps assume that, once NEADS learned at 8:38 that an apparently hijacked airliner was racing towards New York City, it would have immediately had jets scrambled to intercept it. But the Battle Commander at NEADS, Colonel Robert Marr, merely ordered fighter pilots at Otis to "battle stations." He then called the commanding general of NORAD's US Continental Region, Major General Larry Arnold, down in Florida, to seek authorization. Not one to waste time, General Arnold said (he later recalled), "go ahead and scramble them, and we'll get authorities [sic] later" (20). And so the scramble order was finally given at 8:46—just 40 seconds before Flight 11 would crash into the North Tower. Calling Florida had eaten up eight more precious minutes, during which those super-fast F-15s might have saved the North Tower.

INTERLUDE: DID INTERCEPTIONS REQUIRE HIGHEST-LEVEL AUTHORIZATION?

Here, it should be noted, there is another exception to the Commission's account of the need to go up and down the chain of command. General Arnold, according to the Commission's own account, did not believe it necessary to get authorization from the Office of the Secretary of Defense before taking action. Was such authorization really necessary for an interception?

The 9/11 Commission, in support of the claim that it was, cites a memo issued by the Chairman of the Joint Chiefs of Staff, titled "Aircraft Piracy (Hijacking) and Destruction of Derelict Airborne Objects," which was issued June 1, 2001, about 3 months before 9/11.[23] The crucial statement in this document says:

> [T]he NMCC is the focal point within Department of Defense for providing assistance. In the event of a hijacking, the NMCC will be notified by the most expeditious means by the FAA. The NMCC will, *with the exception of immediate responses as authorized by reference d,* forward requests for DOD assistance to the Secretary of Defense for approval. (Emphasis added.)

Some observers have read this statement as saying that all requests for military assistance must get approval from the Office of the Secretary of Defense. But this statement clearly indicates that when a situation requires an immediate response, the secretary of defense need not be consulted in advance. This conclusion is further supported by an examination of "reference d," which points back to a 1997 document, Directive 3025.15, which says: "The DoD Components that receive verbal requests from civil authorities for support in an exigent emergency may initiate informal planning and, if required, immediately respond."[24] This proviso implies that NEADS could have authorized the interceptions on its own.

NEADS NEEDS BETTER RADAR?

It surely was not necessary, therefore, for the "DoD Component" Colonel Marr to waste eight minutes calling Florida. If he in fact did so, he would seem to share the blame with the FAA for the failure to prevent the attack on the North Tower.

The seriousness of the eight-minute phone delay can be seen by looking at the 9/11 Commission's new timeline. It says that NEADS was notified at 8:38 (rather than 8:40, as stated in NORAD's September 18 timeline). And it also places the time of the strike on the North Tower at precisely 8:46:40 (rather than simply 8:46), hence at essentially 8:47. This means that, as the Commission itself says, NEADS was given "nine minutes notice" (21). Allowing a half-minute for the call from NEADS to Otis and then 2.5 minutes for the F-15s to go from scramble order to 29,000 feet, the fighters could have been flying full speed towards New York City by 8:41. At 1,850 miles per hour, they could have traversed the 153 miles from Otis to NYC—the distance given by the Commission (20)—in five minutes. During this period, shoot-down authorization could have been obtained from the Pentagon. Then, arriving at 8:46, the fighter jets would have had 40 seconds to spot and bring down the errant airliner. (Bringing down a hijacked passenger jet over any part of New York City would likely, of course, result in considerable death and destruction. But can anyone say that taking that risk would have been worse than letting hijackers strike their intended target?)

It would seem, then, that this incident alone shows that the 9/11 Commission has failed in its attempt to absolve the military of all blame. The Commission, however, has implicitly supplied a response to any such use of its timeline. This implicit response says, in effect, that even if those eight minutes had not been wasted with the telephone call to Florida, the fighters still would not have been able to intercept Flight 11.

NEADS would not have been able to tell the F-15 pilots where to find this errant airliner, the Commission explains, because the radar system being used by NEADS was too poor. In the Commission's words:

> Because the hijackers had turned off the plane's transponder, NEADS personnel spent the next minutes searching their radar scopes for the primary radar return. American 11 struck the North Tower at 8:46. Shortly after 8:50, while NEADS personnel were still trying to locate the flight, word reached them that a plane had hit the World Trade Center. (20)[25]

This account suggests that the loss of the transponder signal makes it virtually impossible for the US military to track airplanes.

But if that were true, incoming Soviet airplanes during the Cold War could have avoided detection simply by turning off their transponders. Was the US military's defense of the homeland based on the assumption that Soviet pilots would have the courtesy to leave their transponders on? I found no sign in *The 9/11 Commission Report* that this obvious objection was raised. Instead, the Commission apparently accepted, and wrote down with a straight face, the assertion that NEADS personnel spent several minutes trying to find Flight 11 on their radar screens.

But this statement grossly misrepresents the capabilities of the US military's radar systems. For one thing, the military radar system, unlike civilian radar, does not need the transponder to tell the plane's altitude. Also, as Thierry Meyssan has pointed out, the Pentagon's own websites imply that it possesses (in Meyssan's words) "several very sophisticated radar monitoring systems, incomparable with the civilian systems." The website for one of these systems, called PAVE PAWS, says that it is "capable of detecting and monitoring a great number of targets that would be consistent with a massive SLBM [Submarine Launched Ballistic Missile] attack."[26] The PAVE PAWS system is surely not premised on the assumption that those SLBMs would have transponders. Are we to believe that our military's radar systems, which could simultaneously track dozens of missiles in a "massive SLBM attack," could not track a single airliner headed for New York City? The Kean-Zelizow Commission is hence guilty of another major distortion.

THE PAYNE STEWART INCIDENT

Some critics of the response times by the FAA and the US military on

9/11 have pointed to the interception of the private airplane of well-known golfer Payne Stewart as evidence that Flight 11 (as well as the other flights on 9/11) should have been intercepted. Stewart and four passengers, flying a Learjet, left Orlando on October 25, 1999, at 9:20 AM. According to the report from the NTSB (National Transportation Safety Board), there was a regular radio transmission at 9:27. But then when Stewart's plane was given an instruction at 9:34, it failed to respond. (Stewart and his passengers had evidently lost consciousness because of insufficient oxygen in the cabin.) The air traffic controller tried to reestablish contact for 4.5 minutes, then called the military at 9:38.[27] A story in the *Dallas Morning News* reported that,

> according to an Air Force timeline, a series of military planes provided an emergency escort to the stricken Lear, beginning with a pair of F-16 Falcons from the Air National Guard at Tyndall Air Force Base, Florida, about 20 minutes after ground controllers lost contact.[28]

If these reports are accurate, the FAA called the military within 5 minutes of realizing that radio contact had been lost. Then the F-16s arrived about 14 minutes later, at about 9:52.

The official story about Flight 11 makes the response of both the FAA and the military look poor by comparison. Although radio contact was lost at 8:14, the FAA did not contact NEADS until 24 minutes later, at 8:38. And then 9 minutes later, when Flight 11 was crashing into the WTC, NEADS had not even gotten any fighters airborne.

The 9/11 Commission, aware that the Payne Stewart incident has been used for an unfavorable comparison, attempts to undermine this use. Here is that attempt:

> In response to allegations that NORAD responded more quickly to the October 25, 1999, plane crash that killed Payne Stewart than it did to the hijacking of American 11, we compared NORAD's response time for each incident. The last normal transmission from the Stewart flight was at 9:27:10 AM Eastern Daylight Time. The Southeast Air Defense Sector was notified of the event at 9:55, 28 minutes later. In the case of American 11, the last normal communication from the plane was at 8:13 AM EDT. NEADS was notified at 8:38, 25 minutes later. We have concluded there is no significant difference in NORAD's reaction to the two incidents. (459n121)[29]

There are several problems with this statement. First, it implies that radio contact with Stewart's plane was lost at 9:27, whereas that was simply the time of the last normal transmission. It was not until 9:34 that the traffic controller noticed something wrong—as is made clear in the NTSB memo that the Commission cites.[30] Second, it is unclear why the Commission claims that SEADS was not notified until 9:55; that time is not mentioned in the NTSB memo. According to the story in the *Dallas Morning News*, in any case, the F-16s had already arrived by 9:54.

But although there is some confusion about the actual time the first fighter jets arrived in the Payne Stewart incident,[31] the main problem in the Commission's statement is that although it pretends to address the main question—the response time of NORAD on 9/11—it fails to do so. The statement begins by saying that the Commissioners "compared NORAD's response time for each incident." And at the end we read: "We have concluded there is no significant difference in NORAD's reaction to the two incidents." But in between those two statements, as readers can see, there is absolutely nothing about NORAD's reaction time. The only comparison is between the FAA's reaction time—how long it took the FAA to notify SEADS and how long to notify NEADS.

It is difficult to tell here whether the Commission was deliberately attempting to obfuscate the issue, or whether those who wrote and approved this note were simply confused themselves. In any case, the treatment of this issue by the Kean–Zelikow Report simply provides one more reason why readers should approach this supposedly authoritative work with considerable skepticism.

CONCLUSION

The 9/11 Commission clearly meant to defend the US military's claim that it was blameless for the fact that its fighters failed to prevent Flight 11 from striking the North Tower. But this defense is problematic in every respect.

The Commission portrays the FAA as staffed at both the local and the national levels with incompetent people: flight controllers in Boston who could not infer that Flight 11 had been hijacked, although it had confronted them with all the traditional signs, and people at headquarters who, when they were finally notified of the hijacking, would not pick up the phone to alert the US military. The Commission fails, furthermore, to raise the question of why, if FAA personnel had responded so incompetently, no one was fired or even publicly reprimanded. The Commission also provides a self-contradictory treatment of the chain-of-command issue. On the one hand, it accepts the claim that this time-consuming protocol, according to which all requests had to go through every step in the chain of command, was in effect. On the other hand, it praises FAA personnel in Boston for their "initiative" in contacting NEADS directly. The Commission evidently failed to realize that it had thereby thrown into question a central part of its own defense of the official story.

The Commission's treatment of the response by the US military is equally problematic. It fails to inquire into the truth of the claim that McGuire Air Force Base had no fighters on alert. It fails to challenge the claim that NEADS had to call General Arnold in Florida simply to get permission to have fighters scrambled—a claim that is especially problematic in light of Arnold's statement that he himself did not need to call NORAD headquarters. The Commission then fails to explore the question why, even if this call to Florida was deemed necessary, it took eight minutes—a length of time that seems especially strange in light of Arnold's later indication that he was anxious to expedite matters. The Commission likewise fails to point out that, without the waste of these eight minutes, F-15s coming even from Otis would have at least had a chance to prevent the attack on the North Tower (although the Commission, with its treatment of the Payne Stewart incident, seems to be implying that that would not have been enough time). The Commission, finally, fails to confront the absurdity of the claim that NEADS officials lost track of Flight 11 because its transponder was not on.

It seems evident, thus far in any case, that the Commission has not succeeded in removing the grounds for suspicion that the US military had issued stand-down orders for 9/11.

CHAPTER THIRTEEN

The Commission on Flight 175

The problems in the 9/11 Commission's attempt to defend the US military's behavior on 9/11 do not end with its treatment of Flight 11. Indeed, they become, if anything, more severe in relation to the other three flights, partly because in these three cases the Commission revises the previous story quite radically. The present chapter focuses on the Commission's revisions about Flight 175.

Back on September 18, 2001, NORAD told us that the FAA notified NEADS of the possible hijacking of Flight 175 at 8:43. It also told us that the F-15s tried to get to Manhattan in time to intercept Flight 175 but were still 71 miles away when that airliner hit the South Tower.[1] As we saw in Chapter 11, however, that account created problems, because the times did not compute. F-15s going full speed would have arrived in Manhattan well before 9:03.

The 9/11 Commission's solution is to give us a revisionist account, one that implies that NORAD's September 18 timeline was simply wrong. Before looking at this account, I will discuss the nature of revisionist hypotheses—in general and about 9/11 in particular—and criteria for evaluating them.

REVISIONISM AND 9/11

A revisionist account is simply an account that suggests one or more major revisions in what had hitherto been accepted as the true account of some event. Some historians seem to use "revisionism" as a dirty word, so that to describe an account as "revisionist" is ipso facto to reject it. There is, however, nothing wrong with revisionism as such. The received accounts of many historical events have been faulty, so that it has often been only through revisionist accounts that we have come closer to the truth about what really happened.

There is, of course, a kind of revisionism that deservedly has a bad reputation. Some revisionist accounts are not seeking to give a more accurate account of what really happened but instead trying to redescribe historical reality in line with what they want people to believe about it for some ulterior purpose. In revisionist writing of this type, the reconstruction of the facts is driven not by the desire to be more adequate to the factual evidence but by the desire to facilitate the aims of those for whom the reconstruction is being carried out.

Whenever we are reading a revisionist account, we need to be alert to signs of which type it is.

One sign that a revisionist account is of the reputable sort, driven by the desire to give a fuller account of the truth, is that it takes account of all the relevant evidence that is available. It does not simply cite evidence that can be used to bolster its own account while ignoring the rest (a practice often called "cherry picking"). Another sign that a revisionist account is of the truth-seeking sort is that it explains how the previous account, which it seeks to replace, was faulty. It does not merely declare this previous account faulty. It provides evidence to show that it is faulty. And it shows how this evidence against the received account, perhaps along with additional evidence, supports the revisionist account being proffered.

Part and parcel of this task is, of course, to show that the purported evidence is credible. For example, according to the received understanding of the laws of the United States, no person may be elected president more than twice. If President Clinton, after serving his two terms, had told us that he could run for a third term, few of us would have accepted this revisionist understanding simply on the basis of his word. If he produced documents that supported his view, we would have demanded that the most rigorous procedures be employed to authenticate those documents—to show, for example, that they had not been doctored, or had not been produced only after he had decided that he wanted to run for another term.

We should not be any less demanding with the revisionist history of 9/11 that has been presented by the 9/11 Commission. We should accept it only if we conclude that, in light of all the relevant evidence, it is more plausible than the received account. But even that would not be sufficient, because the received account, which was based on the timeline provided by NORAD on September 18, 2001, was itself a revisionist account, compared with the account provided by the military immediately after 9/11. We should accept the 9/11 Commission's revisionist account, therefore, only if it is also more plausible than that first account, according to which no fighter jets were scrambled until after the Pentagon was hit.

There is yet one more condition. We should also demand that the 9/11 Commission's account be more plausible, in light of all the relevant evidence, than competing revisionist accounts, such as those suggesting that the attacks were permitted and perhaps even arranged by elements within the US government. It is, of course, precisely the question of this last comparison that motivated the present book, which asks whether the Commission has provided a superior way to deal with the kinds of evidence on which accounts alleging official complicity are based. In Part I of this study, we saw—or at least I argued—that the Commission had not shown that it could handle a wide variety of evidence of this type in a more plausible way. Indeed, it for the most part simply ignored this evidence.

Here in Part II, the general question being treated is still the same: Has the Commission rendered superfluous all accounts alleging government complicity by providing a narrative that, in portraying the Bush administration and the US military as blameless, takes account of all the relevant facts in a plausible way? But whereas this general question remains the same, it takes a different form. It asks whether the Commission's new timeline, with its description of the behavior of the FAA and the US military, is plausible.

This question arises because, as pointed out earlier, the first version of the official account, according to which no fighters were scrambled until after the Pentagon was hit, implied that the military had failed to follow its own standard operating procedures. That version seemed to imply, in fact, that a stand-down order had been issued. The second version, issued by NORAD on September 18, could be read as intended to avoid this problem by saying that although the military did order planes to be scrambled, they were too late because the FAA had not notified the military in time. As we saw, however, this account still failed to get the military (and by implication the Bush administration) off the hook, simply because this account was not plausible. Given NORAD's own statement of the times that it was notified, its fighters should have been able to prevent the strikes on the World Trade Center and the Pentagon.

The 9/11 Commission's new timeline—which seems to be based almost entirely on recent interviews with, and documents provided by, military leaders—can be read as the military's third attempt to provide an account that shows it to be blameless. Although it succeeds to some extent, we still have the question of whether this revisionist account is plausible. I turn now to the Commission's revisionist account of Flight 175 in particular.

THE F-15S LACK A DIRECTION?

The Commission says that although "F-15 fighters were scrambled at 8:46 from Otis Air Force Base. . . [r]adar data show the Otis fighters were airborne at 8:53" (20). Why did it take the pilots seven minutes simply to get airborne (when, as we saw earlier, they routinely go from scramble order to 29,000 feet in 2.5 minutes)? The Commission's answer is that the pilots had not been told where to go.

> NEADS did not know where to send the alert fighter aircraft, and the officer directing the fighters pressed for more information: "I don't know where I'm scrambling these guys to. I need a direction, a destination." (20)

Evidently, therefore, the F-15s simply sat on the ground waiting to be told which direction to go.

This explanation is very vague. The Commission does clearly say that the Otis officer did not know where to send the fighters. But it does not tell us why. It says only that "NEADS did not know." Does this mean that Colonel Robert Marr, the NEADS commander who had spent eight minutes calling Florida, did not know what direction the pilots should head? How could that be? The Boston Center had told NEADS, "We have a hijacked aircraft headed towards New York" (20). That should have been enough information to get the F-15s up and off in the right direction.

That message, to be sure, had been about Flight 11, not Flight 175. But at the time the scramble order was given to Otis, Flight 11 had not yet struck the WTC, so the F-15s should have been sent after it. Once these F-15s were headed to New York, they could have been given further information about the exact destination. As things developed, this further information would have been to change their target from Flight 11 to Flight 175. Then, by virtue of having departed shortly after 8:46, they would have arrived in plenty of time to locate, intercept, and, if necessary, shoot down Flight 175.

We need not rely, moreover, only on common sense reasoning about what should have happened. We have reports from the time indicating that the F-15s did take off at 8:46 even though they did not know exactly where they were to go. In a story published by Newhouse News Service in January 2002, Hart Seely wrote: "As the first plane hit the World Trade Center, the F-15s were rumbling off the runways at Otis." Seely then quoted Major James Fox—the officer at Otis who reportedly gave the scramble order—as saying: "We had no idea where the aircraft was. We just knew it was over land, so we scrambled them towards land."[2]

James Bamford then adds more detail. He says that once the pilots, Nash and Duffy, were headed towards New York, Duffy called to ask for the location of the target, to which the response was: "Your contact's over Kennedy."[3]

The 9/11 Commission's new timeline, however, implies that these stories are all false, but it provides no explanation as to how these stories arose if they are not true.

The Kean–Zelikow Report's claim here—that the pilots could not take off shortly after 8:46 because they did not know where to go—is clearly important to its defense of the military's failure to intercept Flight 175. Equally clearly, however, this claim makes no sense, besides conflicting with what NORAD officials and news reports had said at the time.

THE F-15S LACK A TARGET?

In any case, even if the F-15s did not become airborne until 8:53, they should still have been able to get to Manhattan in time to prevent the South Tower from being hit at 9:03. The Commission's report, however, says: "Lacking a target, [the F-15s] were vectored towards military-controlled airspace off the Long Island coast," where they remained until 10 minutes after the South Tower was hit (20). Lacking a target?

In the third version of the official account, now told by the 9/11 Commission, the military did not learn that Flight 175 had been hijacked until after this airplane hit the South Tower. The F-15s lacked a target at 8:53, according to the Commission, because Flight 11 had already hit the North Tower and the military had been left in the dark about the hijacking of Flight 175.

This account requires considerable revisionism. I have just mentioned Bamford's story stating that the F-15s were to head to JFK Airport. In Chapter 11, we saw statements by both Duffy and General Larry Arnold, which had been cited by ABC News, MSNBC, and *Slate*, that the F-15s were headed towards New York.[4] I also quoted Duffy's colorful remark that they were going "full-blower all the way."[5]

The 9/11 Commission, however, has simply treated those statements as if they had never been made. Duffy's name is mentioned only three times, and these are simply citations in notes to an interview in January 2004, with no indication of the content of what he said. One of those references occurs in a note to the paragraph claiming that the F-15s did not take off because they had no target. This note contains no indication that Duffy was asked about his earlier testimony, according to which he and Nash knew full well where they were headed—to New York City— or about his widely quoted remark about going "full-blower."

The Commission's new claim about notification, according to which NORAD never received notification about Flight 175 until after it hit the South Tower, is contradicted by earlier claims from NORAD itself. It contradicts NORAD's timeline of September 18, 2001, which said that FAA notified it of Flight 175's hijacking at 8:43. It also contradicts a *Toronto Star* report about a conversation involving Captain Michael Jellinek, a Canadian who on 9/11 was overseeing NORAD's headquarters in Colorado. While on the telephone with NEADS, he reportedly asked, after seeing the crash into the South Tower: "Was that the hijacked aircraft you were dealing with?" The person at NEADS said it was.[6] Like the statements attributed to Duffy and Arnold, it does not fit the new official account, so it is simply excised from history.

Of course, if, as many critics of the official account believe, even those previous statements were untrue—because no fighters whatsoever were scrambled until after the Pentagon was hit—then even if the Commission's new account is untrue, no great crime against historical truth has been committed. Replacing one lie with another is a relatively trivial sin. But this, of course, could not be the Commission's defense. Even if the Commission knew that the earlier statements by Duffy and Arnold were both intentional falsehoods, it could not come right out and say this, or it would have undermined any possible basis for accepting the US military's third version of what really happened on 9/11.

But the Commission also could not implicitly treat those statements as falsehoods by simply acting as if they had not been made. And yet this is what it has done. It has given us a new account with no explanation as to how the old account, now said to be false, had arisen. Were the officials who wrote NORAD's September 18 timeline lying? Were they simply confused? We are not told. We are also not told why that previous account—which we had been asked to take on faith for almost three years—was false. We are now simply asked to take the new version on faith.

THE COMMISSION'S APPEAL TO FAITH

In this particular example, furthermore, the faith is supposed to fill in some pretty big holes in the story. We are told, for one thing, that after the F-15s took off at 8:53, they at some point "were vectored towards military-controlled airspace off the Long Island coast," that they were then "brought down to military airspace to 'hold as needed,'" and that "[f]rom 9:09 to 9:13 the Otis fighters stayed in this holding pattern" (20). But what happened in the sixteen minutes between 8:53 and 9:09? Let us assume that, becoming airborne at 8:53, it took the fighters four minutes to get from Otis to the "controlled airspace" off Long Island. That would still leave twelve minutes completely unaccounted for. Although the Commission's portrayal of what happened that day is sometimes precise about times down to the second, its portrayal of this period is drawn in extremely broad strokes.

There is another hole at the other end of this story. At 9:13, the F-15s, being "about 115 miles away from the city," we are told, "exited their holding pattern and set a course direct for Manhattan. They arrived at 9:25 and established a combat air patrol (CAP) over the city" (24). Although F-15s can cover 360 miles in twelve minutes, the F-15s in the Commission's narrative took twelve minutes to travel merely 115 miles. The Commission has not, therefore, avoided the kinds of problems that were contained in NORAD's 2001 timeline.

Still another problem with the Commission's account of the Otis fighters is that it is in contradiction with the report, mentioned in Chapter 11, that was issued by the staff of the 9/11 Commission two months before the appearance of its final report. According to this report, as we saw, New York Mayor Rudolph Giuliani said that President Bush's deputy political director, Chris Henick, told him that fighter jets had been sent to New York City at about 9:46.[7] My assumption is that Henick's statement would have referred to the time when fighters were scrambled from Otis. If so, it would contradict the Commission's claim that they had been scrambled almost an hour earlier, at 8:53. But one might assume Henick's statement to refer not to the original scramble order but to the decision to move the F-15s out of their holding pattern off Long Island. With this interpretation, however, his statement would contradict the Commission's claim that this happened at 9:13.

It is perhaps not surprising, accordingly, that the Giuliani–Henick conversation did not make its way into the Kean–Zelikow Report.

WHY WERE THE F-15S AIRBORNE AT 8:53?

Even if we ignore the question of whether the entire account provided by NORAD in 2001 and then revised by the Commission is a fictional creation, the strange gaps in the Commission's narrative about the trip from Otis to New York City point to a fundamental problem introduced by the Commission's attempt to revise NORAD's 2001 account. The Commission retains NORAD's assertion that the F-15s were airborne at 8:53. But why were the F-15s airborne at 8:53 if they had no target and were not even assigned to do CAP? NORAD previously had an answer: They were going after Flight 175 but got there a little too late. Now, however, the Commission denies that NORAD knew that Flight 175 had been hijacked. To provide a coherent narrative to support this denial, the Commission should give us a plausible explanation as to why the F-15s took off at 8:53. But the Commission merely glosses over this problem by saying: "Lacking a target, [the F-15s] were vectored towards military-controlled airspace off the coast" (20). That statement, however, merely tells us why the planes did not go on into New York City at that time. It provides no answer whatsoever to the question of why the F-15s were scrambled in the first place.

THE COMMISSION'S FAILURE THUS FAR

The Commission has provided this new but very incomplete account, of course, in support of its new claim—that the US military was not informed by the FAA about the hijacking of Flight 175 at 8:43 and therefore did not send the two F-15s from Otis after it. To make this new account believable, the Commission would need to explain why NORAD had earlier said that it had been notified about Flight 175 at 8:43 and that the F-15s were sent after it. The Commission would also need to explain the origin of all the statements, such as those by Duffy and Arnold, which were part of that account but are now implicitly treated as false. The Commission would also need to present an inherently plausible account of what the F-15s were doing if they were not going after Flight 175. We have seen, however, that the Commission has not done any of those things.

Let us now turn to one more element that would be a necessary ingredient if the Commission were to make its revisionist account of the response to Flight 175 plausible—an explanation of why the FAA did not notify the military about Flight 175.

THE FAA'S DELAYED RECOGNITION

Flight 175, we recall, left Boston at 8:14. Then, according to the sources cited in Chapter 11, the plane went off course and its transponder signal was lost at 8:42, after which, at 8:43, the FAA notified NEADS.

In the 9/11 Commission's account, however, things developed quite differently. The plane did not veer off course until "[m]inutes later" than 8:42, and it was not until 8:47 that anything happened to the transponder (21). (In the Commission's account, furthermore, the transponder signal was not lost, but the "transponder code changed, and then changed again.") Given this account, there was no reason for the FAA to have notified NEADS at 8:43, because the flight had at that time given out no signs suggestive of a hijacking.

Furthermore, we are told, when the flight finally did give out such signs, no FAA personnel noticed them until later yet. The FAA controller assigned to Flight 175 at the Boston Center did not notice the change of course and the transponder problem, we are told, because he, coincidentally, was also the controller for Flight 11, and he was still searching for it—not realizing that it had hit the World Trade Center a minute earlier (21).

This excuse seems strange, given the fact that the Commission had said earlier that this controller's supervisor, after learning that he needed to deal with Flight 11, had "assigned another controller to assist him" (19). Why did not this second controller notice the change of course and the transponder code change? The 9/11 Commission offers no explanation. The reader is perhaps supposed to understand that most of the people working for the FAA are simply incompetent.

COMPARING REVISIONISM WITH THE HISTORICAL RECORD

Skepticism about this account need not, furthermore, be based purely on such *a priori* considerations. There are also news reports, such as a *New York Times* story, published five weeks after 9/11, that contradict the Commission's version of what happened. According to the *Times* story, a flight controller, speaking about Flight 175 at 8:42, said that it "looks like he's heading southbound but there's no transponder no nothing and no one's talking to him."[8] This report indicates that the controller noticed the course change and the transponder problem immediately, because, as a story in *Newsday* indicated, the transponder was turned off for only about 30 seconds, after which the signal returned but with a different code.[9]

If these *Newsday* and *New York Times* stories are correct, then the Commission's account is false. If the Commission's account is false, then the question why the second controller did not notice the change of course and the change of transponder code does not arise, because the controller assigned to Flight 175 noticed them immediately, at 8:42. But the more important implication is that, if the Commission's story is false, we have not been given any credible reason to doubt NORAD's assertion on September 18, 2001, according to which it received notification about the hijacking of Flight 175 at 8:43. In order to see if the Kean–Zelikow Commission gives us some better reason to doubt that earlier claim, we will return to its account of the FAA response to Flight 175.

FAILURES TO COMMUNICATE

According to the Commission's revisionist scenario, the controller finally noticed the transponder change at 8:51, after which he made several futile attempts to contact the pilot (21). He also said to another controller, "we may have a hijack" (22). As we saw earlier, FAA protocol says that if controllers suspect that a hijacking may have occurred, they are to treat the case as an actual hijacking. The US military is to be notified. But neither of these controllers, we are told, initiated this process.

Finally, at 8:55, the controller told an FAA manager in New York City that he believed Flight 175 had been hijacked. This New York manager acted quickly but, according to protocol, she could go only one step further up the chain of command, to the regional managers. Taking this step, however, simply wasted time, because when she tried to notify the regional managers, "she was told that they were discussing hijacked aircraft. . . and refused to be disturbed" (22). Could FAA regional managers really be this irresponsible, especially on a day when one airliner had already been hijacked?

Be that as it may, we are then told that, shortly after 9:01, a New York manager—whether the same one or a different one—contacted the Command Center at Herndon and said: "We have several situations going on here. It's escalating big, big time. We need to get the military involved with us" (22). But the military, we are told, did not hear from Herndon. This claim is important because, if the F-15s were hovering off Long Island, they could have gotten to Manhattan very quickly.

The Commission offers no explanation as to why the Command Center at Herndon, after this very clear call for help, did not pick up the phone and call the NMCC. Perhaps an explanation is supposed to be implicit in the Commission's next comment: "Evidence indicates that this conversation was the only notice received by either FAA headquarters or the Herndon Command Center prior to the second crash that there had been a second hijacking" (22). Is the Commission's point that FAA officials at Herndon are so dense that they would need to get more than one notice before they would call in the military?

In any case, the Commission then states the conclusion towards which its narrative has been heading:

> The first indication that the NORAD air defenders had of the second hijacked aircraft, United 175, came in a phone call from the New York Center to NEADS at 9:03. The notice came at about the time the plane was hitting the South Tower. (23)

For evidence to support this point, the Kean–Zelikow Commission merely cites four interviews. The reader, therefore, must simply take the Commission's word for it.

THE 9/11 COMMISSION'S CALL TO FORGETFULNESS AND FAITH

According to this third version of what happened on 9/11, the military is relieved of any possible blame for the attack on the South Tower. It could not take action to prevent this attack because it did not even know that Flight 175 had been hijacked until this plane was hitting its target.

To believe this account, we must forget many things. We must forget the news reports, in publications such as *Newsday* and the *New York Times*, according to which the flight controller recognized the signs of the hijacking immediately, at 8:42. We must forget the problem of why many mainstream news stories, appearing as early as September 12, would have all reported that NORAD was notified of the hijacking of Flight 175 at 8:43.[10] We must also forget the problem of why NORAD, in its official timeline of September 18, would have said that it was notified about Flight 175 at 8:43. We must forget NORAD's statement in this same timeline that planes were sent from Otis to intercept Flight 175. We must also forget all the statements that were made as part of this earlier account, such as Duffy's statement that he and Nash were flying "full-blower" towards New York. If we can forget all these things, we can perhaps believe the Kean–Zelikow Commission's revisionist account of Flight 175.

But to believe this account also requires considerable faith. We must believe that although Flight 175 began providing clear signs at 8:42 that it had been hijacked, the controller did not reach this conclusion until about ten minutes later. We also must believe that this controller, after finally reaching this conclusion, waited several more minutes before telling a superior. We must then believe that when this superior, a manager at the FAA's New York Center, tried to call the regional managers, they refused to take her call. We must then believe that after a New York manager told the Command Center at Herndon of the need for military assistance, its officials failed to notify the military. We must also believe that, although we are now being informed that what NORAD said on September 18 is false, the US military is now telling us the truth. We must also believe that the US military, in spite of claims to the contrary on its own websites, is by itself virtually blind, being wholly dependent upon the FAA to inform it about what is going on in American airspace. If we can believe all this, we can perhaps believe the Kean–Zelikow Commission's revisionist claim about Flight 175.

A FINAL PROBLEM: ONGOING CONVERSATIONS

There is a final problem with the 9/11 Commission's revisionist account of Flight 175. I am introducing this problem here, at the end of the chapter, because it raises an issue that will also be important for our examinations of the Commission's accounts of Flights 77 and 93. This problem is the existence of five reports indicating that the FAA and the

US military would have been in constant communication for a significant period of time prior to the crash of Flight 175 into the South Tower at 9:03. The Commission repeatedly maintains that no one from the FAA telephoned the military. But if the FAA and the military were in constant communication, as these reports indicate, individual phone calls were not necessarily needed.

One such report is contained in the previously mentioned story by Hart Seely. It says that after the FAA notified NEADS of the hijacking of Flight 11—Seely says at 8:40, the time on NORAD's timeline—the NEADS technicians, by listening to the FAA's Boston Center, learned something more: "At 8:43 a.m., Dooley's technicians, their headsets linked to Boston Center, heard of a second plane, United Flight 175, that also was not responding. It, too, was moving to New York."[11]

If this report is correct, then officials at NEADS would not have required a formal "notification" by the FAA to know about the hijacking of Flight 175. They would have learned about it simply by listening to conversations at the FAA's Boston Center.

THE FAA-INITIATED TELECONFERENCE

A second report involves the establishment of a telephone conference, sometimes called a "phone bridge," connecting FAA, NORAD, and NMCC officials. Setting up such a teleconference during a crisis is part of the standard FAA protocol.

The 9/11 Commission does not dispute this point, but seems to say that no such teleconference was set up until 9:20. "At about 9:20," it says, "security personnel at FAA headquarters set up a hijacking teleconference with several agencies, including the Defense Department" (36). The Commission evidently showed no curiosity as to why the FAA would have waited 15 minutes after the second strike on the World Trade Center before setting up such a teleconference. Perhaps simply one more example of FAA incompetence. The inference we can draw from the Commission's statement, in any case, is that the US military could not have learned about the hijacking of Flight 175 from the FAA-initiated teleconference, since it did not begin until 15 minutes after Flight 175 had crashed into the South Tower.

The 9/11 Commission's assertion, however, is contradicted by a report contained in a memorandum from Laura Brown, the Deputy in

Public Affairs at FAA headquarters. This memo was sent on May 22, 2003, following the testimony by FAA director Jane Garvey at the 9/11 Commission hearing earlier that day. Laura Brown's memo, headed "FAA communications with NORAD on September 11, 2001," began with this statement:

> Within minutes after the first aircraft hit the World Trade Center, the FAA immediately established several phone bridges that included FAA field facilities, the FAA Command Center, FAA headquarters, DoD, the Secret Service, and other government agencies.[12]

According to Laura Brown, therefore, the FAA did not wait until 9:20 to establish a teleconference (phone bridge). It instead established it "immediately"—"within minutes"—after the strike on the North Tower. Since that strike occurred slightly before 8:47, we can assume that the teleconference began about 8:50.

Readers face a clear contradiction here. The 9/11 Commission says that the FAA's teleconference did not begin until "about 9:20," whereas Laura Brown says that it began a half-hour earlier, at about 8:50. How do we decide which testimony to believe? This seems a very difficult choice, at least at first glance.

On the one hand, Laura Brown's office is right there in FAA headquarters. She could see what was going on in the Operations Center. And we must assume that she, as the senior career person in the FAA, found this to be the biggest day of her life. It is hard to believe that a year and a half later, when she wrote her memorandum, her memory of what happened that day could have been fuzzy. So we probably either need to believe her or accuse her of lying.

On the other hand, although the Commission supports its contention by referring to a single document, it is a document that we should be able to take as authoritative. The Commission's note says: "For the time of the teleconference, see FAA record, Chronology ADA-30, Sept. 11, 2001." Reading this, many readers would assume that Laura Brown must have been either lying or confused. Surely the written record from the day must trump her testimony from memory, because even the best memory is fallible.

There are, nevertheless, two reasons to doubt the Commission's time (beyond the fact that the Kean–Zelikow Commission appears biased here, being obviously intent on bolstering its contention that the military did not know about the hijacking of Flight 175 in advance).

One reason is the possibility that the written record of the FAA's chronology has been altered in the intervening years. That idea might at first glance seem absurd. Why, one would ask, would the FAA change the chronology in a way that would make itself look worse? That would indeed be a good question—if we knew that the record of the chronology had remained in the FAA's hands all this time. But, I was told by Laura Brown, the FAA had to turn over all its records from that day to the FBI immediately after 9/11. It was not, she said, unusual for the FAA to turn over its records after some major disaster. But normally the records are turned over to the NTSB (National Transportation Safety Board), not the FBI.[13] Assuming that these records included this chronology, we—at least those of us who are aware that the FBI has appeared less concerned to discover the truth about 9/11 than to cover it up—can see that there could be good reason to suspect that the chronology had been altered.

A second reason to be suspicious of the Commission's time of 9:20 is that, whereas the Commission often supports its points simply by referring to recent interviews, eschewing written documents from the past, in this case the Commission relies solely on this one document, providing no testimony from any interviews. If the teleconference had begun at 9:20, surely there would have been several FAA employees willing to say this. The only testimony we have from an FAA employee, however, contradicts the 9:20 starting time.

If we accept Laura Brown's time for the beginning of the FAA-initiated teleconference, rather than that given in the possibly FBI-corrupted FAA chronology, then we should find quite interesting the next two paragraphs of her memo, "FAA communications with NORAD on September 11, 2001," which say:

> The US Air Force liaison to the FAA immediately joined the FAA headquarters phone bridge and established contact with NORAD on a separate line.
> The FAA shared real-time information on the phone bridges about the unfolding events, including information about loss of communication with aircraft, loss of transponder signals, unauthorized changes in course, and other actions being taken by all the flights of interest. . . . Other parties on the phone bridges, in turn, shared information about actions they were taking.[14]

There are several important points here. One is that NORAD was connected to the phone bridge through the military liaison to the FAA. A second important point is that information about the standard signs indicating hijackings were shared about "all flights of interest," and even the Commission recognizes that Flight 175 had become one of those flights by 8:55. According to its account, the controller noticed the transponder code change at 8:51 and decided at 8:55 that the plane had been hijacked.

If we accept this account, then NORAD would have known about the hijacking of Flight 175 no later than 8:55. And, as we saw before, if NORAD had two F-15s circling off Long Island, it could have had Flight 175 intercepted before 9:03.

THE NMCC-INITIATED TELECONFERENCE

The third report to which I referred is from journalist Tom Flocco. It involves a teleconference set up by the NMCC. Normally this teleconference would have been organized by Brigadier General Montague Winfield, the NMCC's Director of Operations. But he had himself replaced at 8:30 that morning by his deputy. When this deputy, Captain Charles Leidig, testified before the 9/11 Commission on June 17, 2004, he was asked about this teleconference (which began as a "significant event" conference, evidently due to Leidig's inexperience, but was soon upgraded to an "air threat" conference). Leidig, however, was evidently not asked to say when this conference call began. The Commission tells us (37), however, that it started at 9:29.

The Commission provides, however, virtually no support for this starting time. In the note for the paragraph in question, the Commission merely cites an earlier interview with Leidig (April 29, 2004). Unlike similar notes, moreover, this one does not suggest that the transcript of that interview specifies the time. The only comment about time is a footnote saying: "All times given for this conference call are estimates, which we and the Department of Defense believe to be accurate within a ±3 minute margin of error" (37). The sole support for this commencement time for Leidig's teleconference, in other words, is the word of some anonymous person in the Pentagon.

The report by Tom Flocco suggests that the starting time may have been considerably earlier. It is again Laura Brown who is the source of this suggestion.

Flocco was at the June 17, 2004, hearing. Rushing up to the head table before Leidig could leave at the end of the session, Flocco asked him when, approximately, his phone bridges had begun. Leidig twice replied that he could not recall—Flocco would have to check the record.[15]

Flocco then says that back at the first 9/11 Commission hearing in Washington, which took place May 22–23, 2003, he had talked with Laura Brown. She told him, he says, that Leidig's phone bridges had begun around 8:20 or 8:25—"which," Flocco adds, "would be a reasonable assertion since American 11 was determined to be hijacked at 8:13, 8:20 or 8:24 AM." But, Flocco then writes: "After returning to her office and conferring with superiors, Brown sent an email to this writer later that same evening after 7:00 PM, revising her initial assertions for the commencement of Leidig's phone bridges to around 8:45 AM."[16] Flocco clearly suspects that Laura Brown's first statement, before her memory was "refreshed" by superiors, may have been closer to the truth. Another essay by him shows, moreover, that he has good reason for this suspicion. In an essay posted in July 2003, he reports that a source at the Department of Transportation told him that phone bridges, linking officials from NORAD, the Secret Service, the Department of Defense, and the Department of Transportation, were established at 8:20.[17]

However, even if we accept Laura Brown's later time (8:45), this would be 44 minutes earlier than the time given by the Kean–Zelikow Commission for the start of the NMCC-initiated teleconference (9:29). And this 44 minutes would make all the difference with regard to Flight 175, for it would mean that there was yet another route through which the US military could have learned about its hijacking in time to have it intercepted before 9:03.

The fourth report to which I referred comes from Captain Michael Jellinek, who, as mentioned earlier, was NORAD's command director on 9/11. According to news reports in 2002, he said that the NMCC's Air Threat Conference Call was initiated not long after the first strike on the WTC and included leaders of NORAD and the FAA.[18] His statement, as reported, does not support Brown's view that this phone bridge began before the first strike on the WTC (whether at 8:20 or 8:45). It instead says that it began shortly thereafter. That, it should be recalled, is when Laura Brown said that the phone bridge initiated by the FAA began— "within minutes" after the first attack. It is possible that these two phone bridges became confused in some minds. But even if Captain Jellinek meant that the NMCC-initiated conference began shortly after the first strike, his statement would contradict the 9/11 Commission's claim that it did not begin until 9:29. And if we take "not long after the first strike" to mean somewhere between 8:49 and 8:53, his statement provides further support for the view that there was opportunity for the military, if it did not know already, to learn from the FAA about the hijacking of Flight 175 in time to intercept it.

The fifth report comes from Richard Clarke, the National Coordinator for Security and Counterterrorism. He reports that on his way from Cheney's office to the Secure Video Conferencing Center, where he was going for the teleconference he had organized, he passed through the Operations Center of the White House Situation Room. On his way, he says, he was grabbed by the deputy director of the Situation Room, who said: "We're on the line with NORAD, on an air threat conference call."[19] Given the times that Clarke specifies both before and after this encounter, it would seem to have occurred shortly before 9:15. Although Clarke's statement does not say when the air threat conference call had begun, it must have been going on for some time if it had already been upgraded from the status of "significant event" conference, with which it had begun. Clarke's narrative, in any case, clearly indicates that it had begun well before 9:29, because he reports many exchanges that occurred in his teleconference prior to 9:28.[20]

Clarke's report, like those from Laura Brown, Tom Flocco, and Michael Jellinek, suggests that everyone in a position to know disputes the 9/11 Commission's starting time for the NMCC-initiated air threat conference. This starting time appears to have been determined by need, not evidence.

All in all, the Kean–Zelikow Commission's defense of the US military's new line on Flight 175—that it had no idea Flight 175 had been hijacked until after this plane struck the South Tower—is extremely weak. This defense is contradicted by so many reports that it can probably be believed only by those who are not aware of this contrary evidence or who assume that they have good grounds for simply accepting the word of the 9/11 Commission.

CHAPTER FOURTEEN

The Commission on Flight 77

The 9/11 Commission's account of the responses by the FAA and NORAD to Flight 175 constitutes, as we have seen, an example of historical revisionism. The Commission has also provided a revisionist account of Flight 77. Having argued in the previous chapter that the Commission's revisionist account of Flight 175 is implausible, I will here examine its revisionist account of Flight 77.

FAA CONTROLLERS MISS SIGNS OF FLIGHT 77'S HIJACKING

In its timeline of September 18, 2001, NORAD had said that at 9:24, which was 13 or 14 minutes before the Pentagon was hit, the FAA had notified it that Flight 77 may have been hijacked. NORAD had also said that it immediately—also at 9:24—issued a scramble order to Langley Air Force Base. But this story, as we saw in Chapter 11, had raised problems. Even given NORAD's twofold claim that the scramble order went to far-away Langley and that the F-16s were not airborne until 9:30, doing the math showed that the fighters should have reached the Pentagon in time to prevent the attack at 9:38. Another problem, as we also saw, was why, if NORAD had been told at 9:24 that Flight 77 appeared to be headed back towards Washington, the Pentagon was not evacuated. In 13 minutes, it seems, virtually everyone could have gotten out. The strike would not have caused the death of 125 people working in the Pentagon. It is perhaps not surprising, therefore, that the military has provided the 9/11 Commission with a revised account.

According to this new account, Flight 77 did not begin deviating from its course until 8:54. The Commission does not mention the report from 2001 according to which eight minutes earlier, at 8:46, Flight 77 went significantly off course for several minutes—an event that surely would have gotten the attention of the relevant FAA controller, who was in Indianapolis. The fact that the first deviation is not part of the Commission's account may be significant for what it says happens next: At 8:56, when the controller in Indianapolis lost the transponder signal and even the radar track for Flight 77, he concluded that "American 77 had experienced serious electrical or mechanical failure" after which it had crashed (24).

The idea that he believed this, rather than that the plane had been hijacked, would probably be more difficult to accept if the Commission's version had retained the information, provided in the earlier account, that Flight 77 had gone off course at 8:46. The Commission, however, fails to mention this feature of the earlier account, which was widely known due to the flight course provided by *USA Today*.[1] The Commission implicitly denies that this deviation happened, but without explaining why reporters thought it had. This is an example of historical revisionism without evidence.

The idea that the Indianapolis controller believed that Flight 77 had experienced "electrical or mechanical failure," rather than having been hijacked, would also be more difficult to accept if he had known that there had already been a hijacking or two that morning. But, we are told, "He did not know that other aircraft had been hijacked" (24). However, according to accounts in the *Guardian* and the *Village Voice* that appeared shortly after 9/11, Boston flight controllers had at 8:25 notified other regional centers—one of which is Indianapolis—of the hijacking of Flight 11.[2] Failing even to mention this discordant report, the Commission fails to counter the doubt this report casts on its claim.

THE RUMOR THAT FLIGHT 77 CRASHED

The Commission does, however, offer an explanation of the origin of the rumor that Flight 77 had crashed in Ohio or Kentucky—a rumor that, of course, has given support to those who believe that some aircraft other than Flight 77 hit the Pentagon. The Commission, perhaps hoping to put this rumor to rest, says that FAA officials in Indianapolis quickly decided that they were wrong. By 9:20, we are told, Indianapolis "learned that there were other hijacked aircraft, and began to doubt its initial assumption that American 77 had crashed" (24). The Commission does not mention that at the time, the rumor lasted long enough and had sufficient evidence for FAA head Jane Garvey to notify the White House about the crash, and for Dale Watson, the FBI's counterterrorism chief, to mention "a report of a large jet crashed in Kentucky, near the Ohio line," during Richard Clarke's teleconference (at least according to Clarke).[3]

ANOTHER FAA FAILURE TO COMMUNICATE

Indianapolis then shared its doubt with Herndon, and at 9:25 Herndon advised FAA headquarters that it "feared that [Flight 77] may have been hijacked" (24–25). But, then, even though "[b]y 9:25, FAA's Herndon Command Center and FAA headquarters knew two aircraft had crashed into the World Trade Center" and also "knew American 77 was lost" (26), no one called the NMCC. Herndon and FAA headquarters were clearly having a bad day.

HOW FLIGHT 77 GOT LOST AND STAYED LOST

Another question that was raised about NORAD's prior account of Flight 77 was based on the report that this airplane, just before it disappeared from radar, made a U-turn and headed back towards Washington.[4] This notion was used to bolster the official claim that the aircraft that hit the Pentagon was indeed Flight 77. But this notion also tended to undermine a more important part of the official account—namely, that the FAA lost track of Flight 77 after it headed back to Washington. For example, after summarizing news reports that said the plane was missing because flight controllers were looking for its radar signal towards the west, not realizing that the plane was headed east, Paul Thompson asked: "Since the plane had already started turning east before the transponder is turned off, why don't flight controllers look in that direction?"[5]

The 9/11 Commission, however, eliminates the idea that anyone saw Flight 77 turn around. It says that when Flight 77 turned around to head east, the FAA radar in Indianapolis was, for "reasons [that] are technical," not displaying information about this flight. The Commission is then able to repeat the standard answer, which it rather belabors:

> As Indianapolis Center continued searching for the aircraft, two managers and the controller responsible for American 77 looked to the west and southwest along the flight's projected path, not east— where the aircraft was now heading. . . . In sum, Indianapolis Center never saw Flight 77 turn around. By the time it reappeared in primary radar coverage, controllers had either stopped looking for the aircraft. . . or were looking towards the west. (25)

This is the 9/11 Commission's explanation of how "American 77 traveled undetected for 36 minutes on a course heading due east for Washington, D.C." (25).

To believe this explanation, of course, we would need to forget that, whatever the inadequacies of the radar system in Indianapolis and other regional centers, the radar systems at FAA headquarters and even more those at the Pentagon—recall the capacities of the PAVE PAWS system—would have had no trouble seeing Flight 77 make a U-turn. We would also have to avoid thinking that those who are watching the skies from inside the Pentagon might be especially alert to any unidentified objects flying towards the Pentagon itself. If we can avoid those thoughts—and some others to be mentioned later—we can perhaps believe that a Boeing 757 flying towards Washington could have gone undetected for 36 minutes.

REVISING NORAD's PREVIOUS ACCOUNT

The 9/11 Commission evidently did succeed in avoiding those thoughts. It was content, therefore, to argue that the Pentagon did not know Flight 77 was coming because "NEADS never received notice that American 77 was hijacked" (34). This is, in fact, the main point of the Commission's revisionist narrative about Flight 77.

Emphasizing the importance of this point, the Commission explicitly says that when General Larry Arnold stated in testimony to the Commission in 2003 that NEADS had received notification of this hijacking at 9:24, his statement was "incorrect" (34). The Commission also tells us that when other NORAD officials said that fighters at Langley had been scrambled to respond to this notification, their statements were "incorrect" (34). These errors were unfortunate, says the Commission, because they "made it appear that the military was notified in time to respond" (34). The Commission's entire narrative about Flight 77 is aimed at undermining this belief.

The Commission does not explain why Arnold and other NORAD officials made statements that were incorrect. It does not say, in other words, whether they were lying or simply confused. Of course, the Commission could have explained the errors by pointing out that both of these claims had been made in NORAD's timeline of September 18, 2001. But that would have simply pushed the problem back. Were the officials who prepared this timeline lying or were they simply confused? And either answer to this question would have occasioned discomfort. If the Commission said they were confused, it would need to explain how these NORAD officials could have been confused about something that had happened only a week earlier. If the Commission had said that these military officials were lying, that would suggest that the military had something to cover up. We can perhaps understand, therefore, why the Kean–Zelikow Commission preferred simply to say that the statements of Arnold and the other NORAD officials were "incorrect." But that statement merely begs the deeper question.

The main point in the Commission's revisionist account of Flight 77, in any case, is its twofold denial that NORAD was notified about the hijacking of Flight 77 and that Langley F-16s were scrambled to intercept it.

INTERLUDE: THE "PHANTOM AIRCRAFT"

But if the military had not been notified about Flight 77 at 9:24, why were fighters from Langley airborne by 9:30? Here the Commission faced a problem similar to that of explaining why the F-15s were scrambled from Otis at 8:53 even though Flight 11 had already crashed and NORAD did not know that Flight 175 had been hijacked. The Commission in the present case at least proffers an explanation.

This explanation requires the introduction of a new idea—the idea of a "phantom aircraft." What really happened, we are told, was that the FAA had made yet another inexplicable error. NEADS, we are told, heard from the FAA at 9:21—35 minutes after the North Tower had been hit by Flight 11—that Flight 11 was still in the air and heading towards Washington. This was why Langley received a scramble order at 9:24. The scrambled jets were supposed to go to the Baltimore area and position themselves "between the reported southbound American 11 and the nation's capital" (26–27).

Because this idea plays a crucial role in the Commission's narrative, it is understandable that the Commission seems upset that

> this response to a phantom aircraft was not recounted in a single public timeline or statement issued by the FAA or Department of Defense. The inaccurate accounts created the impression that the Langley scramble was a logical response to an actual hijacked aircraft. (34)

The Commission assures us, however, that NEADS really did receive the misinformation from someone in the FAA that Flight 11 was still up and heading toward Washington. This fact, the Commission claims, is clear not just from taped conversations at NEADS but also from taped conversations at FAA centers; contemporaneous logs compiled at NEADS, Continental Region headquarters, and NORAD; and other records. (34)

The note for this paragraph, however, gives no references for the "taped conversations at FAA centers; contemporaneous logs compiled at NEADS, Continental Region headquarters, and NORAD; and other records." We simply have to take the Commission's word about them.

The only reference given is to some NEADS audiofiles (26, 461nn148–152). The crucial audiofile contains a conversation between a NEADS technician and someone at the FAA's Boston Center, who at 9:21 says: "I just had a report that American 11 is still in the air, and it's on its way towards—heading towards Washington" (26). How, we wonder, could someone at the FAA have made such a huge mistake?

This question is intensified by the evidence that the traffic controllers at the Boston Center were reportedly very clear about the fate of Flight 11. According to a story in the *Christian Science Monitor* two days after 9/11, flight controllers said that they never lost sight of the flight.[6] Flight controller Mark Hodgkins later said: "I watched the target of American 11 the whole way down."[7] Other stories say that as soon as the Boston flight controllers heard that a plane had hit the WTC, they knew that it was Flight 11, because they had been tracking it continuously since it had begun behaving erratically.[8]

Given this situation, how could one of these controllers at the Boston Center have decided, some 30 minutes later, that Flight 11 was actually alive and well and headed toward Washington? Even if there was something to cause this controller to suspect that this was the case, how can we believe that he or she was sufficiently confident of this belief to pass it on to NEADS as confirmed truth? We will, however, not get an answer to this question because we cannot interrogate this person. The Commission says, with apparent unconcern: "We have been unable to identify the source of this mistaken FAA information" (26).

That claim, of course, is another puzzling feature of the Commission's narrative about the phantom aircraft. Nowadays the identities of people can be determined with great precision from their voices. The Commission says that NEADS has a tape in which this conversation was recorded. Since NEADS and the FAA must have tapes with the voices of all their controllers, why could the identities of the two people not be determined from their voices? Surely this would have been a worthy part of the "exacting investigative work" carried out by the Commission's staff. But the Commission does not tell us why it could not determine the identities of the two people. As with a great many of the things the Commission tells us, we must simply take its word.

This story is made even more implausible by the fact that the Commission has generally portrayed FAA personnel as reluctant to notify the military even after they are absolutely confident that a hijacking has occurred. But now we are told that a controller, having a suspicion that must have seemed extremely counterintuitive, expressed this suspicion as a conviction with such confidence to a NEADS technician that this technician passed it on as definite truth to the NEADS commander.

If all this were not implausible enough, we then have to believe that the NEADS commander would, without verifying the truth of this implausible message with the managers at the Boston Center, give Langley a scramble order. The 9/11 Commission has usually insisted that all such communications had to follow the chain-of-command protocol. But we are here told that a conversation between some person at the Boston Center and some technician at NEADS—neither of whom can now be identified—was sufficient to cause the US military to swing into action. According to the 9/11 Commission's report, nothing else did that day. The US military did not scramble fighters to go after Flight 11, Flight 175, Flight 77, or (as we will see below) Flight 93. The only time fighters were scrambled on this day, they were sent after a phantom.

The Commission, however, was apparently unconcerned about any of these problems. The only important thing, from its perspective, was that the NEADS audiofile does contain this conversation between the two unidentified people, along with other conversations about the phantom aircraft. And that should indeed settle the question, at least the question as to whether this conversation actually took place—if we can assume that these audiofiles faithfully reflect real events.

But can we safely assume this? In the first place, given the fact that the only proffered evidence—the NEADS audiofile—has been in the hands of the US military all this time, we cannot simply assume that it has not been doctored. In any serious criminal trial with an analogous situation, the prosecution would demand that rigorous tests be performed to exclude this possibility. And yet the Commission, acting more like the counsel for the defense (as well as judge and jury), provides no sign that it had such tests performed. In the second place, the Commission itself points out that the idea that Flight 11 had not hit the World Trade Center, but was instead headed toward Washington, is a brand new idea, which had never before been brought up by either the FAA or the Department of Defense. That is certainly suspicious on its face. In the third place, the Kean–Zelikow Commission has distorted so many other matters—a fact that will become even clearer in Chapter 15—that we have no basis for trusting it on this one.

This story—that the Langley Fighters were scrambled at 9:24 in response to Phantom Flight 11 instead of Flight 77—is so important to the 9/11 Commission's narrative of what really happened that day, and to our judgment of whether we can trust the Commission, that it will be helpful to examine the exchange during the Commission's hearings that dealt with this issue. This exchange was between Commissioner Richard Ben-Veniste and General Larry Arnold, who, as we have seen, was the NORAD Commander for the Continental United States.

> MR. BEN-VENISTE: General Arnold. Why did no one mention the false report received from FAA that Flight 11 was heading south during your initial appearance before the 9/11 Commission back in May of last year? And why was there no report to us that contrary to the statements made at the time, that there had been no notification to NORAD that Flight 77 was a hijack?
>
> GEN. LARRY ARNOLD: Well, the first part of your question— Mr. Commissioner, first of all, I would like to say that a lot of the information that you have found out in your study of this 9/11, the things that happened on that day, helped us reconstruct what was going on.
>
> And if you're talking about the American 11, in particular, the call of American 11, is that what you are referring to?
>
> MR. BEN-VENISTE: Yes.
>
> GEN. ARNOLD: The American 11, that was—call after it had impacted, is that what you're referring to?
>
> MR. BEN-VENISTE: No. I'm talking about the fact that there was

miscommunication that Flight 11 was still heading south instead of having impacted—

GEN. ARNOLD: That's what I'm referring to. That's correct. As we—as we worked with your committee in looking at that, that was probably the point in time where we were concerned—remember, that call, as I recall, actually came after United 175, as well as American 11, had already impacted the North and South Towers of the World Trade Center. And then we became very concerned, not knowing what the call signs of those aircraft were that had hit the World Trade Center, we became very concerned at that particular point that those aircraft, that some aircraft might be heading toward Washington, D.C.

MR. BEN-VENISTE: General, is it not a fact that the failure to call our attention to the miscommunication and the notion of a phantom Flight 11 continuing from New York City south in fact skewed the whole reporting of 9/11, it skewed the official Air Force report, which is contained in a book called *The Air War Over America*, which does not contain any information about the fact that you were following, or thinking of a continuation of Flight 11, and that you had not received notification that Flight 77 had been hijacked?

GEN. ARNOLD: Well, as I recall, first of all, I didn't know the call signs of the airplanes when these things happened. When the call came that American 11 was possible hijacked aircraft, that aircraft just led me to come to the conclusion that there were other aircraft in the system that were a threat to the United States.

MR. BEN-VENISTE: General Arnold, surely by May of last year, when you testified before this commission, you knew those facts.

GEN. ARNOLD: I didn't recall those facts in May of last year. That's the correct answer to that. In fact, as I recall, during that time frame, my concern was, why did—the question that came to me was, why did we scramble the aircraft out of Langley Air Force Base, the F-16s out of Langley Air Force Base? And there had been statements made by some that we scrambled that aircraft the report of American 77, which was not the case, and I knew that.

And I was trying to remember in my own mind what was it that persuaded us to scramble those aircraft. And I thought at the time it was United 93. But as I was able to—we did not have the times when these things were—when we were notified of this. I did not have that information at that time. I didn't have it.

MR. BEN-VENISTE: General Arnold—

MR. ARNOLD: And so we scrambled those aircraft to get them over Washington D.C. to protect Washington D.C.

MR. BEN-VENISTE: According to our staff, you know that there was a substantial problem in getting information from NORAD, that we received information, we were told that the information was complete. We went out into the field, our staff did, and did a number of interviews. And as a result of those interviews, we found that there were tapes which reflected the facts relating to Flight 11.

And we found additional information by which we were able, through assiduous and painstaking work, listening to any number of tape recordings, to reconstruct what actually occurred, as you have heard in the Staff Statement.

I take it you have no disagreement with the facts put forward in the Staff Statement. That's been produced in advance for comment, and I take it you're in agreement now with our staff's conclusions with respect to those facts.

MR. ARNOLD: I am.

MR. BEN-VENISTE: We have—and I'm not going to go through it, but it is disturbing to see that there were efforts at after-action reports which were available shortly after 9/11. There were communications which our staff has received with respect to e-mails that reflect some of the facts on nearly a contemporaneous basis with the 9/11 catastrophe that reflect a story which unfortunately is different from the one which was presented to this commission earlier.

When you . . . were asked about the existence of tape recordings reflecting these open-line communications, . . . you indicated that you had no such recollections. . . .

MR. ARNOLD: Yeah, the Northeast Air Defense Sector apparently had a tape that we were unaware of at the time. And your—to the best of my knowledge, what I've been told by your staff is that they were unable to make that tape run. But they were later able to—your staff was able, through a contractor, to get that tape to run.

And so, to the best of my knowledge, that was an accurate statement in May that I did not know of any tape recordings. If I had had them available to me, I certainly would have been able to give you more accurate information.

Our focus was on when the events occurred, and we did not focus on when we—we didn't have a record—I did not have a record of when we had been told different things.[9]

This painfully embarrassing testimony certainly provides no basis for increased confidence in the 9/11 Commission's claims about Flight 77 and Phantom Flight 11. Elsewhere the Commission told us that Colonel Robert Marr, the head of NEADS, had to call General Arnold to get permission to scramble fighters to go after the real Flight 11. But now we are being asked to believe that planes were scrambled for phantom Flight 11 without Arnold's having heard anything about such a flight. We are also asked to believe that he later learned the truth about this phantom flight but could "not recall" it when he had previously testified before the Commission. Our confidence in the Commission's story is also not helped by seeing the way in which General Arnold had to be coached and coaxed into giving his verbal assent to it.

In sum, given all the problems inherent in the Commission's claim about Phantom Flight 11, my own view is that until there is an investigation of the evidence for this new idea by some truly neutral investigative body, we have reason to wonder whether the "phantom aircraft" is not itself a phantom.

NEADS LEARNS THAT FLIGHT 77 IS LOST

The Commission's argument, in any case, is that Langley was ordered to scramble jets at 9:24 because of this phantom aircraft, not because NEADS had learned that Flight 77 had been hijacked.

However, perhaps as an attempt to explain how that idea came about, the Commission says that NEADS did learn something about Flight 77 at that time.

NORAD officials stated that at 9:24, NEADS received notification of the hijacking of American 77. This statement was . . . incorrect. The notice NEADS received at 9:24 was that American 11 had not hit the World Trade Center and was heading for Washington, D.C. (34)

But this statement by the Commission is itself incorrect, at least within its own narrative. According to this narrative (26, 32), the false information about American 11 came at 9:21, not 9:24. So this claim does not work as an explanation of the origin of the idea that NEADS had learned about Flight 77's hijacking at 9:24.

In any case, what NEADS officials really learned, according to the Commission's narrative, was only that Flight 77 had been lost. And they learned this at 9:34, not 9:24. NEADS allegedly learned this, furthermore, purely "by chance."

According to the Kean–Zelikow Commission, NEADS had called a manager at the FAA's Washington Center to talk about Flight 11, and during this conversation, this manager said—evidently as an aside— "We're looking—we also lost American 77" (27). The Commission, continuing to develop its portrait of the FAA as staffed by incompetent people, says: "If NEADS had not placed that call, the NEADS air defenders would have received no information whatsoever that the flight was even missing." This information, however, did no good because, as the Commission again insists: "No one at FAA headquarters ever asked for military assistance with American 77" (27).

WHY THE LANGLEY JETS WERE SO FAR AWAY

If we accept the Phantom Flight 11 story as the explanation of why jets were scrambled from Langley, we still might wonder why these jets were not over Washington when Flight 77 arrived. The official story in its previous incarnation, as we saw in Chapter 11, said that although the F-16s left Langley at 9:30, they were still 105 miles away at 9:38, when the Pentagon was struck. No explanation was forthcoming as to why jets that can fly 1,500 mph had traveled only 25 miles in eight minutes. The Commission's new account of Flight 77 does explain why the jets were far from Washington without violating elementary mathematics. This explanation again involves incompetence, but this time the pilots manifested this malady, which was certainly going around that day.

At 9:36, we are told, the FAA's Boston Center notified NEADS that there was an unidentified aircraft, six miles southwest of the White House, which was closing in (27). This unidentified aircraft is, in the Commission's narrative, really none other than Flight 77, which had made it all the way back to Washington without being spotted (9, 27). In any case, given this startling news, the mission crew commander at NEADS ordered the Langley fighters to race toward the White House. "He then discovered, to his surprise, that the Langley fighters were not headed north toward the Baltimore area as instructed, but east over the ocean." They had misunderstood their instructions. Accordingly, when the Pentagon was struck at 9:38, "[t]he Langley fighters were about 150 miles away"—even farther away, therefore, than the 105 miles that NORAD had previously claimed (27).[10]

BLAMING THE PILOT, ABSOLVING THE MILITARY

The Commission's report has thereby explained why the Langley fighters, in spite of being scrambled at 9:24, were nowhere close to the Pentagon when it was struck. It has, moreover, absolved the military of any blame by explaining—this being the main point of the story—that

> the military did not have 14 minutes to respond to American 77, as testimony to the Commission in May 2003 suggested. It had at most one or two minutes to react to the unidentified plane approaching Washington, and the fighters were in the wrong place to be able to help. They had been responding to a report about an aircraft that did not exist. (34)

Of course, this account does not completely absolve "the military" in the sense of all its personnel, because it implies that the three Langley pilots, especially the lead pilot, made a terrible mistake—a mistake that allowed the Pentagon to be attacked. But this account does absolve "the military" in the sense of its top brass—along with its civilian boss, Secretary Rumsfeld—and that is, of course, what is important. There was no stand-down order or even any slow-down order, but only an honest mistake by a pilot.

The mistake by this lead pilot obviously plays a crucial role in the new narrative told by the military through the 9/11 Commission. This narrative is evidently intended to explain why it had previously been thought, falsely, that Langley fighters had been scrambled at 9:24 in response to word that Flight 77 had been hijacked. That false belief would have arisen through a fusion of two elements in what really happened. On the one hand, Langley fighters were indeed scrambled at 9:24 (although they were scrambled in response to "Phantom Flight 11" and then went the wrong way). On the other hand, the FAA did indeed notify the military about Flight 77 (although this occurred at 9:34, rather than 9:24, and it was merely a notification that Flight 77 was lost, so no scramble order was needed). Evidently these facts somehow got fused, in the minds of some NORAD officials, into the belief that Langley fighters had been scrambled at 9:24.

With that problem cleared up, all that was needed was an explanation as to why there were no planes over Washington to stop Flight 77 from hitting the Pentagon. This explanation is provided by the claim that the pilots went the wrong way.

EXPLAINING THE PILOTS' ERROR

But does the 9/11 Commission make this claim plausible? Here is its attempt:

> The Langley pilots were heading east, not north, for three reasons. First, unlike a normal scramble order, this order did not include a distance to the target or the target's location. Second, a "generic" flight plan—prepared to get the aircraft airborne and out of local airspace quickly—incorrectly led the Langley fighters to believe they were ordered to fly due east (090) for 60 miles. Third, the lead pilot and local FAA controller incorrectly assumed the flight plan instruction to go "090 for 60" superseded the original scramble order. (27)

But what kind of an explanation is this? Not a very good one.

With regard to the first point, we are not told why the order did not include a distance or a target. But there was no mystery—the flights were supposed to go to Baltimore.

With regard to the second point, we are given no good reason why there was only a "generic" flight plan, since the F-16s were supposed to head to Baltimore. And the fact that the planes were to get "airborne and out of local airspace quickly" provides no reason for a merely "generic" flight plan. All scrambled fighter jets are supposed to get airborne quickly, and they are not slowed down by being told where they are supposed to go. Indeed, the F-15s at Otis were supposedly slowed down because they did not know where they were supposed to go. Furthermore, far from being airborne quickly, these Langley pilots took six minutes to get up (the new timeline says, like the old one, that the scramble order came at 9:24 but that the F-16s were not airborne until 9:30).

With regard to the third point, it is not clear what exactly the point is. Part of the point is that, not surprisingly, an FAA person was involved in the glitch, so the fault was not entirely that of the military pilot. But insofar as the rest of the point depends on an incorrect assumption having been made by both the lead pilot and the FAA controller, it is prima facie implausible. Surely the FAA controller knew by then that the nation was dealing with domestic hijackings, not a threat from "overseas." But if so, why would he or she assume the F-16s should head out to sea? Would he or she not have double-checked such a strange order?

EVIDENCE FOR THE STORY ABOUT PILOT ERROR

The need for discussion of all these problems brings us to the second question to ask about this revisionist explanation of why the F-16s were so far from Washington: What evidence are we provided for it? There is a reference to an interview in December 2003 with Dean Eckmann, the lead pilot, but with no quotations from this interview (27, 461n153).[11] And there are two FAA memos from September of 2003 (461n153), with no evidence that the documents from 2001 they are supposedly based on were checked for authenticity.

Given the fact that we are dealing here with an explanation that involves an enormous blunder on the part of a highly trained pilot and a highly trained FAA controller—a blunder that led to a successful attack on the military headquarters of the most powerful military force in history—should we not be offered more evidence for this revisionist account? Should the people involved—such as the pilots, the FAA controller, and the military officer who gave the scramble order—not be intensely interrogated, under oath, and with lie detectors? Philip Zelikow is a historian. He knows that if he presented a revisionist case about some controversial historical event—such as the division of Germany at the outset of the Cold War—and wanted this case to be taken seriously, he would need to present far better evidence than his Commission has presented here.

I mean this point to apply, furthermore, not just to this story about the pilot's error, but to all the crucial claims in the Commission's account of Flight 77: the claim that FAA headquarters had not notified its regional centers about earlier hijackings until 9:20; the claim that Flight 77 traveled undetected toward the Pentagon for 36 minutes; the idea that although American Airlines and most flight controllers at the Boston Center knew that Flight 11 had hit the North Tower, someone at Boston told someone at NEADS that it was still aloft; and the claim that the FAA never asked the military for assistance with regard to Flight 77.

ONGOING CONVERSATIONS BETWEEN THE FAA AND THE US MILITARY

The Commission's main revisionist claim about Flight 77, as we have seen, is that the FAA did not notify the military that it had been hijacked at 9:24 or at any other time prior to 9:38, when the strike on the Pentagon occurred. The Kean–Zelikow Commission, combining this claim with its assumption that the US military is generally unaware about what is going on in American airspace unless it is informed by the FAA, concludes that no one in the Pentagon knew that Flight 77 was headed towards it. As with the Commission's similar claim about Flight 175, however, there are reports that suggest that this claim is untrue.

Laura Brown's Memo: One of these is Laura Brown's memo of May 23, 2003, in which she reported on the phone bridge established by the FAA. She said, as we saw earlier, that this teleconference, which involved both the Department of Defense and a military liaison connected to NORAD, began "within minutes" after the first strike, hence about 8:50. She then said, in a statement not fully quoted before, that the FAA shared "real-time information" about "all the flights of interest, including Flight 77."

Finally, she explicitly took issue with General Larry Arnold's statement, made in testimony to the 9/11 Commission that day, that the FAA did not notify NORAD about Flight 77 until 9:24. (In making this statement, of course, Arnold was simply reaffirming NORAD's timeline of September 18, 2001.) She said:

> NORAD logs indicate that the FAA made formal notification about American Flight 77 at 9:24 a.m., but information about the flight was conveyed continuously during the phone bridges before the formal notification.

During my telephone conversation with Laura Brown, she emphasized the importance of this distinction, saying that the "formal notification" was primarily a formality and hence irrelevant to the question of when the military knew about Flight 77. The important point, she made clear, was that military officials were receiving "real-time information" about Flight 77 on an ongoing basis by means of the phone bridge that was established by the FAA at about 8:50. Although she spoke in a matter-of-fact way, she clearly was upset that military leaders would claim that, prior to the time of the formal notification, they had no idea that Flight 77 had been hijacked.

And now—as if that earlier claim by the military were not bad enough from the perspective of FAA personnel such as Laura Brown—the 9/11 Commission claims that even the notification at 9:24 did not happen. General Arnold's previously orthodox statement is declared "incorrect." The new orthodoxy, which the Kean–Zelikow Commission hopes to establish, declares that the FAA never notified the military about Flight 77 before the Pentagon was struck. The conversation between the FAA and the US military about Flight 77, to which Laura Brown referred in her memo, is deleted from history, because the 9/11 Commission has declared that the FAA-initiated conference—which Brown said began within minutes of the first strike on the World Trade Center—did not really begin until 9:20 (36).

Laura Brown on the NMCC Teleconference: The Commission also seeks to exclude the possibility that a conversation about Flight 77 could have taken place during the NMCC-initiated teleconference. The Commission declares, as we saw, that it was not until 9:29 that the conference initiated by Captain Leidig began (37). As we saw, however, Laura Brown at first said that it began about 8:25. She later revised this, perhaps under pressure, but she revised it only to 8:45, so she has this teleconference beginning at least 44 minutes earlier than the Commission says.

If we believe her, we have to conclude that the military is now using the 9/11 Commission to perpetrate a lie. The suspicion that it is Laura Brown, rather than the military, who is here telling the truth is suggested by the fact that, as we saw earlier, Tom Flocco reported that Captain Leidig himself could "not recall" when the teleconference began—even though it, as the first such teleconference he had ever directed, must have been one of the biggest moments of his life.

Matthew Wald's NYT Story: It is, moreover, not just a question of Laura Brown's word against that of the current spokespersons for the US military. Her perspective on this matter is supported by a second report that contradicts the 9/11 Commission. Matthew Wald's well-known story, published in the *New York Times* four days after 9/11, began with this statement:

> During the hour or so that American Airlines Flight 77 was under the control of hijackers, up to the moment it struck the west side of the Pentagon, military officials in a command center on the east side of the building were urgently talking to law enforcement and air traffic control officials about what to do.[12]

The "command center on the east side" is, of course, the NMCC. And the "air traffic control officials" are personnel of the FAA.

Here again we see that it was commonly accepted that the NMCC had been in conversation with FAA—and about Flight 77 in particular—for a long time. How long? When Wald wrote that story, he believed that the Pentagon had been hit at 9:45. Even with this late time, however, his statement that the conversation had been going on an "hour or so" would support Laura Brown's view that conversations began, at least in the NMCC-initiated teleconference, before the first strike on the WTC—which makes sense, given the fact that everyone agrees that the US military knew about the hijacking of Flight 11 no later than 8:40. In relation to Flight 77 and the Pentagon, of course, that distinction—whether the conference began before or after the strike on the North Tower—is of trivial importance.

The central point is that according to Matthew Wald of the *New York Times* as well as Laura Brown of the FAA, the US military would have known about the signs that Flight 77 had been hijacked shortly after these signs occurred and were being discussed within the FAA. Wald's article was, in fact, headed: "Pentagon Tracked Deadly Jet but Found No Way to Stop It." The mere desire of the 9/11 Commission to deny that the Pentagon knew that Flight 77 was hijacked cannot delete such reports from the historical record.

Richard Clarke's Account of the White House Teleconference: The existence of conversations involving the FAA and the US military going on long before the strike on the Pentagon is also supported by Richard Clarke. As we saw in the previous chapter, Clarke's narrative of that morning supports the view that by 9:15, the NMCC's "air threat" conference call had been going on for some time. Clarke also, as mentioned earlier, ran his own teleconference from the White House. The 9/11 Commission, appealing to the log of the White House Situation Room, says that Clarke's conference did not begin until 9:25. The Commission even adds: "Indeed, it is not clear to us that the video teleconference was fully under way before 9:37, when the Pentagon was struck" (36). But Clarke's own account suggests that it began closer to 9:15. Let us see why.

Assuming the rough accuracy of this account, we can infer from the two times that Clarke notes that his teleconference began sometime between 9:10 and 9:28. On the one hand, he says that, having noted that it was 9:03 as he was rushing to the White House, he was told when he arrived that "[t]he other tower was just hit." We can infer, accordingly, that he must have gotten there at about 9:05. He then rushed to Cheney's office, where he had what would seem to have been about a five-minute conversation. Assuming he got to Cheney's office at about 9:06, he would have left at about 9:11, at which time, he reports, he went to the Video Conferencing Center off the Situation Room. On the other hand, he says that at one later point he noted that it was 9:28—shortly after which his conference paused while the president's talk, which began at 9:30, was being televised. So his teleconference must have started sometime between 9:10 and 9:28.

That Clarke's conference must have begun considerably before 9:28, perhaps a little before 9:15, can then be inferred from the discussions that occurred, according to his account, during that period. At the outset of his teleconference, he reports, he discussed the protocol for the teleconference. He then had an extended conversation with Jane Garvey, representing the FAA. During this conversation, they discussed the two attacks on the WTC, the whereabouts of Secretary of Transportation Norman Mineta, the question of whether Garvey could order all air traffic stopped, the number of planes that may have been hijacked, and the fact that it was Ben Sliney's first day on the job as the FAA's National Operations Manager. This exchange had to take several minutes.

Clarke then reports that Norman Mineta arrived at the White House and came to the Situation Room, after which Clarke suggested that he join the vice president down in the shelter conference room, officially known as the Presidential Emergency Operations Center, or PEOC.

Clarke next reports that he had an exchange with General Richard Myers, representing the Joint Chiefs of Staff, during which they discussed the question of scrambling fighters and placing Combat Air Patrol over Washington. It was at this point, when he asked Myers how long this would take, that he noted that it was 9:28.[13]

All of that, it seems, would have taken at least 10 minutes, probably more. Clarke's account strongly contradicts, therefore, the 9/11 Commission's estimation that this White House teleconference did not begin until 9:25. All those discussions could not have occurred in three minutes.

The earlier starting time for Clarke's conference is also supported by testimony to the 9/11 Commission, given by Norman Mineta himself. In this testimony on May 23, 2003, Mineta reported that after he arrived at the White House that morning, he met briefly with Clarke, then was taken down to the PEOC, where he arrived at 9:20.[14] Since in Clarke's narrative, Mineta seemed to arrive at the White House about 5 minutes after Clarke's video teleconference had begun, Mineta's 9:20 time for arriving at the PEOC would mean that Clarke's conference had begun by 9:15.

The Commission's suggestion that Clarke's conference might not have been "fully under way" even at "9:37, when the Pentagon was struck," is strongly contradicted by the next part of Clarke's account. He says that when he resumed the teleconference, after the president's speech was finished, he turned back to Jane Garvey, who discussed other potential hijacks, including United 93—at which time Brian Stafford, the Director of the Secret Service, handed him a note saying that an aircraft was headed in their direction so that he was going to order a general evacuation of the White House. And then Ralph Seigler, the deputy director of the Situation Room, stuck his head in the room and said: "there has been an explosion in the Pentagon parking lot, maybe a car bomb!" Following a brief discussion of CoG (Continuity of Government), Clarke's deputy, Roger Cressey, announced: "A plane just hit the Pentagon." With regard to the concern about how destructive the strike had been, Clarke commented: "I can still see Rumsfeld on the screen, so the whole building didn't get hit."[15] So, even if it did not seem clear to the 9/11 Commissioners that Clarke's teleconference had gotten fully under way before the Pentagon was struck, it evidently seemed clear enough to Clarke himself.

But how do we decide whether to believe Clarke or the Commission? On the one hand, if we accept the Commission's account, we must believe that Richard Clarke was lying or that his memory of that morning was very faulty. But can we suppose that he would have lied about the time his conference began—suggesting that it had begun about 15 minutes before the president's 9:30 talk—even though a videotape of the teleconference could be released to prove him wrong? If not, can we suppose that his memory could have been so faulty about the first 15 minutes or so of what must have been one of the biggest mornings of his professional life? On the other hand, can we doubt the Commission's starting time of 9:25, given the fact that it is vouchsafed, the Commission says, by the Communications Log of the White House Situation Room?

However, although that final sentence looks like a rhetorical question, it is not. There is a basis for us to doubt the Commission's starting time, in spite of its appeal to this log. We, after all, simply have to take the Commission's word that this is what the log says. We have little basis for confidence that, if it said something else, the Bush White House would inform us of this fact. Of course, the Commission, publishing its report in July 2004, had to suppose that the Bush–Cheney administration might be replaced by a Democratic administration, which might indeed release the log. But even this eventually could have been protected against. After all, this log could have simply been revised to make it fit the Commission's timeline. Getting such a revision made could have been one of the benefits of the tight relationship between the Bush White House and the Commission's executive director.

At this point, to be sure, a careful reader of the notes at the end of *The 9/11 Commission Report* could point out that the 9:25 starting time is said also to be vouchsafed by the FAA chronology for September 11, 2001 (462n189). As we saw in Chapter 13, however, that chronology has been not been in the hands of the FAA or the NTSB all this time, as it normally would have been, but in the hands of the FBI. If the Kean–Zelikow Commission had the log of the White House Situation Room changed, it would have also had the FAA chronology changed.

To think that members of the Commission or its staff would do this, of course, we would need to believe that they would deliberately lie and tamper with evidence. An informed judgment about this should be based on the performance of the Commission in relation to other questions. My own reading of the Kean–Zelikow Commission does not inspire confidence that it—that is, some members of the Commission and/or its staff—would not lie and tamper with evidence if they thought it necessary to defend their case.

Another serious conflict between Clarke's account and that of the 9/11 Commission involves participation by the FAA and the Pentagon.

In Clarke's account, the FAA's Jane Garvey is there from the outset, evidently answering questions before 9:20. But the Commission, in line with its claim that no significant interchange occurred in any teleconferences between the FAA and the military, says that Garvey did not join Clarke's teleconference until 9:40—which would have been, of course, after the Pentagon had been struck (36). In Clarke's account, as we have seen, the first conversation, which was with Garvey, was about hijacked airliners and grounding air traffic, whereas the Commission says that the first topic was "the physical security of the President, the White House, and federal agencies" (36). The Commission has this discussion begin at 9:40, which is also said to be the time at which the FAA joined the teleconference. It then says: "Immediately thereafter it was reported that a plane had hit the Pentagon." (36) The Commission's timeline thereby excludes the possibility that the FAA might have conveyed something of importance to the representative(s) from the US military prior to the strike on the Pentagon. We again have to decide whether to believe Clarke or the Kean–Zelikow Commission.

With regard to the Pentagon's participation, the Commission's account does not directly contradict Clarke's account. But it does, by failing to confirm it, imply its untruth. Here is what the Commission says:

> We do not know who from Defense participated, but we know that in the first hour none of the personnel involved in managing the crisis did. And none of the information conveyed in the White House video teleconference, at least in the first hour, was being passed to the NMCC. (36)

In other words, although the Commissioners do not know who was representing the Defense Department, they somehow know that it was not anyone important. They also somehow know that this person was not passing on any information to the NMCC. But if they do not know who it was, how do they know what he or she was not doing? How, in fact, do they know it was not someone from the NMCC itself?

These apparent self-contradictions do not, however, constitute the most serious problem with the 9/11 Commission's statement. This problem is its claim that it does "not know who from Defense participated." How can we believe this? Surely many people in the Pentagon would have known who participated in the White House's teleconference. As already suggested, furthermore, the videotape from this conference was surely retained. If no one at the Pentagon could remember, the staff, as part of its exacting investigative work, could have gotten this videotape and played it. And from this tape the staff would have learned—assuming the basic truth of Richard Clarke's account—that the participants from the Department of Defense were two rather important people: General Richard Myers, Acting Chairman of the Joint Chiefs of Staff, and Donald Rumsfeld, the Secretary of Defense. The Commission's staff, in fact, did not even need to ferret out this videotape. Its members could have simply read Clarke's book, which was the talk of Washington and the news shows for several weeks after its appearance early in 2004.

I have pointed to the White House teleconference run by Richard Clarke as a further example of the evidence that FAA and US military officials had ongoing conversations on the morning of 9/11, including conversations for a considerable period prior to the strike on the Pentagon. But the 9/11 Commission denies that there was any opportunity for the US military to have learned about Flight 77 from the FAA in time to do anything about it. Here is the Commission's general claim about all the teleconferences, followed by its claim about this teleconference and this flight in particular:

> The FAA, the White House, and the Defense Department each initiated a multiagency teleconference before 9:30. Because none of these teleconferences—at least before 10:00—included the right officials from both the FAA and the Defense Department, none succeeded in meaningfully coordinating the military and FAA response to the hijackings . . . . We found no evidence that [Richard Clarke's] video teleconference participants had any prior information that American 77 had been hijacked. (36)

These two claims are crucial to the 9/11 Commission's argument that the military had no idea that Flight 77 had been hijacked.

Unfortunately for the first claim, Clarke's account suggests that his teleconference included exactly the right people: Jane Garvey, Richard Myers, and Donald Rumsfeld.

With regard to the second claim, Clarke's account does not directly contradict the Commission's, because he does not say that Flight 77 was mentioned prior to the Pentagon strike, whether by Garvey or anyone else. But Clarke does have Garvey of the FAA joined in the same video teleconference with Myers and Rumsfeld of the Pentagon. And Garvey surely would have known at this time about the signs suggesting that Flight 77 had been hijacked. Laura Brown's memo, as we saw, indicated that the FAA was keeping military officials in the FAA-initiated teleconference abreast of developments about Flight 77. Clarke's White House teleconference provided, therefore, one more context in which the US military—if it did not already know—could have learned about the hijacking of Flight 77.

The 9/11 Commission's claim that the US military did not even know that Flight 77 had been hijacked seems to based not on an impartial scrutiny of the evidence but purely on the conclusion that this claim is needed to protect the US military from suspicion that it deliberately allowed the Pentagon to be attacked. NORAD's September 18 timeline, with its already extreme claim that it was not notified by the FAA until 9:24, had not succeeded in removing this suspicion. This claim, therefore, had to be declared "incorrect" and replaced with the even more extreme claim that the US military was never notified about the hijacking of Flight 77. Those who care more about evidence and common sense than about the reputation of the US military, however, will likely find this new claim dubious.

THE COMMISSION'S STRANGE DENIAL ABOUT MYERS AND RUMSFELD

One loose end remains from the discussion in the previous section. There I suggested some reasons to consider completely implausible the 9/11 Commission's denial that it knew who from the Defense Department had participated in the Clarke's video teleconference. It is, indeed, hard to consider this denial as anything other than an outright lie. As I mentioned above, however, suspecting a lie means suspecting a motive to lie. What motive would the Commission have for pretending that it did not know that Myers and Rumsfeld were participating in Clarke's conference?

The Commission would have had such a motive if Myers and Rumsfeld had said that they were doing something else at the time. Let us imagine that they had, and then that the 9/11 Commission had checked the videotape and found that these two men had instead been participating in Clarke's teleconference. Let us imagine that the Commission had then reported this fact. This exposure of these lies by Myers and Rumsfeld would have thrown into doubt all their other statements. Readers would have reasonably inferred that, if Myers and Rumsfeld lied about this, they must have been trying to cover up something and, therefore, probably lied about other things. This would have undermined the Commission's own account of 9/11, because it relies heavily on interviews with Rumsfeld, Myers, and other leaders of the US military. Accordingly, if Myers and Rumsfeld had lied about what they were doing that morning, the Commission might well have felt the need to cover up those lies, so as not to throw into doubt the credibility of the primary authorities for its own narrative about the day of 9/11.

And Myers and Rumsfeld did, in fact, say that they were doing other things that morning. I will first look at Myers' account of his own behavior, then compare it with Clarke's account. I will then do the same for Rumsfeld.

Myers on Myers: In a note, the Commission says: "The Vice Chairman was on Capitol Hill when the Pentagon was struck, and he saw smoke as his car made its way back to the building (Richard Myers interview, Feb. 17, 2004)." (463n199)

As we can see, this statement about the whereabouts of Richard Myers seems to be based solely on an interview with Myers himself. The Commission could have, to be sure, cited Secretary Rumsfeld's statement, according to which when he (Rumsfeld) entered the NMCC at 10:30, "Myers 'had just returned from Capitol Hill.'"[16] This, however, would have provided poor support, because according to Myers himself, he had been back for about 50 minutes, and the Commission itself has him in the NMCC by 10:00 (38). It is perhaps understandable, therefore, that the Commission did not cite Rumsfeld's supporting testimony. So it was left with Myers himself as the only one to testify that he had been to Capitol Hill.

Furthermore, lest one think that someone on the Commission staff simply misunderstood what Myers said, we can see from other sources that the Commission's statement fits with a rather elaborate tale Myers has evidently told about what he was doing on Capitol Hill. In James Bamford's book, *A Pretext for War*, we read the following account:

> Air Force General Richard Myers, the Vice Chairman [of the Joint Chiefs of Staff, was] in charge of the country's armed forces. But incredibly, he would remain unaware of what was going on around him during the entire series of attacks.
>
> Myers was on Capitol Hill waiting to meet with Georgia Senator Max Cleland about his upcoming confirmation hearings to become the new Joint Chiefs chairman. While in Cleland's outer office, he watched live television reports following the first crash into the World Trade Center and then went into Cleland's office for his routine meeting. There he would remain for the next forty-five minutes, self-promoting his talents to lead the military. . . .
>
> Through it all, the general in charge of the country's military was completely ignorant of the fact that the United States was under its worst attack in nearly two centuries.[17]

As his source for this information, Bamford cites an article by Sgt. Kathleen Rhem of the US military, which was published by the American Forces Press Service about six weeks after 9/11.[18]

As Bamford's final paragraph implies, this story is incredible. We are supposed to believe that after the North Tower of the World Trade Center was struck by an airplane, Air Force General Myers, the Acting Chairman of the Joint Chiefs, simply sat there watching TV coverage like an ordinary American citizen. We are supposed to believe that he did not call the NMCC, and that no one from it called him. We are then supposed to believe that he went into Cleland's office without telling Cleland's secretary to notify him if the TV coverage reported any further developments. We are then supposed to believe that even after the South Tower was struck, the secretary did not inform him and also that no one from the NMCC or anywhere else in the Pentagon called to notify and consult with him. We are even supposed to believe that he was still not called when the Pentagon itself was struck.

Given the incredible nature of this story, Bamford surely should have checked Sgt. Rhem's account against accounts provided by people who were not beneath Myers in the military chain of command. Of course, Bamford, who in a previous book exposed Operations Northwoods,[19] may not actually believe Rhem's account; he may simply be presenting it as part of the official story. In any case, we cannot fault Bamford for not comparing Rhem's account with the account provided by Richard Clarke, because Bamford's and Clarke's books came out at about the same time (early in 2004). But this is not true of *The 9/11 Commission Report*, which was not put into final form until many months after Clarke's book appeared. So let us look more closely at the story told by Myers, as reflected in the accounts given by Bamford and the Commission, then compare it with what is said about Myers in Clarke's narrative.

According to Bamford's account, Myers watched live TV coverage after the first crash, which occurred at 8:46, but then went into Cleland's office prior to the second crash, which occurred at 9:03. We can assume, accordingly, that he would have gone into Cleland's office between 8:55 and 9:02. He then reportedly remained there until about 9:40. This supposition would fit with the Commission's account, according to which "Myers was on Capitol Hill when the Pentagon was struck, and he saw smoke as his car made its way back to the building."

Clarke on Myers: Richard Clarke's account of his video teleconference— which, we recall, must have started about 9:15—begins with these statements:

> As I entered the Video Center, . . . I could see people rushing into studios around the city: Donald Rumsfeld at Defense and George Tenet at CIA. . . . Air Force four-star General Dick Myers was filling in for the Chairman of the Joint Chiefs, Hugh Shelton, who was over the Atlantic. Bob Mueller was at the FBI . . . .

Later, after Clarke's discussion with Jane Garvey, he had the following exchange with Myers:

> "JCS, JCS. I assume NORAD has scrambled fighters. . . ."

> "Not a pretty picture Dick." Dick Myers, himself a fighter pilot, [said,] "We are in the midst of Vigilant Warrior, a NORAD exercise, but . . . Langley is trying to get two [fighters] up now."

> "Okay, how long to CAP over D.C.?" . . . .

> "Fast as we can. Fifteen minutes?" Myers asked, looking at the generals and colonels around him. It was now 9:28.[20]

That account fits with NORAD's timeline of September 18, 2001. According to that timeline, it was at 9:24 that Langley received the scramble order. At 9:28, it would have still been trying to get two fighters up.

Clarke's narrative next tells about the pause (for the president's address), further discussions, the strike on the Pentagon, and the report that Cheney had said that the president had given shootdown authorization. After that, according to Clarke: "General Myers asked, 'Okay, shoot-down aircraft, but what are the ROE [Rules of Engagement]?'"[21] A little later, after a break, Clarke writes:

> We resumed the video conference. "DOD, DOD, go." I asked the Pentagon for an update on the fighter cover.
> Dick Myers had a status report. "We have three F-16s from Langley over the Pentagon. Andrews is launching fighters from the D.C. Air National Guard. . . ."[22]

Still later, after Clarke had returned from a trip down to the shelter conference room to see Cheney, several more topics were discussed. In the final sentence of Clarke's account of his video conference, which referred to discussions shortly after 3:00, we read: "'There are forty-two major Taliban bombing targets,' General Myers said, reviewing a briefing handed to him."[23]

According to Richard Clarke, therefore, General Myers participated in the White House video conference from the beginning and evidently—perhaps off and on—until the end. If Clarke's account is correct about this, the Commissioners could have learned about the participation of Myers simply by reading Clarke's book, the accuracy of which they could have confirmed by viewing the videotape. On the other hand, if they had discovered that Myers had not participated, they should have told us that Clarke's account is false. But the Commission fails even to mention Clarke's account, which has Myers not only in the Pentagon, but actively involved in a NORAD exercise. This failure makes it hard not to conclude that the Commission was deliberately attempting to protect Myers' own account from challenge.

We should also remind ourselves that the Commission could have easily cleared up this controversy if only Max Cleland had remained a member. As I reported in *The New Pearl Harbor*,[24] Cleland, a Democrat who had lost his Senate seat in the previous election, needed a job with a salary. Senate Democrats had recommended him for a Democratic slot on the board of the Export-Import Bank, and the White House sent this nomination to the Senate near the end of 2003. Being legally forbidden from holding both positions, Cleland resigned from the Commission (after which he was replaced by former Senator Bob Kerrey). But if Cleland had remained on the Commission, he could simply have confirmed or disconfirmed Myers' presence in his office from 8:45 to 9:45 on the morning of 9/11. Of course, having Cleland physically present at the Commission hearing was not necessary. The Commissioners could have simply telephoned Cleland to ask him about this, but it evidently did not occur to them to make this call. So we are simply left with the contradiction between the accounts by Myers and Clarke.

Rumsfeld on Rumsfeld: I turn now to the conflict between Clarke's statements about Rumsfeld, on the one hand, and Rumsfeld's account of his own behavior, on the other. Complicating this comparison is the fact that there are (at least) three versions of Rumsfeld's activities, all three of which were evidently authorized by Rumsfeld himself.

Version 1: Shortly after 9/11, Rumsfeld said that when the Pentagon was hit, he was in his office, which is on the fourth floor. He said that he then went downstairs to see what happened and was told that a plane had hit the Pentagon. He then started helping put people on stretchers and carry them to ambulances. He was "out there for awhile," after which he decided he should go back to his office and figure out what to do. This account was carried on the Department of Defense website as well as being in many newspaper and television stories.[25]

As for how long "awhile" was, a Defense Department statement four days after 9/11 said that it was "about half an hour."[26] Given the fact that Rumsfeld's office, which is located in the East Wing, is about 2,000 feet from the West Wing, it would have surely taken him at least 10 minutes simply to walk there and back. If he was then in the parking lot for 30 minutes, he would have been away from his office from about 9:40 until about 10:20.

Version 2: When he testified to the 9/11 Commission, Rumsfeld evidently told a rather revised tale. According to a Commission staff report issued in March, 2004, Rumsfeld said:

> I was in my office with a CIA briefer . . . . [A]t 9:38, the Pentagon shook with an explosion of then unknown origin. . . . I went outside

to determine what had happened. I was not there long because I was back in the Pentagon with a crisis action team shortly before or after 10:00 AM.[27]

In this account, there is nothing about his putting people on stretchers or otherwise helping out. He simply went out to see what happened, then got back to his office by about 10:00. He must have stayed a very short period, since much of the 20 minutes would have been consumed by walking there and back. He certainly did not stay "half an hour."

So, either Rumsfeld was not telling the truth to the Commission or else he and other people put untruths on the Department of Defense website. But the 9/11 Commission, in spite of its attempt to provide "the fullest possible account" of 9/11, evidently did not press Rumsfeld to clarify which of the two accounts, if either, was correct.

Version 3: In any case, *The 9/11 Commission Report* has produced still another version of Rumsfeld's activities during this period. It says: "After the Pentagon was struck, Secretary Rumsfeld went to the parking lot to assist with rescue efforts" (37).[28] The Commission also reports that at 9:44, NORAD was unable to locate Rumsfeld (38). It then says:

> He went from the parking lot to his office (where he spoke to the President [shortly after 10:00]), then to the Executive Support Center, where he participated in the White House video teleconference. He moved to the NMCC shortly before 10:30, in order to join Vice Chairman Myers. (43–44)

Here, interestingly, the Commission shows that it did know that Rumsfeld participated in Clarke's video conference, if only briefly. But the main problem with the Commission's version is that it simply combines the two previous ones, in spite of the contradiction between them. Like the first version, the Commission's version has Rumsfeld helping with rescue efforts. But like the second version, the Commission's version has him getting back to his office by 10:00. The Commission's version, accordingly, must be false.

The even more important question is whether all the versions of Rumsfeld's story are false. This possibility would be raised if it is true— as it has been suggested—that there may be a lack of any photographs or eyewitnesses to confirm that Rumsfeld was at the crash site at all.[29] We would, in any case, be forced to conclude that all three versions of

Rumsfeld on Rumsfeld are indeed false if we accept the truth of Richard Clarke's statements about Rumsfeld.

Clarke on Rumsfeld: As we saw earlier, Clarke's account begins thus: "As I entered the Video Center, . . . I could see people rushing into studios around the city: Donald Rumsfeld at Defense and George Tenet at CIA." Later in Clarke's narrative, after word was received about the strike on the Pentagon, Clarke said: "I can still see Rumsfeld on the screen." Shortly thereafter, Clarke writes:

> Rumsfeld said that smoke was getting into the Pentagon secure teleconferencing studio. Franklin Miller urged him to helicopter to DoD's alternate site. "I am too goddamn old to go to an alternate site," the Secretary answered. Rumsfeld moved to another studio in the Pentagon.

Still later, after Clarke had returned from a trip down to the shelter conference room to see Cheney, several more topics were discussed, and then: "CIA Director George Tenet was up next. . . . Defense Secretary Don Rumsfeld briefed on the status of forces.[30]

In Clarke's account, accordingly, Rumsfeld was not in his office when the Pentagon struck, as he said in his own account of his activities, but in the "secure teleconferencing studio" in the Pentagon. After the Pentagon was hit, furthermore, he did not walk down to the west wing to see what happened. He simply moved to another studio.

For the purposes of the present chapter, there are two main implications that follow from this discussion of the accounts of Rumsfeld's activities. First, the Commission was surely aware that these mutually inconsistent versions of Rumsfeld's activities exist, and yet it chose not to mention the fact. It would appear, therefore, that the Commission deliberately covered up the fact that Rumsfeld had lied in two and perhaps all three of his versions. A second implication is that if Clarke's account is true, then Rumsfeld, like Myers, would have been present to hear anything that might have been said about Flight 77, in spite of the Commission's attempt to claim the contrary.

NORMAN MINETA'S ACCOUNT

In the previous two sections, we have looked at accounts pointing to the possibility for the Pentagon to have learned from the FAA that an aircraft was headed towards the Pentagon. But another account, provided by Secretary of Transportation Norman Mineta, suggests that Vice President Cheney, at least, had direct knowledge of such an aircraft.

As we saw earlier, Mineta said, in his testimony before the 9/11 Commission on May 23, 2003, that he arrived at the Presidential Emergency Operations Center, where Vice President Cheney was in charge, at 9:20. During Mineta's testimony, he described the following episode:

> During the time that the airplane was coming in to the Pentagon, there was a young man who would come in and say to the Vice President, "The plane is 50 miles out." "The plane is 30 miles out." And when it got down to "the plane is 10 miles out," the young man also said to the Vice President, "Do the orders still stand?" And the Vice President turned and whipped his neck around and said, "Of course the orders still stand. Have you heard anything to the contrary?"[31]

When asked by Commissioner Timothy Roemer how long this conversation occurred after he arrived, Mineta said: "Probably about five or six minutes," which, as Roemer pointed out, would mean "about 9:25 or 9:26." With regard to what "the orders" referred to, Mineta assumed that they were orders to have the plane shot down.

There are, however, three problems with Mineta's assumption. In the first place, this interpretation would imply that Cheney had given shoot-down authorization at some time before 9:25, which is much earlier, as we will see below, than even Clarke says. Second, Mineta's interpretation would not fit with the subsequent facts, because the aircraft headed towards the Pentagon was *not* shot down. Third, Mineta's interpretation would not make the episode intelligible. Had Cheney given the expected order—the order to have an aircraft approaching the Pentagon shot down—we could not explain why the young man asked if the order still stood. It would have been abundantly obvious to him that it would continue to stand until the aircraft was actually shot down. His question would make sense, however, if "the orders" were ones that seemed unusual.

Some critics of the official account have suggested, therefore, that "the orders" in question were orders *not* to have the aircraft shot down. But of course this interpretation, while arguably being the more natural one, would also be very threatening to the Bush administration and the Pentagon.

It is not surprising, therefore, that although Mineta's account was released in the 9/11 Commission's staff report in May 2003, this account is not included, or even mentioned, in the Commission's final report. This omission provides rather clear evidence that the Commission's real mission was not to provide the fullest possible account of 9/11 but to defend the account provided by the Bush administration and the Pentagon.

WHEN WAS THE "UNIDENTIFIED AIRCRAFT" FIRST REPORTED?

Mineta's account, had it been included, would have created yet another problem for the 9/11 Commission's main claim about the strike on the Pentagon, which is that there was no warning about an unidentified aircraft heading towards Washington until 9:36 and hence only "one or two minutes" before the Pentagon was struck (34). Contrary to NORAD's 2001 timeline as well as to testimony by NORAD officials in May 2003, therefore, the Kean–Zelikow Commission says that "the military did not have 14 minutes "to protect the Pentagon." It had at most one or two minutes to react to the unidentified plane approaching Washington."(34). But Mineta's account, with its report that the approaching aircraft was 50 miles out, then 30, then 10, implies that government officials had far more than two minutes' notice.

With regard to the question of which account to believe, an investigation interested in the facts would have noted that Mineta's account agrees with previous accounts reported by the press. Virtually the same account—with the reports about the aircraft's being 50, 30, and then 10 miles out—was given by ABC News a year after 9/11. The only difference is that ABC said that the 50-mile report was given at 9:27 whereas Mineta placed it at "about 9:25 or 9:26."[32] Accordingly, the Mineta–ABC account says that Vice President Cheney knew about the unidentified aircraft about nine minutes earlier than the Commission now claims. So the government would have had 11 or 12 minutes to respond, not merely "one or two minutes."

Of course, the Commission's claim, strictly speaking, is that it was the military that had only one or two minutes to react, whereas the reports given by Mineta and ABC News refer to knowledge had by Vice President Cheney and others with him in the underground shelter. The Commission could have reconciled these stories by simply saying that neither Cheney, his Secret Service agents, nor the military liaison in the PEOC reported this information to the Pentagon. But that, of course, would not do. So the contradiction stands.

Moreover, besides the fact that the Commission's account contradicts press reports from the time and the testimony of the Bush administration's secretary of transportation, it contains an even more serious problem: It contradicts itself.

On the one hand, the Kean–Zelikow Commission tells us that the "one or two minutes" gave the Pentagon only sufficient time to get the previously unidentified aircraft identified. After the Pentagon learned about this unidentified aircraft at 9:36, it reportedly ordered an unarmed military C-130H cargo airplane that was already in the air "to identify and follow the suspicious aircraft." After which:

> The C-130H pilot spotted it, identified it as a Boeing 757, attempted to follow its path, and at 9:38, seconds after impact, reported to the control tower: 'looks like that aircraft crashed into the Pentagon sir.'" (25–26)

This element of its narrative is important, of course, because it, if true, would refute the allegation that the aircraft that hit the Pentagon was not a Boeing 757. Useful as it may be, however, this account seems difficult to reconcile with what we had been told earlier.

As saw in Chapter 1, the Commission repeated the well-known report about the amazing maneuver made by the aircraft before it struck the Pentagon. In this account, it was at 9:34—not 9:36—that the Secret Service got word from the airport about an unidentified aircraft. In this account, furthermore, we were told:

> American 77 was then 5 miles west-southwest of the Pentagon and began a 330-degree turn. At the end of the turn, it was descending through 2,200 feet, pointed towards the Pentagon. (9)

This element of the story, as we saw earlier, was referred to much later in *The 9/11 Commission Report*, where it remarked about the president's being impressed by "Hanjour's high-speed dive into the Pentagon" (334).

In the later report about getting the flight identified as a Boeing 757, however, there is nothing about this. The military pilot, after identifying the aircraft, simply "attempted to follow its path," then reported that it "looks like that aircraft crashed into the Pentagon" (25–26). Given the other story, we would expect the C-130H pilot to have made some comment about how difficult it was to "follow its path" while it was making that 330-degree downward spiral. And we would have expected this military pilot to have been at least as impressed as was the president that this other pilot could have performed such an amazing maneuver in a Boeing 757.

Besides evidently having trouble deciding exactly what story to tell about the final minutes of the aircraft that hit the Pentagon, the Commission also evidently had trouble deciding what time to assign to the first notification about this aircraft received by Cheney's Secret Service agents. On page 27 and 34, as we saw, the agents received this notification at 9:36. On page 9, they received it at 9:34. At the 9/11 Commission staff report on June 17, 2004, the agents received this notification at 9:32.

These internal contradictions within the Commission itself, in conjunction with the contradiction between the Commission's account (with any of its three times) and the reports by Mineta and ABC News (which say 9:25–9:27), suggest that the Commission finally settled on 9:36 not because of empirical evidence but because this time allowed it to claim that the military "had at most one or two minutes to react to the unidentified plane approaching Washington."

WHY WERE FIGHTER JETS NOT OVER WASHINGTON LONG BEFORE?

Most of the elements in the 9/11 Commission's account that we have discussed thus far—the FAA's failure to notify the military, the losing of Flight 77, the phantom aircraft, the error by the FAA controller and the lead pilot, the idea that there was no ongoing discussion between the FAA and the military, and the idea that the military had only one or two minutes' notice about an incoming aircraft—have served to explain why there were no military aircraft over Washington to prevent the strike on the Pentagon. Why, however, were there not fighter jets placed over the nation's capital even earlier—as soon as it was apparent that the nation was under attack? Why, in other words, was CAP not placed over Washington immediately after 9:03, when the second tower was struck?

NORAD's excuse is that the FAA did not tell it that Flight 77 was headed towards Washington. But would it not be obvious, once the military realized that a terrorist attack using airplanes was underway, that it should have sent up fighters to protect the nation's capital, even without the report of a specific threat?

This question is especially pressing in light of a 2002 story by William B. Scott in *Aviation Week and Space Technology*. After the second attack on the World Trade Center, according to Scott,

> Calls from fighter units . . . started pouring into NORAD and sector operations centers, asking, "What can we do to help?" At Syracuse, N.Y., an ANG commander told [NEADS Commander] Marr, "Give me 10 minutes and I can give you hot guns. Give me 30 minutes and I'll have heat-seeker [missiles]. Give me an hour and I can give you slammers." Marr replied, "I want it all."[33]

If this story is true, however, why were none of these fighters over Washington by 9:37? One would assume that the 9/11 Commission would have asked Colonel Marr or General Ralph Eberhart, the head of NORAD, why, if these offers "started pouring into NORAD," they were declined. If such offers were indeed declined and then NORAD later claimed that the Pentagon was struck because no fighters were available to protect Washington, it would appear that NORAD had deliberately left the nation's capital unprotected. This appearance, one would think, should have been worth a few minutes of the Commission's time. *The 9/11 Commission Report*, however, makes no mention of the report of these offers.

STILL MORE EVIDENCE AGAINST THE COMMISSION'S CLAIM

The evidence that challenges the Commission's account of Flight 77 and the strike on the Pentagon, we should recall, is not limited to the evidence provided in this chapter. Much of the strongest evidence was given in Chapter 3, which provided a cumulative argument against the claim that the aircraft that hit the Pentagon was Flight 77. The elements in this cumulative argument were: (1) the fact that Hani Hanjour, the alleged pilot of Flight 77, could not have performed the maneuver required for the aircraft to hit the Pentagon's west wing; (2) the fact that the Pentagon's west wing was the least likely part of the Pentagon for terrorists to strike; (3) the fact that photographs taken shortly after the strike show that the facade of the west wing had not yet collapsed and that the entrance hole created by the attacking aircraft was very small; (4) the fact that no remains of a Boeing 757 were visible either outside or inside the Pentagon (combined with the fact that fires, especially ordinary hydrocarbon fires, do not melt—let alone vaporize—airplanes); (5) the fact that any commercial aircraft, by virtue of not having a military transponder, would have been automatically shot down by the Pentagon's anti-missile batteries; and (6) the fact that the Pentagon has failed to release any videos showing that the attacking aircraft was indeed a Boeing 757.

For people who know about all this evidence, the refusal of the Commission even to mention it suggests that the Commissioners realized that it could not be countered. The Commission's only gesture in this direction is its attempt to provide evidence that the "unidentified aircraft" headed towards the Pentagon was, in fact, a Boeing 757. As we saw, however, the Commission's story about getting this identification made just before the aircraft struck the Pentagon conflicts with another account of the last minutes of this aircraft's journey. The Commission's sole rebuttal to all the above-cited evidence, in other words, is testimony that is contradicted on other pages of the Kean–Zelikow Report itself.

CONCLUSION

The 9/11 Commission has attempted to defend the US military against suspicion that it was guilty of complicity in the attack on the Pentagon. For those who know the problematic facts, however, this attempt does not even approach success.

The Commission has, in the first place, simply ignored virtually all the evidence suggesting that the aircraft that struck the Pentagon could not have been Flight 77 because it could not have been a Boeing 757.

In the second place, the Commission, in its determination to show that the US military had virtually no notice before the Pentagon was struck, has created a narrative filled with implausibilities, omissions, contradictions of other credible reports, and even self-contradictions. The implausibilities include the stories of Phantom Flight 11 and the Langley pilots flying out to sea. The omissions include the report that the FAA's Indianapolis Center did know about the hijacking of Flight 11 before Flight 77's erratic behavior began, the fact that the sophistication of the US military radar systems renders absurd the idea that Flight 77 could have been lost for over a half hour, and, most important, the evidence that the FAA and the US military had been in conversation about Flight 77 for a long period—a likelihood that the 9/11 Commission went to extreme lengths to refute, even to the point of covering up the inconsistencies in the accounts of the activities of Myers and Rumsfeld. The contradictions of other credible reports include those by Clarke and Mineta. The self-contradictions include the three different times given for the notification about the incoming aircraft and the two accounts of the final minutes of that aircraft before it struck the Pentagon.

The Commission's attempt to defend the US military's behavior in relation to Flight 77 is as unsuccessful as its attempts in relation to Flights 11 and 175. I turn now to its attempt to do the same thing—albeit with a different set of problems—in relation to Flight 93.

CHAPTER FIFTEEN

The Commission on Flight 93

At this point, the Commission has attempted to demonstrate, three-fourths of the central thesis of its first chapter. This thesis consists of the twofold claim that:

(1) The "nine minutes' notice" that NEADS received about Flight 11 before it struck the North Tower "was the most the military would receive of any of the four hijackings" (21).

(2) The military, in fact, received "no advance notice on the second [plane], no advance notice on the third, and no advance notice on the fourth" (31). Now, having argued its case regarding the first three planes, the Commission sets out to make its case about the fourth one, Flight 93. According to the Commission's report, here is what really happened.

THE FAA AGAIN FAILS TO MAKE THE CALL

The controller at the FAA's Cleveland Center received the last normal transmission from United Flight 93 at 9:27. Less than a minute later, this controller heard "unintelligible sounds of possible screaming," then noticed that Flight 93 had descended 700 feet. At 9:32, the controller heard a voice saying: "Keep remaining sitting. We have a bomb on board." The controller quickly notified his supervisor, and word quickly went up the chain of command: "By 9:34, word of the hijacking had reached FAA headquarters" (28).

But the quickness stopped there. At 9:36, the FAA's Cleveland Center asked the Herndon Command Center whether anyone had requested the military to intercept the flight. Cleveland even volunteered to make the call directly. "The Command Center," however, "told Cleveland that FAA personnel well above them in the chain of command had to make the decision to seek military assistance and were working on the issue" (28–29). This is perhaps the Commission's strongest assertion of its claim that the chain-of-command protocol prevented regional FAA centers from calling the military directly. The Commission is here also suggesting that FAA officials at Herndon and FAA headquarters stubbornly refused to call the military even when they were implored to do so by FAA personnel in the field.

If we believe this account, we must believe that Monte Belger, the Acting Deputy Administrator at FAA headquarters, and Ben Sliney, the new National Operations Manager at the Herndon Command Center, perhaps along with other officials at those places, had to debate whether the report of a hijacked airliner with a bomb on board was sufficient to justify bothering the military. They would, furthermore, have debated this question for a long time. Another ten minutes later, at 9:46, Herndon told FAA headquarters that United 93 was "twenty-nine minutes out of Washington, D.C." (29). One would suppose that this report would finally have prodded the FAA's hijack coordinator—who was in Washington, where the plane was headed—to pick up the phone and call the NMCC. But instead, another 3 minutes later, at 9:49 ("13 minutes after Cleveland Center had asked about getting military help"), the following conversation between Herndon and FAA headquarters reportedly occurred:

> COMMAND CENTER: Uh, do we want to think, uh, about scrambling aircraft?
>
> FAA HEADQUARTERS: Oh, God, I don't know.
>
> COMMAND CENTER: Uh, that's a decision somebody's gonna have to make probably in the next ten minutes.
>
> FAA HEADQUARTERS: Uh, ya know everybody just left the room. (29)

The Commission's point in printing this exchange was clearly to convey the impression that incompetence continued to reign at the FAA.

In any case, at 9:53, we are told, Monte Belger was discussing with Peter Challan, the deputy director for air traffic services, whether to ask the military to have planes scrambled. Or at least someone reported that they were discussing this—both of them say that they cannot remember the conversation (29–30, 461n167). But whether they had the conversation or not, they did not make the call. During the next 10 minutes, according to the Commission's narrative, FAA headquarters continued to receive more information about the progress of Flight 93— until this flight, at 10:03, crashed near Shanksville, Pennsylvania, 125 miles from Washington (30).

MILITARY IGNORANCE OF THE HIJACKING OF FLIGHT 93

In case some readers missed the main point of this narrative, the Kean–Zelikow Report provides a summary statement:

Despite the discussions about military assistance, no one from FAA headquarters requested military assistance regarding United 93. Nor did any manager at FAA headquarters pass any of the information it had about United 93 to the military. (30)

This conclusion is of utmost importance, of course, because from the beginning there have been suspicions that Flight 93 was shot down by the US military. We saw in Chapter 11, furthermore, that there is much evidence to support this suspicion. The 9/11 Commission's report does not, however, mention any of this evidence. It simply says: "The NEADS air defenders never located the flight or followed it on their radar scopes. The flight had already crashed by the time they learned it was hijacked" (31).

This is the central claim of the Commission's discussion about Flight 93, as is shown by the fact that it is repeated three more times:

By the time the military learned about the flight, it had crashed. (34)
By 10:03, when United 93 crashed in Pennsylvania, there had been no mention of its hijacking [to the military]. (38)
NORAD did not even know the plane was hijacked until after it had crashed. (44)

The implication of this oft-repeated claim is that, since the military did not know that Flight 93 had been hijacked, it could not possibly have shot it down. That would follow, of course, if the claim is true.

But there are reasons to believe that it is not true. In regard to Flights 175 and 77, as we saw, the teleconferences were nemeses for the Commission's claims. It argued that the US military did not know that Flights 175 and 77 had been hijacked because (1) the military did not receive telephone calls making formal notification about these hijackings and (2) the teleconferences began too late to be of any help. In each case, however, the claim about the teleconferences was contradicted by several reports to the contrary by people in position to know. The Commission's claim with regard to Flight 93—that "[b]y the time the military learned about the flight, it had crashed"—is also challenged by reports about teleconferences.

WORTHLESS TELECONFERENCES?

With regard to Flight 93, the Kean–Zelikow Report cannot try to protect the military's ignorance by claiming that the teleconferences began too late. Even its own extremely late timeline entails that all three teleconferences had begun by 9:30. What it does instead is to claim that all the teleconferences were essentially worthless—at least with respect to the possibility that the military might have learned about the hijacking of UA 93 from the FAA. I will look at the Commission's treatments, in turn, of the FAA-initiated teleconference, the NMCC-initiated teleconference, and the White House video teleconference.

The FAA-Initiated Teleconference: The Commission's concern to isolate the FAA from the Defense Department is evident in its description of the FAA-initiated conference. It says:

> At about 9:20, security personnel at FAA headquarters set up a hijacking teleconference with several agencies, including the Defense Department. The NMCC officer who participated told us that the call was monitored only periodically because the information was sporadic, it was of little value, and there were other important tasks. (36)

Clearly, given the Commission's account, the NMCC could have learned nothing from this teleconference—except that it was "of little value."

The NMCC-Initiated Teleconference: The Kean–Zelikow Commission says:

> Inside the NMCC, the deputy director for operations called for an all-purpose "significant event" conference. It began at 9:29 with a brief recap. . . . The FAA was asked to provide an update, but the line was silent because the FAA had not been added to the call. (37)

So, the NMCC first refuses to participate in the FAA teleconference, then fails to add the FAA to its own teleconference. In any case, we are next told that, after a brief pause:

> [T]he call resumed at 9:37 as an air threat conference call, which lasted more than eight hours. The President, Vice President, Secretary of Defense, Vice Chairman of the Joint Chiefs of Staff, and Deputy National Security Advisor Stephen Hadley all

participated in this teleconference at various times, as did military personnel from the White House underground shelter and the President's military aide on Air Force One.

Operators worked feverishly to include the FAA, but they had equipment problems and difficulty finding secure phone numbers. (37)

In other words, the NMCC was somehow able to get everyone included in its call except the FAA. The Pentagon operators had no "equipment problems and difficulty finding secure phone numbers" in relation to "[t]he President, Vice President, Secretary of Defense, Vice Chairman of the Joint Chiefs of Staff, . . . Deputy National Security Advisor Stephen Hadley" or "military personnel from the White House underground shelter and the President's military aide on Air Force One." The NMCC had problems getting connected only with the FAA—the primary organization that regularly, by means of secure telephones, informs the NMCC about potential crises involving airplanes.

The Commission's comedy-of-errors account then continues with this statement:

> NORAD asked three times to confirm the presence of the FAA in the teleconference. The FAA representative who finally joined the call at 10:17 had no familiarity with or responsibility for hijackings, no access to decisionmakers, and none of the information available to senior FAA officials. (37)

This statement—besides emphasizing that NORAD really did want to hear from the FAA—informs us that when the FAA did finally get joined to the NMCC teleconference, it put an ignoramus on the phone. We are also informed, however, that this ultimately made no difference, because this did not happen until 10:17, by which time Flight 93 had already crashed. Once again there was no chance for the FAA to let the military know about this hijacked airliner.

Clarke's White House Video Teleconference: The Commission admits that both the FAA and the Defense Department were represented in Richard Clarke's teleconference. But it says that "none of the information conveyed in the White House video teleconference, at least in the first hour, was being passed to the NMCC" (36). Given the Commission's claim that Clarke's conference did not start until 9:25, this "first hour" would have run from 9:25 until 10:25. It would, therefore, have covered the period during which the shootdown authorization was given and transmitted and UA Flight 93 crashed.

If we had only the Commission's account of this teleconference, we would have no basis for challenging its claim that no information could have been passed from the FAA to the NMCC about Flight 93. As we have seen, however, we have Clarke's own account, and it paints a very different picture.

For one thing, the Commission claims, as we saw in Chapter 14, that "none of [the three] teleconferences—at least before 10:00—included the right officials from both the FAA and the Defense Department." However, according to Clarke's account, as we also saw, that statement is not true, because his conference involved FAA head Jane Garvey, Secretary of Defense Donald Rumsfeld, and Acting Chairman of the Joint Chiefs Richard Myers.

Another feature of Clarke's account is even more directly threatening to the Commission's claim that the US military did not learn about the hijacking of Flight 93 until after it crashed. According to Clarke, when his teleconference resumed, after the pause to listen to the president at 9:30, the following exchange occurred:

> "FAA, FAA, go, Status report. How many aircraft do you still carry as hijacked?"
> Garvey read from a list: "All aircraft have been ordered to land at the nearest field. Here's what we have as potential hijacks: Delta 1989 over West Virginia, United 93 over Pennsylvania. . ."
> [Secret Service Director Brian] Stafford slipped me a note. "Radar shows aircraft headed this way." Secret Service had a system that allowed them to see what FAA's radar was seeing.
> Ralph Seigler stuck his head into the room, "There's been an explosion in the Pentagon parking lot, maybe a car bomb!"[1]

After this, as we saw in the previous chapter, Clarke reported still seeing Rumsfeld on the screen and then talking to Myers.

According to Clarke's account, then, both Rumsfeld and Myers would have learned before 9:40 that United 93 had likely been hijacked. And surely, assuming the attacks on the WTC and the Pentagon to be surprise attacks by foreign terrorists, Rumsfeld and Myers would have immediately conveyed Garvey's information about Flight 93 to the

NMCC. If Clarke's account is accepted as accurate at this point, therefore, the 9/11 Commission's claim about the military's ignorance about Flight 93 is completely undermined.

Clarke's account here, incidentally, undermines not only the Commission's claim about Flight 93 but also its claims about the other flights, at least UA 175 and AA 77. I refer to his revelation, mentioned in Chapter 4, that the Secret Service can see everything the FAA does. And we can certainly call this a "revelation," rather than simply an "allegation," because there can be little doubt as to its truth. If the Secret Service has the job of protecting the president, it would surely be hooked into the FAA's radar systems. And if this is the case, then the Commission's case, built on the idea that only the FAA knew about the hijackings, collapses.

If we accept Clarke's account, furthermore, we have a basis for questioning a central feature of the Commission's account of the NMCC-initiated conference. The Kean–Zelikow Report says:

> At 9:48, a representative from the White House shelter asked if there were any indications of another hijacked aircraft. The deputy director for operations mentioned the Delta flight and concluded that "that would be the fourth possible hijack." . . .
> By 10:03, when United 93 crashed in Pennsylvania, there had been no mention of its hijacking and the FAA had not yet been added to the teleconference. (38)

Even if we accepted the final clause—which shows again the Commission's intense desire to convince us that not a single message could have been conveyed from the FAA to the US military until after Flight 93 had crashed—we would still have a basis for questioning the assertion that "there had been no mention of [United 93's] hijacking." If Clarke's account can be trusted, as we saw above, Rumsfeld and Myers would have heard Garvey talk about not only Delta 1989 but also United 93. And they would have surely told the NMCC.

One of the many failings of the Kean–Zelikow Report was its failure to deal with Clarke's account in spite of its direct challenge to the Commission's own.

WHY WERE THERE THREE TELECONFERENCES?

Another failing was the fact that, although the Commission reported that there were three teleconferences, it did not ask why. The Commission does say that these teleconferences were in some competition with each other and that this competition contributed to the fact that, at least in the eyes of the Commission, they were largely worthless. In making this point, the Commission quotes one witness as saying: "[It] was almost like there were parallel decisionmaking processes going on. . . . [I]n my mind they were competing venues for command and control and decisionmaking" (36). But if in the Commission's mind, the fact that there were three simultaneous teleconferences was one of the major contributors to the success of the attack on the Pentagon and the failure to intercept Flight 93 (so that, in the Commission's thinking, it probably would have struck the White House or the Capitol Building if the passengers had not caused it to crash [44–45]), then finding out why there were three teleconferences should have been a major item on the Commission's agenda.

Had the Commissioners asked Laura Brown of the FAA about this, she would presumably have told them what she told me by telephone— that the normal protocol was for the FAA to initiate phone bridges that connected FAA headquarters, the FAA Command Center at Herndon, and regional FAA facilities with the NMCC and NORAD (as well as with the Secret Service and other governmental agencies). It was not normal protocol, she emphasized, for the NMCC to initiate its own teleconference. If that is the case, then the Commission should have asked those in charge of the NMCC why they thought it wise to violate the normal protocol by establishing their own teleconference, rather than participating fully and actively in the FAA-initiated teleconference.

One reason why this question needed to be asked arises from the very fact—at least the alleged fact—that the competition between the teleconferences hindered communication between the FAA and the US military. On the one hand, we are told that the NMCC, in spite of sincere efforts, was unable to get the FAA connected to its teleconference until 10:17. On the other hand, we are told that although the NMCC was successfully connected to the FAA by means of the FAA-initiated conference call, "the call was monitored only periodically [by the NMCC] because the information was sporadic, it was of little value, and there were other important tasks." The more important tasks presumably included participating in the NMCC's own teleconference, which, unfortunately, could not get connected to the FAA because of "equipment problems and difficulty finding secure phone numbers."

A serious investigation would have asked whether this was not just all too convenient for the military's story, according to which the military received no information about the flights in time to intercept them. Given the fact that sometimes motive can be inferred from consequence (as part of the more general truth that cause can often be inferred from effect), should the Commission not have explored the possibility that the NMCC violated standard protocol by setting up its own teleconference precisely in order to be able to make this claim? The fact that the Kean–Zelikow Commission's final report shows no sign of having explored this question is one more reason to conclude that it was not a serious investigation actually aimed at getting the truth.

WHY DID GENERAL WINFIELD HAVE HIMSELF REPLACED BY CAPTAIN LEIDIG?

As we saw above, the 9/11 Commission referred to the fact that the NMCC-initiated conference call was made by "the deputy director for operations" (37). As I pointed out earlier, this deputy director was Captain Charles Leidig, who was running the operation because the director, Brigadier General Montague Winfield, had asked him to sit in for him. Leidig himself explained this to the Commission during his testimony on June 17, 2004, reading this prepared statement:

> On 10 September 2001, Brigadier General Winfield, U.S. Army, asked that I stand a portion of his duty as Deputy Director for Operations, NMCC, on the following day. I agreed and relieved Brigadier General Winfield at 0830 on 11 September 2001.[2]

Leidig also pointed out that he had only recently qualified to perform this duty. He had become the Deputy for NMCC Operations about two months before 9/11 and had only qualified in August to stand watch in Winfield's place. As far as we can tell from his statement, 9/11 was his first day actually to do this.

One might think that the 9/11 Commission would have found all this curious, namely:

1. That Winfield had planned the day before to turn over his duties to his deputy for part of the day that turned out to be the most dramatic and fateful day of the NMCC's existence;

2. That the time at which Winfield actually asked Leidig to take over on 9/11 was 8:30 AM—which was 15 minutes after Flight 11 had shown

the standard signs of a hijacking and 10 minutes after phone bridges connecting the FAA and the NMCC had been initiated—at least, Tom Flocco tells us, according to Laura Brown (at first) and someone from the Department of Transportation.

3. That Leidig was inexperienced in this role—as suggested by the fact that he originally initiated the teleconference as merely a "significant event" call—which would, as the Commission explains, merely "seek to gather information"—so that it later had to be upgraded to an "air threat" call (37, 463n194).

Suspicious minds, looking at all this, might wonder if the NMCC was building in an "inexperience" defense, meaning that what appeared to be failures by the NMCC could be dismissed as failures of communication, explainable by Leidig's inexperience in directing teleconferences.

Tom Flocco has such a mind. Pointing out that reports at the time commented on the "confusion and chaos" and "abysmal handling of communications" during that day, Flocco entitles his essay about the substitution "Rookie in the 9-11 Hot Seat?" Flocco makes his point clear by referring to the possibility of "an overt military stand-down on 9/11— seemingly masked by feigned confusion, chaos, and screwed up communications."[3]

The Kean–Zelikow Commission, however, revealed no sign in its final report that it harbored any such suspicions. One would think that, at the very least, the Commission would have asked Winfield why he did not resume his duties after the first attack on the World Trade Center, or at least after the second attack. Would his failure to do so not constitute extreme dereliction of duty? Would a responsible general leave a "rookie in the hot seat" on such a day? But apparently even this question was not raised.

The president, furthermore, seemed to share the Commission's judgment that there was no reason to question the performance of either Winfield or Leidig. "In May, 2003," Flocco reports, "Bush nominated Brigadier General Montague Winfield for promotion to the two-star rank of Major General and Captain Charles Leidig has recently been nominated by the President to the two-star rank of Navy Admiral."[4] They were both evidently perceived as having performed their respective duties well.

WHEN WAS THE SHOOT-DOWN AUTHORIZATION GIVEN?

The Commission's central claim about Flight 93 is, as we have seen, that "[b]y the time the military learned about the flight, it had crashed." This claim, which is explicitly made, is primarily important for the support it gives to the Commission's implicit claim—that the US military did not shoot down Flight 93. The fact that this negative claim remains merely implicit suggests, perhaps, that the Commission considered the very mention of it, even for the purpose of refuting it, too dangerous. In any case, one attempt by the Commission to support this claim, which we examined above, was its argument that the military could not have learned about Flight 93 from any of the teleconferences.

But the Commission's main support for its claim about Flight 93 is a new timeline for the events surrounding the authorization finally given to fighter pilots to shoot down hijacked airliners. If this new timeline is accepted, it clinches the Commission's case for its implicit negative claim. As we will see, however, this new timeline contradicts prior reports of when the events in question happened.

The shoot-down authorization, everyone seems to agree, was given by Vice President Cheney while he was in the "shelter conference room," the informal name for the Presidential Emergency Operations Center (PEOC), which is under the east wing of the White House. According to the 9/11 Commission, here is how and when this came about.

At 10:02, the Secret Service agents with the vice president received word from the FAA that an aircraft was headed towards Washington (41). Then between 10:10 and 10:15, the FAA reported that this aircraft was only 80 miles away (41). The FAA meant UA 93, but this plane had, of course, crashed at 10:03, so the FAA had made another big mistake (30). But neither the military nor Cheney's Secret Service agents knew this, so the military asked Cheney for permission to engage, and he gave it, said Libby later, "in about the time it takes a batter to decide to swing" (41).[5]

However, since this was seven to twelve minutes after Flight 93 had crashed, the implication is that this plane could not have possibly been shot down by the US military. The Commission further strengthens this argument by claiming not only that the military would probably never shoot down a plane without White House authorization (45), but also that it was not until 10:31 that this authorization was communicated to the military (45, 42).[6]

The Commission's case here has evidently been widely accepted. For example, in the program on National Public Radio that I mentioned in the Introduction, it was said that one of the things "we now know," thanks to *The 9/11 Commission Report*, is that Vice President Cheney's authorization to the US military to shoot down any remaining hijacked airliners "came too late."

The Commission makes this case, however, only by contradicting many reports that have been widely accepted. Having mentioned these in Chapter 11, I will here simply list most of them, after discussing the first one at greater length, for illustrative purposes. The Commission contradicts:

1. The report that fighter jets were given shoot-down orders shortly after 9:56 (rather than at 10:30). This report was contained in stories published by *USA Today*, the *Washington Post*, ABC News, and CBS News.[7] To illustrate, I will quote some of the account provided by James Bamford, who based it on the transcript of the ABC News program, which was entitled "9/11." Bamford writes:

> As United 93 got closer and closer to the White House, . . . Cheney conferred with Secretary of Defense Donald Rumsfeld and then asked Bush to order the United jetliner shot down. . . . Bush, however, immediately passed the buck back to Cheney, leaving the decision to him as to whether to give the final okay to shoot down the plane. . . . A few minutes later, Cheney passed the order to . . . the Pentagon's War Room. . . . Sitting in the glassed-in Battle Cab of NORAD's Northeast Air Defense Sector Operations Center at Rome, New York, Air Force Colonel Robert Marr received the call. Then he sent out word to air traffic controllers to instruct fighter pilots to destroy the United jetliner. . . . "United Airlines Flight 93 will not be allowed to reach Washington, D.C.," said Marr.[8]

Bamford concludes, as did the ABC program, with the official story, according to which the military did not need to shoot down UA 93, because the passengers caused it to crash.

The present point, however, is that Bamford's account illustrates how well publicized the then-standard view was, according to which the shoot-down authorization was not only given specifically for Flight 93 but was also given before it crashed. If that story was false, as the Kean–Zelikow Report now insists, must we not wonder why the White House and the Pentagon did not call press conferences in order to set the record straight? Why did they not demand a retraction from ABC News and other news organizations that were telling the same story? In any case, having discussed this first report at some length, I will now simply summarize a number of reports that are contradicted.

2. A report that shortly after the Secret Service, following the strike on the Pentagon, told Andrews Air Force Base, "Get in the air now!", someone from the White House declared the Washington area a "free-fire zone." One of the pilots later said: "That meant we were given authority to use force, if the situation required it, in defense of the nation's capital, its property and people."[9] This story suggests that the shoot-down authorization may have been given at 9:45 or even a little earlier.

3. Reports in stories published by the *Pittsburgh Post-Gazette* and the *Washington Post* that the information that the aircraft was 80 miles out, followed by Cheney's permission to engage it, came before Flight 93 crashed (rather than afterwards, between 10:10 and 10:15), and that then, after this permission was granted, an F-16 went in pursuit of Flight 93.[10]

4. Reports by CBS television and a flight controller that Flight 93 was being tailed by at least one F-16.[11]

5. Reports on September 15, 2001, in the *Boston Herald* and the *New York Times*, according to which Deputy Secretary of Defense Paul Wolfowitz said that "the Air Force was tracking the hijacked plane that crashed in Pennsylvania . . . and had been in a position to bring it down if necessary."[12]

6. The statement by Major Daniel Nash, one of the two F-15 pilots sent to New York City, that he was told that a military F-16 had shot down an airliner in Pennsylvania.[13]

7. Reports from people both inside UA 93 and on the ground, summarized in Chapter 11, suggesting that the plane was brought down by a military missile.

The Commission does not refute any of these earlier reports, which had been generally accepted. It simply ignores them. We again have revisionism without evidence or even argument.

RICHARD CLARKE ON THE SHOOT-DOWN AUTHORIZATION

The Commission's account is also contradicted by Richard Clarke's narrative. Clarke says that he telephoned down to the shelter conference room shortly after 9:30. Reaching his liaison to Cheney, Clarke told him to

request authorization for "the Air Force to shoot down any aircraft—
including a hijacked passenger flight—that looks like it is threatening to
attack and cause large-scale death on the ground." Although Clarke says
that he expected the decision to be slow in coming, his liaison called back
some time before Air Force One had taken off—which it finally did at
about 9:55—to say: "Tell the Pentagon they have authority from the
President to shoot down hostile aircraft, repeat, they have authority to shoot
down hostile aircraft." Clarke reports that he was "amazed at the speed of
the decisions coming from Cheney and through him, from Bush."[14]

As we saw before, several news sources, including ABC and CBS
News and the *New York Times*, had said that the shoot-down
authorization came shortly after 9:56—that is, shortly after Air Force
One had become airborne. Clarke's narrative puts it before the
presidential plane had taken off, hence several minutes earlier. Clarke, in
fact, suggests that he learned of Cheney's order just after the evacuation
of the White House began at about 9:45. Clarke, therefore, seems to
suggest that he learned of the authorization by 9:50.[15] Clarke's narrative
is supported, furthermore, by the second of the six reports summarized
above, according to which the Secret Service told fighter pilots, perhaps
prior to 9:45, to treat the airspace over Washington as a "free-fire zone."

The Commission does not directly challenge Clarke's narrative. It
simply says: "Clarke reported that they were asking the President for
authority to shoot down aircraft. Confirmation of that authority came at
10:25" (37). So, although the Commission acknowledges the truth of
Clarke's report that he was involved in seeking shoot-down authorization,
it simply ignores his own report as to when he received word of this
authorization, blithely saying that he received it at 10:25, more than 35
minutes later than Clarke himself suggests. The Commission does not
explain how Clarke's memory could have been so confused, or why he
would have lied. It simply gives a much later time.

To be credible, as we saw earlier, a revisionist account must explain
why the received account is false. It should also explain the origin of the
reports on which the received account was based. The Commission,
however, does not refute any of these previously accepted reports. It also
does not explain how, if they were false, they arose. The Commission
simply gives its own new timeline, then rests its claim—that the
shootdown authorization was not given until after 10:10—on this new
timeline. Its implicit argument appears to be: Given this timeline, these

other reports could not possibly be true. That logic is impeccable. But the Commission would first need to give us a credible case for its revisionist timeline, and this it has not done.

WHEN DID CHENEY GO TO THE SHELTER?

This revisionist timeline, furthermore, contradicts still other reports. The new timeline, as we saw, claims that it was not until 10:02 that the Secret Service agents with the Vice President received word of an aircraft approaching Washington. This claim is bolstered by the Commission's claim that Cheney did not arrive in the PEOC until "shortly before 10:00, perhaps at 9:58" (40).

This time is in turn bolstered by the Commission's way of responding to the report, contained in the received account (having been told even by Cheney himself), that the vice president was hustled down to the shelter conference room after word was received that a plane was headed towards the White House. The Commission says that at 9:33, a tower supervisor at Reagan National Airport told the Secret Service that "an aircraft [is] coming at you and not talking with us." The Commission claims, however, that the Secret Service agents immediately received another message, telling them that the aircraft had turned away from the White House, so "[n]o move was made to evacuate the Vice President at this time" (39).

Having dismissed that earlier time for the Vice President's journey downstairs, the Commission then tells us that the Secret Service did not order Cheney's evacuation until "just before 9:36," so that Cheney did not enter the underground corridor until 9:37. The Commission next claims that even then Cheney did not go straight to the shelter conference room at the other end of the corridor. Rather:

> Once inside, Vice President Cheney and the agents paused in an area of the tunnel that had a secure phone, a bench, and television. The Vice President asked to speak to the President, but it took time for the call to be connected. He learned in the tunnel that the Pentagon had been hit, and he saw television coverage of the smoke coming from the building. (40)

We next learn that getting the call connected, watching TV, and talking to the president took a long time—20 minutes or so:

The Secret Service logged Mrs. Cheney's arrival at the White House and she joined her husband in the tunnel. According to contemporaneous notes, at 9:55 the Vice President was still on the phone with the President. . . . After the call ended, Mrs. Cheney and the Vice President moved from the tunnel to the shelter conference room. . . . We have concluded, from available evidence, that the Vice President arrived in the room shortly before 10:00, perhaps at 9:58. (40)

This timeline, however, contradicts earlier reports, according to which the Secret Service agents took Cheney to the corridor leading to the shelter conference room much earlier than 9:36. The *New York Times* and the *Telegraph* said it was about 9:06. An eyewitness account—by David Bohrer, a White House photographer—said it occurred "just after 9:00."[16] The Commission, accordingly, has given a time far later than the previously reported times. Its time of 9:36 is also contradicted by the report by ABC News that Cheney was already in the PEOC at 9:27 when he was told that a flight was 50 miles from Washington.[17] So either those reporters were terribly misinformed or else the 9/11 Commission is trying to revise history not for the purpose of providing a more accurate account but solely for the purpose of defending the US military against the suspicion that it shot down Flight 93.

The Commission's time is also contradicted by Richard Clarke. From his account of what happened that morning, we can infer that he went to Cheney's office, where Condoleezza Rice was meeting with the vice president, at about 9:06. (Clarke reports, as we saw earlier, that he rushed directly to Cheney's office after arriving at the White House just after the South Tower had been hit, hence only a few minutes after 9:03.) After what appears to have been no more than a five-minute conversation, Rice reportedly said that the Secret Service wanted Cheney and her to go to the bomb shelter (meaning the PEOC). Cheney then began gathering up his papers to go with the eight Secret Service agents who were waiting outside his office. Clarke's account, therefore, seems to suggest that Cheney went below at about 9:12.[18]

That Cheney actually went down at about that time is also suggested by subsequent developments in Clarke's narrative. He says that he and Rice went directly to the Video Teleconferencing Center for their teleconference, which evidently began about 9:15. After spending a few minutes there, Rice reportedly said: "I'm going to the PEOC to be with the Vice President. Tell us what you need." Clarke replied: "What I need is an open line to Cheney and you." Clarke then reports, as we saw, that he forwarded requests for Cheney on that line shortly after 9:30, then had answers back before 9:55.[19] Clarke's account, accordingly, fits with the various news reports saying that Cheney went to the PEOC much earlier than the Kean–Zelikow Report now claims.

In constructing its new historical reality, in fact, the Kean–Zelikow Report even contradicts Cheney's own account, provided on *Meet the Press* just five days after 9/11.[20] In this interview with Tim Russert, Cheney said that shortly after witnessing the second strike on the World Trade Center (9:03), he talked by telephone with the president about what the latter would say in his address to the nation. Cheney then reported that it was only "several minutes" later when the Secret Service agents came into his office, grabbed him, and moved him "very rapidly" to the underground corridor, "because they had received a report that an airplane was headed for the White House." (In Cheney's account, unlike that of the 9/11 Commission, that report did not immediately get canceled.) In this account, Cheney's telephone conversation with the president had to occur sometime between "shortly before 9:15," when Bush left the classroom (39), and 9:25, when a photograph shows Bush sitting in a holding room, waiting to give his address (which began at 9:30).[21] Indeed, the president's own daily diary says that the call began at 9:15, as a note in the Commission's report points out (463n204). Even if we suppose that this conversation ran until 3 minutes before the 9:25 photograph was taken, it would have ended at 9:22. If it was only "several minutes" later that Cheney was hurried to the underground corridor, Cheney himself would seem to have supported the report from ABC News, according to which he was already in the underground facility at 9:27.

Finally, as we have seen, the Commission's reconstruction is flatly and convincingly contradicted by Norman Mineta's eyewitness testimony. Besides reporting that when he arrived at the PEOC, Cheney was already there, Mineta also indicated that Cheney had already been there long enough to give "orders" (which Mineta, perhaps wrongly, assumed to be shoot-down orders). Mineta's account would seem, therefore, to support Clarke's narrative, which suggests that Cheney left for the shelter by about 9:12.

For the Commission now to claim that Cheney was not even ordered to go underground until 9:36, therefore, is revisionism of a rather audacious sort.

This revisionism is, furthermore, unsupported. The Commission makes no attempt, for example, to explain how Cheney could have gotten the time wrong only five days after the event. Although it cites a Cheney interview with *Newsweek* on November 19, 2001, the Commission makes no mention of Cheney's much better known interview with Tim Russert on September 16, in which he implied that he had gone below at about 9:25. The main support for the Commission's view is a Secret Service report, which allegedly says that the Vice President was not taken into the underground corridor until 9:37. The Commission admits, however, that it was told in a 2004 briefing with the Secret Service that "the 9:37 entry time in their timeline was based on alarm data, which is no longer retrievable" (464n209). This aspect of the Commission's new timeline, accordingly, has no documentation.

Worse, it is flatly contradicted by the eyewitness testimony given before the Commission by Norman Mineta, the Secretary of Transportation. In constructing its revisionary timeline, the Kean–Zelikow Commission implies that either Mineta was lying or else his memory of his experiences that morning had become very confused. But it is hard to imagine what motive Mineta would have for lying about his time of arrival at the PEOC and about what he observed there. It is equally hard to suppose that the events of a morning like that would not be permanently seared into his memory. Furthermore, as we saw earlier, his and Clarke's accounts agree, and he and ABC News agree almost to the minute as to the time of the conversation about the plane that was at first 50 miles out.

We must conclude, therefore, that the timeline of the Kean–Zelikow Commission has been reconstructed not on the basis of new evidence but purely to support the claim that Cheney could not have given his shoot-down order until after Flight 93 had already crashed.

SHOOT-DOWN AUTHORIZATION FROM THE PRESIDENT: A RED HERRING?

From the outset, the official story about 9/11 has involved the notion that authorization to shoot down hijacked airliners can come only from the president of the United States. In his appearance on *Meet the Press*, Vice President Cheney even suggested that the "question of whether or not we would intercept commercial aircraft" was "a presidential-level decision."[22] Most informed commentators, realizing that interception is a fairly routine matter, which is carried out about 100 times a year, have not been taken in by this obfuscation. But the belief that only the president can authorize the shooting down of airplanes has persisted. Without that belief, most of the controversies that have surrounded the shoot-down authorization would not exist.

We have already explored one of these controversies—the question of exactly when Vice President Cheney received the authorization from the president and then conveyed this authorization to the US military. The Commission, as we have seen, places this event much later than every prior source.

Another question has been whether Cheney actually did discuss this matter with the president or whether he gave the authorization on his own. The existence of this controversy is mildly reflected in the following remarkable passage in the Commission's report:

> The Vice President remembered placing a call to the President just after entering the shelter conference room. . . . The Vice President stated that he called the President to discuss the rules of engagement for the CAP. He recalled feeling that it did no good to establish the CAP unless the pilots had instructions on whether they were authorized to shoot if the plane would not divert. He said the President signed off on that concept. The President said he remembered such a conversation, and . . . emphasized to us that he had authorized the shootdown of hijacked aircraft. . . . Rice . . . remembered hearing [the Vice President] inform the President, "Sir, the CAPs are up. Sir, they're going to want to know what to do." Then she recalled hearing him say, "Yes sir." . . . Among the sources that reflect other important events of that morning, there is no documentary evidence for this call. . . . Others nearby who were taking notes, such as the Vice President's chief of staff, Scooter Libby, who sat next to him, and Mrs. Cheney, did not note a call between the President and Vice President immediately after the Vice President entered the conference room. (40–41)

This is the closest the Commission comes to accusing the president and the vice president of lying about any issue. And this issue, like the issue of whether there was any link between al-Qaeda and Iraq, provided material for much discussion in the press. *Newsweek* even reported that although "some on the commission staff were, in fact, highly skeptical of the vice president's account and made their views clearer in an earlier draft of their staff report," vigorous lobbying from the White House resulted in the report's being "watered down."[23]

Is it possible, however, that the whole issue is a red herring? The Commission's narrative seems to reflect concern on its part to reinforce the idea that shoot-down authorization can properly come only from the president. Besides the passage just quoted, in which the point is made implicitly (by suggesting that Cheney might have improperly given the authorization without consulting Bush), the Commission says:

> Prior to 9/11, it was understood that an order to shoot down a commercial aircraft would have to be issued by the National Command Authority (a phrase used to describe the president and secretary of defense). (17)

This passage seems deliberately ambiguous, failing to make clear whether the order can come from either the president or the secretary of defense or whether it must come from both the president and the secretary of defense. The Commissioners cannot mean the latter, however, because in their own narrative they have the order made by the president and the vice president, without the involvement of the secretary of defense (43). But if the "Command Authority" means either the president or the secretary of defense, then the decision could equally be made by the secretary, without the president (or the vice president).[24] That clearly would not do.

The Commission states what it really wants to say more clearly in the following passage:

> In most cases, the chain of command authorizing the use of force runs from the president to the secretary of defense and from the secretary to the combatant commander. The President apparently spoke to Secretary Rumsfeld for the first time that morning shortly after 10:00. . . . It was a brief call in which the subject of shoot-down authority was not discussed. (43)

The point of this passage, in saying that this is the chain of command (only) "in most cases," is not to suggest that in some cases the president could be bypassed. The point, instead, is that in some cases the secretary might not be involved.

This point is also reinforced by other comments. For example, the Commission quotes military officials as saying that they could send fighter jets after an aircraft on their own but "would need 'executive' orders to shoot it down" (458n98).

The Commission's most extreme statement about the need, at least in practice, for authorization from the president comes in a "what if" discussion of Flight 93. In imagining what might have happened if the passengers on Flight 93 had not caused it to crash, the Commission says:

> It is possible that NORAD commanders would have ordered a shootdown in the absence of the authorization communicated by the Vice President, but given the gravity of the decision to shoot down a commercial airliner, and NORAD's caution that a mistake not be made, we view this possibility as unlikely. (45)

But is it actually true that only the president can authorize shoot-downs, as a general rule? Evidence that it is not is contained in the following quotation from a document issued June 1, 2001, which was quoted in Chapter 12:

> In the event of a hijacking, the NMCC will be notified by the most expeditious means by the FAA. The NMCC will, with the exception of requests needing an immediate response . . . forward requests for DoD [Department of Defense] assistance to the Secretary of Defense for approval.[25]

There is nothing here about the White House. "DoD assistance," furthermore, does not mean simply interception. It includes the possibility of shooting down a hijacked airliner. As we saw in Chapter 11, Glen Johnson of the *Boston Globe* summarized the description by NORAD spokesman Mike Snyder in the following way:

> When planes are intercepted, they typically are handled with graduated response. The approaching fighter may rock its wingtips to attract the pilot's attention, or make a pass in front of the aircraft. Eventually, it can fire tracer rounds in the airplane's path, or, under certain circumstances, down it with a missile.[26]

I emphasize this point because of the utter lack of realism and historical accuracy in the Commission's discussion of interception. It says, by contrast:

> The FAA and NORAD had developed protocols for working together in the event of a hijacking. . . . If a hijack was confirmed, procedures called for the hijack coordinator on duty to contact the Pentagon's National Military Command Center (NMCC) and to ask for a military escort aircraft to follow the flight [and] report anything unusual . . . .The protocols did not contemplate an intercept. They assumed the fighter escort would be discreet, "vectored to a position five miles directly behind the hijacked aircraft," where it could perform its mission to monitor the aircraft's flight path. (17–18)

The Commission could have given us some evidence for this claim about the "protocols" by discussing some of the occasions on which fighters have been scrambled in recent times. According to press reports, NORAD fighters were scrambled on 129 occasions in 2000.[27] The Associated Press reports, furthermore, that there had been 67 scrambles between September 2001 and June 2002.[28] Assuming the truth of the Commission's description of the protocols that were in effect prior to 9/11, it presumably could have shown that although these fighters scrambled, they did not actually intercept the airplanes but were "discreet," remaining five miles behind the suspect airplanes, merely monitoring their behavior. But the Commission does not do this. Given this lack of evidence, should we not assume that Mike Snyder and others at NORAD are finding this description of scrambling protocol by the Kean–Zelikow Commission a source of considerable amusement?

To return to Snyder's description—and hence to the real world, in which fighters not only intercept but might even shoot down hijacked aircraft: The pilots can "down [the hijacked airplane] with a missile," to be sure, only if they have authorization. But this authorization, as the June 1 document reaffirms, normally comes from the Office of the Secretary of Defense. It need not come from White House—as if the president would have to be awakened in the middle of the night, or pulled out of a concert, or interrupted in the middle of a State of the Union address, if there were a situation in which immediate authorization for a shoot-down were required to prevent a disaster.

In such emergencies, moreover, the authorization need not even come from the Office of the Secretary of Defense (and certainly not from the secretary personally). This point has already been documented in Chapter 12 (see page 165–166), which I would encourage the reader to review.

Accordingly, the Commission's twofold question of presidential authorization—*when* and even *if* President Bush authorized the military to shoot down Flight 93—is a red herring. As such it has distracted reporters and the public from following the trail of the failures of 9/11 to the Pentagon, which had not only the authority but also the mandate to shoot down hijacked airliners when such action was necessary "to save lives, prevent human suffering, or mitigate great property damage." The Kean–Zelikow Report's attempt to argue that the US military is blameless for its disastrous failure to do this on 9/11 must itself be judged a failure.

WHEN DID FLIGHT 93 CRASH?

The central aim of the Commission's narrative about Flight 93, as we have seen, has been to convince readers that the US military neither did nor could have shot down this plane. One of the central disputes involved in this question concerns the exact time at which Flight 93 crashed. The Commission admits, in fact, that "'[t]he precise crash time has been the subject of some dispute" (30). NORAD put the time at 10:03, and the Commission endorses this time while refining it to 10:03:11. The FAA, however, said 10:07.[29] A seismic study authorized by the US army came closer to the FAA time, giving 10:06:05 as the exact time of the crash (461n168).[30] This latter time has been widely accepted,[31] but the Kean–Zelikow Commission, of course, rejects it.

This dispute is important for two reasons. First, the Commission's preferred time of 10:03 puts even more minutes between the crash time and the earliest possible time, according to the Commission, that Cheney could have given the shoot-down authorization (10:10). The 10:03 time, therefore, makes it seem even more unlikely that the plane could have been shot down. Second, the tape of the cockpit recording ends at 10:02. If the crash occurred at 10:03, not much of the tape would be missing. But if the crash occurred at 10:06, then there is a four-minute gap.[32] Of course, the missing time is suspicious in any case, even it be only a one-minute gap. According to a story in the *New York Observer*, "Some of the relatives are keen to find out why, at the peak of this struggle, the tape suddenly stops recording voices and all that is heard in the last 60 seconds or so is engine noise."[33] But to have four minutes missing would be even more suspicious, so it is certainly better for the Bush administration and the US military if the 10:03 time is accepted.

On what basis, however, can the Commission challenge the results of the seismic study? The Commission combines three approaches. In the first place, the Commission says:

> The 10:03:11 impact time is supported by previous National Transportation Safety Board analysis and by evidence from the Commission's staff's analysis of radar, the flight data recorder, the cockpit voice recorder, infrared satellite data, and air traffic control transmissions. (30)

This claim is, however, triply problematic. In the first place, we are given no reference for the "previous National Transportation Safety Board analysis." In the second place, Mary Schiavo, former Inspector General of the Transportation Department, was quoted in February 2004 as saying: "We don't have a NTSB [National Transportation Safety Board] investigation here."[34] In the third place, all the other alleged evidence is based on "the Commission's staff's analysis." We simply have to trust it and, frankly, this Zelikow-directed staff has not proven itself worthy of our trust.

The Commission's second approach is simply to say that the seismic study is not reliable. Here is the Commission's argument:

> [T]he seismic data on which [the two authors of the seismic study] based this estimate are far too weak in signal-to-noise ratio and far too speculative in terms of signal source to be used as a means of contradicting the impact time established by the very accurate combination of FDR, CVR, ATC, radar, and impact site data sets. These data sets constrain United 93's impact time to within 1 second, are airplane- and crash-site specific, and are based on time codes automatically recorded in the ATC audiotapes for the FAA centers and correlated with each data set in a process internationally accepted within the aviation accident investigation community. (462n169)

But this argument, while it might on first hearing sound impressive, is simply a string of assertions. No evidence that any of us could check is cited. We again simply have to take the word of the Kean–Zelikow Commission.

Furthermore, when we look at the actual seismic study—which was carried out at the request of the US Army by Won-Young Kim of the Lamont-Doherty Earth Observatory of Columbia University and Gerald R. Baum of the Maryland Geological Survey—it seems far less "speculative" than the Commission suggests. Kim and Baum, who were asked to do studies for all four crashes, said that only the signal from the crash into the Pentagon was too weak for them to determine a definite time (a fact, interestingly, that provides further support for the view that the Pentagon was not hit by a giant airliner). With regard to the crash of UA 93, they examined the seismic records from four stations near the crash site. Whereas the signal-to-noise ratio was very low for two of these (about 1:1), it was about 2.5:1 at one of the stations (SSPA). Kim and Baum concluded:

> Although seismic signals across the network are not as strong and clear as the WTC case . . . , three component records at station SSPA . . . are quite clear. . . . [From these records] we infer that the Flight 93 crashed around 14:06:05 5 (UTC) (10:06:05 EDT).[35]

It appears, therefore, that the Commission was engaging in wishful-reading.

The Commission's third approach is to say that "one of the study's principal authors now concedes that 'seismic data is not definitive for the impact of UA 93.'"[36] However, besides the fact that we do not know under what conditions and with what qualifications this author, Won-Young Kim, may have made this concession, we also can infer that the other principal author of that seismic study, Dr. Gerald Baum, does *not* concede that the seismic data are not definitive for establishing the time at which Flight 93 crashed.

The Commission has, in sum, not made a good case for its early time for the crash of UA Flight 93. But even if the Commission's time proves to be correct, this will do little to bolster its case against the shoot-down.

ANOTHER REPORT ABOUT GENERAL WINFIELD

As we saw earlier, Brigadier General Montague Winfield, Director of Operations for the NMCC, had himself replaced at 8:30 on the morning of 9/11 by Captain Charles Leidig, his deputy. As discussed above, this substitution was, at the least, interesting. But there was also another interesting dimension to this episode. Captain Leidig, who told the 9/11 Commission about the substitution, also told them that shortly before Flight 93 crashed, Winfield resumed his duties.[37]

That report makes especially interesting a dimension of James Bamford's account of those moments that was not quoted earlier.

> As United 93 got closer and closer to the White House, . . . Cheney . . . asked Bush to order the United jetliner shot down. . . . Bush, however, . . . [left] the decision to him . . . A few minutes later, Cheney passed the order to Army Brig. Gen. W. Montague Winfield in the Pentagon's War Room. "The President had given us permission to shoot down innocent civilian aircraft that threatened Washington, D.C." Winfield said. . . . Air Force Colonel Robert Marr . . . sent out word to air traffic controllers to instruct fighter pilots to destroy the United jetliner.[38]

Bamford's account is made especially interesting, in turn, by the fact that General Winfield was later quoted as saying, in relation to Flight 93: "At some point, the closure time came and went, and nothing happened, so you can imagine everything was very tense at the NMCC."[39]

What could "the closure time" mean here except the time at which they expected the fighter jet to reach Flight 93? This is at least a question that the Kean–Zelikow Commission should have asked General Winfield.

SUMMARY AND CONCLUSION

As we have seen, there is considerable evidence to support the conclusion that the US military shot down UA Flight 93, namely:

1. Multiple evidence that the shoot-down authorization was given before 10:00, perhaps about 9:45.

2. Reports that after this authorization was transmitted, an F-16 was sent after UA 93.

3. Reports from CBS News, a flight controller, and Paul Wolfowitz that Flight 93 was being tailed by an F-16.

4. The reported statement by General Montague Winfield, which seemed to say that he and others in the NMCC expected Flight 93 to be shot down.

5. Rumors within the military that one of its F-16s shot down an airliner in Pennsylvania.

6. Reports from people in UA Flight 93 and on the ground

suggesting that it was downed by a missile.

The evidence for the conclusion that Flight 93 was shot down by the US military is indeed very strong.

The Kean–Zelikow Commission, in seeking to refute this conclusion, did not take on any of this evidence directly, or even mention it. The Commission instead rested its case on two claims: (1) the claim that the military did not even know that Flight 93 had been hijacked until after it crashed; (2) the claim that the shoot-down authorization announced by Vice President Cheney came after Flight 93 had crashed. As we have seen, however, the Commission's arguments for these claims are unconvincing.

The first claim, that the military did not know Flight 93 was hijacked, rests on the twofold assertion that the FAA never specifically called the military about this flight and that the teleconferences provided no opportunity for this information to be transmitted. But there are reasons to doubt this assertion. Insofar as the FAA and NMCC teleconferences really were worthless for transmitting information from the FAA to the military, that would appear to have been deliberate sabotage on the part of the NMCC—setting up its own teleconference, putting a rookie in charge of it, claiming an inability to get connected with the FAA, and not listening to the FAA teleconference. There are, furthermore, reasons to doubt that these teleconferences really were so worthless. Let us recall Laura Brown's memorandum, "FAA communications with NORAD on September 11, 2001." According to this memo, the FAA, immediately after the first crash into the WTC, established phone bridges, which included both the Pentagon and NORAD. And then:

> The FAA shared real-time information on the phone bridges about the unfolding events, including information about loss of communication with aircraft, loss of transponder signals, unauthorized changes in course, and other actions being taken by all the flights of interest.[40]

And even the Kean–Zelikow Report agrees that UA 93 was a "flight of interest" for the FAA by 9:34.

The Commission's assertion about the worthlessness of the teleconferences is also undermined by Clarke's account, according to which Jane Garvey announced the probable hijacking at about 9:40, while Myers and Rumsfeld were both participating. Clarke also revealed that the Secret Service, which is interconnected with every agency involved with national security, watches the FAA radar.

The first claim of the *Report*—that the military had no knowledge about the hijacking of Flight 93 until after it crashed—is, therefore, highly implausible (even apart from the fact, mentioned in Chapter 11, that some NORAD officials had been notified at 9:16).

The same is true of its second claim, according to which the shoot-down authorization came too late—seven or more minutes after Flight 93 had crashed. Besides the fact that the Commission's claim that this authorization did not come until after 10:10 is flatly contradicted by numerous prior reports, including that of Richard Clarke himself, the new timeline for Vice President Cheney's arrival in the shelter conference room is probably the feature of the Commission's case that is most patently false. In addition to the fact that there is admittedly no evidence for it, it is contradicted by many other reports, including those of three eyewitnesses: Richard Clarke, Norman Mineta, and White House photographer David Bohrer. The other element in the Commission's case—the argument that UA really crashed three minutes earlier than the seismic study indicates—must be judged weak at best. The lengths to which the Kean–Zelikow Commission went in trying to establish this three-minute difference suggests, furthermore, that its main concern was to try to remove the suspicion that the tape of the flight recorder was actually missing the last four minutes—minutes that may have revealed why the plane really crashed.

Given the complete failure of the Kean–Zelikow Report to show that the US military could not have shot down Flight 93, combined with its failure to refute any of the strands of evidence supporting the conclusion that the military did shoot it down, this probability remains unrefuted. Indeed, we now have additional evidence for its truth: the very fact that the Kean–Zelikow Commission, besides failing to confront any of the evidence directly, engaged in such obvious distortions in its desperate attempt to rule out this possibility.

CHAPTER SIXTEEN

The FAA Takes the Fall

C entral to the Commission's narrative about the day of 9/11 itself, as we have seen, is the goal of refuting the suspicion that the military failed to respond appropriately. The central claim in this argument is that the FAA did not inform the military of the hijackings in time for the attacks to be prevented. Accounts suggesting that the military was notified in time to respond, the Kean–Zelikow Commission declares, "overstated the FAA's ability to provide the military with timely and useful information that morning" (34).

We have, however, seen reason to suspect that the FAA is being asked to take the fall to protect the US military. In this chapter, we will explore this question more directly. I will look first at the Commission's treatment of the US military, then its treatment of the FAA.

THE COMMISSION'S TREATMENT OF THE US MILITARY

In discussing the 9/11 Commission's treatment of the US military, I will first review the support given to the military by the Commission's new timeline, then look at some other dimensions.

Accepting the Military's New Timeline: The Kean–Zelikow Report exonerated the military of any complicity or even serious incompetence in two ways. It accepted, and perhaps at places even created, the military's new timeline, especially for the latter three flights. And it glossed over obscurities and other difficulties in this timeline.

With regard to Flight 11, the Commission did not press to find out why the telephone call from NEADS to General Arnold in Florida took eight minutes—or whether this call was even necessary. It did not demand clarification about why the Otis fighters, after being given a scramble order at 8:46, were not airborne until 8:53.

With regard to Flight 175, the Commission did not demand to know why, if NORAD had really not been notified at 8:43 about this hijacking, NORAD had maintained for almost three years that it had. The

Commission did not press for clarification as to why, if Flight 11 had already crashed at 8:53 and the military had not yet been alerted about Flight 175, the Otis fighters were airborne at all. Nor did it press NEADS officials to clear up obscurities in the story about what the fighters did after taking off, including the question of why they were hovering off Long Island rather than being sent into the city to establish Combat Air Patrol.

With regard to Flight 77, the Commission accepted the military's new claim that, contrary to what NORAD had said back in 2001, it was not notified at 9:24 about this plane's hijacking. In support of this new claim, the Commission failed to press NORAD officials as to why they had given out that misinformation in 2001. The Commission also, in support of the new claim, provided an elaborate tale with several new elements—the newly discovered Phantom Flight 11, the newly discovered journey of the Langley pilots out to sea, and the newly discovered realization that NEADS had learned from the FAA only that Flight 77 was lost, not that it had been hijacked. In support of the Pentagon's claim that it had no idea that an aircraft was headed towards it, the Commission suppressed testimony to the Commission itself by Norman Mineta, who said that Vice President Cheney knew about this unidentified aircraft while it was still 50 miles out. The Commission also, in accepting the story about the military pilot identifying the incoming aircraft as a Boeing 757, overlooked the contradiction between this story and the other story about this aircraft's last few minutes, according to which it had to make an amazing downward spiral in order to hit the west wing. Finally, the Commission simply ignored all the physical evidence suggesting that the aircraft that hit the Pentagon could not have been a giant airliner and hence could not have been Flight 77.

With regard to Flight 93, the Kean–Zelikow Commission went to great lengths to create a timeline according to which it would be implausible to think the military had shot the flight down. In order to make this point, the Commission not only placed the crash-time three minutes earlier than does the seismic study. It also put the shootdown authorization at least 20 minutes later than did earlier reports. To support this late authorization time, furthermore, the Kean–Zelikow Report, in what is probably its most obviously fabricated episode, portrayed the vice president as going into the shelter conference room some 45 minutes later than indicated in other reports—including those of two members of the Bush administration: Richard Clarke and Norman Mineta. This report also, of course, simply ignored all the evidence supporting the thesis that Flight 93 was shot down by the US military.

Finally, with regard to all the flights, especially the latter three, the Commission worked mightily to convince us that the military could not have possibly learned about them from the FAA through any of the three teleconferences, even though this effort required contradicting not only common sense but also the testimony of Richard Clarke and the FAA's Laura Brown.

Not Asking about Other Available Fighters: The military's claim, as we have seen, is that no planes got to New York or Washington in time to prevent the attacks partly because there were no available fighters close enough. There are reports, however, that suggest otherwise.

According to one of these reports, three F-16s from Andrews Air Force Base were on a training mission in North Carolina when the North Tower was hit at 8:46. Being only 207 miles from Washington, they could have been back by 9:00 to establish CAP until replacements were sent. And yet they did not begin flying over Washington until 10:45.[1]

It would seem that this report should have been the source of a lively conversation with Colonel Marr and Generals Myers, Eberhart, and Arnold. And yet we have no indication in *The 9/11 Commission Report* that the subject was ever brought up.

There is, however, a slight allusion to a similar story. In a curious passage, we read, in relation to the response to the hijacking of Flight 11: "Boston Center . . . tried to contact a former alert site in Atlantic City, unaware it had been phased out" (20). The story behind this passage, which the Commission does not report, is that the 177th Fighter Wing, based at the Atlantic City International Airport in Pomona, New Jersey, was fully active, and that two of its F-16s were at that moment conducting bombing sorties only eight minutes from Manhattan. These facts are reported in a story by Mike Kelly in New Jersey's *Bergen Record.*[2]

We might suppose that these facts were not mentioned because the Commission was unaware of them. However, both Chairman Kean and one of the Commission's lead investigators, John Farmer, were interviewed by Kelly and quoted in his story. But although Farmer personally read the staff statement at the hearing on June 17, 2004, which dealt with these matters, there is no mention of these F-15s.

Peter Lance, who tells this story in his recent book, *Cover Up,* then quotes Lorie van Auken, whose husband died in the North Tower, as saying:

> I'm frankly stunned by this. . . . If two fighters were only eight minutes away, the Commission should have done an exhaustive study on why they didn't get called. To leave them out of the official hearing record is unbelievable.[3]

Perhaps one of the reasons this story had to be omitted is that it would have been in tension with the notion, which the Commission accepts, that NEADS had only two sites with fighters on alert. James Bamford, who also reports the story about the F-16s being only eight miles from Manhattan, says, in fact, that NEADS could call on "alert fighter pilots at National Guard units at Burlington, Vermont; Atlantic City, New Jersey; Cape Cod, Massachusetts; and Duluth, Minnesota."[4] Adding these to Langley, Virginia, gives us five, and adding Andrews would give us six. Perhaps one of the many ways in which the Commission protected the military was by not publishing or even saying anything that would have challenged General Myers' claim that in September, 2001, NEADS had only two bases that kept fighters on alert.

Accepting the Military's "External Posture" Excuse: Besides accepting the military's new timeline, which puts all the serious blame on the FAA, the 9/11 Commission also accepted the military's excuses for why it was not more prepared for the kinds of attacks that occurred on 9/11. The problem, explained the Commission, was that the "protocols," which NORAD and the FAA had developed "for working together in the event of a hijacking," were "unsuited in every respect for what was about to happen" (17, 18). These protocols, to be more precise, falsely presumed that:

- the hijacked aircraft would be readily identifiable and would not attempt to disappear;

- there would be time to address the problem through the appropriate FAA and NORAD chains of command; and

- the hijacking would take the traditional form: that is, it would not be a suicide hijacking designed to convert the aircraft into a guided missile. (18)

I will look at these three alleged presumptions in order.

The first alleged presumption, that the aircraft "would not attempt to disappear," simply means that it would not turn off its transponder. Rather, the pilot would use the transponder to "squawk" the universal code to signal a hijacking (17). And then the transponder signal would make the plane easy to track, without having to resort to primary radar. It is certainly the case that one of the transponder's functions is to allow the pilot to send this universal 4-digit code. And it is also the case that if the pilot does this, there is little room for doubt as to whether a hijacking has occurred.

But we have already looked at the absurdity of the twofold suggestion that the FAA did not expect hijackers to turn off the transponder and that, if they do so, the plane virtually "disappears." The FAA manual mentions the disappearance of the transponder signal as one of the three standard signs that a plane has been hijacked. One of the sillier statements in the Kean–Zelikow Report, accordingly, is the assertion that "[t]he defense of U.S. airspace on 9/11 was . . . improvised by civilians who had never handled a hijacked aircraft that attempted to disappear" (31). Maybe they hadn't, but they were certainly trained to deal with aircraft not giving out signals from their transponders. We have also seen that it is equally absurd to suggest that the military's radar systems are premised on the assumption that, for example, Soviet bomber pilots would not have been so discourteous as to turn off their transponders. I will, therefore, say no more about this first alleged presumption, but will instead focus on the second and third ones.

The second alleged presumption—that "there would be time to address the problem through the appropriate FAA and NORAD chains of command"—involves two issues. One is the idea that, prior to 9/11, the protocol involved a rigid "chain of command," in which ten or more minutes would be required simply to get a scramble order issued. We have already addressed this issue, within both the FAA and the military, sufficiently. I will here, therefore, treat only the second issue, which is the claim that insofar as the military was expecting airplane threats against the homeland, they expected the flights to originate from overseas. In Chapter 5, we looked at the Commission's use of the "looking overseas" argument to excuse the intelligence agencies. Here we will look at its use to excuse the military.

The idea that the military was prepared only to respond to threats coming from abroad was put forward primarily by General Myers. In his opening statement before the Commission on June 17, 2004, he said: "[O]ur military posture on 9/11, by law, by policy and in practice, was focused on responding to external threats, threats originating outside of our borders." Later, under questioning from Commissioner John Lehman, he made clear that this "posture" had implications for radar coverage, saying: "[W]e were clearly looking outward. We did not have the situational awareness inward because we did not have the radar coverage."[5]

Commissioner Jamie Gorelick challenged Myers about this "posture" claim, saying:

> I think that the question that has to be on the minds of the American people is, where was our military when it should have been defending us, and I think that is a fair question. . . . And the response of NORAD . . . is that NORAD was not postured to defend us domestically unless someone was coming at us from abroad, and that has lots of implications. . . . That's why I come back to this word posture, we were postured against an external threat.
>
> In my experience, the military is very clear about its charters, and who is supposed to do what. So if you go back and you look at the foundational documents for NORAD, they do not say defend us only against a threat coming in from across the ocean, or across our borders. It has two missions, and one of them is control of the airspace above the domestic United States, and aerospace control is defined as providing surveillance and control of the airspace of Canada and the United States. To me that air sovereignty concept means that you have a role which, if you were postured only externally, you defined out of the job.

Myers then replied with an absurd argument, saying: "What we try to do is follow the law, and the law is pretty clear on Posse Comitatus and that is whether or not the military should be involved in domestic law enforcement. . . ."

Gorelick quickly pointed out the absurdity of this argument, saying:

> Let me just interrupt, when I was general counsel of the Defense Department, I repeatedly advised, and I believe others have advised that the Posse Comitatus says, you can't arrest people. It doesn't mean that the military has no authority, obligation, or ability to

defend the United States from attacks that happen to happen in the domestic United States.

Nevertheless, although Gorelick had thoroughly undermined Myers' case, Myers' view became that of the Kean–Zelikow Report, in which we read the following statement:

NORAD's mission was, and is, to defend the airspace of North America. . . . That mission does not distinguish between internal and external threats; but because NORAD was created to counter the Soviet threat, it came to define its job as defending against external attacks. (16)

The truth of Gorelick's point is recognized. But it is recognized purely as a statement about how NORAD *should* have understood its mission. I myself would interpret her point more critically, taking it to express incredulity at the idea that NORAD could really have been thinking that its mission was only to defend against external threats. The Kean–Zelikow Report, however, takes Myers at his word. Rightly or wrongly, it says, NORAD did in fact "define its job [solely] as defending against external attacks." We find this statement repeated near the end of the book:

America's homeland defenders faced outward. . . .[NORAD's] planning scenarios occasionally considered the danger of hijacked aircraft being guided to American targets, but only aircraft that were coming from overseas. (352)

The Commission, at this point, actually makes a criticism of the military, saying:

We recognize that a costly change in NORAD's defense posture to deal with the danger of suicide hijackers, before such a threat had ever actually been realized, would have been a tough sell. But NORAD did not canvass available intelligence and try to make the case. (352)

This is, however, pretty mild criticism. The Commission says only that NORAD's leaders were guilty of bureaucratic incompetence— they should have been more proactive in trying to get what they needed.

Possibly relevant here is Michael Parenti's observation that "policymakers [sometimes] seize upon incompetence as a cover"—that is, as a way to deny their active involvement in some illegal operation. This admission of incompetence is then "eagerly embraced by various commentators," because they prefer to see their leaders as suffering from incompetence "rather than to see deliberate deception."[6] We need only to replace "policymakers" with "military leaders" to ask if the same dynamic may have been exemplified in relation to various statements made by US military leaders. In the present case, we have Myers' statements showing that he misunderstood the meaning of Posse Comitatus and hence the nature of NORAD's assignment, followed by the Commission's correction of his separation between internal and external threats and its criticism of his (and more generally NORAD's) failure to request the money to get inward-looking radar.

Accepting the Military's "No Recognition" Claim: The third alleged presumption was that any hijacking of an American airliner would not be "a suicide hijacking designed to convert the aircraft into a guided missile" (18). Because of that presumption, the 9/11 Commission claimed, we had "a military unprepared for the transformation of commercial aircraft into weapons of mass destruction" (31).

This presumption again came from the testimony of General Myers, who justified the military's outward looking "posture" by appeal to the absence of prior threats of the kinds of hijackings that occurred on 9/11. In his testimony, he said:

> [T]he use of aircraft as a weapon, as a missile, other than World War II and the Kamikaze situation, I'm not aware, and I've tried to research this, and the best information I get, I am not aware that an aircraft has ever been used as a weapon. Now, there have been landings on the White House lawn . . . . There was talk about crashing airplanes into the CIA. But, in most of that threat reporting leading up to 9/11, it was hijacking an airplane and in the normal hijack mode, not in the mode of a weapon. . . . Even the work that was done and the hijackings that were planned for the Philippines, which is a well-known plot, they planned to hijack the airplanes and blow them up primarily. So . . . the intelligence did not point to this kind of threat, and I think that explains our posture.[7]

Myers claimed, in other words, that NORAD's outward looking posture was justified by the absence of any significant incidents, or even threats, in which hijacked airplanes were used as weapons.

The 9/11 Commission followed Myers' lead in connecting these two issues. That is, although the Commission distinguished between the second and the third alleged presumptions, it actually treated them together, saying: "The threat of terrorists hijacking commercial airlines within the United States—and using them as guided missiles—was not recognized by NORAD before 9/11" (17). Basing this "no recognition" claim on a private interview with NORAD's Commander in Chief, General Ralph E. Eberhart (458n98), the Kean–Zelikow Report constructed a significant portion of its defense of the US military around this claim.

This defense contained, to be sure, a criticism. The criticism is that there was a "failure of the imagination." The Commission derived this phrase from Paul Wolfowitz. In a memo to Rumsfeld shortly after 9/11, Wolfowitz commented on the 1995 Manila air plot, which envisaged crashing an explosives-laden plane into CIA headquarters.[8] In light of the fact that US authorities knew about this plot, Wolfowitz blamed a "failure of imagination" for the fact that little thought had been devoted to the potential threat from suicide hijackers (335). The Commission adopted and developed this notion. In so doing, it was leveling a criticism of sorts at the defense establishment.

But that criticism, like the previous criticism of bureaucratic incompetence, is not very serious compared with the charge of complicity. Military officials are probably not terribly bothered by this criticism, given that it is made for the sake of precluding the more serious charge. A mere charge of incompetence does not bring with it a threat of prosecution for, among other things, mass murder.

In any case, the mild criticism of a "failure of imagination" is made as part of the Commission's defense of what we can call NORAD's "failures of interception." Those failures, we are told, are understandable and even excusable because NORAD officials, being deficient in imaginative abilities, simply failed to recognize the "threat of terrorists hijacking commercial airlines within the United States—and using them as guided missiles" (17).

Of course, for this defense to be credible, the "no recognition" claim must itself be credible.

The contention that the threat really was not recognized was based partly on the fact that the Kean–Zelikow Report combined the second and third presumption into a single twofold presumption—that commercial airliners would not be (1) hijacked within the United States and then (2) used as guided missiles by suicide hijackers. Given the fact that both conditions would need to be met to have a counter-instance to Eberhart's "no recognition" claim, the Kean–Zelikow Report can dismiss several seeming counter-instances by pointing out that one or the other of the two conditions was not met. The Report mentioned, for example, a proposed readiness test for NORAD based on the idea of "a hijacked airliner coming from overseas and crashing into the Pentagon" (346). This example, by having the aircraft coming from overseas, provided no refutation of the contention that no one had imagined a plane hijacked within the United States and then use to strike the Pentagon—the crucial difference being that if the plane was coming from overseas, there would be plenty of time to identify the aircraft and scramble interceptors.

However, even with the stipulation that both conditions would have to be met, there is considerable evidence that counts against the credibility of Eberhart's claim.

Some of this evidence is, surprisingly enough, provided by the Commission itself. I will list nine examples provided in the Kean–Zelikow Report that either clearly do, or at least may, contradict the Report's endorsement of Eberhart's "no recognition" claim:

1. "[A]n Algerian group hijacked an airliner in 1994, . . . possibly to crash it into the Eiffel Tower" (345). The airplane was hijacked in Algiers. But since the distance from Algiers to Paris is less than the distance across the United States, there might have been less time to intercept it than is available to intercept a plane hijacked within this country. It would, therefore, not take much imagination to transfer the scenario to the United States.

2. "In early 1995, Abdul Hakim Murad—Ramzi Yousef's accomplice in the Manila airlines bombing plot—told Philippine authorities that he and Yousef had discussed flying a plane into CIA headquarters" (345). It was, we saw, this plan that provided the basis for Wolfowitz's "failure of imagination" comment.

3. "In August of [1998], the intelligence community had received information that a group of Libyans hoped to crash a plane

into the World Trade Center" (344–45). The Commission does not explicitly say that the plane would be hijacked from within the United States, but it also does not explicitly say otherwise.

4. "[Richard] Clarke had been concerned about the danger posed by aircraft since at least the 1996 Atlanta Olympics. . . . In 1998, Clarke chaired an exercise [that] involved a scenario in which a group of terrorists commandeered a Learjet on the ground in Atlanta, loaded it with explosives, and flew it towards a target in Washington, D.C." (345). The Commission elsewhere concluded the description of this exercise by saying that the terrorist group "took off for a suicide mission to Washington" (457–58n98).

5. "After the 1999–2000 millennium alerts, . . . Clarke held a meeting of his Counterterrorism Security Group devoted largely to the possibility of a possible airplane hijacking by al Qaeda. . . . [T]he possibility was imaginable, and imagined" (345).

6. "In early August 1999, the FAA's Civil Aviation Security intelligence office summarized the Bin Ladin hijacking threat. . . . [T]he paper identified a few principal scenarios, one of which was a 'suicide hijacking operation'" (345).

7. A CIA report on June 12, 2001, said that KSM "was recruiting people to travel to the United States to meet with colleagues already there so that they might conduct terrorist attacks on Bin Ladin's behalf. On June 22, the CIA notified all its station chiefs about intelligence suggesting a possible al Qaeda suicide attack on a U.S. target over the next few days" (256).

8. "In late July [2001], because of threats, Italy closed the airspace over Genoa and mounted antiaircraft batteries at the Genoa airport during the G-8 summit, which President Bush attended" (258). We learn elsewhere that the Italians kept fighters in the air over the city, and that the threat was taken so seriously that Bush stayed overnight offshore, on an aircraft carrier.[9] Although this example, like the first one, is about a threat in Europe, not the United States, it obviously counts against the thesis that there was a "failure of imagination" with regard to the possibility that terrorists might try to use airplanes to attack President Bush. (Another puzzling thing about this example is that the Commission, in mentioning that "antiaircraft batteries" had to be mounted at the

Genoa airport, failed to point out that the White House and the Pentagon already have their own antiaircraft batteries, which would shoot down any aircraft except one with a transponder signal indicating that it belongs to the US military.)

9. On August 6, 2001, the Presidential Daily Brief included an intelligence memo stating, among other things, that "[one threat report said] that Bin Ladin wanted to hijack a US aircraft. . . . FBI information since that time indicates patterns of suspicious activity in this country consistent with preparations for hijackings or other types of attacks. . . . CIA and the FBI are investigating a call to our Embassy in the UAE in May saying that a group of Bin Ladin supporters was in the US planning attacks with explosives" (262).

Strangely, therefore, although the Kean–Zelikow Report endorsed Eberhart's claim that "[t]he threat of terrorists hijacking commercial airlines within the United States—and using them as guided missiles— was not recognized by NORAD before 9/11," this claim is undermined by examples provided within this document itself.

The claim is even further undermined if we look outside this document. I will provide six examples.

1. In 1993, a panel of experts commissioned by the Pentagon suggested that airplanes could be used as missiles to bomb national landmarks. In 1994, one of these experts wrote in the *Futurist* magazine:

> Targets such as the World Trade Center not only provide the requisite casualties but, because of their symbolic nature, provide more bang for the buck. In order to maximize their odds for success, terrorist groups will likely consider mounting multiple, simultaneous operations.[10]

2. In 1995, Senator Sam Nunn, in *Time* magazine's cover story, described a scenario in which terrorists crash a radio-controlled airplane into the US Capitol Building.[11]

3. In 1999, the National Intelligence Council, which advises the President and US intelligence agencies on emerging threats, said in a special report on terrorism: "Al-Qaeda's expected retaliation for the US cruise missile attack [of 1998]. . . could take several forms of terrorist attack in the nation's capitol. Suicide bombers belonging to al-Qaeda's Martyrdom Battalion could crash-land an aircraft packed with high

explosives . . . into the Pentagon, the headquarters of the Central Intelligence Agency (CIA), or the White House."[12]

4. In October 2000, Pentagon officials carried out an emergency drill to prepare for the possibility that a hijacked airliner might be crashed into the Pentagon.[13]

5. In July 2001, according to an article headed "NORAD Had Drills of Jets as Weapons," the military planned a drill in which hijacked airliners, originating in the United States, were used as weapons to crash into targets, including the World Trade Center.[14]

6. At 9:00 on the morning of 9/11, the National Reconnaissance Office, which operates spy satellites and draws its personnel from the military and the CIA, had planned to simulate the accidental crashing of an airplane into its headquarters, four miles from Dulles Airport in Washington. The simulation was evidently to be run by John Fulton "and his team at the CIA."[15]

From all these examples, we can see that Eberhart's "no recognition" claim is simply not plausible and that the 9/11 Commission must have known this. We can conclude, therefore, that the Commission's support for the claim reflected less its belief that the claim was true than its commitment to protecting the military's reputation, even if that required distorting historical reality.

Not Probing Mysteries Surrounding Pentagon Officials: As we have seen, there are mysteries about the behavior of at least three of the leading Pentagon officials on the morning of 9/11. The report by General Richard Myers on his own activities during the attacks, besides being implausible in itself, is contradicted by Richard Clarke's account of Myers' participation in the White House video teleconference. Clarke's account also contradicts three reports about and by Secretary of Defense Rumsfeld, which are themselves mutually self-contradictory. And it was certainly odd that General Montague Winfield would have his role, as director of communications in the NMCC, assumed by his deputy, who had only recently qualified to take over that role, and then that Winfield did not take back his position after it was clear that a terrorist attack was underway.

The Kean–Zelikow Commission, however, showed no interest in pressing these gentlemen to try to clarify what they did that morning. After reading *The 9/11 Commission Report*, therefore, we have no idea what Myers and Rumsfeld were doing, say, between 8:00 and 9:15 (although—to anticipate the next issue—Clarke indicated that he was participating in a war game). We have no idea that Winfield was doing for most of the morning. Perhaps these men were not doing anything terrible. But the Kean–Zelikow Report has tried to protect them, at least, from the charge of lying. And, of course, people generally lie about their whereabouts at a particular time only when they were doing something they want kept secret. It is possible, therefore, that in not probing the question of whether these Pentagon leaders lied, the 9/11 Commission helped them cover up even greater misdeeds.

Not Probing the "War Games" Issue: Some critics of the official account of 9/11 believe that if we ever get a full account of how the attacks were able to succeed, we will see that a vital role was played by some military exercises, sometimes called "war games," that had been scheduled for that morning.[16]

   The 9/11 Commission Report does not completely omit discussion of this issue, but the discussion is very brief. The issue is introduced in a conversation between the FAA and NEADS about Flight 11. After the FAA person says that they have a hijacked aircraft headed towards New York and "need someone to scramble some F-16s or something up there," the person at NEADS says: "Is this real-world or exercise?" (20). The note to this discussion then explains:

> On 9/11, NORAD was scheduled to conduct a military exercise, Vigilant Guardian, which postulated a bomber attack from the former Soviet Union. We investigated whether military preparations for the large-scale exercise compromised the military's response to the real-world terrorist attack on 9/11. According to General Eberhart, "it took about 30 seconds" to make the adjustment to the real-world situation. . . . We found that the response was, if anything, expedited by the increased number of staff at the sectors and at NORAD because of the scheduled exercise. (458n116)

Those who believe that war games played a major role in the events of that day consider this cursory treatment a cover-up. For example, Michael Kane, taking issue with the implication that Vigilant Guardian was the only war game being run that morning,[17] says: "There were at least three, as has been documented by the mainstream press, and there may have been more than five such exercises running."[18] The best known, aside from Vigilant Guardian, is Vigilant Warrior, in Richard Clarke's book.[19] Still another was called Northern Vigilance.[20] A fourth was the exercise being run by the National Reconnaissance Office.

The importance attached to this issue by many students of 9/11 is shown by the fact that audience members at the final 9/11 hearing shouted out, as Commissioner Jamie Gorelick was about to begin her questioning: "Tell us about the war games."[21] But Gorelick did not ask about them. When asked afterwards why not, she replied—thereby illustrating the power of Zelikow's staff to determine which topics were explored—that "the staff concluded [that the war games] were not an inhibition to the military doing its job and therefore I wasn't going to waste my time with that."[22]

The one Commission member to ask a question about the military exercises being run that morning, Kane reports, was Timothy Roemer. Saying to General Eberhart, "you were postured for an exercise against the former Soviet Union," Roemer asked:

Did that help or hurt? Did that help in terms of were more people prepared? Did you have more people ready? Were more fighters fueled with more fuel? Or did this hurt in terms of people thinking, "No, there's no possibility that this is real world; we're engaged in an exercise," and delay things?

In response, Eberhart said: "my belief is that it helped because of the manning, because of the focus."

Kane then reports that he, after General Eberhart's testimony was over, asked him who was in charge of coordinating the multiple war games running on 9/11, to which Eberhart replied: "No comment." Kane writes: "If the war games helped 'because of the focus,' why was General Eberhart reluctant to comment on just who was at the center of that focus?"[23]

It would appear, accordingly, that the issue of the war games being run on 9/11 was yet another issue on which the 9/11 Commission helped the military avoid embarrassing questions.

Not Mentioning Operation Northwoods: The 9/11 Commission also protected the military from suspicion by not bringing up "incidents" that have in the past been provoked by the US military to justify war. America's wars of conquest against both Mexico and the Philippines were, for example, provoked by incidents engineered by the US military.[24] The sinking of the *Maine*, which provided a pretext for the United States to invade Cuba in 1898—under the battle cry "Remember the *Maine*, the hell with Spain"—is often included in the list of such incidents, but the explosion that sank the ship may have been an accident.[25] In any case, defenders of the US military could dismiss the relevance of those incidents, saying that they happened in a different era, before today's standards of integrity had been institutionalized. More relevant, therefore, would be the plan known as Operation Northwoods, which has become widely known through James Bamford's 2001 book, *Body of Secrets*.[26]

The plan was developed early in the Kennedy administration. The former president, Dwight Eisenhower, had asked the CIA to come up with a pretext to invade Cuba. The goal of the resulting plan was "the replacement of the Castro regime with one more devoted to the true interests of the Cuban people and more acceptable to the U.S., in such a manner to avoid any appearance of U.S. intervention."[27] Although Eisenhower approved this plan, Kennedy, after the Bay of Pigs fiasco, transferred planning for Cuba to the Defense Department. Early in 1962, the Joint Chiefs of Staff, led by its chairman, General Lyman Lemnitzer, gave Kennedy a plan called Operation Northwoods.

This Top Secret plan described "pretexts which would provide justification for US military intervention in Cuba."[28] A decision to intervene in Cuba, the document says, "will result from a period of heightened US–Cuban tensions which place the United States in the position of suffering justifiable grievances." The plan would also make the world ready for US intervention "by developing the image of the Cuban government as rash and irresponsible, and as an alarming and unpredictable threat to the peace of the Western Hemisphere."[29]

The plan then listed a series of possible actions to create this image. For example: "We could develop a Communist Cuban terror campaign in the Miami area, in other Florida cities and even in Washington. . . . We could sink a boatload of Cubans enroute to Florida (real or simulated)."[30] Particularly interesting, in light of some of the proposed scenarios as to what really happened on 9/11, is the following idea:

> It is possible to create an incident which will demonstrate convincingly that a Cuban aircraft has attacked and shot down a

chartered civil airliner. . . . The destination would be chosen only to cause the flight plan route to cross Cuba. . . .

   a. An aircraft at Eglin AFB would be painted and numbered as an exact duplication for a civil registered aircraft belonging to a CIA proprietary organization in the Miami area. At a designated time the duplication would be substituted for the actual civil aircraft and would be loaded with the selected passengers, all boarded under carefully prepared aliases. The actual registered aircraft would be converted to a drone.

   b. Take off times of the drone aircraft and the actual aircraft will be scheduled to allow a rendezvous south of Florida. From the rendezvous point the passenger-carrying aircraft will descend to minimum altitude and go directly into an auxiliary field . . . . The drone aircraft meanwhile will continue to fly the filed flight plan. When over Cuba the drone will being [sic] transmitting on the international distress frequency a "MAY DAY" message stating he is under attack by Cuban MIG aircraft. The transmission will be interrupted by destruction of the aircraft which will be triggered by radio signal.[31]

Fake casualty lists would then be placed in US newspapers to "cause a wave of national indignation."[32]

In some of the schemes, such as the plan to "sink a boatload of Cubans," real deaths would be caused. And in some, real deaths of Americans, as in a "Remember the *Maine*" incident: "We could blow up a U.S. ship in Guantánamo Bay and blame Cuba."[33]

Although Kennedy rejected this scheme, the point at hand is that these military leaders proposed a commission that would have reported on Operation Northwoods would have thereby informed the American public that Generals Myers, Eberhart, and Winfield belong to a tradition in which such planning is not unknown. Such a commission would have asked whether the attacks of 9/11 might have been the latest in a series of pretexts for war created by the US military.

The Kean–Zelikow Commission, however, was not that kind of commission. Operation Northwoods was never once mentioned. Keeping silent about this part of the military tradition was one more way in which the Commission protected the military from suspicion.

THE COMMISSION'S TREATMENT OF THE FAA

As we have seen in previous chapters, the 9/11 Commission's treatment of the FAA is radically different from its treatment of the military. But then the 9/11 Commissioners, in harmony with their apparent determination not to blame anyone for the attacks of 9/11, say, amazingly: "We do not believe that the true picture of that morning reflects discredit on the operational personnel at . . . FAA facilities" (31).

How can the Commissioners say this? Flight controllers and supervisors, according to the Commission's narrative, were consistently slow to realize that their planes had been hijacked, even if these planes hit the Trifecta, showing all three of the standard tell-tale signs. When the truth finally forced its way through their dense skulls, they were slow to contact their superiors. And if the FAA personnel in the field were incompetent, their superiors were even worse. Flight 175 was not stopped partly because the regional managers refused to take the call that would have told them it was hijacked. Worst of all were the officials in Washington. Although they learned about three of the flights in time to have had them intercepted, they failed in each case to alert the military. Although the Commissioners say that their aim was not "to assign individual blame," they have in effect portrayed officials at FAA headquarters as guilty of criminal negligence of the most extreme sort.

The Commission seeks to give partial absolution by saying that the FAA was "unprepared for the type of attacks launched against the United States on September 11, 2001." The FAA officials, we are told, struggled "to improvise" to meet a "challenge they had never before encountered and had never trained to meet" (45). The problem, in particular, was that "[n]o one at the FAA . . . that day had ever dealt with multiple hijackings" (10).

There are, however, three problems with this explanation. In the first place, most of the failures by FAA personnel, as portrayed in the Commission's report, were unrelated to the fact that there were several hijackings that day.

In the second place, the FAA did, as the Commission pointed out, have one truly unprecedented task to perform that day—the task of landing all the aircraft in the country. And yet the Commission reported that the FAA "execut[ed] that unprecedented order flawlessly" (31). Is it not strange that the FAA personnel carried out that unprecedented task so flawlessly and yet failed so miserably with the tasks they had long been performing on a regular basis?

In the third place, personnel from the FAA have disputed the Commission's portrayal of the FAA's response that day. As we have seen, Laura Brown, in her memo of May 22, 2003, stated emphatically that the FAA established a phone bridge immediately after the first strike on the World Trade Center, then

> shared real-time information on the phone bridges about the unfolding events, including information about loss of communication with aircraft, loss of transponder signals, unauthorized changes in course, and other actions being taken by all the flights of interest.

She thereby disputed in advance the Commission's conclusion that the military received "no advance notice on the second [plane], no advance notice on the third, and no advance notice on the fourth" (31). The 9/11 Commission claimed that the FAA failed in each of these cases to call the Department of Defense. According to Laura Brown, however, the FAA was in continuous contact with the Department of Defense from about 8:50 on.

If we consider the fact that the Kean–Zelikow Report simply accepts without question all the explanations and excuses provided by the military, together with the fact that its portrayal of the FAA is too negative to be believable, it would seem that the FAA is being forced to take the fall to protect the US military—and, thereby, the Bush administration.

Given all the evidence that points in this direction, the most surreal moment in the hearings surely occurred when Commissioner Bob Kerrey suggested that exactly the opposite was occurring. In the hearing on June 17, 2004, the following exchange occurred:

> MR. KERREY: General Eberhart. . . . Do you know what NORAD's experience is in intercepting planes prior to 9/11?

> GEN. EBERHART: Sir, we can provide that for the record. . . .

> MR. KERREY: I've got some concern for the military in this whole situation, because the optics for me is, you all are taking a bullet for the FAA. I appreciate that may be wrong, but that's how it appears, because, General Arnold, you in particular on the day covered

yourself in glory. I think the military performed, under the circumstances, exceptionally well, and I don't understand why the— . . . [T]here was a briefing at the White House on the 17th of September. And it feels like something happened in that briefing that produced almost a necessity to deliver a story that's different than what actually happened on that day.

General Arnold, is that an unfair optic on my part? As I said, if you look at what you all did on that day, it's hard to find fault. And we really haven't uncovered this stuff, it was readily available, the facts were all there. So it leaves the impression that there is an attempt to create a unified story there, and has you all, as I said, taking a bullet for the FAA, because the FAA should have told you what was going on—it seems to me. . . . Help me out here. Am I looking at this wrong? Because, as I said, it looks like you guys did a good job on that day, and now it—you know, it just gives the appearance that you're standing in front of the FAA, and unnecessarily so.

GEN. EBERHART: Sir, I'd like to answer that question. And, first of all, there's no scheme here or plot to spin this story to try to cover or take a bullet for anyone. And I for one, from the day after 9/11 to today, do not get into FAA bashing, because as I can imagine being on those screens that morning, as I can imagine being in their shoes, and the confusion that existed that morning—obviously we know we could have done it better. . . . But I can assure you that there was—we didn't get together and decide that we were going to cover for anybody or take a bullet for anybody. . . .

MR. KERREY: . . . General Arnold, are you—I presume you didn't accompany and weren't a part of that briefing?

MR. ARNOLD: Well, the only thing I can add is that the FAA— we were dependent on the FAA on 9/11. Had the FAA—I felt we worked very well together, in spite of the fact that we were not postured to handle that threat. . . .

MR. KERREY: Well, I appreciate your wanting not to bash the FAA, but, my God, the Cleveland Center said somebody needs to notify the military and scramble planes, and they didn't. You would have an additional 30 minutes of notification. Now it turns out that passengers on 93 took care of it for us. But it's—you know, I don't consider it to be bashing just to say to them, My God, you guys should have notified us—and didn't. And that's a fairly significant breakdown.[34]

This exchange in June of 2004 came over a year after Laura Brown's memo, which was sent in May of 2003. It appeared that this memo had no effect on the Commission's final report. In her telephone conversation with me, in fact, she said that the claim that the NMCC was not called by the FAA was simply not true. This and much other information was given to the 9/11 Commission, she said, but on disputed issues, the Commission always gave the benefit of the doubt to the military, never to the FAA.[35] Her statement, which is certainly consistent with the Commission's treatments of the military and the FAA, provides further reason to believe that the biggest distortion in the Kean–Zelikow Report is this twofold distortion: Making the FAA look as if it failed to follow its standard procedures on 9/11 in order to disguise the fact that the US military in fact did not follow its standard procedures.

CONCLUSION

The purpose of the 9/11 Commission, it should be abundantly clear by now, was not to provide "the fullest possible account of the events surrounding 9/11." The purpose was to argue, implicitly, that the US government was not itself complicit in the attacks of 9/11. As we have seen, however, the Commission could make this argument only by distorting, or completely omitting, dozens of facts.

In Chapter 1, we reviewed facts that were omitted about the alleged suicide hijackers—that at least six of them are reportedly still alive; that some of them, including Mohamed Atta, did not behave like devout Muslims ready to meet their Maker; that Hani Hanjour did not have the piloting skills to do what Flight 77 allegedly did (a fact that the Commission acknowledged and then ignored); and that flight manifests showing these nineteen men to have been on those planes have never been produced.

In Chapter 2, we saw that the Commission ignored various facts that contradict the theory that the WTC buildings were brought down by fire (perhaps, in the case of the Twin Towers, in conjunction with the impact of the airplanes)—namely, that fire has never before brought down steel-frame high-rise buildings; that the fires, especially in the South Tower and Building 7, were not very big, hot, or long-lasting; and that the wrong tower fell first. In providing an implicit explanation of how the towers could have collapsed, the Commission, amazingly, simply denied their most important feature—47 massive steel columns constituting the core of each tower. The Commission then omitted any mention of the collapse that is universally recognized as the most difficult to explain, that of Building 7. It, of course, also omitted Larry Silverstein's apparent confession that this building was brought down by controlled demolition. The Commission also failed to discuss the fact that the collapses of all three buildings exemplified ten standard features of controlled demolitions (even while alluding to two of them—the fact that the towers came straight down and at virtually free-fall speed). It failed to discuss Mayor Giuliani's reported statement suggesting that he had advance knowledge that the towers were going to collapse. It failed to mention that a brother and a cousin of President Bush were principals in the company that handled security for the WTC. And it failed to discuss the quick removal of the steel beams and columns, even though this removal of evidence from a crime scene would normally be a federal crime.

In Chapter 3, as we saw, the Kean–Zelikow Report failed to discuss various facts about the strike on the Pentagon that are inconsistent with the official story—namely, that the west wing was the least likely, as well as a very difficult, part of the Pentagon for terrorists to strike; that the facade of the west wing did not collapse for a half hour after allegedly being hit by a Boeing 757 going several hundred miles per hour; that the entrance hole was big enough only for the nose of a Boeing 757; that a Boeing airliner was visible neither outside nor inside the Pentagon; and that the government, besides not releasing videos proving that the aircraft was a Boeing airliner, had the video from the nearby gas station confiscated. Finally, the Commission explained the hijackers' decision not to attack a nuclear plant in terms of fear that, because of the restricted airspace around a nuclear plant, their plane would be shot down. But the Commission then simply ignored the fact that the airspace around the Pentagon is surely equally restricted, so that only a military aircraft could get through without activating the anti-missile batteries.

We saw in Chapter 4 that while the Commission went to considerable lengths to show that it was not fear on the president's part that kept him away from Washington after the attacks, the Commission dealt only superficially with the more serious problem, namely: Why did both the president and the Secret Service show a *lack* of fear during the hour when they should have been very much afraid? We saw, moreover, that the Commission failed to challenge the Secret Service's distorted presentation of the options available, as if the only alternative to running out the door was to remain at the school another half hour.

In Chapter 5, we saw that the Commission omitted any discussion of the advance warnings evidently received by Attorney General Ashcroft, Mayor Willie Brown, and several Pentagon officials. It failed to mention the advance warnings David Schippers claims to have received from several FBI agents. The Commission also failed to mention these FBI agents, who said that they knew the date and targets of the attacks long in advance. The Commission likewise failed to explore whether the NSA, which reportedly intercepted a call from KSM to Mohamed Atta the day before 9/11, giving him final authorization to execute the plan, was really not translated until after 9/11. Finally, with regard to the massive purchases of put options on companies whose stock prices were sure to plummet after the attacks, the Commission denied that they involved insider trading by simply begging the question.

In Chapter 6, we saw that the omissions in the Kean–Zelikow Report also included evidence that OBL had spent time shortly before 9/11 in an American hospital, where he was visited by a CIA agent; evidence that OBL had not really been disowned by his own family and the Saudi royal family; evidence that the effort to capture him in Afghanistan was a charade; and Posner's report that according to Abu Zubaydah, at least three members of the Saudi royal family knew that al-Qaeda attacks on America were scheduled for 9/11. The final report of the 9/11 Commission, moreover, clearly distorted known facts in denying any Saudi funding of al-Qaeda and denying, in particular, that Princess Haifa gave money to al-Qaeda members even indirectly.

Chapter 7 revealed several more distortions by the Commission: its ignoring, in relation to the September 13 flight carrying Saudis, the distinction between private and commercial flights, which had been emphasized by Craig Unger; its ignoring of the evidence that some 300 Saudis left the country in the ensuing days; its false suggestion that everyone who should have been considered a "person of interest" was thoroughly interrogated; and its pretense that Prince Bandar was not heavily involved in arranging the Saudi flights. The Kean–Zelikow Commission also failed to point out that either the president himself or some subordinate was, by authorizing these hasty departures, guilty of obstructing a criminal investigation.

In Chapter 8, which dealt with omissions about the FBI, we saw that the Commission failed to mention FBI agent Robert Wright's serious allegations about obstruction by FBI headquarters; that it omitted Minneapolis agent Coleen Rowley's accusation of sabotage by FBI headquarters in the Moussaoui case; that it left out her crucial complaint, which is that an agent at headquarters altered her FISA petition before forwarding it; that the Commission struck from the record all the damning details presented in the 3.5-hour testimony by Sibel Edmonds; and that it evidently did not interview any of the FBI agents Edmonds accused of gross misconduct, such as Mike Feghali and Thomas Frields. Finally, putting Edmonds' letter to Chairman Kean together with the letter from former federal employees to the US Congress, which was quoted in the Introduction, we can infer that the Commission treated in

a similar way the testimony of the 24 other former federal employees
who, in addition to Edmonds, signed this letter, which said:

> Omission is one of the major flaws in the Commission's report. We
> are aware of significant issues and cases that were duly reported to
> the commission by those of us with direct knowledge. . . . Serious
> problems and shortcomings within government agencies likewise
> were reported to the Commission but were not included in the
> report.[1]

If those 24 other people had, like Edmonds, written a public letter
spelling out the nature of their testimony, we would surely have a much
longer list of the Commission's omissions.

In any case, we then saw in Chapter 9 that the Kean–Zelikow Report
omitted various facts that, if widely known, might threaten continued aid
to, and cooperation with, Pakistan and its ISI: the presence of ISI chief
Mahmoud Ahmad in Washington the week prior to 9/11; evidence that
Ahmad ordered an ISI agent to wire $100,000 to Mohamed Atta;
evidence that US officials, after word of this payment got out, pressured
the Pakistani government to "retire" him; evidence of ISI participation in
the assassination of Ahmad Shah Masood; evidence that KSM, who
reportedly gave Mohamed Atta the final authorization for the 9/11
hijackings, was linked to the ISI; evidence that Daniel Pearl was murdered
by ISI agents, perhaps KSM; evidence that Mushaf Ali Mir, a military
officer with ISI links, knew of the 9/11 attacks in advance; and evidence
that in 1999, ISI agent Rajaa Gulum Abbas predicted the destruction of
the towers. We saw, finally, that the Commission, while surely familiar
with the evidence of the ISI payment to Atta, claimed to have seen "no
evidence" that any foreign government supplied funding to al-Qaeda.

In Chapter 10, we saw that the 9/11 Commission omitted reference
to various facts suggesting that the Bush administration had interests of
the type that could have provided motives for arranging or at least
allowing the attacks of 9/11. The Commission's report excluded, in
particular, the Bush administration's reference to the 9/11 attacks as
"opportunities"; the PNAC statement that "a new Pearl Harbor" would
be helpful for bringing about its desired transformation of the military;
the fact that Rumsfeld, Myers, and Eberhart, who were in charge of the
air defense of America on 9/11, were enthusiastic promoters of the US
Space Command, for which Rumsfeld obtained increased funding on the

basis of the 9/11 attacks; evidence that the war in Afghanistan was about gas, oil, and increased military presence in Central Asia, not peace and human rights; evidence that several members of the Bush administration had long been anxious for a war to gain control of Iraq; and the fact that Rumsfeld's memo indicated he wanted to attack Iraq whether it was involved in 9/11 or not.

Beyond all these omissions and distortions, furthermore, there are all the ones mentioned in Part II. Assuming, however, that these are sufficiently fresh in the reader's mind, I will not summarize them here. I will add, however, that even after we have enumerated all the omissions and distortions in this book, we would surely not have close to a complete listing of the omissions and distortions in *The 9/11 Commission Report*. This is because I have, of course, mentioned only those I know about because of my previous study of evidence pointing to complicity in the attacks of 9/11 by the Bush administration. But there are major portions of the Kean–Zelikow Report that are simply ignored in the present book. I have no idea how many omissions and distortions there may be in those portions.

But I have learned, from the omissions and distortions discussed here, that the Commission's final report simply cannot be trusted. One of the clearest indications of this fact is the Commission's obviously false claim that on the morning of 9/11, Vice President Cheney did not arrive in the shelter conference room until shortly before 10:00. If we are certain that the Commission is fabricating here, how can we trust it in all the places in which we do not have independent knowledge of the facts, one way or the other?

If this supposedly authoritative report is not authoritative, we need an explanation as to why not. After all, people usually do not distort the truth for no reason at all. In the Introduction, I suggested that at least part of the explanation could be found in the conflicts of interest inherent in the Commission's executive director. Given Philip Zelikow's close personal, professional, and ideological ties to the Bush White House, he could hardly lead the 9/11 staff in an objective, independent, impartial search for the truth about the attacks of 9/11, especially if the White House was complicit in those attacks (whether by intention or merely inattention).

I have emphasized this problem inherent in the 9/11 Commission, along with the fact that its two most powerful members were Republicans, by calling it the Kean–Zelikow Commission. I will now elaborate on this point, then broaden the explanation by discussing other conflicts of interest within the Commission and its staff. I will base this discussion on information provided in the 2004 book by investigative reporter Peter Lance, *Cover Up*.[2]

PHILIP ZELIKOW AND THE WHITE HOUSE

In the Introduction to the present book, I wrote that "the Commission's investigation was essentially run by Zelikow." This judgment is confirmed, Peter Lance reports, by a member of the Commission's staff who became a confidential source for him. This source said that of the Commission's eight investigative teams, the only team leader who was not controlled by Zelikow was John Farmer—"a former New Jersey attorney general who was close to Chairman Tom Kean." As a consequence, the source said, "Farmer is really butting heads with him." By contrast, he said, "The other teams are completely controlled by Zelikow." More generally, Lance's source said, "Zelikow is calling the shots. He's skewing the investigation and running it his own way."[3]

Lance reports, furthermore, that he had some first-hand experience with the way Zelikow exercised his control over the investigation. On the basis of Lance's previous book, *1000 Years for Revenge: International Terrorism and the FBI: The Untold Story*, he requested an opportunity to testify to the Commission. He was originally turned down by Zelikow. But then, after Lance's book was brought to the attention of Chairman Kean, he was invited to testify. Zelikow assigned the task of taking Lance's testimony to staff member Dietrich L. Snell.

This assignment, however, was problematic. On the one hand, Lance's book revolved around Ramzi Yousef, who was the architect of the 1993 World Trade Center bombing and also of the "Bojinka" plot to blow up a dozen US airplanes. Lance's account of Yousef was in strong tension with the account presented by the prosecuting attorneys in the 1996 Bojinka trial, in which Yousef was convicted. Dietrich Snell, on the other hand, just happened to be one of the prosecuting attorneys in that trial. So Lance was assigned by Zelikow to give his testimony to a 9/11 Commission staff member who had a professional interest in having Lance's account rejected.

Lance was not completely surprised, he reports, to find that most of the points he had made to Snell were either omitted, distorted, or disputed in the final report.[4] The details of, and the reasons for, these differences are too complex to summarize here. The main point for now, in any case, is simply that Lance had some personal experience with the way in which Zelikow, with his power to "call the shots," could "skew the investigation."

I have also suggested that because of Zelikow's power to shape the investigation and the final report, combined with his close relationship to the Bush White House, the Commission's investigation was probably no more "impartial" and "independent" than if it had been conducted by Condoleezza Rice, Dick Cheney, or George Bush. Lance, in fact, quotes Lorie van Auken, speaking for the Family Steering Committee or at least the four Jersey Girls, as saying: "It's our sense today that they decided early on what they wanted the public to know and then geared the hearings to fit this pre-conceived script."[5] The Commission, in other words, was not really conducting an investigation but merely engaging in a performance to instill in the public mind what "they decided early on." The "they" in this statement would refer primarily to the executive director.

Lance has emphasized, furthermore, that the influence of the White House on the production of the final report was not limited to the influence mediated through Zelikow. In this regard, Lance points to a UPI story published July 1, 2004, which revealed that the various Staff Reports—many of which found their way into the final report with few changes—were cleared by the White House in advance. This story, written by Shaun Waterman, also revealed that the chapters of the final report were sent to the Department of Justice before being cleared for publication.[6] The official reason was that these clearances would guarantee that, unlike the final report of the Joint Inquiry, none of the Commission's report would need to be blacked out in the interests of national security. Lance, however, quotes Kristen Breitweiser's observation that this process allows the administration, in the name of protecting national security, "to hide information that is just embarrassing or inconvenient."[7] Or, a more suspicious mind might add, even worse.

The Commission's close working relationship with the White House explains some things about the Commission's final report that might otherwise be puzzling. One of these is the fact that it contains no criticism of the president, in spite of the obstacles he had placed in the way of the Commission. These obstacles were several. The first was simply the long resistance even to having such a commission. The president agreed only after the families of the victims and then revelations from the Joint Inquiry created so much pressure that the White House had little choice but to agree.[8]

A second obstacle to having a commission that might discover the truth about 9/11 was the president's appointment of Henry Kissinger to be its chairman. This appointment produced widespread incredulity, with the *New York Times* saying that "it is tempting to wonder if the choice of Mr. Kissinger is not a clever maneuver by the White House to contain an investigation it long opposed."[9] Scepticism about Kissinger's capacity to run an independent investigation was based in part on evidence that he was receiving consulting fees not only from corporations with heavy investments in Saudi Arabia but also from Unocal—the oil company that, as we saw in Chapter 10, wanted to build a pipeline through Afghanistan—if only the Taliban could be replaced by a government that would provide the needed stability.[10] When there were cries that Kissinger needed to reveal his business clients, the president said that this would not be necessary. The Congressional Research Service declared, however, that Kissinger had to reveal his clients, but Kissinger resigned rather than do so.[11] It was only after this failed effort that Bush appointed Kean and Zelikow—a decision that would, of course, not be portrayed by the authors of the final report as yet another obstacle.

At that point, in any case, the obstacles to be placed before the Commission's work had only begun. The president refused to give it adequate funding. Whereas the investigation of the Challenger disaster received $50 million, Bush promised only $3 million for the investigation of the much more deadly and complex disaster of 9/11. He then initially resisted when the Commission asked for an additional $8 million.[12] After that we witnessed delays in issuing security clearances; resistance to providing documents; insistence that federal employees have "minders" present when they were testifying; resistance to having White House officials testify, especially under oath; and resistance to extending the deadline when the Commission realized that, because of the many delays, it needed more time.

The Commission's frustration with the White House because of these delays boiled over into the public domain, often becoming the stuff of headlines. For example, when the security clearance for Slade Gorton, a former senator very familiar with intelligence issues, was being delayed, Vice-Chairman Lee Hamilton called it "astounding that someone like Senator Gorton can't get immediate clearance." Chairman Kean interpreted the insistence on having minders as an attempt at "intimidation." Referring to the delay in obtaining White House documents, Max Cleland, said: "It's obvious that the White House wants to run out the clock here. . . . [W]e're still in negotiations with some assistant White House counsel about getting these documents— it's disgusting." Slade Gorton made this complaint bipartisan, saying that the "lack of cooperation" would make it "very difficult" for the commission to complete its work by the deadline. At one point, after a subpoena had been issued to the FAA, Chairman Kean said that this subpoena would "put other agencies on notice that our document requests must be taken as seriously as a subpoena." Kean even indicated that he was ready to subpoena the White House itself, saying: "Any document that has to do with this investigation cannot be beyond our reach. . . . I will not stand for [stonewalling]. . . . We will use every tool at our command to get hold of every document."[13]

In reading *The 9/11 Commission Report*, however, one would have no idea that such conflicts had ever occurred. In their Preface, Kean and Hamilton make no mention of the "White House" and have only one reference to President Bush: After thanking their fellow commissioners and the staff, they say, "We thank the Congress and the President" (xvii). So, in the same statement in which they announced their aim "to provide the fullest possible account" of the "facts and circumstances" relating to 9/11, Kean and Hamilton made no mention of one of the seemingly most inexplicable facts about 9/11—that after the biggest terrorist attack ever suffered by the United States, the president wanted no investigation into this attack and then, once he was forced to accept this investigation, seemingly did everything in his power to delay and obstruct it. Is it not mysterious that the 9/11 Commission would, in its final report, make no reference to these facts? Perhaps—until we recall that the White House had a hand, both indirectly through Zelikow and directly, in producing the final report.

The omissions and distortions in the final report, however, are not entirely explainable in terms of the influence of Zelikow and the White House. At least some of the Commissioners themselves and the members of the Commission's staff had conflicts of interest.

OTHER CONFLICTS OF INTEREST

Conflicts of interest in the Commissioners can be illustrated by reference to Chairman Kean himself. He was a member of the Board of Directors for the oil company Amerada Hess, which joined with Delta Oil of Saudi Arabia—one of the companies in the CentGas consortium—to form Hess–Delta.[14] The replacement of Kissinger with Kean, therefore, did not remove the danger that the chairman of the 9/11 Commission might be conflicted with regard to exposing information of two kinds: information that could create problems for US–Saudi relations, and information suggesting that the war in Afghanistan had something to do with allowing the CentGas pipeline project to go forward. As we have seen, in fact, information of both kinds was omitted from *The 9/11 Commission Report.*

News reports have, furthermore, indicated that all the other Commissioners had at least one possible conflict of interest.[15]

There were also serious problems within the Commission's staff. If we look at the pages of *The 9/11 Commission Report* on which the members of the staff are listed (xiii–xiv), we get no idea of who these people are. We are told only that, for example, Dietrich Snell served as a "Senior Counsel & Team Leader." We are not told that he was formerly an attorney for the Department of Justice and that he was a prosecutor in Ramzi Yousef's Bojinka trial. We have no reason to suspect, therefore, that these "staff members" had conflicts of interest, ones that might have given them motives to conceal some of the facts dug up by their investigative work.

Lance reports, however, that Dietrich Snell was not an exception. Rather, he says: "Nearly half of the Commission staff members had ties to the very agencies they were charged with examining."[16]

Getting more specific, Lance says:

> Of the seventy-five staffers listed on the Commission's Web site, nine worked for the Department of Justice . . . , another six had worked for the CIA, and six others were FBI veterans. Four staffers had worked at the White House, three at the State Department, and five others at the Pentagon. The Commission staff also included representatives of the INS and the NTSB . . . , and one staff worker who served on a key intelligence oversight committee.[17]

When the Commissioners themselves are added, furthermore, some of those numbers are increased. For example, three of the Commissioners— Jamie Gorelick, Richard Ben-Veniste, and James Thompson—had worked for the Department of Justice (DoJ).

We might, upon first thought, think that it was good that the Commission had members with those backgrounds, because they would thereby be in a better position to evaluate the work of those agencies in relation to 9/11.

However, although there were surely some advantages to having members with experience in the various agencies the Commission was to investigate, these advantages were surely outweighed by the dangers. One danger was simply that these members, by virtue of loyalties to those agencies and ties to people still working for them, would be tempted to conceal facts that might lead to embarrassment, dismissal, or even criminal prosecution. An even greater danger, in the sense of constituting an even greater conflict of interest, was that some of these members may have been personally involved in cases that were, or at least should have been, investigated by the Commission. According to Lance, in fact, this was often true. I will summarize examples he gives of such conflicts involving former CIA, FBI, and DoJ employees.

Conflicts of Interest with Respect to the CIA: In reviewing one of the reports by the Commission's staff, Lance comments that it went "particularly easy on the CIA" when describing what he terms an "extraordinary agency blunder."[18] Suspecting that this may have something to do with the fact that six of the members of the staff had previously worked for the CIA, he illustrates the problem in terms of one of those members, Douglas MacEachin. Examining Staff Statement Number 11, which treated "The Performance of the Intelligence Community," Lance is especially critical of its treatment of the planes-as-weapons idea, which some al-Qaeda operatives, such as Ramzi Yousef, were discussing by 1994. The staff report, Lance mentions, does offer a criticism of the CIA, but one that does not get specific:

> Noting that the Counterterrorism Center (CTC) at the CIA "did not analyze how a hijacked aircraft or other explosives-laden aircraft might be used as a weapon," the staff statement singles out no one for blame. That may be because one of its authors was staff member Douglas MacEachin—who served as deputy director of intelligence at the CIA until 1995.

To underline the problem here, Lance quotes Lorie van Auken as asking: "How does the Commission use a senior retired CIA official to evaluate the work of the CIA during his tenure? How can they possibly expect a transparent, objective analysis?"[19]

Conflicts of Interest with Respect to the FBI: In my own summaries of reports about obstructions of 9/11-related investigations, both prior to and after the attacks, the FBI has easily been the major agency involved. For example, the stories involving Sibel Edmonds, Coleen Rowley, David Schippers, and Robert Wright all involved the FBI. And yet there is little if any serious criticism of the FBI within *The 9/11 Commission Report.* The report, indeed, seems to go out of its way to conceal reports of FBI misconduct.

This fact is less surprising if we keep in mind Lance's observations about the make-up of the Commission. Besides having six former FBI employees, two of the Commissioners who had been prosecutors for the DoJ—Richard Ben-Veniste and James Thompson—had worked closely with the FBI.[20] Given these facts, it is perhaps not surprising to learn from Lance that "[i]n all of its public hearings, the staff and the Commissioners never permitted a single witness outside of the government to offer testimony critical of the FBI."[21] From the Commissioners themselves, furthermore, the FBI, rather than receiving criticism, received praise. In one of the hearings, Ben-Veniste declared: "The FBI is the finest law enforcement agency in the world, bar none."[22]

Lance then gives an example of how this attitude prevented any evidence to the contrary from surfacing. Prior to the hearing in April that was to deal with the FBI, he reports, "the Jersey widows pushed hard to get the 9/11 Commission to address [Sibel] Edmonds's charges." But, as we saw in Chapter 8, the Commission had no questions for FBI Director Mueller about any of the matters that Edmonds had laid out in great detail to the Commission's staff. Lance then adds this fact:

> The only reference to the issue came in a cryptic comment from Richard Ben-Veniste . . . . "There's one area I want to put off to the side," he said, "and that's the area of FBI translators. I understand there are active investigations with respect to some of the allegations that have been made. I don't want to get into those facts now. I don't think it's appropriate."[23]

So, although Edmonds had reported incidents suggesting deliberate FBI sabotage of FBI investigations and even collusion with organizations that the FBI was supposed to be investigating, the 9/11 Commission, set up to investigate all the "facts and circumstances" relating to 9/11, would not discuss her charges, thinking it more "appropriate" to let them be investigated by the FBI and the DoJ—the very agencies against which the charges were made.

In Chapter Eight, we examined four of the eight points contained in the open letter to Chairman Kean sent by Edmonds, who explained that these were the matters about which she had informed his Commission's staff. With regard to our present concern, however, it will be helpful to look at one of the points not mentioned earlier. In what was, in fact, the first of the specific charges stated in her letter, she said:

> After the terrorist attacks of September 11 we, the translators at the FBI's largest and most important translation unit, were told to slow down, even stop, translation of critical information related to terrorist activities so that the FBI could present the United States Congress with a record of "extensive backlog of untranslated documents," and justify its request for budget and staff increases. While FBI agents from various field offices were desperately seeking leads and suspects, and completely depending on FBI HQ and its language units to provide them with needed translated information, hundreds of translators were being told by their administrative supervisors not to translate and to let the work pile up. . . . This issue has been confirmed by the Senate Judiciary Committee [and] substantiated by the Department of Justice Inspector General Report (Please refer to DoJ–IG report Re: Sibel Edmonds and FBI Translation, provided to you prior to the completion of your report). I provided your investigators with a detailed and specific account of this issue and the names of other witnesses willing to corroborate this.

This was one of the items that the Commission deemed it inappropriate to discuss.

Given this background, it is interesting to see what the Commission's final report had to say about FBI translators. In the section on the FBI, we see that the Commission did point out that the FBI was not doing a very effective job. We also find out, however, that the main problem was lack of adequate funding. At the end of the paragraph on the inadequacies of the FBI's "intelligence collection effort," accordingly, we read that the FBI "lacked sufficient translators proficient in Arabic and other key languages, resulting in a significant backlog of untranslated intercepts" (77). Then, in the note to this paragraph, we read: "Since 9/11, the FBI has [added] nearly 700 new translators" (273n25).

Here, then, is the sequence of events after 9/11. First, translators were told to slow down, even stop, translating vital documents so that the "extensive backlog of untranslated documents" could be used to justify budget and staff increases. Second, Sibel Edmonds tried to blow the whistle on this scam (among other things) but was silenced. Third, the FBI's scam worked—it got its increases. Fourth, the 9/11 Commission had Edmonds' testimony taken in private but refused to mention it publicly. Fifth, the Commission justified the FBI's budget and staff increases by reference to the "significant backlog of untranslated intercepts." The FBI must have been pleased to have so many friends on the Commission. (For a discussion of conflicts of interest involving former members of the Department of Justice, especially Jamie Gorelick, and the FBI, see the Appendix.)

LIMITED CRITICISMS

Given the make-up of the 9/11 Commission, the nature of its criticisms is not surprising. The Commission does offer criticisms of various agencies, including the US military. The Commission can thereby portray itself as having carried out its assignment. But the criticisms are innocuous. No individuals are singled out for blame. And the blameworthy deeds are failures of imagination, failures to communicate, and the like, not prosecutable crimes. If the Kean-Zelikow Report is the final reckoning, Martha Stewart will spend more time in prison than anyone responsible for the deaths of the almost 3,000 people killed on 9/11.

THE SILENCED COMMISSIONER

Peter Lance devotes a page to one member of the Commission who had threatened to be trouble from the White House's point of view, Max Cleland. As I mentioned in Chapter Fourteen, Cleland had to leave the Commission when he was named to fill an opening on the board of the Export–Import Bank. Lance points out, in a section headed "Silencing Senator Cleland," that "it was only after his open attacks on the Bush Administration that the White House sent his nomination to the Senate."[24]

Lance is referring to criticisms by Cleland that were published in an interview titled "The President Ought to be Ashamed." In this interview, Cleland was especially criticizing a deal that was worked out between the Commission and the White House with regard to access to the Presidential Daily Briefs, according to which most of the Commissioners would not see them. Indeed, only Philip Zelikow and Jamie Gorelick were to be allowed full access.[25] Cleland declared that "that decision compromised the mission of the 9/11 commission, pure and simple." Cleland also, after saying that "the Warren Commission blew it," added:

> I'm not going to be part of that. I'm not going to be part of looking at information only partially. I'm not going to be part of just coming to quick conclusions. I'm not going to be part of political pressure to do this or not do that. I'm not going to be part of that.[26]

And, of course, he was not—by virtue of leaving the Commission. We will, of course, never know what the outcome would have been if he had remained. My own suspicion is that his remaining would have had little effect on the shape of the final report, given the fact that it is in reality the Kean–Zelikow Report. But I also suspect that, had Cleland remained, Kean and Hamilton could not have announced, in the Preface, that the ten Commissioners came together "to present this report without dissent" (xv).

FINAL THOUGHTS

In any case, whatever might have been the case, we need to respond to the final report that has in fact been delivered. This book constitutes a response from the perspective of what I consider the most important question: Does *The 9/11 Commission Report* do anything to dispel the suspicion, which is held by many people in America and around the world, that the attacks of 9/11 were able to succeed only with the complicity of the US government? In the first part of this critique, I pointed out that the Commission, far from refuting any of the evidence that points in this direction, simply ignored most of it and distorted the rest. In the second part, I suggested that the Commission's attempt to defend the US military in particular against this suspicion is at best seriously flawed, at worst a set of audacious lies. Accordingly, the Kean–Zelikow Report, far from lessening my suspicions about official complicity, has served to confirm them. Why would the minds in charge of this final report engage in such deception if they were not trying to cover up very high crimes?[27]

As this book was going to press, I learned that *The 9/11 Commission Report* had been included among the finalists for the National Book Awards. I would not have been shocked by this news except for the fact that the nomination was in the nonfiction category.

Appendix

Conflicts of Interest involving Former DoJ–FBI Members

If we think of the Department of Justice and the FBI as essentially one entity, the DoJ–FBI, there were eighteen members of the Commission with ties to it. In light of the discussions in the Conclusion of conflicts of interest, we would expect these ties involving the DoJ to have created some additional conflicts of interest. Peter Lance's narrative in *Cover Up*, in fact, revolves around such conflicts involving Ramzi Yousef. Although a good understanding of Lance's complex narrative can be obtained only by reading his book, I will summarize enough of the main points to explain some of these conflicts.

One main point is that the true cause of the crash of TWA Flight 800 on July 17, 1996, was deliberately covered up by the DoJ–FBI. Although the official explanation became "mechanical failure," the evidence showed that the plane was brought down by a bomb, which had been placed in the cabin above the fuel tank, causing it to explode. On August 22, the FBI was ready to announce this finding. A *New York Times* story reporting that "an explosive devise was detonated inside the passenger cabin" was already in the works.[1] Later that day, however, the FBI suddenly reversed itself. To understand Lance's explanation of what happened, we need to know some essential elements in his narrative.

One of these elements is that although Yousef is rightly credited with the so-called Bojinka plot (which was discovered in Manila in January 1996), he had two quite different plots involving planes. The Bojinka plot was to blow up a dozen US airliners headed home from Asia, using a new bomb invented by Yousef, which would be placed under a seat above the fuel tank. The second plot was to hijack airplanes and use them as weapons, crashing them into buildings such as the World Trade Center, the Pentagon, CIA headquarters, and a nuclear plant.[2]

Another essential element in Lance's narrative is that while Yousef was in a New York jail awaiting trial (after being captured in February

1995), the cell between his and that of other al-Qaeda members was assigned to Gregory Scarpa, Jr., a member of the notorious Colombo family. Yousef started using Scarpa to pass information to his associates and Scarpa, hoping to get a lighter sentence, began giving that information to federal agents. After Yousef realized he was going to be convicted in the Bojinka trial, Scarpa learned that he was arranging to have KSM and other al-Qaeda associates use one of his bombs to bring down an American airliner in order to create a mistrial (the idea being that his lawyer could claim that the similarity to the bombings planned in the Bojinka plot would prejudice the jury).[3]

A third essential element in Lance's story is that the evidence of Yousef's responsibility for the destruction of TWA 800 was overwhelming. The bomb design that Scarpa received from Yousef was like the bomb Yousef had used for a test on a flight from Manila.[4] Prior to TWA 800, the center fuel tank of a Boeing 747 had never exploded in mid-air, and the chemicals found in the passenger cabin above the fuel tank were those recommended by Yousef. Yousef had told Scarpa his motive. And Scarpa, besides reporting that Yousef had given the order, provided additional evidence of al-Qaeda responsibility.[5] The FBI knew all this and yet did not use it. Why not?

This brings us to a fourth essential point, which is that Greg Scarpa, Jr., was also set to give testimony in a police corruption case involving his father, who had been an FBI informant as well as a notorious "killing machine." Greg Scarpa, Sr., had informed for FBI agent Lindley DeVecchio, with whom he had developed an extremely corrupt relationship.[6] Greg Scarpa, Jr., besides being prepared to testify against Yousef, was to be the primary witness against DeVecchio.[7]

With those background points, we can understand the FBI–DoJ reversal on the cause of the crash of TWA 800. On August 22 (1996), FBI Director Louis Freeh, to whom DeVecchio's lawyer had earlier appealed, summoned the head of the FBI's New York office, who was in charge of the TWA investigation, to a high-level meeting, which was also attended by Deputy Attorney General Jamie Gorelick. At this meeting, it was decided that exposing the DeVecchio–Scarpa relationship would have disastrous consequences. Besides creating a scandal, it would undermine at least nine high-profile cases against mobsters.[8] To prevent the conviction of DeVecchio, the credibility of Greg Scarpa, Jr., had to be undermined.[9]

It followed, therefore, that if Scarpa's testimony against his own father was to be considered not credible, his testimony against Yousef could not be used, so it was dismissed as "a hoax."[10] And if Yousef was not to be blamed, the whole idea that the flight had been brought down by a bomb had to be discredited. This was done primarily by falsely claiming that the chemicals found in the cabin had resulted from spills during a recent test for a bomb-sniffing dog.[11] So although Yousef and (secretly) KSM were convicted in the Bojinka plot, they were not even indicted for the bombing of TWA 800.

One respect in which Lance's narrative is directly relevant to the 9/11 Commission involves two researchers who tried to bring information to the attention of the Commission. Angela Clemente and Dr. Stephen Dresch had spent much time researching the relationship between Yousef and Greg Scarpa, Jr., even discovering the letters Yousef had given Scarpa and FBI memos proving their authenticity. Their conclusion was that Scarpa's reports about Yousef were "one hundred per cent truthful," from which it followed that KSM and other al-Qaeda operatives were responsible for the crash of TWA 800. Assuming the 9/11 Commission would be anxious to learn about this information, Clemente and Dresch sent a letter to the 9/11 Commission, detailing their discoveries and offering to testify. But they received no reply.[12]

We can, of course, understand why, with its large DoJ–FBI membership, the Commission would have been resistant to information supporting the view that TWA 800 was indeed, as the FBI had originally suspected, brought down by al-Qaeda operatives. After all, if that was the case, then the downing of this flight, which killed 230 people, was then the "biggest mass murder in American history."[13] Those in the DoJ–FBI who decided to cover up the truth about this crash, such as Jamie Gorelick, may well have believed that their decision was justifiable. Nevertheless, they would surely, especially after 9/11, not want to help reveal the fact that they had lied and, in so doing, covered up this prior al-Qaeda attack on America.

Lance also suggests that those with DoJ–FBI ties would have had a second reason to ignore the testimony being proffered by Clemente and Dresch. Given the information the FBI had received from Scarpa about Yousef's plans and cohorts, it "could have thwarted the TWA 800 crash."[14] As stated in the *New York Times* story of August 23, 1996 (which the FBI was unable to kill), "in loss of life, the downing of TWA

Flight 800 would stand as the most serious crime in American history."[15] The FBI would not want the public to know that it could have prevented this crime.

Still another part of the story about 1996 that DoJ–FBI loyalists would not want revealed is that the FBI turned down an opportunity to meet with one of Yousef's associates and hence an opportunity to monitor the al-Qaeda cell in New York City.[16]

Lance reports on still further respects in which it was not in the interest of some members of the Commission to have the full story about Ramzi Yousef revealed. Some of those respects, too complex to summarize here, help explain why Dietrich Snell, as one of Yousef's prosecutors, would have been resistant to parts of Yousef's story that Lance himself sought to bring to the Commission's attention. The portion of Lance's narrative that I have summarized, however, is sufficient to illustrate the way in which the presence on the Commission of eighteen former DoJ–FBI employees may have worked against its mandate to provide "the fullest possible account of the events surrounding 9/11."

As Lance's book shows, it seems that the more we learn about the 9/11 Commission, the more we see that it was exactly *not* the kind of body that would have revealed the truth about 9/11. A radically different kind of investigation is needed.

Notes

Introduction

[1] The official name of the 9/11 Commission is the National Commission on Terrorist Attacks upon the United States. This name is reflected in the full title of its final report, given in the following note.

[2] All page numbers in the text refer to *The 9/11 Commission Report: Final Report of the National Commission on Terrorist Attacks upon the United States*, Authorized Edition (New York: W. W. Norton, 2004).

[3] "Poll Shocker: Nearly Half Support McKinney's 9/11 Conspiracy Theory," Newsmax, Wednesday, April 17, 2002 (www.newsmax.com/showinside.shtml?a=2002/4/17/144136). The title of this story reflects the false but widely held belief that Cynthia McKinney had accused the Bush administration of foreknowledge. I discussed this flap in NPH 161–64, 207–08nn48–49 (for "NPH," see note 8, below).

[4] "CBS Poll: 56% Think There Is a 9/11 Cover-Up," *CBS/New York Times* Poll, April 23–27, 2004 (www.cbsnews.com/htdocs/CBSNews_polls/042804_poll.pdf; also available at http://www.pollingreport.com). Unfortunately the title referred only to the 56% who said the Bush administration was "hiding something," ignoring the 16% who said it was "mostly lying."

[5] See "Half of New Yorkers Believe US Leaders Had Foreknowledge of Impending 9-11 Attacks and 'Consciously Failed' to Act; 66% Call for New Probe of Unanswered Questions by Congress or New York's Attorney General, New Zogby International Poll Reveals" (www.zogby.com/news/ReadNews.dbm?ID=855). The poll had a 3.5 margin of error. A complete breakdown of its results is available at www.911truth.org/dossier/zogby911.pdf.

[6] Conducted by Maritz Thompson Lightstone, a national survey research firm, this poll is said to be accurate within 3.58 percent, 19 times out of 20. The results were reported in the *Toronto Star*, May 26, 2004.

[7] Ian Johnson, "Conspiracy Theories about Sept. 11 Get Hearing in Germany," *Wall Street Journal*, September 29, 2003.

[8] *The New Pearl Harbor: Disturbing Questions about the Bush Administration and 9/11* (Northampton, Mass.: Interlink Books/Olive Branch Press, March, 2004), henceforth NPH. In August 2004, a second edition appeared, labeled "Updated Edition with a New Afterword." When referring to material that is only in the Updated Edition (otherwise the pagination is the same), the note will say "NPH, 2nd ed."

[9] Even this division of the alternative theory into only two versions is somewhat crude. In an earlier discussion of the idea that elements within the US

government were "complicit" in the attacks, I pointed to the existence of at least eight possible levels of complicity, beginning with the mildest—though still impeachable—offense of constructing a false account of what happened (NPH xxi–xxii).

[10] Paul Sperry, "Is Fix in at 9/11 Commission?" Antiwar.com, March 31, 2004 (http://antiwar.com/sperry/?articleid=2209).

[11] Philip Zelikow and Condoleezza Rice, *Germany Unified and Europe Transformed: A Study in Statecraft* (Cambridge: Harvard University Press, 1997).

[12] Associated Press, December 27, 2003; David Corn, "Probing 9/11," *Nation*, 277/1 (July 7: 2003): 14–18, at 16; Paul Sperry, "Is Fix in at 9/11 Commission?"; Emad Mekay, "Iraq Was Invaded 'to Protect Israel'—US Official," *Asia Times*, March 31, 2004 (www.atimes.com/atimes/Front_Page/FC31Aa01.html).

[13] This call, made earlier, was repeated in the Family Steering Committee's press release of March 20, 2004 (www.911independentcommission.org/mar202004.html).

[14] Sperry, "Is Fix in at 9/11 Commission?"

[15] See NPH 147–56 and below, 283–85.

[16] Philip Shenon, "9/11 Commission Could Subpoena Oval Office Files," *New York Times*, October 26, 2003.

[17] In Emad Mekay's article headed "Iraq Was Invaded 'to Protect Israel'—US Official" (see note 12, above), the US official referred to was Philip Zelikow. He was quoted as speaking of "the threat that dare not speak its name," thereby referring to the threat that Iraq posed not to the United States but to Israel. His point was that at least one of the prime motives behind the US invasion of Iraq in 2003 was the desire of the Bush administration to eliminate this threat. In explaining why this threat "dare not speak its name," Zelikow reportedly said that "the American government doesn't want to lean too hard on it rhetorically, because it is not a popular sell."

[18] "When we wrote the report," said Zelikow, "we were also careful not to answer all the theories. It's like playing Whack-A-Mole. You're never going to whack them all." Quoted in Carol Morello, "Conspiracy Theories Flourish on the Internet," *Washington Post*, October 7, 2004 (www.washingtonpost.com/wp-dyn/articles/A13059-2004Oct6.html?sub=AR). Nicholas Levis, after quoting Zelikow's statement, writes: "Now we know [a basic] rule of the Kean Commission: Don't test theories. Just whack them, if you can, and otherwise do your best to ignore them" ("Zelikow: Losing to the Bacteria: Open Letter to Philip Zelikow and the *Washington Post*," October 7, 2004 [www.911truth.org/article.php?story=20041009142411882]).

[19] This letter of September 13, 2004, under the title "Open Letter: National Security Experts Speak Out: 9/11 Commission Falls Short," is available at www.911CitizensWatch.org.

PART ONE
CHAPTER ONE: THE ALLEGED HIJACKERS

[1] Waleed al-Shehri, reports Thierry Meyssan, "gave an interview to the Arab-language daily, *Al-Quds al-Arabi*, based in London." See Thierry Meyssan, *9/11: The Big Lie* (London: Carnot, 2002), 54.

[2] Associated Press, September 22, 2001, cited in Meyssan, *9/11: The Big Lie*, 54.

[3] David Harrison, "Revealed: The Men with Stolen Identities," *Telegraph*, September 23, 2001 (www.portal.telegraph.co.uk/news/main.jhtml?xml=/news/2001/09/23/widen23.xml).

[4] BBC News, September 23, 2001 (http://news.bbc.co.uk/2/hi/world/middle_east/1559151.stm).

[5] Meyssan, *9/11: The Big Lie*, 54.

[6] Harrison, "Revealed: The Men with Stolen Identities."

[7] *Independent*, September 17, 2001 (http://news.independent.co.uk/world/middle_east/story.jsp?story=94438); BBC News, September 23, 2001 (http://news.bbc.co.uk/2/hi/world/middle_east/1559151.stm).

[8] NPH 86, citing *Newsweek*, October 15, 2001, and *San Francisco Chronicle*, October 4, 2001.

[9] See Daniel Hopsicker, *Welcome to Terrorland: Mohamed Atta and the 9/11 Cover-up in Florida* (Eugene: MacCowPress, 2004). These details from Hopsicker's book are summarized in his "Top Ten Things You Never Knew About Mohamed Atta," Mad Cow Morning News, June 7, 2004 (www.madcowprod.com/index60.html), and in an interview in the Guerrilla News Forum, June 17, 2004 (www.guerrillanews.com/intelligence/doc4660.html), summarized in NPH, 2nd ed., 243n1.

[10] "Terrorist Stag Parties," *Wall Street Journal*, October 10, 2001 (http://www.opinionjournal.com/best/?id=95001298).

[11] Associated Press, October 5, 2001; *Boston Globe*, September 18, 2001; *Independent*, September 29, 2001.

[12] Seymour Hersh, "What Went Wrong?" *New Yorker*, October 1, 2001.

[13] Marc Fisher and Don Phillips, "On Flight 77: 'Our Plane Is Being Hijacked,'" *Washington Post*, September 12, 2001 (www.washingtonpost.com/wp-dyn/articles/A14365-2001Sep11.html).

[14] The flight manifest for AA 11 that was published by CNN can be seen at www.cnn.com/SPECIALS/2001/trade.center/victims/AA11.victims.html. The manifests for the other flights can be located by simply changing that part of the URL. The manifest for UA 93, for example, is at www.cnn.com/SPECIALS/2001/trade.center/victims/ua93.victims.html.

[15] For example, Icelander Elias Davidsson told me that after he recently

wrote to American Airlines, asking for the final flight manifest for AA 11 on September 11, 2001, he received the following reply (I received a copy of this letter from Elias Davidsson on September 9, 2004. I believe he had received it from American Airlines the same day):

Dear Mr. Davidsson:
Thank you for your email dated August 5 [2004]. Please accept my apologies for the delay in responding to you.
At the time of the incidents we released the actual passenger manifests to the appropriate government agencies who in turn released certain information to the media. These lists were published in many major periodicals and are now considered public record. At this time we are not in a position to release further information or to republish what the government agencies provided to the media. Instead, should you require a copy of these lists may we suggest that you research major periodicals for copies of their publications containing the information you seek.
Mr. Davidsson, I trust this information will be of use to you.
Sincerely,
Karen Temmerman
Customer Relations, American Airlines

CHAPTER TWO: THE COLLAPSE OF THE WORLD TRADE CENTER BUILDINGS
[1] In a report by FEMA (the Federal Emergency Management Agency), the results of the fire in the office building at One Meridian Plaza in Philadelphia in 1991 are described thus: "Beams and girders sagged and twisted . . . under severe fire exposures. . . . Despite this extraordinary exposure, the columns continued to support their loads without obvious damage." See "High-Rise Office Building Fire One Meridian Plaza Philadelphia, Pennsylvania" (http://usfa.fema.gov/fire-service/techreports/tr049.shtm).
[2] See FEMA Report #403, *World Trade Center Building Performance Study*, May 2002 (www.fema.gov/library/wtcstudy.shtm), Appendix A, which states: "In the mid-1990s British Steel and the Building Research Establishment performed a series of six experiments . . . to investigate the behavior of steel frame buildings. . . . Despite the temperature of the steel beams reaching 800–900° C (1,500–1,700° F) in three of the tests. . . , no collapse was observed in any of the six experiments." Note that there is a very big difference between merely having the *fire* reach these temperatures and actually having the steel beams and columns get this hot. Few if any of the columns and beams in the Twin Towers would have even approached these temperatures.
[3] The Commission does, to be sure, say on the same page that "an EMS

paramedic approached the FDNY Chief of Department and advised that an engineer in front of 7 WTC had just remarked that the Twin Towers in fact were in imminent danger of a total collapse" (302). But this third-hand comment, based on alleged remarks from two unnamed sources, cannot be taken as serious evidence that any expert opinion expected the towers to collapse.

[4] For photographs and descriptions of the North and South Tower fireballs, see Eric Hufschmid, *Painful Questions: An Analysis of the September 11th Attack* (Goleta, Calif.: Endpoint Software, 2002; available at www.EricHufschmid.Net), 30–32. Hufschmid makes the point about the inability of the fire to spread (38).

[5] One can compare the fires in Building 7 with those in Buildings 5 and 6 by turning to Figures 5–30, 6–2, and 6–3 in Hufschmid, *Painful Questions*. See also my discussion in NPH 12–17.

[6] *New York Times*, September 11, 2002. Even if the statement about the South Tower is not quite true, the story illustrates the big difference between the two fires.

[7] See NPH 17–18.

[8] "The Wrong Tower Fell First" is the title of a section in Fintan Dunne, "The Split-second Error: Exposing the WTC Bomb Plot" (www.psyopnews.com or www.serendipity.li).

[9] I point this out in NPH 12–13, citing Thomas Eagar, professor of materials engineering at MIT.

[10] FEMA, *World Trade Center Building Performance Study*, Ch. 5, Sect. 6.2, "Probable Collapse Sequence," discussed in NPH 22.

[11] This point is more true of Building 7, because of the fact mentioned in the fourth point.

[12] On points 3 and 4, see Jim Hoffman, "The North Tower's Dust Cloud: Analysis of Energy Requirements for the Expansion of the Dust Cloud following the Collapse of 1 World Trade Center," Version 3.1, January 5, 2004 (http://911research.wtc7.net/papers/dustvolume/volume.html), discussed in NPH, 2nd ed., 177–79.

[13] For visual evidence of these first six characteristics, see Eric Hufschmid's *Painful Questions*, his video "Painful Deceptions" (available at www.EricHufschmid.Net) and several presentations on websites, such as Jeff King, "The World Trade Center Collapse: How Strong is the Evidence for a Controlled Demolition?" Plaguepuppy (http://st12.startlogic.com/~xenonpup/collapse%20update). The quoted phrase in point 6 is taken from King's article.

[14] Therefore they, in the words of Jim Hoffman, "could be easily loaded onto the equipment that was cleaning up Ground Zero." See Jim Hoffman, "Your Eyes Don't Lie: Common Sense, Physics, and the World Trade Center Collapses," originally an interview on KPFA, January 21, 2004 (available at

http://911research.wtc7.net/talks/radio/youreyesdontlie/index.html), quoted in
NPH, 2nd ed., 177. Coincidentally, the company given the job of cleaning up
the rubble at the WTC—Controlled Demolition, Inc.—says in its publicity that
its systems "segment steel components into pieces matching the lifting capacity
of the available equipment" (quoted in Eric Hufschmid's video, "Painful
Deceptions" and in NPH, 2nd ed., 178).

[15] See NPH 179n74.

[16] For points 9 and 10, see NPH 19–20.

[17] Thomas Eagar, mentioned in note 9, tried to provide such an explanation
in "The Collapse: An Engineer's Perspective," NOVA interview
(www.pbs.org/wgbh/nova/wtc/collapse.html) and in "Why did the World Trade
Center Collapse? Science, Engineering, and Speculation" (with Christopher
Musso), *JOM* 53/12 (2001), 8–11. However, as I have pointed out (NPH
13–19), there are numerous problems with his theory. First, the fires were
neither large enough nor long-lasting enough to heat the steel to the temperature
Eagar himself says would be necessary. Second, his theory requires that the floors
above the floor where the fire was most intense collapsed on it, and that all these
floors then fell on the floor beneath it, causing it to break loose, and so on
down. But even if this were conceivable, each floor would have provided at least
some resistance, making it impossible for 110 floors to collapse in 10 to 15
seconds, meaning the speed at which the material would fall if it were finding
little or no resistance. Third, for each floor to fall in this way, hundreds of steel
joints on 236 exterior columns and 47 core columns had to break almost
simultaneously. Fourth, Eagar's pancake theory, according to which the floors fell
like records on an old phonograph with a spindle up the middle of the records,
cannot account for the fact that each collapse was total. Why did the equivalent
of the spindle—the 47 core columns—also come crashing down? Fifth, his
theory cannot explain why most of the steel columns came down in 30-foot
pieces, ready to be loaded on trucks (see n. 14). Sixth, his theory cannot explain
why the South Tower collapsed first.

[18] I am indebted to Eric Hufschmid for this information. Pictures of some
of these columns can be seen on page 23 of Hufschmid's *Painful Questions*.

[19] See NPH 16–17.

[20] The book itself contains no index. But readers can search for any word or
name in the book at http://vivisimo.com/911.

[21] "America Rebuilds," PBS documentary, 2002, now available as PBS
Home Video, ISBN 0-7806-4006-3 (www.pbs.org/americarebuilds). Silverstein's
statement can be viewed (http://www.infowars.com/Video/911/wtc7_pbs.WMV)
or heard on audio file (http://VestigialConscience.com/PullIt.mp3 or
http://sirdave.com/mp3/PullIt.mp3). For a discussion, see Jeremy Baker, "PBS
Documentary: Silverstein, FDNY Razed WTC 7," Infowars.com
(www.infowars.com/print/Sept11/FDNY.htm); also available at Rense.com

(http://www.rense.com/general47/pulled.htm). Silverstein's comments have been discussed at some length on the *Alex Jones Show*, "WTC-7 Imploded by Silverstein, FDNY and Others," January 19, 2004 (see www.prisonplanet.com/011904wtc7.html), discussed in NPH, 2nd ed., 175–77.

[22] CBS News, September 11, 2001. Videos of the collapse of Building 7, which have seldom appeared on mainstream television, can be viewed at various websites, including http://wtc7net/videos.html and www.geocities.com/killtown/wtc7.html. Particularly good for this purpose is Eric Hufschmid's DVD, "Painful Deceptions" (available at www.EricHufschmid.Net).

[23] For photographs and discussion, see Eric Hufschmid, *Painful Questions*, 62–65.

[24] "WTC-7 Imploded by Silverstein, FDNY and Others," *Alex Jones Show*, January 19, 2004 (see www.prisonplanet.com/011904wtc7.html).

[25] The official investigators found that they had less authority than the clean-up crews, a fact that led the Science Committee of the House of Representatives to report that "the lack of authority of investigators to impound pieces of steel for examination before they were recycled led to the loss of important pieces of evidence" (see the report at http://www.house.gov/science/hot/wtc/wtc-report/WTC_ch5.pdf).

[26] *New York Times*, December 25, 2001, and *Fire Engineering*, January 2002.

[27] Quoted on the *Alex Jones Show*, "WTC-7 Imploded by Silverstein, FDNY and Others," and in NPH 181–82.

[28] See Margie Burns, "Secrecy Surrounds a Bush Brother's Role in 9/11 Security," *American Reporter* 9/2021 (January 20, 2003); Wayne Madsen, "Marvin Bush Employee's Mysterious Death—Connections to 9/11?" From the Wilderness Publications, 2003 (www.betterworld.com/getreallist/article.php?story=20040127223419798); and NPH, 2nd ed., 180.

[29] Craig Unger, *House of Bush, House of Saud: The Secret Relationship between the World's Two Most Powerful Dynasties* (New York & London: Scribner, 2004), 249. The company at the time was named Securacom.

[30] Ibid., 249n. In speaking of al-Sabah as a coinvestor, Unger is referring to KuwAm, a Kuwaiti–American investment firm that has provided financial backing for Stratesec, previously called Securacom. See Wayne Madsen, "Marvin Bush Employee's Mysterious Death—Connections to 9/11?", discussed in NPH, 2nd ed., 246n31. On the false testimony about Kuwaiti babies, see Chalmers Johnson, *The Sorrows of Empire: Militarism, Secrecy, and the End of the Republic* (New York: Henry Holt, 2004), 230.

[31] One can search for these and other names at http://vivisimo.com/911.

CHAPTER THREE: THE STRIKE ON THE PENTAGON

[1] *Los Angeles Times,* September 16, 2001.

[2] Meyssan, *9/11: The Big Lie,* 20.

[3] Nafeez Mosaddeq Ahmed, *The War on Freedom: How and Why America was Attacked September 11, 2001* (Joshua Tree, Calif.: Tree of Life, 2002), 299–300; Meyssan, *9/11: The Big Lie,* 20.

[4] See Thierry Meyssan, *Pentagate* (London: Carnot Publishing, 2002), page VI of the photo section. This picture can also be viewed on Meyssan's website called "Hunt the Boeing. Test Your Perceptions" (www.asile.org/citoyens/numero13/pentagone/erreurs_en.htm).

[5] *New York Times* and CNN, September 12, 2001.

[6] See Paul Thompson and the Center for Cooperative Research, *The Terror Timeline: Year by Year, Day by Day, Minute by Minute: A Comprehensive Chronicle of the Road to 9/11—and America's Response* (New York: HarperCollins/ReganBooks, 2004), 455, from which I learned about these news stories. The only later publication mentioned is *NPFA Journal,* November 1, 2001

[7] Marc Fisher and Don Phillips, "On Flight 77: 'Our Plane is Being Hijacked,'" *Washington Post,* September 12, 2001.

[8] See Thierry Meyssan, *9:11: The Big Lie* (London: Carnot, 2002), "Hunt the Boeing," and a video entitled "Pentagon Strike" (www.freedomunderground.org/memoryhole/pentagon.php).

[9] "DoD News Briefing," Defense Link, Department of Defense, September 12, 2001 (www.defenselink.mil/news/Sep2001/t09122001_t0912asd.html).

[10] "DoD News Briefing on Pentagon Renovation," Defense Link, Department of Defense, September 15, 2001.

[11] The only citations to Ed Plaugher are to statements he made later. As I pointed out (NPH 34), a month later, after there was time for his memory to be refreshed, Plaugher said that he did remember having seen "pieces of the fuselage, the wings, the landing gear, pieces of the engine." But the Commission, not quoting either of these statements, did not have to explain why we should prefer his later to his earlier memory.

[12] *NFPA Journal,* November 1, 2001. This argument, Meyssan points out (*Pentagate,* 14–17), has been articulated by many defenders of the official account (see NPH 216n44).

[13] *Washington Post,* November 21, 2001, and *Mercury,* January 11, 2002.

[14] See "Images Show September 11 Pentagon Crash," posted on CNN, March 8, 2002 (www.cnn.com/2002/US/03/07/gen.pentagon.pictures/index.html).

[15] Dick Eastman, "What Convinced Me that Flight 77 Was Not the Killer Jet," Part 1, American Patriot Friends Network (http://www.apfn.org/apfn/77_deastman1.htm).

[16] *Richmond Times-Dispatch*, December 11, 2001.

[17] Carol Morello, "Conspiracy Theories Flourish on the Internet," *Washington Post*, October 7, 2004 (www.washingtonpost.com/wp-dyn/articles/A13059-2004Oct6.html?sub=AR).

[18] See NPH 26–27.

[19] See NPH 26, 36–39.

[20] This statement is contained in the transcript of an interview by *Parade* magazine with Rumsfeld on October 12, 2001, available at www.defenselink.mil/news/nov2001/t11182001_t1012pm.html/.

[21] See Meyssan's website (www.effroyable-imposture.net).

CHAPTER FOUR: THE BEHAVIOR OF BUSH AND HIS SECRET SERVICE

[1] Bill Sammon, *Fighting Back: The War on Terrorism from Inside the Bush White House* (Washington: Regnery, 2002), 90.

[2] *Sarasota Herald-Tribune*, September 10, 2002.

[3] *New York Times*, September 16, 2001; *Telegraph*, December 16, 2001; ABC News, September 14, 2002; *Washington Post*, January 27, 2002.

[4] Allan Wood and Paul Thompson, "An Interesting Day: President Bush's Movements and Actions on 9/11," Center for Cooperative Research (www.cooperativeresearch.org), under the section headed "Why Stay?"

[5] NBC, *Meet the Press*, September 16, 2001.

[6] Richard A. Clarke, *Against All Enemies: Inside America's War on Terror* (New York: Free Press, 2004), 6.

[7] Ibid., 4.

[8] *New York Times*, September 16, 2001; *Telegraph*, December 16, 2001; *Dallas Morning News*, August 28, 2002.

[9] Paul Thompson and the Center for Cooperative Research, *The Terror Timeline: Year by Year, Day by Day, Minute by Minute: A Comprehensive Chronicle of the Road to 9/11—and America's Response* (New York: HarperCollins/ReganBooks, 2004), 461.

[10] *Salon*, September 12, 2001; CBS New, September 11, 2002; *Dallas Morning News*, August 28, 2002; all cited in Thompson, *The Terror Timeline*, 460.

[11] Clarke, *Against All Enemies*, 6.

[12] Ibid., 7, 8.

[13] *Washington Post*, January 27, 2002.

[14] MSNBC, September 16, 2001, quoted in Thompson, *The Terror Timeline*, 375.

[15] Clarke, *Against All Enemies*, 7.

[16] Ibid., 2–3.

CHAPTER FIVE: ADVANCE INFORMATION ABOUT THE ATTACKS

[1] Whereas I have continued to use the spelling "Laden," which is common in the US press, the Commission spells the name "Ladin," which has been prevalent—as part of "Usama bin Ladin"—in US government publications and in the British press. The Commission also capitalizes "Bin," hence writing his name "Usama Bin Ladin."

[2] Associated Press, May 16, 2002; *San Francisco Chronicle*, June 3, 2002; *Washington Post*, May 27, 2002.

[3] Associated Press, May 16, 2002 (available at www.foxnews.com/story/0,2933,52982,00.html).

[4] The index for *The 9/11 Commission Report* is, to repeat, available at http://vivisimo.com/911.

[5] Although one Commissioner did ask Ashcroft about this in a public session, this discussion was evidently one of the items not deemed important enough to include in the final report.

[6] *Alex Jones Show*, October 10; *World Net Daily*, October 21; "David Schippers Goes Public: The FBI Was Warned," *Indianapolis Star*, October 13; and "Active FBI Special Agent Files Complaint Concerning Obstructed FBI Anti-Terrorist Investigations," *Judicial Watch*, November 14, 2001. This story was reported in NPH 84.

[7] William Norman Grigg, "Did We Know What Was Coming?", *The New American* 18/5: March 11, 2002 (www.thenewamerican.com), quoted in NPH 85.

[8] Kyle F. Hence, "Billions in Pre-911 Insider Trading Profits Leave a Hot Trail," Centre for Research on Globalisation, April 21, 2002 (www.globalresearch.ca/articles/HEN204B.html).

[9] *San Francisco Chronicle*, September 29, 2001.

[10] Allen Poteshman, "Unusual Option Market Activity and the Terrorist Attacks of September 11, 2001," *Journal of Business* (forthcoming in 2005 or 2006; until then available at www.business.uiuc.edu/poteshma).

[11] *Independent*, October 14, 2001.

[12] See NPH 72, where I cited both UPI (February 13, 2001) and former detective Michael Ruppert, who has said: "It is well documented that the CIA has long monitored such trades—in real time—as potential warnings of terrorist attacks and other economic moves contrary to U.S. interests" ("Suppressed Details of Criminal Insider Trading Lead Directly into the CIA's Highest Ranks," From the Wilderness Publications [www.fromthewilderness.com or www.copvcia.com], October 9, 2001).

[13] Here are the references at the end of the note: "Joseph Cella interview (Sept. 16, 2003; May 7, 2004; May 10–11, 2004); FBI briefing (Aug. 15, 2003); SEC memo, Division of Enforcement to SEC Chair and Commissioners,

"Pre-September 11, 2001 Trading Review," May 15, 2002; Ken Breen interview (Apr. 23, 2004); Ed G. interview (Feb. 3, 2004)."

[14] *San Francisco Chronicle,* September 12 and 14, 2001.

[15] Evan Thomas and Mark Hosenball, "Bush: 'We're At War,'" *Newsweek,* September 24, 2001 (available at www.WantToKnow.info/010924newsweek).

[16] *Independent,* September 15, 2002.

[17] Summary of the Final Report of the Joint Inquiry (http://intelligence.senate.gov/press.htm).

[18] *Los Angeles Times,* December 12, 2003, cited in NPH 73.

[19] As one can see by connecting to http://vivisimo.com/911 and typing in KSM.

CHAPTER SIX: OSAMA, THE BIN LADENS, AND THE SAUDI ROYAL FAMILY

[1] Richard Labeviere, "CIA Agent Allegedly Met Bin Laden in July," *Le Figaro,* October 31, 2001. This story was also reported in Anthony Sampson, "CIA Agent Alleged to Have Met Bin Laden in July," *Guardian,* November 1; Adam Sage, "Ailing bin Laden 'Treated for Kidney Disease,'" *London Times,* Nov. 1; Agence France Presse, November 1; Radio France International, November 1; and Reuters, November 10, all 2001.

[2] Department of Defense, April 6, 2002 (www.defenselink.mil/news/Apr2002/t04082002_t407genm.html), quoted in NPH 107.

[3] *Daily Mirror,* November 16, 2001.

[4] *Telegraph,* February 23, 2002.

[5] Labeviere, "CIA Agent Allegedly Met Bin Laden in July," quoted in Nafeez Mosaddeq Ahmed, *The War on Freedom: How and Why America was Attacked September 11, 2001* (Joshua Tree, Calif.: Tree of Life, 2002), 179.

[6] Craig Unger, "Unasked Questions: The 9/11 Commission Should Ask Who Authorized the Evacuation of Saudi Nationals in the Days Following the Attacks," *Boston Globe,* April 11, 2004. For more evidence counting against the portrait of OBL as the disowned black sheep of the family, see Ahmed, *The War on Freedom,* 178–79.

[7] Prince Faisal's statement is quoted in Michael O'Keffee, "Man of Mystery," *New York Daily News,* May 22, 2004 (www.nydailynews.com/sports/story/196031p–169336c.html).

[8] For more evidence suggestive of a covert alliance involving OBL, the Saudi government, and the US government, see Ahmed, *The War on Freedom,* 187–202. The idea of a covert alliance may be untrue. But the 9/11 Commission should at least have discussed the evidence that seems to support it.

[9] Gerald Posner, *Why America Slept: The Failure to Prevent 9/11* (New York: Random House, 2003), 181–94.

[10] Ibid., 188–90.

[11] Ibid., 190.

[12] Ibid., 180n.

[13] Ibid., 188–93, 267–69.

[14] Craig Unger, *House of Bush, House of Saud: The Secret Relationship between the World's Two Most Powerful Dynasties* (New York & London: Scribner, 2004), 264–66.

[15] O'Keffee, "Man of Mystery."

[16] Unger, *House of Bush*, 255, 266–68.

[17] Later the story was changed to say that Prince Ahmed was hospitalized because of a stomach problem and an addiction to painkillers (O'Keffee, "Man of Mystery").

[18] This explanation is cited, without necessarily being endorsed, in O'Keffee, "Man of Mystery," which also mentions the deaths of the two other men.

[19] Posner, *Why America Slept*, xi, xii, 35, 44–47, 59, 142, 146, 150, 155, 169, 173, 178.

[20] Gerald Posner, *Case Closed: Lee Harvey Oswald and the Assassination of JFK* (New York: Random House, 1993).

[21] Ibid., 190.

[22] Josh Meyer, "2 Allies Aided Bin Laden, Say Panel Members," *Los Angeles Times*, June 20, 2004 (http://www.latimes.com/news/nationworld/world/la-fg-alqaeda20jun20,1,440629.story).

[23] Ibid.

[24] Bob Graham, *Intelligence Matters: The CIA, the FBI, Saudi Arabia, and the Failure of America's War on Terror* (New York: Random House, 2004), 215.

[25] *The New Pearl Harbor*, 119–20; citing *Washington Post*, December 29, 2001; *Newsweek*, September 24, 2002; *Los Angeles Times*, September 24, 2002; and *New York Times*, July 25, 2003.

[26] Graham, *Intelligence Matters*, 12–13, 224.

[27] Ibid., 24, 167.

[28] Ibid., 168, 223, 225.

[29] Ibid., 169, citing Dana Priest, "White House, CIA Kept Key Portions of Report Classified," *Washington Post*, July 25, 2003.

[30] Ibid., 224, quoting an Associated Press story of March 24, 2004, "FBI Concludes 2 Saudis Not Intel Agents."

[31] Ibid., 226–29.

[32] Ibid., 166.

[33] Ibid., 166, 216.

[34] Ibid., xiv.

[35] Unger, *House of Bush*, 179–80; Graham, *Intelligence Matters*, 168. Unger spells the name Basnan, Graham spells it Bassnan. I have followed Unger's spelling. In this summary, I have drawn on both counts, somewhat more from Graham's.

[36] Craig Unger, *House of Bush*, 179–80.

[37] Unger, *House of Bush*, 179n.

CHAPTER SEVEN: THE SAUDI FLIGHTS

[1] Unger, "Unasked Questions," *Bostton Globe*, April11, 2004.

[2] Kathy Steele, with Brenna Kelly and Elizabeth Lee Brown, "Phantom Flight from Florida," *Tampa Tribune*, October 5, 2001.

[3] Unger, *House of Bush*, 8–9; "Unasked Questions."

[4] Unger, "Unasked Questions."

[5] Jean Heller, "TIA Now Verifies Flight of Saudis," *St. Petersburg Times*, June 9, 2004 (www.saintpetersburgtimes.com/2004/06/09/Tampabay/TIA_now_verifies_flig.shtml).

[6] "Phantom Flight" was, of course, the name used in the original article in the *Tampa Tribune*, cited in note 2, above.

[7] Unger, *House of Bush*, 9, citing Steele, "Phantom Flight from Florida."

[8] Unger, "Unasked Questions."

[9] Unger, *House of Bush*, 9.

[10] Ibid., 256.

[11] Ibid., 9. One odd feature of the Commission's treatment of this issue is that Jean Heller's story, "TIA Now Verifies Flight of Saudis," contains an assertion that the Commission seemingly could have used to bolster its case but did not. Heller said: "most of the aircraft allowed to fly in US airspace on Sept. 13 were empty airliners being ferried from the airports where they made quick landings on Sept. 11. The reopening of airspace included paid charter flights, but not private, non-revenue flights. 'Whether such a (LearJet) flight would have been legal hinges on whether somebody paid for it,' said FAA spokesman William Shumann. 'That's the key.'" Why did the Commission not refer to this distinction? Did it simply not know about it? Or did it discover that Shumann's distinction was one that was invented after the fact? To answer these questions, we would need to see whether there is evidence that this distinction was made and publicized at the time. Was it, for example, made in the NOTAM broadcast at 10:57 AM, which Unger reported? My assumption that the Commission's failure to refer to this distinction reflected its judgment that the distinction would not hold up under scrutiny because it had been invented later. When I asked Craig Unger himself if this was the case, he replied, "Yes, this is, as you

put it, a later-invented distinction. When I asked the FAA if the flights were legal, they assured me that the flights did not take place—as did the FBI and White House on many occasions" (e-mail of Monday, September 27, 2004).

[12] One more dimension of this incompleteness involves a story in the *New York Times* saying that, in Unger's summary statement, "before September 14, members of the bin Laden family were driven or flown under FBI supervision first to a secret assembly point in Texas and later in Washington" (*House of Bush*, 256, referring to Patrick E. Tyler, "Fearing Harm, Bin Laden Kin Fled From U.S.," *New York Times*, September 30, 2001). If this report is correct—the FBI said it was "erroneous," but as Unger shows, their other denials about these stories proved false—there would have been at least one more flight on September 13 or even earlier. But the Commission's report does not mention this possibility.

[13] As mentioned in an earlier note, this name is spelled in various ways, especially Osama bin Laden (abbreviated OBL), Usama bin Ladin, and Usama Bin Ladin (the latter two abbreviated UBL). *The 9/11 Commission Report* has adopted the third of these conventions.

[14] Unger, *House of Bush*, 178–79.

[15] Ibid., 258.

[16] Ibid., 12.

[17] Ibid., 257.

[18] Unger, "Unasked Questions."

[19] Ibid.

[20] Unger, *House of Bush*, 7.

[21] Ibid., 269.

[22] Unger, "Unasked Questions."

[23] Unger, *House of Bush*, 255.

[24] Craig Unger, "The Great Escape," *New York Times*, June 1, 2004 (www.nytimes.com/2004/06/01/opinion/01UNGE.html), referring to a Judicial Watch press release of March 25, 2004 (www.judicialwatch.org/3569.shtml).

[25] Craig Unger, "Bin Laden Manifests," July 22 (www.houseofbush.com/index.php?p=11).

[26] Unger, "Unasked Questions."

[27] Unger, *House of Bush*, 7.

[28] Ibid. 3,15.

[29] Ibid., 145.

[30] Ibid., 2, 7.

[31] Ibid., 14–15, 8.

[32] Although Unger had not specified that the meeting between Bandar and

Bush occurred prior to the authorization of the flights, Senator Bob Graham, after describing the meeting, says that the flights took off "later that day" (Graham, *Intelligence Matters*, 26).

[33] Unger, *House of Bush*, 7.

[34] Ibid., 16.

[35] Ibid., 11.

[36] Ibid., 255.

[37] Ibid., 254, citing CNN's "Daybreak," March 19, 2002.

[38] NBC, *Meet the Press*, April 25, 2004 (http://www.msnbc.msn.com/id/4829855). This interview is posted at http://archive.salon.com/politics/war_room/2004/04/26/bandar.

[39] Ibid., 253.

[40] Posner, *Why America Slept*, 193.

[41] See note 1 of Chapter 6, above.

[42] Posner, *Why America Slept*, 193.

CHAPTER EIGHT: ALLEGATIONS ABOUT FBI HEADQUARTERS

[1] *New York Times*, May 19 and 20, 2002, and *Los Angeles Times*, May 26, 2002.

[2] *Time*, May 21, 2002, and the Senate Intelligence Committee, October 17, 2002. Rowley's letter is discussed in Patrick Martin, "September 11 Cover-Up Crumbles: Who Was Covering for Moussaoui, and Why?" World Socialist Website, May 29, 2002 (www.wsws.org/articles/2002/may2002/sept-m29.shtml).

[3] In NPH (148), having said that there is "reason to believe that intimidation may have dampened some of the members' investigative zeal," I pointed out that there were reports "that on August of 2002, FBI agents had questioned nearly all 37 members of the Senate and House intelligence committees about 9/11-related information leaks." According to these reports, "[t]he agents even demanded that these senators and representatives submit to lie detector tests and turn over phone records and appointment calendars." I also cited a law professor who, commenting on this demand, said: "It creates a great chilling effect on those who would be critical of the FBI" (*Washington Post*, August 2, 2002). Finally, I pointed out that some senators and representatives expressed grave concern about the violation of the separation of powers, with Senator John McCain saying, "What you have here is an organization compiling dossiers on people who are investigating the same organization," and another senator saying that the FBI is "trying to put a damper on our activities and I think they will be successful" (*Washington Post*, August 3 and 24; Associated Press, August 29, 2002).

[4] See NPH 82–83. The three internal quotations came, respectively, from UPI, May 30, 2002; *LA Weekly*, August 2, 2002; and ABC News, November 26, 2002.

[5] See the previous note. Also, *The New Pearl Harbor*, with its summary of

Wright's case, was provided to the Commissioners.

[6] See *Time*, December 22, 2002.

[7] NPH 80–81, 122. The references for the internal quotations are, respectively: *New York Times*, February 8, 2002; *Time*, August 4, 2002; *Newsweek*, May 20, 2002; *Time*, May 21 and 27, 2001; *Time*, July 21 and 27, 2002; *Time*, May 27, 2002; and *Star Tribune*, December 22, 2002.

[8] See James V. Grimaldi, "2 FBI Whistle-Blowers Allege Lax Security, Possible Espionage," *Washington Post*, June 19, 2002 (www.washingtonpost.com/ac2/wpdyn?pagename=article&node=&contentId=A 7829-2002Jun18&notFound=true/); also stories by Cox News, August 14, 2002, and Associated Press, October 18, 2002.

[9] See NPH 83–84. I have recently noticed, however, that this discussion of Edmonds is in the wrong chapter in NPH. It should be in Chapter 8, which deals with obstructions *after* 9/11.

[10] NPH, 2nd ed., 189–92.

[11] Sibel Edmonds, "Our Broken System," July 9, 2004 (available at www.911citizenswatch.org/print.php?sid=329 or www.scoop.co.nz/mason/stories/HL0408/S00012.htm). This article begins thus: "On Tuesday, July 6, 2004, Judge Reggie Walton made a decision and ruled on my case. Under his ruling, I, an American citizen, am not entitled to pursue my 1st and 5th Amendment rights guaranteed under the Constitution of the United States. The vague reasoning cited, without any explanation, is to protect 'certain diplomatic relations for national security.' Judge Walton reached this decision after sitting on this case with no activity for almost two years. He arrived at this decision without allowing my attorney and I any due process: NO status hearing, NO briefings, NO oral argument, and NO discovery. He made his decision after allowing the government attorneys to present their case to him, privately, in camera, ex parte; we were not allowed to participate in these cozy sessions. Is this the American system of justice we believe in? Is this the due process we read about in our civics 101 courses? Is this the judicial branch of our government that is supposed to be separate from the other two branches in order to protect the people's rights and freedom?"

[12] Sibel Edmonds, "Letter to Thomas Kean from Sibel Edmonds," 9/11 Citizens Watch, August 1, 2004 (www.911citizenswatch.org/modules.php?op=modload&name=News&file=articl e&sid=373); also available as "An Open Letter to the 9/11 Panel," Antiwar.com, August 2, 2004 (http://antiwar.com/edmonds/?articleid=3230).

[13] Ibid.

[14] Ibid.

[15] Ibid.

[16] Ibid.

[17] Ibid.

CHAPTER NINE: PAKISTAN AND ITS ISI

[1] See NPH 108–09.

[2] *New York Times*, September 13, 2001, quoted in Michel Chossudovsky, *War and Globalisation: The Truth Behind September 11* (Canada: Global Outlook, 2002), 51.

[3] Senator Graham reports that on the morning of 9/11, he, as chairman of the Senate Intelligence Committee, Porter Goss, as chairman of the House Intelligence Committee, and Senator Jon Kyl, a member of the Senate Intelligence Committee, along with several staff members, had a breakfast meeting with General Ahmad "in reciprocation for General Ahmed's [Graham's spelling] hospitality during our trip to Pakistan two weeks earlier." However, he reports, the meeting, which began at 8:00, was disbanded as soon as word was received of the attack on the second tower of the World Trade Center (*Intelligence Matters*, ix–xi).

[4] *Wall Street Journal*, October 10, 2001 (http://www.opinionjournal.com/best/?id=95001298).

[5] Agence France Presse, October 10, 2001, cited in Chossudovsky, *War and Globalisation*, 58.

[6] CNN, March 14, 2002; *Los Angeles Times*, March 15, 2002.

[7] Chossudovsky, *War and Globalisation*, 156–58.

[8] Manoj Joshi, "India Helped FBI Trace ISI–Terrorist Links," *Times of India*, October 9, 2001.

[9] Josh Meyer, "2 Allies Aided Bin Laden, Say Panel Members," *Los Angeles Times*, June 20, 2004 (http://www.latimes.com/news/nationworld/world/la-fg-alqaeda20jun20,1,440629.story).

[10] See NPH 112.

[11] Manoj Joshi, "India Helped FBI Trace ISI–Terrorist Links," quoted in NPH 113.

[12] Steve Coll, *Ghost Wars: The Secret History of the CIA, Afghanistan, and bin Laden, from the Soviet Invasion to September 10, 2001* (New York: Penguin, 2004), 504–05.

[13] Nafeez Mosaddeq Ahmed, *The War on Freedom*, 224–25.

[14] "Our Friends the Pakistanis," *Wall Street Journal*, October 10, 2001 (http://www.opinionjournal.com/best/?id=95001298).

[15] As I had pointed out (NPH 192n3), there are many spellings of this man's name. I have followed Chossudovsky's preference, "Masood," but *The 9/11 Commission Report*, along with Steve Coll, writes "Massoud."

[16] Chossudovsky, *War and Globalisation*, 52–54, 60.

[17] Coll, *Ghost Wars*, 329.

[18] Coll, *Ghost Wars*, 4.

NOTES TO CHAPTER TEN   313

[19] Ibid., 567–69, 574–75.

[20] Reuters, September 15, 2001, quoted in Chossudovsky, *War and Globalisation*, 53.

[21] Coll, *Ghost Wars*, 439, 452. (In this latter statement, Coll is reporting that George Tenet never publicly made this statement. But Coll says this in such a way as to indicate that the statement *could* have been truthfully made.)

[22] NPH 116, citing UPI, September 30, 2002.

[23] *Washington Post*, February 23, 2002.

[24] *Boston Globe*, February 7, 2002; *Observer*, February 24, 2002; *Newsweek*, March 11, 2002; *Vanity Fair*, August 2002.

[25] *Time*, January 26, 2003; UPI, September 30, 2002; John J. Lumpkin, "New Theory on Pearl Slaying: 9/11 Mastermind Believed to Have Killed *Wall Street Journal* Reporter," APAP, October 21, 2003.

[26] *Guardian*, April 5, 2002.

[27] Gerald Posner, *Why America Slept: The Failure to Prevent 9/11* (New York: Random House, 2003), 189, 191, 193, summarized in NPH, 109.

[28] WPBF Channel 25, August 5, 2002; Cox News, August 2, 2002; *Palm Beach Post*, October 17, 2002; quoted in NPH 117.

CHAPTER TEN: POSSIBLE MOTIVES OF THE BUSH ADMINISTRATION

[1] Ian Johnson, "Conspiracy Theories about Sept. 11 Get Hearing in Germany," *Wall Street Journal*, September 29, 2003.

[2] Bob Woodward, *Bush at War* (New York: Simon & Schuster, 2002), 32.

[3] "Secretary Rumsfeld Interview with the *New York Times*," *New York Times*, October 12, 2001. For Rice's statement, see Chalmers Johnson, *The Sorrows of Empire: Militarism, Secrecy, and the End of the Republic* (New York: Henry Holt, 2004), 229.

[4] *The National Security Strategy of the United States of America*, September 2002 (available at www.whitehouse.gov/nsc/nss.html).

[5] The only statement I have seen that even comes close is the Commission's statement that "[t]he President noted that the attacks provided a great opportunity to engage Russia and China" (330).

[6] The Project for the New American Century (henceforth PNAC) *Rebuilding America's Defenses: Strategy, Forces and Resources for a New Century*, September 2000 (www.newamericancentury.org).

[7] Johnson, *The Sorrows of Empire*, 178.

[8] Lehman, who was secretary of the navy during two Reagan administrations, signed PNAC's "Letter to President Bush on the War on Terrorism," September 20, 2001 (www.newamericancentury.org/Bushletter.htm).

[9] PNAC, *Rebuilding America's Defenses*, 51.

[10] *Washington Post*, January 27, 2002.

[11] Henry Kissinger, "Destroy the Network," *Washington Post*, September 11, 2001.

[12] Greg Miller, "Al Qaeda Finances Down, Panel Says," *Los Angeles Times*, August 22, 2004.

[13] This document, which I downloaded in 2003, gives www.spacecom.af.mil/usspace as the website for the US Space Command. But in August 2004, I found that I could no longer access this site.

[14] An earlier version of this document, entitled "Joint Vision 2010," is discussed in Jack Hitt, "The Next Battlefield May Be in Outer Space," *New York Times Magazine*, August 5, 2001, and in Karl Grossman, *Weapons in Space* (New York: Seven Stories, 2001).

[15] The developments that had been achieved already by 1998 are described in George Friedman and Meredith Friedman, *The Future of War: Power, Technology and American World Dominance in the 21st Century* (New York: St. Martin's, 1998).

[16] For a brief overview of this project, see Grossman, *Weapons in Space*.

[17] PNAC, *Rebuilding America's Defenses*, 54, quoted and discussed in Rahul Mahajan, *Full Spectrum Dominance: U.S. Power in Iraq and Beyond* (New York: Seven Stories Press, 2003), 53–54. The idea is that if some country the United States wishes to attack has a modest number of nuclear missiles, we could eliminate most of them with a first strike. If the country then launched its few surviving missiles at the United States, they would probably not get through our missile defense shield. Although this shield would probably not protect America from a first strike in which many missiles were fired, it would, the theory is, knock down all the missiles in a small-scale attack. The foreign country would have good reason to believe, therefore, that the United States might go ahead and attack it in spite of its possession of nuclear weapons. It would, therefore, realize that its efforts to deter the United States with threats to retaliate would be futile. As a result, the United States could simply take over the country without needing to attack its nuclear missiles.

[18] Paul O'Neill, the first Secretary of the Treasury in the Bush–Cheney administration, reports that a memo written by Secretary of Defense Donald Rumsfeld, a member of PNAC, said that threats to US security were being created by the fact that regional powers hostile to the United States were "arming to deter us." See Ron Susskind, *The Price of Loyalty: George W. Bush, the White House, and the Education of Paul O'Neill* (New York: Simon & Schuster, 2004), 81.

[19] This figure is reported in the *Global Network Space Newsletter #14* (Fall, 2003), which is posted on the website of the Global Network Against Weapons and Nuclear Power in Space (www.space4peace.org).

[20] Any possible doubt about the statement's meaning was reportedly dispelled by Christopher Maletz, assistant director of PNAC. Christopher Bollyn says that when he asked Maletz what was meant by the need for "a new Pearl Harbor," he replied: "They needed more money to up the defense budget for raises, new arms, and future capabilities," and neither the politicians nor the military would have approved "without some disaster or catastrophic event." Christopher Bollyn, "America 'Pearl Harbored,'" American Free Press, updated April 12, 2004 (www.americanfreepress.net/12_24_02/America_Pearl_Harbored/america_pearl_harbored.html).

[21] *Report of the Commission to Assess U.S. National Security Space Management and Organization* (www.defenselink.mil/cgi-bin/dlprint.cgi).

[22] Ibid., quoted in Thierry Meyssan *9/11: The Big Lie* (London: Carnot, 2002), 151–52.

[23] Department of Defense News Briefing on Pentagon Attack (www.defenselink.mil/cgi-bin/dlprint.cgi), quoted in Meyssan, *9/11: The Big Lie*, 152.

[24] This point is emphasized in Meyssan, *9/11: The Big Lie*, 154.

[25] An examination of the Commission's report shows that Rumsfeld is mentioned in 53 paragraphs, Myers in 18, and Eberhart in 8. Many of these places cite interviews with them as sources of information. None of them reflect any questions implying that any aspects of their behavior that day might have been less than exemplary, or that any of their statements may have been less than fully truthful.

[26] See Ahmed Rashid, *Taliban: Militant Islam, Oil and Fundamentalism in Central Asia* (New Haven: Yale University Press, 2001), 145. Rashid first used this name in "The New Great Game: The Battle for Central Asia's Oil," *Far Eastern Economic Review*, April 10, 1997. He also uses it for Part 3 of *The Taliban*. Chalmers Johnson refers to Rashid as "the preeminent authority on the politics of Central Asia" (*The Sorrows of Empire*, 179).

[27] See Steve Coll, *Ghost Wars*, 305.

[28] Rashid, *Taliban*, Chs. 12 and 13.

[29] Ibid., 163.

[30] Coll, *Ghost Wars*, 308; Rashid, *Taliban*, 167, 171; Johnson, *The Sorrows of Empire*, 177.

[31] Coll, *Ghost Wars*, 338.

[32] Rashid, 166.

[33] Rashid, *Taliban*, 168.

[34] Ibid., 166. Although, as Rashid reports, the State Department quickly retracted this announcement, the revelation of its true sympathies had been made.

[35] Coll, *Ghost Wars*, 330.

[36] Rashid, *Taliban*, 166.

[37] *Telegraph*, August 13, 1998, quoted in NPH 90.

[38] Rashid, *Taliban*, 75–79, 175.

[39] Ibid., 175.

[40] Quoted in Jean-Charles Brisard and Guillaume Dasquié, *Forbidden Truth: U.S.–Taliban Secret Oil Diplomacy and the Failed Hunt for Bin Laden* (New York: Nation Books/Thunder's Mouth Press, 2002), and NPH 91.

[41] George Arney, "U.S. 'Planned Attack on Taleban'," BBC News, September 18, 2001 ("Taleban" is a spelling preferred by some British writers).

[42] The basis for this attack was provided on 9/11 itself. In the president's statement to the nation that evening, he declared: "We will make no distinction between the terrorists who committed these acts and those who harbor them." Then in a meeting of the National Security Council, which followed immediately, CIA Director Tenet reportedly said that al-Qaeda and the Taliban are essentially one and the same, after which Bush said to tell the Taliban that we were finished with them (*Washington Post*, January 27, 2002).

[43] Chalmers Johnson, *The Sorrows of Empire*, 178–79.

[44] *The Frontier Post*, October 10, 2001, cited in Ahmed, *The War on Freedom*, 227.

[45] *Chicago Tribune*, March 18, 2002, quoting from the Israeli newspaper *Ma'ariv*.

[46] Johnson, *The Sorrows of Empire*, 176.

[47] Ibid., 182–83.

[48] Zbigniew Brzezinski, *The Grand Chessboard: American Primacy and Its Geostrategic Imperatives* (New York: Basic Books, 1997), 210.

[49] Ibid., 35–36.

[50] Ibid., 36.

[51] Ibid., 212, 24–25.

[52] Reported in David E. Sanger and Robin Toner, "Bush, Cheney Talk of Iraq and al-Qaida Link," *New York Times*, June 18, 2004.

[53] William Safire, *New York Times*, June 21, 2004; Susan Jo Keller, "Political Uproar: 9/11 Panel Members Debate Qaeda–Iraq 'Tie,'" *New York Times*, June 21, 2004 (http://www.nytimes.com/2004/06/21/politics/21PANE.html); Joe Conason, "9/11 Panel Becomes Cheney's Nightmare" (available at www.911citizenswatch.org/modules.php?op=modload&name=News&file=article&sid=319).

[54] The Commission added that Wolfowitz said the chances of Saddam's involvement were high partly because he suspected that Saddam was behind the 1993 attack on the World Trade Center—a theory for which the Commission says it found no credible evidence (336, 559n73).

[55] Johnson, *The Sorrows of Empire*, 227.

[56] Although Johnson does not name it, he probably has in mind the Pentagon's 1992 "Defense Planning Guidance" (DPG), authored primarily by Paul Wolfowitz, then the undersecretary of defense for policy, and Lewis "Scooter" Libby.

[57] The Institute for Advanced Strategic and Political Studies, "A Clean Break: A New Strategy for Securing the Realm," July 8, 1996 (http://www.israeleconomy.org/strat1.htm).

[58] James Bamford, *A Pretext for War* (New York: Doubleday, 2004), 263.

[59] Paul D. Wolfowitz and Zalmay M. Khalilzad, "Saddam Must Go," *Weekly Standard* (December 1997).

[60] PNAC, "Letter to President Clinton on Iraq," January 26, 1998 (www.newamericancentury.org); PNAC, "Letter to Gingrich and Lott," May 29, 1998 (www.newamericancentury.org).

[61] PNAC, *Rebuilding America's Defenses*, 14, 17.

[62] Johnson, *The Sorrows of Empire*, 228–29.

[63] See Ron Susskind, *The Price of Loyalty*, 75, 91. In an interview on CBS's "60 Minutes" in January 2004, O'Neill, who as Secretary of the Treasury was a member of the National Security Council, said that the main topic within days of the inauguration was going after Saddam, with the question being not "Why Saddam?" or "Why Now?" but merely "finding a way to do it" (www.cbsnews.com/stories/2004/01/09/60minutes/main592330.shtml). "[H]e is right," says Richard Clarke about O'Neill's claim. "The administration of the second George Bush did begin with Iraq on its agenda." Richard A. Clarke, *Against All Enemies: Inside America's War on Terror* (New York: Free Press, 2004), 264.

[64] These notes were quoted in "Plans for Iraq Attack Began on 9/11," CBS News, September 4, 2002.

[65] Bamford, *A Pretext for War*, 285.

[66] Susskind, *The Price of Loyalty*, 96.

[67] Stephen Gowans, "Regime Change in Iraq: A New Government by and for US Capital," ZNet, April 20, 2003; the internal quote is from Robert Fisk, *Independent*, April 14, 2003.

[68] Johnson, *The Sorrows of Empire*, 226.

[69] PNAC, *Rebuilding America's Defenses*, 14.

PART TWO
CHAPTER ELEVEN: PROBLEMS IN EARLIER ACCOUNTS OF THE FLIGHTS

[1] The FAA's *Aeronautical Information Manual: Official Guide to Basic Flight Information and Air Traffic Control (ATC) Procedures* (www.faa.gov).

[2] Chairman of the Joint Chiefs of Staff Instruction 3610.01A, June 1, 2001,

"Aircraft Piracy (Hijacking) and Destruction of Derelict Airborne Objects" (www.dtic.mil).

[3] Glen Johnson, "Otis Fighter Jets Scrambled Too Late to Halt the Attacks," *Boston Globe*, September 15 (http://nl.newsbank.com/nl-search/we/Archives?p_action=print).

[4] Ibid.

[5] FAA News Release, August 9, 2002; cited in William Thomas, "Pentagon Says 9/11 Interceptors Flew: Too Far, Too Slow, Too Late," in Jim Marrs, *Inside Job: Unmasking the 9/11 Conspiracies* (San Rafael: Origin Press, 2004), 145–49.

[6] Congressional testimony by NORAD's commander, General Ralph E. Eberhart, made in October 2002, and *Slate* magazine, January 16, 2002.

[7] Cited in Nafeez Mosaddeq Ahmed, *The War on Freedom: How and Why America Was Attacked September 11, 2001* (Joshua Tree, Calif.: Tree of Life Publications, 2002), 151.

[8] Air Traffic Control Center, "ATCC Controller's Read Binder" (available at www.xavius.com/080198.htm, quoted in Ahmed, *The War on Freedom*, 148).

[9] "U.S. Senator Carl Levin (D-MI) Holds Hearing on Nomination of General Richard Myers to be Chairman of The Joint Chiefs of Staff," Senate Armed Services Committee, Washington D.C., September 13, 2001. The portion of this interview in question is printed in Meyssan, *9/11: The Big Lie*, 161–63.

[10] Glen Johnson, "Otis Fighter Jets."

[11] CBS News, September 14, 2001.

[12] Johnson, "Otis Fighter Jets."

[13] Matthew Wald, "After the Attacks: Sky Rules; Pentagon Tracked Deadly Jet but Found No Way to Stop It," *New York Times*, September 15, 2001.

[14] The 9/11 Commission, Staff Report, May 19, 2004. Cited in Paul Thompson, *The Terror Timeline*, 439.

[15] This show, besides being mentioned by Johnson, was mentioned as the first articulation of the new story, soon to become the official version, in George Szamuely, "Scrambled Messages," *New York Press*, 14/50 (www.nypress.com/14/50/taki/bunker.cfm).

[16] "NORAD's Response Times," News Release by the North American Aerospace Defense Command, September 18, 2001 (available at www.standdown.net/noradseptember182001pressrelease.htm).

[17] *Christian Science Monitor*, September 13, 2001; MSNBC, September 15, 2001; *New York Times*, October 16, 2001; Associated Press, August 12, 2002.

[18] ABC News, September 14, 2001; *New York Times*, September 15, 2001.

[19] *Boston Globe*, November 23, 2001; ABC News, July 18, 2002.

[20] *New York Times*, September 12, 2001; *Guardian*, October 17, 2001;

Boston Globe, November 23, 2001. Ben Sliney, the new Operations Manager at the FAA's Command Center, reported later that he soon heard about the message with the phrase, "We have some planes," and that this phrase haunted him all morning (*USA Today*, August 18, 2002).

[21] *Village Voice*, September 13, 2001.

[22] *Guardian*, October 17, 2001.

[23] *Christian Science Monitor*, September 13, 2001.

[24] CNN, September 17, 2001; *Washington Post*, September 12, 2001; NORAD, September 18, 2001.

[25] ABC News, September 14, 2001.

[26] "NORAD's Response Times," September 18, 2001 (available at www.standdown.net/noradseptember182001pressrelease.htm).

[27] *Guardian*, October 17, 2001; *New York Times*, October 16, 2001; *Boston Globe*, November 23, 2001.

[28] *Boston Globe*, November 23, 2001; *New York Times*, November 16, 2001.

[29] *Washington Post*, September 12, 2001; CNN, September 17, 2001; "NORAD's Response Times," September 18, 2001.

[30] ABC News, September 11, 2002; MSNBC, September 23, 2001; *Slate*, January 17, 2002.

[31] William B. Scott, "Exercise Jump-Starts Response to Attacks," *Aviation Week and Space Technology*, June 3, 2002 (www.aviationnow.com/content/publication/awst/20020603/avi_stor.htm).

[32] *Air Force News*, July 30, 1997.

[33] A story in the *Cape Cod Times* (September 16, 2001) quoted an Otis spokesman as saying that an "F-15 departing from Otis can reach New York City in 10 to 12 minutes." But this statement, which presupposed an average speed of only about 1000 mph, perhaps factored in the scramble and take-off times.

[34] "NORAD's Response Times," September 18, 2001.

[35] Stan Goff, "The So-Called Evidence is a Farce," *Narco News* #14: October 10, 2001 (www.narconews.com); George Szamuely, "Scrambled Messages," *New York Press*, 14/50 (www.nypress.com/14/50/taki/bunker.cfm).

[36] This deviation was shown in the flight course for AA 77 provided by *USA Today* shown on the first page of Paul Thompson's timeline for Flight 77 (www.cooperativeresearch.org/timeline.jsp?timeline=complete_911_timeline&day_of_911=aa77).

[37] *Guardian*, October 17, 2001; *New York Times*, October 17, 2001; *Boston Globe*, November 23, 2001.

[38] *New York Times*, September 15, 2001.

[39] *Newsday*, September 23, 2001; *Guardian*, October 17, 2001; *Boston Globe*, November 23, 2001.

[40] *Washington Post*, September 12, 2001; *Newsday*, September 23, 2001.

[41] *New York Times*, October 16, 2001.

[42] *Washington Post*, September 12, 2001; CNN, September 17, 2001; Associated Press, August 19, 2002; "NORAD's Response Times," September 18, 2001.

[43] *The 9/11 Commission Report* says 9:37:46 (33).

[44] "NORAD's Response Times," September 18, 2001 (see note 69, below); *Newsday*, September 23, 2001.

[45] George Szamuely, "Nothing Urgent," *New York Press* 15/2 (www.nypress.com/15/2/taki/bunker.cfm).

[46] *Telegraph*, September 16, 2001.

[47] "Air Attack on Pentagon Indicates Weaknesses," *Newsday*, September 23, 2001.

[48] *Pittsburgh Post-Gazette*, October 29, 2001; *Boston Globe*, November 23, 2001; Jere Longman, *Among the Heroes: United Flight 93 and the Passengers and Crew Who Fought Back* (New York: HarperCollins, 2002), 208.

[49] *Guardian*, October 17, 2001; *Boston Globe*, November 23, 2001; MSNBC, July 30, 2002.

[50] CNN September 17, 2001; MSNBC, September 3, 2002.

[51] *Newsweek*, September 22, 2001; *Pittsburgh Post-Gazette*, October 28, 2001.

[52] Available at www.9-11commission.gov/archive/hearing2/9-11Commission_Hearing_2003-05-23.htm.

[53] There *is* a dispute about the time, but only whether the time was 10:03 or 10:06, as will be discussed later.

[54] *USA Today*, September 16, 2001; *Washington Post*, January 27, 2002; ABC News and CBS News, September 11, 2002.

[55] *Pittsburgh Post-Gazette*, October 28, 2001; *Washington Post*, January 27, 2002.

[56] CBS News, September 11, 2001; Associated Press, September 13, 2001; *Nashua Telegraph*, September 13, 2001.

[57] *Boston Herald*, September 15, 2001. Wolfowitz's statement was also referred to in Matthew Wald's *New York Times* article of that day, "After the Attacks: Sky Rules."

[58] Cleveland Newschannel 5, September 11, 2001; *Philadelphia Daily News*, November 15, 2001; *Pittsburgh Post-Gazette*, September 12, 2001; *St. Petersburg Times*, September 12, 2001.

[59] Reuters News Service, September 13, 2001; CBS News, May 23, 2002; *Pittsburgh Tribune-Review*, September 14, 2001.

[60] *Pittsburgh Post-Gazette*, September 13, 2001.

[61] *Independent*, August 13, 2002; *Philadelphia Daily News*, November 15, 2001.

[62] MSNBC, September 11, 2002; Jere Longman, *Among the Heroes*, 110.

[63] *Newsweek*, September 22, 2001; *Pittsburgh Post-Gazette*, October 28, 2001; *Telegraph*, August 6, 2002.

[64] *Pittsburgh Post-Gazette*, September 28, 2002; Longman, *Among the Heroes*, 180.

[65] ABC News, September 11, 2001; Associated Press, September 12, 2001. Longman (264) and the *Mirror* report that although the FBI later denied that the recording of this call contained any mention of smoke or an explosion, the person who took this call was not allowed to speak to the media.

[66] The *Mirror*, September 13, 2002; Longman, *Among the Heroes*, 180.

[67] William B. Scott, "Exercise Jump-Starts Response to Attacks," *Aviation Week and Space Technology*, June 3, 2001; *Cape Cod Times*, August 21, 2002.

[68] This exchange is quoted in Meyssan, *9/11: The Big Lie*, 162.

[69] Based on "NORAD's Response Times," September 18, 2001 (available at www.standdown.net/noradseptember182001pressrelease.htm).

CHAPTER TWELVE: THE COMMISSION ON FLIGHT 11

[1] As stated in Chapter 11, news reports at the time said that the transponder went off right after radio contact was lost, hence at about 8:15. But the 9/11 Commission, entirely on the basis of interviews, puts the time at 8:21 (18). Colonel Robert Marr, head of NEADS, had put the time even later, saying the transponder went off sometime after 8:30 (ABC News, September 11, 2002). The Commission does not mention either of these alternative times.

[2] MSNBC, September 12, 2001.

[3] This account, with its 40-minute delay between transmission and translation, may or may not contradict Ben Sliney's statement quoted in note 20 of Ch. 11, above, in which he reported that he learned about this phrase "soon" after it was transmitted.

[4] NORAD's timeline had estimated 8:46 as the time. It is specified as 8:46:40 by the 9/11 Commission (32), then rounded off to 8:47.

[5] Quoted in James Bamford, *A Pretext for War* (New York: Doubleday, 2004), 60–61.

[6] Ibid., 4.

[7] *Newsday*, September 23, 2001; quoted in Paul Thompson, *The Terror Timeline*, 108.

[8] See, for example, Illarion Bykov and Jared Israel, "Guilty for 9-11: Bush, Rumsfeld, Myers, Section 1: Why Were None of the Hijacked Planes Intercepted?" (www.emperors-clothes.com/indict/911page.htm; listed in the

Table of Contents under "Evidence of high-level government conspiracy in the events of 9-11").

[9] *San Diego Union-Tribune*, September 12, 2001.

[10] *USA Today*, September 17, 2001.

[11] MSNBC, September 23, 2001.

[12] Emails from Kyle Hence, 9/11 CitizensWatch, September 23 and 29, 2004.

[13] *Telegraph*, September 16, 2001; *Denver Post*, September 11, 2001.

[14] *Aviation Week and Space Technology*, September 9, 2002.

[15] Ibid.

[16] *San Diego Union-Tribune*, September 12, 2001.

[17] Although some readers might consider this possibility unrealistic, James Bamford reports that Colonel Marr stated—with respect to what unarmed fighters going after Flight 93 could do—that (in Bamford's indirect quotation) "the only solution would be for one of the fighter pilots to give up his own life by crashing into the United Airlines jet" (*A Pretext for War*, 67, citing the transcript for "9/11," ABC News, September 11, 2002).

[18] To find these statements, try www.dcmilitary.com; or go to www.archive.org and enter www.andrews.af.mil; failing both of those routes, go to emperors-clothes.com/9-11backups/dcmilsep.htm and emperors-clothes.com/9-11backups/dcmil.htm to locate backups for the DC Military web pages for September and November.

[19] Quoted in Bykov and Israel, "Guilty for 9-11," and Ahmed, *The War on Freedom*, 154–55, citing DC Military (www.dcmilitary.com).

[20] On this change, see Bykov and Israel, "Update to Guilty for 9-11: Bush, Rumsfeld, Myers: Section 1," The Emperors New Clothes (www.emperors-clothes.com/indict/911page.htm), or Thompson, "September 11" (After 9:03 AM).

[21] Bykov and Israel, reported, however, that the DC Military website could still be accessed through www.archive.org by entering "www.andrews.af.mil." They further report, in any case, that they maintain backups of the DC Military web pages for September and November, so that they can be compared, at emperors-clothes.com/9-11backups/dcmilsep.htm and emperors-clothes.com/9-11backups/dcmil.htm.

[22] Richard A. Clarke, *Against All Enemies: Inside America's War on Terror* (New York: Free Press, 2004), 12.

[23] This document, often referred to simply as CJCSI 3610.01A, is available at www.dtic.mil/doctrine/jel/cjcsd/cjcsi/3610_01a.pdf. See Afterword, NPH, 2nd ed.

[24] The idea that no standard procedures should prevent "immediate responses" in emergency situations is also stated in other places in this memo of

June 1, 2001. Section 4.4, after saying that the secretary of defense retains approval authority for various types of support, concludes by saying: "Nothing in this Directive prevents a commander from exercising his or her immediate emergency response authority as outlined in DoD Directive 3025.1." And Section 4.5 begins with these words: "With the exception of immediate responses under imminently serious conditions, as provided in paragraph 4.7.1., below. . . . " I have discussed this issue at greater length in the Afterword to the second edition of NPH.

[25] "Because of a technical issue," we are told, "there are no NEADS recordings available of the NEADS senior weapons director and weapons director technician position responsible for controlling the Otis scramble" (459n20). This explanation was apparently good enough for the Commission.

[26] Thierry Meyssan, *Pentagate* (London: Carnot Publishing, 2002), 115, quoting "PAVE PAWS, Watching North America's Skies, 24 Hours a Day" (www.pavepaws.org).

[27] NTSB (National Transportation Safety Board), Aircraft Accident Brief for Payne Stewart Incident, October 25, 1999 (http://www.ntsb.gov/Publictn/2000/aab0001.htm).

[28] Lynn Lunsford, "Loss of Oxygen Cited as Possible Cause of Jet's Wayward Flight, Crash," Knight-Ridder Tribune Business News: *The Dallas Morning News*, October 26, 1999 (available at www.wanttoknow.info/991026dallasmorningnews).

[29] The note (459n121) concludes with these references: "See NTSB memo, Aircraft Accident Brief for Payne Stewart incident, Oct. 25, 1999; FAA email, Gahris to Myers, 'ZJX Timeline for N47BA accident,' Feb. 17, 2004."

[30] NTSB, "Aircraft Accident Brief for Payne Stewart Incident."

[31] The NTSB memo, unfortunately, gets very confused, making it very difficult for anyone to figure out from it what happened. Part of the confusion seems to be the failure to account for the difference between time zones, but the confusion appears deeper than this. Partly for this reason, and partly because of the conflicts between the various news reports (perhaps due in large part to the confusions in this memo), I myself do not cite the Payne Stewart incident as an example of rapid response time (although it may well have been).

CHAPTER THIRTEEN: THE COMMISSION ON FLIGHT 175

[1] "NORAD's Response Times," NORAD News Release, September 18, 2001 (available at www.standdown.net/noradseptember182001pressrelease.htm).

[2] Hart Seely, "Amid Crisis Simulation, 'We Were Suddenly No-Kidding Under Attack,'" Newhouse News Service, January 25, 2002.

[3] James Bamford, *A Pretext for War* (New York: Doubleday, 2004), 15, quoting the transcript for "9/11," ABC News, September 11, 2002.

[4] ABC News, September 11, 2002; MSNBC, September 23, 2001; *Slate*, January 17, 2002.

[5] William B. Scott, "Exercise Jump-Starts Response to Attacks," *Aviation Week and Space Technology*, June 3, 2002 (www.aviationnow.com/content/publication/awst/20020603/avi_stor.htm).

[6] *Toronto Star*, December 9, 2001, cited in Thompson, *The Terror Timeline*, 392.

[7] The 9/11 Commission, Staff Report, May 19, 2004, cited in Paul Thompson, *The Terror Timeline*, 439.

[8] *New York Times*, October 16, 2001.

[9] *Newsday*, September 10, 2002.

[10] *Washington Post*, September 12, 2001; CNN, September 17, 2001; "NORAD's Response Times," September 18, 2001; *Newsday*, September 10, 2002; Associated Press, August 19, 2002.

[11] Hart Seely, "Amid Crisis Simulation, 'We Were Suddenly No-Kidding Under Attack,'" Newhouse News Service, January 25, 2002.

[12] I obtained a copy of this memo from Kyle Hence, co-founder of 9/11 CitizensWatch, who was one of its original recipients.

[13] Laura Brown told me this in a telephone conversation I had with her on Sunday, August 15, 2004.

[14] Posted at www.911truth.org/article.pup?story=2004081200421797.

[15] Tom Flocco, "Rookie in the 9-11 Hot Seat?" tomflocco.com, June 17, 2004 (http://tomflocco.com/modules.php?name=News&file=article&sid=65); also available at Los Angeles Independent Media Center, June 17, 2004 (http://la.indymedia.org/news/2004/06/113002.php).

[16] Ibid.

[17] Tom Flocco, "9-11 Probe Continues to Bypass Executive Branch Testimony," tomflocco.com, October 13, 2003 (http://tomflocco.com/modules.php?name=News&file=article&sid=10).

[18] CNN, September 4, 2002; ABC News, September 11, 2002; William B. Scott, "Exercise Jump-Starts Response to Attacks," *Aviation Week and Space Technology*, June 3, 2002.

[19] Richard A. Clarke, *Against All Enemies: Inside America's War on Terror* (New York: Free Press, 2004), 2.

[20] Ibid., 3–5.

CHAPTER FOURTEEN: THE COMMISSION ON FLIGHT 77

[1] This flight course for AA 77 provided by *USA Today* is shown on the first page of Paul Thompson's timeline for Flight 77 (www.cooperativeresearch.org/timeline.jsp?timeline=complete_911_timeline&day_of_911=aa77).

[2] *Village Voice*, September 13, 2001; *Guardian*, October 17, 2001.

[3] *USA Today*, August 13, 2002. Clarke, *Against All Enemies*, 13.

[4] *Washington Post*, September 12, 2001; *Newsday*, September 23, 2001.

[5] Paul Thompson, "September 11: Minute-by-Minute" (8:56), available at www.cooperativeresearch.org.

[6] *Christian Science Monitor*, September 13, 2001.

[7] ABC News, September 6, 2002.

[8] *New York Times*, September 13, 2001; Hart Seely, "Amid Crisis Simulation, 'We Were Suddenly No-Kidding Under Attack,'" Newhouse News Service, January 25, 2002.

[9] National Commission on Terrorist Attacks Upon the United States, 12th Public Hearing, June 17, 2004 (www.9-11commission.gov/archive/hearing12/9-11Commission_Hearing_2004-06-17.htm).

[10] Since the previous account said that the F-16s were 105 (instead of 150) miles away, one could wonder if the Commission meant to suggest that this idea arose from transposing the "5" and the "0."

[11] It is on page 45 of *The 9/11 Commission Report* that we learn that Eckmann was the lead pilot.

[12] Matthew Wald, "After the Attacks: Sky Rules; Pentagon Tracked Deadly Jet but Found No Way to Stop It," *New York Times*, September 15, 2001.

[13] Clarke, *Against All Enemies*, 3–5.

[14] "Statement of Secretary of Transportation Norman Y. Mineta before the National Commission on Terrorist Attacks upon the United States, May 23, 2003," available at www.cooperativeresearch.org/timeline/2003/commissiontestimony052303.htm.

[15] Clarke, *Against All Enemies*, 7–8.

[16] Department of Defense, March 23, 2004.

[17] Bamford, *A Pretext for War*, 38–39.

[18] Sgt. 1st Class Kathleen T. Rhem, USA, "Myers and Sept. 11: 'We Hadn't Thought About This,'" American Forces Press Service, October 23, 2001.

[19] James Bamford, *Body of Secrets: Anatomy of the Ultra-Secret National Security Agency* (2001; New York: Anchor Books, 2002), 82–91.

[20] Clarke, *Against All Enemies*, 5.

[21] Ibid., 7–9.

[22] Ibid., 12.

[23] Ibid., 23.

[24] NPH 238n27.

[25] Department of Defense, October 12, 2001; *Minneapolis Star Tribune*, September 12, 2001; CNN, December 5, 2001; ABC News, September 11,

2002. A brief version of this account is also given in Bob Woodward, *Bush at War* (New York: Simon & Schuster, 2002), 24–25.

[26] Department of Defense, September 15, 2001.

[27] 9/11 Commission Staff Report, March 23, 2004, quoted in Paul Thompson, *The Terror Timeline*, 424, 426.

[28] For this account, according to which Rumsfeld again helps with rescue efforts, the Commission cites an interview it had with Rumsfeld in December 2002, along with a Department of Defense memo and an interview with Rumsfeld's assistant, Stephen Cambone, in 2004 (463n193).

[29] This problem is raised by Paul Thompson (*The Terror Timeline*, 426).

[30] Clarke, *Against All Enemies*, 22.

[31] "Statement of Secretary of Transportation Norman Y. Mineta before the National Commission on Terrorist Attacks upon the United States, May 23, 2003," available at www.cooperativeresearch.org/timeline/2003/commissiontestimony052303.htm.

[32] ABC News, September 11, 2002.

[33] William B. Scott, "Exercise Jump-Starts Response to Attacks," *Aviation Week and Space Technology*, June 3, 2002 (www.aviationnow.com/content/publication/awst/20020603/avi_stor.htm).

CHAPTER FIFTEEN: THE COMMISSION ON FLIGHT 93

[1] Clarke, *Against All Enemies*, 7.

[2] The National Commission on Terrorist Attacks upon the United States, June 17, 2004; quoted in Tom Flocco, "Rookie in the 9-11 Hot Seat?" tomflocco.com, June 17, 2004 (http://tomflocco.com/modules.php?name=News&file=article&sid=65).

[3] Flocco, "Rookie in the 9-11 Hot Seat?"

[4] Ibid.

[5] According to Elizabeth Drew (*New York Review of Books*, September 23, 2004, 8) the White House was very anxious for this phrase, showing Cheney's decisiveness, to be included.

[6] I have left out of my discussion in the text the following passage in the Kean–Zelikow Report about what happened after the shoot-down authorization was finally communicated to NORAD: "The NEADS commander [Colonel Robert Marr] told us he did not pass along the order because he was unaware of its ramifications. Both the mission commander and the senior weapons director indicated they did not pass the order to the fighters circling Washington and New York because they were unsure how the pilots would, or should, proceed with this guidance" (43). I will not comment on the absurdities in these statements except to point out that here the Kean–Zelikow Report has succeeded

in making military officials appear as ridiculous as it normally makes FAA officials appear. Of course, people do say absurd things when they are creating or at least going along with a false story (which is how I account for the hesitations and absurdities in the General Larry Arnold's testimony before the Commission quoted in Chapter 12). My point is simply that we should not confuse these statements by Marr and the senior weapons director with what really occurred. But the Commission, treating the statements as actual history, makes it seem as if military personnel can simply decide not to obey an order if they happen to be "unaware of its ramifications" or they are "unsure how [others] would, or should, proceed with this guidance."

[7] *USA Today,* September 16, 2001; *Washington Post,* January 27, 2002; ABC News and CBS News, September 11, 2002.

[8] Bamford, *A Pretext for War,* 65–66.

[9] *Aviation Week and Space Technology,* September 9, 2002.

[10] *Pittsburgh Post-Gazette,* October 28, 2001; *Washington Post,* January 27, 2002.

[11] CBS News, September 11, 2001; Associated Press, September 13, 2001; *Nashua Telegraph,* September 13, 2001.

[12] The direct quotation is from the *Boston Herald,* September 15, 2001. Matthew Wald's *New York Times* article of that day, "After the Attacks: Sky Rules," paraphrased the statement.

[13] William B. Scott, "Exercise Jump-Starts Response to Attacks," *Aviation Week and Space Technology,* June 3, 2002; *Cape Cod Times,* August 21, 2002.

[14] Richard Clarke, *Against All Enemies,* 7–8.

[15] *New York Times,* September 12, 2001; MSNBC, September 22, 2001; *Washington Post,* January 27, 2002.

[16] *New York Times,* September 16, 2001; *Telegraph,* December 16, 2001; ABC News, September 14, 2002.

[17] ABC News, September 11, 2002.

[18] Clarke, *Against All Enemies,* 2.

[19] Ibid., 3–8. It was before 9:55 because it was before Air Force One took off.

[20] NBC, *Meet the Press,* September 16, 2001.

[21] This photograph, which includes a clock showing the time to be 9:25, can be seen on the White House website or on Paul Thompson's "September 11."

[22] NBC, *Meet the Press,* September 16, 2001.

[23] *Newsweek,* June 20, 2004, quoted in Thompson, *The Terror Timeline,* 443–44.

[24] Accordingly, if Cheney gave the authorization on his own, even though the president was neither incapacitated nor incommunicado, his authorization

would have been improper, even if it is not true that the authorization can come only from the president. So the question is important.

[25] Chairman of the Joint Chiefs of Staff Instruction 3610.01A, June 1, 2001, "Aircraft Piracy (Hijacking) and Destruction of Derelict Airborne Objects" (www.dtic.mil/doctrine/jel/cjcsd/cjcsi/3610_01a.pdf).

[26] Glen Johnson, "Otis Fighter Jets Scrambled Too Late to Halt the Attacks," *Boston Globe*, September 15 (http://nl.newsbank.com/nl-search/we/Archives?p_action=print).

[27] *Calgary Herald*, October 13, 2001.

[28] Associated Press, August 13, 2002.

[29] *New York Observer*, February 11, 2004.

[30] Won-Young Kim and G. R. Baum, "Seismic Observations during September 11, 2001, Terrorist Attack," Spring 2002 (report to the Maryland Department of Natural Resources), cited in *The 9/11 Commission Report*, 461n168.

[31] *San Francisco Chronicle*, December 9, 2002; *Philadelphia Daily News*, September 16, 2002.

[32] See William Bunch, "Three-Minute Discrepancy in Tape," *Philadelphia Daily News*, September 16, 2002.

[33] *New York Observer*, June 17, 2004, cited in Thompson, *The Terror Timeline*, 445.

[34] *New York Observer*, February 11, 2004, quoted in Thompson, *The Terror Timeline*, 446.

[35] Won-Young Kim and G. R. Baum, "Seismic Observations during September 11, 2001, Terrorist Attack," Spring 2002 (available at www.cooperativeresearch.org). "UTC" refers to Universal Coordinated Time, which has largely superseded GMT (Greenwich Mean Time).

[36] Citing an email letter from Won-Young Kim, "Re: UA Flight 93," July 7, 2004.

[37] Tom Flocco reports that Leidig, in his testimony before the 9/11 Commission on June 17, 2004, "told [John] Lehman and [Timothy] Roemer that Winfield . . . reassumed his duties as Deputy Director for Operations for the NMCC just before United Flight 93 crashed in Pennsylvania" ("Rookie in the 9-11 Hot Seat?").

[38] Bamford, *A Pretext for War*, 65–66.

[39] ABC News, September 15, 2002.

[40] This memorandum was quoted above in Chapter 13 under "The FAA-Initiated Teleconference."

CHAPTER SIXTEEN: THE FAA TAKES THE FALL

[1] *Aviation Week and Space Technology*, September 9, 2002.

[2] Mike Kelly, "Atlantic City F-16 Fighters Were Eight Minutes Away from 9/11 Hijacked Planes," *Bergen Record*, December 5, 2003.

[3] Peter Lance, *Cover Up: What the Government is Still Hiding about the War on Terror* (New York: Harper-Collins/ReganBooks, 2004), 230–31.

[4] Bamford, *A Pretext for War*, 4, 15.

[5] National Commission on Terrorist Attacks Upon the United States, 12th Public Hearing, June 17, 2004 (www.9-11commission.gov/archive/hearing12/9-11Commission_Hearing_2004-06-17.htm).

[6] Michael Parenti, *The Terrorism Trap: September 11 and Beyond* (San Francisco: City Lights, 2002), 93–94.

[7] Ibid.

[8] As can be seen in the Appendix, Wolfowitz thereby expressed a very narrow view of the "Manila plot."

[9] *Los Angeles Times*, September 27, 2001; CNN, July 18, 2001.

[10] *Washington Post*, October 2, 2001.

[11] *New York Times*, November 3, 2001; *Time*, April 4, 1995.

[12] Associated Press, April 18, 2002.

[13] MDW News Service, November 3, 2000; *Mirror*, May 24, 2002.

[14] *USA Today*, April 18, 2004.

[15] John J. Lumpkin, "Agency was to Crash Plane on 9-11," Associated Press, August 22, 2002; Pamela Hess, "U.S. Agencies—Strange 9/11 Coincidence," UPI, August 22, 2002.

[16] This idea is central to Michael C. Ruppert, *Crossing the Rubicon: The Decline of American Empire at the End of the Age of Oil* (Gabriola Island, British Columbia: New Society Publishers, 2004).

[17] Vigilant Guardian is the exercise referred to in the previously cited article by Hart Seely, "Amid Crisis Simulation, 'We Were Suddenly No-Kidding Under Attack,'" Newhouse News Service, January 25, 2002. This exercise is also mentioned in James Bamford, *A Pretext for War*, 4, but Bamford says that 9/11 was Day 4 of that exercise, whereas Seely had said that it was Day 2.

[18] Michael Kane, "Analyzing the 9/11 Report: Chapter 1: Omissions, Contradictions and Falsehoods," August 17, 2004 (http://inn.globalfreepress.com/modules/news/article.php?storyid=693). Besides the four war games mentioned in the text, Kane also mentions one called Northern Guardian.

[19] Richard Clarke, *Against All Enemies*, 5.

[20] Peter Lance, *Cover Up*, 226, citing William B. Scott, "Exercise Jump-

Starts Response to Attacks," *Aviation Week and Space Technology,* June 3, 2002 (www.aviationnow.com/content/publication/awst/20020603/avi_stor.htm), and Mike Kelly, "Atlantic City F-16 Fighters Were Eight Minutes Away from 9/11 Hijacked Planes."

[21] Michael Kane, "The Final Fraud: 9/11 Commission Closes Its Doors to the Public: Cover-Up Complete," From the Wilderness Publications (www.fromthewilderness.com/members/071204_final_fraud.shtml). The comments of these audience members were, Kane reports, published in the Associated Press transcript of the hearing (http://wid.ap.org/transcripts/040617commission911_1.html).

[22] Ibid.

[23] Ibid.

[24] See Richard Van Alstyne, *The Rising American Empire* (1960; New York, Norton, 1974), 143; Howard Zinn, *A People's History of the United States* (1980; New York: HarperPerennial, 1990), 155, 307. This practice is not, to be sure, unique to the US military tradition. For example, Walter LaFeber, articulating a view that is widespread among historians, says that the "Mukden incident," in which an explosion destroyed part of the Japanese railway in Manchuria, was engineered by Japanese army officers "as an excuse to conquer Manchuria." See Walter LaFeber, *The Clash: U.S.–Japanese Relations throughout History* (New York: Norton, 1997), 166. The Reichstag fire, said by the Nazis to have been started by Communists, is widely thought to have been started by the Nazis themselves (but for an argument to the contrary, see Ian Kershaw, *Hitler: 1889–1936: Hubris* [New York: Norton, 1998]).

[25] See Geoffrey Perret, *A Country Made by War: From the Revolution to Vietnam—the Story of America's Rise to Power* (New York: Random House, 1989), 280n.

[26] James Bamford, *Body of Secrets: Anatomy of the Ultra-secret National Security Agency* (2001: New York: Anchor Books, 2002), 82–91.

[27] CIA, "A Program of Covert Operations Against the Castro Regime," April 16, 1961 (declassified CIA document), quoted in Thierry Meyssan, *9/11: The Big Lie,* 140.

[28] This memorandum is printed in Meyssan, *9/11: The Big Lie,* 198. It can also be read on the ABC website (http://abcnews.go.com/sections/us/DailyNews/jointchiefs_010501.html).

[29] This memorandum is printed in Meyssan, *9/11: The Big Lie,* 199–205. The passages quoted in this paragraph are on page 199.

[30] Ibid., 202–203.

[31] Ibid., 204.

[32] Ibid., 202.

[33] Ibid., 202.

[34] National Commission on Terrorist Attacks Upon the United States, 12th Public Hearing, June 17, 2004 (www.9-11commission.gov/archive/hearing12/9-11Commission_Hearing_2004-06-17.htm).

[35] Telephone interview with Laura Brown, August 15, 2004.

CONCLUSION

[1] "Open Letter: National Security Experts Speak Out: 9/11 Commission Falls Short," available at www.911CitizensWatch.org.

[2] Peter Lance, *Cover Up: What the Government is Still Hiding about the War on Terror* (New York: Harper-Collins/ReganBooks, 2004).

[3] Ibid., 139–40.

[4] Ibid., 215–220.

[5] Ibid., 3.

[6] Ibid., 243–44, citing Shaun Waterman, "9/11 Commission Finishes First Chapters," UPI, July 1, 2004.

[7] Ibid., 243–44.

[8] *Newsweek*, September 22, 2002.

[9] CNN, November 30, 2001; *Pittsburgh Post-Gazette*, December 3, 2001; *Washington Post*, December 1, 2001; *Chicago Sun-Times*, December 13, 2002; *New York Times*, November 29, 2002.

[10] *Newsweek*, December 15, 2002; *Washington Post*, October 5, 1998; *Salon*, December 3, 2002.

[11] *New York Times*, December 12, 2001; MSNBC, December 13, 2001; *Seattle Times*, December 14, 2002.

[12] Associated Press, January 27, 2003; *Time*, March 26, 2003.

[13] *Seattle Times*, March 12, 2003; "White House Accused of Stalling 9-11 Panel," Associated Press, October 26, 2003; Philip Shenon, "9/11 Commission Could Subpoena Oval Office Files," *New York Times*, October 26, 2003. I have discussed these various obstacles in NPH 149–50.

[14] *Multinational Monitor*, November, 1997; Associated Press, January 20, 2003; *Boston Herald*, December 11, 2001.

[15] CBS News, March 5, 2003, Associated Press, December 12, 2002; Associated Press, January 1, 2003; Associated Press, February 14, 2003; Associated Press, March 27, 2003.

[16] Lance, *Cover Up*, 208.

[17] Ibid., 208.

[18] Ibid., 161.

[19] Ibid., 197.

[20] Ibid., 208.

[21] Ibid., 222.

[22] Ibid., 202.

[23] Ibid., 2002.

[24] Ibid., 141, citing Philip Shenon, "Ex-Senator Will Soon Quit 9/11 Panel, Leaving Gap for Victim's Advocates," *New York Times*, December 5, 2003.

[25] I discussed this deal in NPH 154–55.

[26] Eric Boehlert, "The President Ought to be Ashamed: Interview with Max Cleland," Salon.com, Nov. 13, 2003.

[27] A video entitled "The Great Conspiracy" (www.greatconspiracy.ca), produced and narrated by Canadian media critic Barrie Zwicker, directly raises the question of conspiracy on the part of the Bush administration in the course of providing an excellent introduction to many of the problems in the official account of 9/11.

APPENDIX

[1] Peter Lance, *Cover Up: What the Government is Still Hiding about the War on Terror* (New York: Harper-Collins/ReganBooks, 2004), 67.

[2] Ibid., 38, 44, 284–85.

[3] Ibid., 5, 49–54, 62, 64.

[4] Ibid., 41, 52, 103.

[5] Ibid., 52, 56–57, 66–68, 71–72, 97.

[6] Ibid., 19–20, 86, 91.

[7] Ibid., 90, 95.

[8] Ibid., 6, 68–69, 82, 97–98, 103, 127.

[9] Ibid., 90–91, 98, 106.

[10] Ibid., 72, 105.

[11] Lance convincingly shows that the plane in which the test in question was carried out could not have been the plane used for TWA Flight 800 (ibid., 69–70, 83–90).

[12] Ibid., 127.

[13] Ibid., 5.

[14] Ibid., 103.

[15] Ibid., 68.

[16] Ibid., 6, 58, 103.

INDEX OF NAMES

Z

Z/11   10 9/10